OFFICE WITHOUT POWER
Secretary-General
Sir Eric Drummond
1919–1933

Sir Eric Drummond

by

Sir Gerald Kelly

(Palais des Nations, Geneva. Reproduced by courtesy of the United Nations and Lady Kelly).

OFFICE WITHOUT POWER

POWER

Secretary-General
Sir Eric Drummond
1919–1933

By

JAMES BARROS

CLARENDON PRESS • OXFORD

1979

Oxford University Press, Walton Street, Oxford OX2 6DP

OXFORD LONDON GLASGOW

NEW YORK TORONTO MELBOURNE WELLINGTON

KUALA LUMPUR SINGAPORE JAKARTA HONG KONG TOKYO

DELHI BOMBAY CALCUTTA MADRAS KARACHI

IBADAN NAIROBI DAR ES SALAAM CAPE TOWN

*Published in the United States
by Oxford University Press, New York*

British Library Cataloguing in Publication Data

Barros, James
    Office without power.
    1. Drummond, *Sir* Eric
    I. Title
    341.22′092′4   JX1975   78-40312
    ISBN 0-19-822551-2

*Typeset by CCC and printed and bound at
William Clowes & Sons Limited
Beccles and London*

TO

LELAND M. GOODRICH

James T. Shotwell Professor Emeritus
Columbia University
Gentleman, Teacher, Scholar

PREFACE

This volume examines the tenure of Sir Eric Drummond as the first Secretary-General of the League of Nations. Of the secretaries-general who have served the world community since 1919 Drummond's fourteen years of service was the longest. He organized the League's multinational Secretariat in 1919–20 and during the years that followed acquired the reputation, at least to the uninitiated, of an unflappable and efficient administrator— which he surely was—but nothing more. How Drummond used his office, the range of his influence, his personal and political contacts, and his intervention behind the scenes in political issues facing the world organization will be examined in the pages that follow. By investigating how Drummond actually operated, as opposed to how people thought he operated, I hope that Drummond's role as Secretary-General can be evaluated. Moreover, Drummond's use of his high office and the precedents he established will perhaps give us a better understanding of the possibilities and limitations inherent in the office, and help frame some generalizations about its use in international politics.

ACKNOWLEDGEMENTS

I would like to thank the trustees of the Carnegie Endowment for International Peace whose support made it possible for me to examine the League of Nations Archives during the period 1966–7. In particular I am indebted to the Carnegie Endowment's Geneva Office, its director, John Goormaghtigh, and his associate, Jean Siotis, for their great assistance during the period I worked in Switzerland. I am especially obligated to the Canada Council whose generosity made it possible on two separate occasions to consult papers in London, Ottawa, and Washington. Research in Edinburgh was made possible by the International Studies Programme of the University of Toronto. The time needed to write this volume was made possible by the Earhart Foundation of Ann Arbor, Michigan, and I would like to thank the trustees of the foundation for their invaluable assistance.

For critical comments and suggestions which did much to improve this study I would like to thank Leland M. Goodrich, James T. Shotwell Professor Emeritus of Columbia University, and Leon Gordenker of the Department of Politics of Princeton University. Sir Eric Drummond's son, the present Lord Perth, also found time in a busy schedule to read the study and to clarify certain factual matters.

Lastly, it should be noted that the views and opinions expressed in this study are my own and do not necessarily reflect those of the institutions or persons who have assisted me in this endeavour.

ERINDALE COLLEGE   J.B.
DEPARTMENT OF POLITICAL ECONOMY
UNIVERSITY OF TORONTO
TORONTO, ONTARIO, CANADA

CONTENTS

ABBREVIATIONS

ADAP 1918–1945	Germany, Auswärtiges Amt, *Akten zur deutschen auswärtigen Politik 1918–1945* (Göttingen: Vandenhoeck and Ruprecht, 1966–)
BLL	Beaverbrook Library, London
BLOU	Bodleian Library, Oxford University
BL	British Library, London
CC	Churchill College, Cambridge
CU	Cambridge University
CUNY	Columbia University, New York
DBFP, 1919–1939	Great Britain, Foreign Office, *Documents on British Foreign Policy, 1919–1939* (London: H.M. Stationery Office, 1947–)
DCER	Canada, Department of External Affairs, *Documents on Canadian External Relations* (Ottawa: Queen's Printer, 1967–)
DDB 1920–1940	Belgium, Ministère des Affaires Étrangères, *Documents diplomatiques belges 1920–1940*; *La Politique de sécurité extérieure* (Bruxelles: Palais des Académies, 1964–)
DDF 1932–1939	France, Ministère des Affaires Étrangères, Commission de Publication des Documents Relatif aux Origines de la Guerre 1939–1945, *Documents diplomatiques français 1932–1939* (Paris: Imprimerie Nationale, 1963–)
DDI	Italy, Ministero degli Affari Esteri, Commissione per la Pubblicazione dei Documenti Diplomatici, *I documenti diplomatici italiani* (Roma: Libreria dello Stato, 1952–)
DGFP 1918–1945	Germany, Auswärtiges Amt, *Documents on German Foreign Policy 1918–1945* (Washington, D.C.: Government Printing Office, 1949–)
FO	Foreign Office records, Public Record Office, London
IOL	India Office Library, London
LC	Library of Congress, Washington, D.C.
LNA	League of Nations Archives, United Nations Library, Palais des Nations, Geneva
LSEPS	London School of Economics and Political Science
NA	National Archives of the United States, Washington, D.C.
NCO	New College, Oxford
NRA	National Register of Archives (Scotland), Edinburgh
PAC	Public Archives of Canada, Ottawa

PACRMB	Public Archives of Canada, Records Management Branch, Ottawa
PRFRUS...	U.S. Department of State, *Papers Relating to the Foreign Relations of the United States* ... (Washington, D.C.: Government Printing Office)
PRO	Public Record Office, London
PU	Princeton University
Simon Papers	The Personal Papers of Sir John Simon, Devon
SRO	Scottish Record Office, Edinburgh
UB	University of Birmingham
YUNH	Yale University, New Haven
YUT	York University, Toronto

I

PARIS 1919

The Chancellor

At the Paris Peace Conference's plenary session of 28 April 1919, President Wilson proposed and the conference accepted the appointment of Sir James Eric Drummond, K.C.M.G., C.B., as first Secretary-General of the League of Nations. The conference's action implemented paragraph two Article 6, of the proposed Covenant of the League of Nations that its Secretary-General would be chosen by the peace conference.[1] Thus, in his early forties and after nineteen years of service in the British Foreign Office, Drummond was seconded to head the new world organization.

Drummond, however, had not been everyone's first choice as Secretary-General. Lord Robert Cecil, a member of the British delegation who played a paramount role in drafting the Covenant and in organizing the League, had explained to the Imperial War Cabinet on Christmas Eve of 1918 that the plan was to have 'a permanent organization presided over by a man of the greatest possible ability'.[2] Cecil wanted him to be called the 'Chancellor' and be both head of the League's international secretariat and the 'international representative of the League—its mouthpiece—and the suggester, if not the director, of its policy'. The position was to be bestowed upon some eminent political person; he 'should be rather more than what we know as a permanent official'. He was to be influential politically.[3]

[1] *PRFRUS, The Paris Peace Conference 1919*, iii. 288.

[2] CAB/23/42, PRO. See also, David Lloyd George, *The Truth about the Peace Treaties* (London: Gollancz, 1938), i. 629.

[3] Lord Robert Cecil, *All the Way* (London: Hodder and Stoughton, 1949), p. 150. According to Philip Noel-Baker, who was Cecil's assistant at Paris in 1919, it had been 'hoped that the "Chancellor" would be a statesman of great international position, who should be in his own person the embodiment of the League and the guardian of the Covenant . . . that his relation to the members of the Council should be that of an equal among equals, and that his international authority would be a factor of great importance in establishing

(continued)

Cecil felt that the great danger for the League would be that governments, especially those of small states, would be unwilling to take political initiatives, that they would lack political courage. The Chancellor therefore would not only have the power to take political initiatives but would also have to be a person who would not be afraid to expose himself to international criticism.[1] Thus one of his powers would have been to summon on his own initiative meetings of the League Council, maybe even meetings of the League Assembly.[2]

What Cecil failed to see, however, was that any international official who had such power and used it would soon find himself at odds with the state against which his action was directed. Indeed, his subsequent relations with that state would be strained and his ability to offer advice or moderate the actions of that state would be compromised. In fact, under the powers proposed for the Chancellor there was no assurance that either the Council or the Assembly would respond to his call or even act on his complaint. Cecil's proposal of the Chancellor was idealistic in the extreme, based as it was on the assumption that a single individual acting on his own initiative and possessing no real power could merely by his personality and prestige affect the course of international relations.

Nevertheless Cecil decided in early 1919 to approach the Greek Prime Minister, Eleftherios Venizelos, and to offer him the Chancellorship. Cecil had first proposed Venizelos's name to the Imperial War Cabinet during the Christmas Eve session of 1918.[3] His choice was no altruistic act but based, as we shall see,

the practical utility and the moral authority of the League'. Philip [Noel-] Baker, 'The Making of the Covenant from the British Point of View', in Rask-Ørsted Fondet, *Les Origines et l'œuvre de la Société des Nations*, ed. Peter Munch (Copenhague: Gyldendal, 1924), ii. 41.

[1] Interview with Philip Noel-Baker, 24 July 1971.

[2] [Noel-]Baker, 'The Making of the Covenant from the British Point of View', p. 41. See also, Charles Howard-Ellis, *The Origin, Structure and Working of the League of Nations* (London: Allen and Unwin, 1928), p. 163 and fn. Of course, the Secretary-General of the United Nations under Article 99 of the Charter can summon on his own initiative meetings of the Security Council. According to Drummond the Chancellor would have had even wider political power than the Secretary-General of the United Nations. Stephen M. Schwebel, *The Secretary-General of the United Nations* (Cambridge: Harvard University Press, 1952), p. 4.

[3] CAB/23/42, PRO; Cecil, *All the Way*, p. 150; Lloyd George, i. 629.

on the belief that Venizelos was pro-British—which he was—
and that he could manage and control President Wilson. The
possibility of selecting Venizelos as Chancellor had probably
been triggered in Cecil's mind by a letter sent on 18 December
from Captain Gerald Talbot, the naval attaché in Athens
assigned to Venizelos as aide-de-camp during his stay in London,
to Admiral Sir Reginald Hall, the Director of Naval Intelligence.
In his letter Captain Talbot asked Admiral Hall whether in
certain situations 'it would not perhaps be useful to use M.
Veniselos as a, so to speak, neutral means of inspiring certain of
our Allies . . . with a view more clearly in accord' with those of
Great Britain in regard to certain questions, if they existed,
where London was likely to be in disagreement with its Allies. In
saying this Captain Talbot had the United States and her
president in mind. He thought that opportunities would 'often
occur where one could, of course, quite unofficially, get
[Venizelos] to follow a desired line or to urge a suitable idea or
theory'. There were, he observed, 'probably very few men
endowed with his gift of argument and persuasion, and he
exercises, as a rule, a very remarkable influence on the person
with whom he is discussing; I think that this would apply
especially in the case of Americans, who are not, I imagine,
particularly "au fait" with all the complex conditions in Europe'.

Since it was British policy during this period to accommodate
both the United States and President Wilson, and since
Venizelos's personal qualities would be invaluable in any
Chancellor, Venizelos undoubtedly seemed to Cecil the type of
man he was looking for. 'This is a suggestion that should be kept
in mind. We ought to work closely with M. Venizelos', Cecil
noted in red ink after this letter was communicated to him on 23
December by Sir William Tyrrell, the Foreign Office's Assistant
Under-Secretary, who assured Cecil that Captain Talbot was an
officer of 'ability, tact & discretion'.[1]

Venizelos was a natural person for the position. He was well
known to both London and Paris. A leader of a small state, he
was then at the height of his intellectual and political powers. He
was an experienced diplomat and a statesman of European if not

[1] [Talbot] to Hall, 18 Dec. 1918, and the attached note by W[illiam]
T[yrrell] to Cecil, 23 Dec. [1918], as well as a minute by R[obert] C[ecil], [23
Dec. 1918?], Philip Noel-Baker Papers, FO/800/249.

world-wide reputation. Loyal to the Entente Powers during the war he had brought Greece to their side against the wishes of the king and at the price of a constitutional and political crisis. Moreover, like any leader of a small state interested in maintaining the post-war *status quo* Venizelos was 'very keen', as Captain Talbot informed Cecil, on the idea of the League. He was also, again according to the captain, very Anglophile and greatly preferred England to France,[1] a not unimportant consideration keeping in mind the international political role that the Chancellor was scheduled to play.

On 8 January 1919, several days after his arrival in Paris, Cecil broached his plan to three of the young academics attached to the American delegation (Messrs. James T. Shotwell, George Louis Beer, and A. A. Young). They strongly supported the idea.[2] So Cecil arranged to dine with Venizelos who, according to Captain Talbot, desired to talk to Cecil about the League.[3] When offered the Chancellorship by Cecil on behalf of the British Government, probably on the evening of 12 January,[4] Venizelos declined it, explaining that his own country needed him.[5]

Venizelos's decision undoubtedly disappointed Cecil a great deal, but it was not a death blow to the idea of a Chancellor for there were other potential candidates for the office. President Wilson thought about it at one point, and South Africa's Defence Minister, General Smuts, was mentioned along with Czechoslovakia's President, Tomas Masaryk, and Cecil himself.[6] Wilson,

---

[1] Cecil Diary, 10 Jan. 1919, p. 7, Add. MS. 51131, Robert Cecil Papers, BL. See also Jean Siotis, *Essai sur le Secrétariat international* (Genève: Droz, 1963), pp. 61–2; Cecil, *All the Way*, p. 150.

[2] Cecil Diary, 8 Jan. 1919, p. 5, Add. MS. 51131, Robert Cecil Papers, BL.

[3] Cecil Diary, 10 Jan. 1919, p. 7, ibid.

[4] Cecil Diary, 12 Jan. 1919, p. 11, ibid.

[5] Cecil, *All the Way*, pp. 150–1; Lord Robert Cecil, *A Great Experiment* (London: Jonathan Cape, 1941), p. 89.

[6] Lord Salter, *Memoirs of a Public Servant* (London: Faber and Faber, 1961), p. 146; Lord Salter, 'James Eric Drummond', *DNB 1951–1960* (London: Oxford University Press, 1971), p. 314; Raymond B. Fosdick, *The League and the United Nations after Fifty Years. The Six Secretaries-General* (privately printed, 1972), p. 13 fn.; Arthur W. Rovine, *The First Fifty Years. The Secretaries-General in World Politics 1920–1970* (Leyden: Sijthoff, 1970), p. 24; Siotis, p. 61; F. Yeats-Brown, 'The League of Nations. The Character of Sir Eric Drummond', *The Spectator*, 5 Jan. 1929, p. 14.

it appears, relinquished the idea of resigning the presidency and accepting the Chancellorship when he realized that his primary obligation was to see the Versailles Treaty through the Senate.[1] The far greater power that could have been exercised by an American President in world affairs might also explain Wilson's rejection of the idea. In the case of Smuts, the Chancellorship must have been an unattractive position compared with the influence and power that he could wield among political circles in London.

After Venizelos, Masaryk was probably the next most attractive candidate. He possessed many of Venizelos's advantages. He was the leader of a small state, intelligent, known to London and Paris, committed to the idea of the League, supporter of the Entente Powers during the war, and very friendly toward the Anglo-French. Masaryk, however, refused the Chancellorship on the grounds that he could not abandon his newly independent countrymen during that critical hour in their history. Acceptance of the Chancellorship would give the Czechs the impression that they were being abandoned by the very man who had brought them their freedom. Cecil, it appears, was passed over at his own request because his selection as Chancellor would have provoked a negative reaction from Georges Clemenceau, the French Prime Minister. He would have viewed Cecil's appointment as an indication of the growing British diplomatic influence in the drafting of the Covenant. Moreover, it should be noted that though the Prime Minister, Lloyd George, appears to have been favourably disposed to the idea of the Chancellor, Clemenceau and Vittorio Orlando, the Italian Prime Minister, were not 'particularly enthusiastic' about a Chancellor possessing real executive powers.[2]

With no other acceptable person available to play the political

---

[1] Fosdick, *The League and the United Nations After Fifty Years*, p. 13 fn.

[2] Siotis, pp. 61, 64; Lloyd George, i. 629. There is some evidence to show that the French were opposed to the Chancellorship idea. According to Drummond some French official circles felt that the Secretariat did not need to be large or consist of eminent men. The French 'idea was that international cooperation should be effected through continual meetings of responsible statesmen, and that a Secretariat was required only to note down decisions arrived at [during] those meetings'. Minutes of a Meeting held in the Secretary-General's Room, 3 Dec. 1919, General 1919: 40/2278/854, LNA.

role envisaged for Venizelos,[1] Cecil was forced to reconsider and to modify both the nature and the title of the office. He decided to de-emphasize and to depoliticize the Chancellor's office. Moreover, it was to be called the office of the Secretary-General and the position was to be that of a non-political functionary patterned along the lines of a senior government civil servant.[2] At Paris they had decided, Drummond noted years later, that they did not want to establish an international dictator.[3]

Cecil's initial draft of the Covenant on 11 January,[4] and the one tendered by Cecil and the British delegation on 20 January clearly reflected the metamorphosis of the Chancellor's office. In his 11 January sketch of the Covenant written before his conversation with Venizelos, Cecil desired that the Secretary-General or Chancellor 'should be appointed by the Great Powers, if possible choosing a national of some other country'—an obvious allusion to Venizelos. By 20 January, however, after Venizelos's rejection of the offer the draft Covenant was changed to read that the Chancellor should hold office at the Council's pleasure and to be named in the Covenant, his successor to be appointed by the Council. The draft Covenant of 27 January by Cecil and David Hunter Miller, the chief legal adviser of the American delegation, and the revised draft written on 2 February by Miller and his British counterpart, Sir Cecil Hurst, completed the process of making the office more administrative and less political.[5] Finally, on 13 February, the peace conference's League of Nations Commission completed the process. Undoubtedly to have the title of the office reflect more accurately its intended non-political role a proposal of the Commission's

[1] According to Drummond, the Chancellorship hinged on Venizelos's appointment. When it was discovered that they could not 'get the highest caliber man for the job', the whole question was reconsidered. Schwebel, p. 4.

[2] Cecil, *All the Way*, p. 151; Cecil, *A Great Experiment*, pp. 89–90; Salter, *Memoirs of a Public Servant*, p. 146; [Noel-] Baker, 'The Making of the Covenant from the British Point of View', pp. 40–1.

[3] Schwebel, p. 4. Five years after the event Philip Noel-Baker wrote that it had been decided at Paris that to lay the responsibility of Chancellor 'upon a single man was hardly possible'. [Noel-] Baker, 'The Making of the Covenant from the British Point of View', p. 41.

[4] Robert Cecil, Draft Sketch of a League of Nations, 11 Jan. 1919, FO/608/242.

[5] David Hunter Miller, *The Drafting of the Covenant* (New York: G. P. Putnam's Sons, 1928), ii. 61–4, 106–16, 131–41, 231–7.

Drafting Committee was accepted, substituting the title 'Secretary-General' for that of 'Chancellor' in the draft Covenant.[1] In the end the political powers given to the Secretary-General in the Covenant were minimal. According to the Covenant he was to act 'in that capacity in all meetings of the Assembly and of the Council'; Drummond's successor was to be appointed by the Council with the approval of a majority of the Assembly; the Secretary-General would appoint the secretariat staff subject to the Council's approval; the Secretary-General and the secretariat officials would have diplomatic privileges and immunities; in the case of war or threat of war the Secretary-General was on the request of a League member to summon immediately a Council meeting; and finally, the Secretary-General was to make all arrangements for a complete investigation and consideration of a dispute submitted to the Council which any party to the dispute believed would lead to a rupture.[2]

Drummond's Selection

Since the office of the Chancellor was to be downgraded the search to find someone to fill it moved away from the political personage and in the direction of the trained civil servant and functionary. Cecil's choice fell on Sir Maurice Hankey, the Secretary to the Cabinet, the Committee of Imperial Defence, and the Imperial War Cabinet.[3] Hankey had allowed his 'name to be mentioned informally' if the peace conference desired a British national for the position.[4] He was a natural choice as Secretary-General. He had discussed as early as January 1918 in a memorandum to the cabinet how the League might be developed.[5] Curiously, in mid-October 1918, almost a month before the armistice, he had a vision that he was destined to become the League's first Secretary-General.[6] By informally offering his name for consideration Hankey was obviously interested in the position and the possibilities that it offered. He did, however, have his reservations for he had warned Lloyd

---

[1] Ibid., pp. 302, 305.

[2] Articles 6, 7, 11, and 15 of the League Covenant.

[3] Cecil, *All the Way*, p. 151.

[4] Hankey to Esher, 16 Feb. 1919, Volume XI, Esher Papers, CC.

[5] G.T. 3344, M.P.A. Hankey, The League of Nations. Observations by the Secretary, 16 Jan. 1918, CAB/24/39, PRO.

[6] Stephen Roskill, *Hankey: Man of Secrets* (London: Collins, 1970), i. 613.

George that the general discussions about the League at the peace conference left him uneasy. His uneasiness can probably be traced to those clauses in the League Covenant dealing with the applications of sanctions against an aggressor state.[1]

Cecil approached Hankey probably on 13 February, the very day the peace conference's League of Nations Commission substituted the title Secretary-General for that of Chancellor in the draft Covenant.[2] Several days later Sir William Wiseman, who headed the British Secret Service in the United States during the war, took the matter up with his friend, Colonel Edward M. House, President Wilson's chief political adviser, 'who was quite agreeable' to Hankey's appointment.[3]

The selection of Hankey likewise raised no objections from the French who were desirous, for reasons of prestige, to assume the chairmanship of the peace conference's various commissions. The British tack appears to have been that though they would not press the question of chairmanships they wished the French to understand that having waived its claim London would insist on the chairmanship of future peace conference commissions and 'other such leading positions in connection with the Peace Conference'.[4] Who was to be Secretary-General was to be largely an Anglo-American question.

Though Hankey appears to have been initially attracted by Cecil's offer,[5] in the end Hankey's inclination and the advice that he received especially on the British side, made him decline it. Lord Esher, a fellow member of the Committee of Imperial Defence, told Hankey that he could play a more important political role not in an untried League but by continuing as the Secretary to the Cabinet 'at the right hand of the Prime Minister of the day'.[6] On the other hand, the Foreign Secretary, Arthur

---

[1] Ibid., ii. 56–7 and 60, 61.

[2] Cecil Diary, 13 Feb. 1919, p. 63, Add. MS. 51131, Robert Cecil Papers, BL.

[3] Cecil Diary, 16 Feb. 1919, p. 66, ibid.

[4] Hankey to [Lloyd George], 16 Feb. 1919, File F/23/4/14, Lloyd George Papers, BLL.

[5] Ian Malcolm Diary, 17 Feb. [1919], SRO-NRA.

[6] Hankey to Esher, 16 Feb. 1919, and Esher to Hankey, 18 Feb. [sic] 1919, Volume XI, Esher Papers, CC; see also Roskill, ii. 64–5. The last letter misdated 18 February is partially reproduced in Reginald Baliol Brett Esher, *Journals and Letters of Reginald, Viscount Esher*, ed. Oliver, Viscount Esher (London: Nicolson and Watson, 1938), iv. 226–8.

Balfour, and the Colonial Secretary, Lord Milner, advised him to accept the offer. Faced by conflicting advice Hankey was undecided and explained to Cecil that he could make no decision until he consulted with Lloyd George. Hankey's indecision and doubts were now the main stumbling block, for Colonel House made it clear to Cecil as he had to Wiseman that he 'warmly accepted the suggestion' of Hankey's appointment for the post.[1]

Colonel House's acceptance of Hankey, however, was based solely on political considerations dealing with British acceptance of the League and its administration. As he explained to President Wilson, he had approved of Hankey's possible appointment because Hankey had during the war done the type of work contemplated for the Secretary-General and because it would make Lloyd George and his colleagues, who had little faith in the League, more enthusiastic for the future world organization. There were also other advantages in having an English Secretary-General. It would lessen American difficulties and not place Washington at a disadvantage as would the selection of a French or Italian Secretary-General. In fact, it would enable the United States, if she so desired, to assume as a trade-off the chairmanship of the League Council.[2]

At the end of February Hankey solicited Lloyd George's advice, trying to ascertain the type of support that London might give the League.[3] Since Lloyd George had a penchant for oral messages we can safely assume that no written reply was ever made, but judging from Hankey's subsequent comments and actions Lloyd George probably advised him to delay any decision until the structure of the League was more definite and the nature of the peace settlement better known. As February gave way to March the pressure on Hankey to accept the position

---

[1] Cecil Diary, 27 Feb. 1919, pp. 73, 75, Add. MS. 51131, Robert Cecil Papers, BL.

[2] House (Paris) to Wilson, 27 Feb. 1919, Drawer 49, Folder 12, Edward M. House Papers, YUNH. A slightly different version misdated 28 Feb. 1919 is in the folder marked 28 Feb. 1919, Series 5B, Woodrow Wilson Papers, LC. House's message is partially reproduced in Edward M. House, *The Intimate Papers of Colonel House*, ed. Charles Seymour (New York: Houghton Mifflin, 1928), iv. 352.

[3] Hankey to [Lloyd George], 28 Feb. 1919, File F/23/4/7, Lloyd George Papers, BLL. See also, Roskill, ii. 66–7.

persisted.[1] Though he still doubted if he would accept he did during this period sketch an interesting plan for the organization and the working of the League as well as a provisional plan for the organization of the Secretariat.[2]

By 4 April, however, time was running out and the question of Hankey's appointment was again raised by Cecil who pressed Lloyd George for a decision.[3] This same day Hankey asked the advice of Lord Curzon, the Acting Foreign Secretary. He queried whether he would be 'more useful as an international official than as a British official?' 'I advised in favour of his remaining at home', Lord Curzon scribbled across the top of Hankey's letter.[4] The future Foreign Secretary strongly doubted whether the League was 'going to be the great and potent and world-pacifying instrument that its creators' desired. Like Esher he recommended that Hankey continue as Secretary to the Cabinet, a post that Curzon considered more powerful and important. Decline 'the gilded chair at Geneva', he submitted.[5]

Among those who also 'advised strongly' against accepting Cecil's offer was Hurst. He argued that his American counterpart, Miller, was certain, despite Wilson's confidence, that the Senate would reject American membership in the League.[6] This comment undoubtedly impressed Hankey for without American representation the League's effectiveness would suffer a serious blow.

Finally, on 17 April after a long discussion with Hankey, Lloyd George agreed that he should reject Cecil's offer.[7] What would he rather be, Lloyd George asked him, the Secretary to the Cabinet, the heart of a great empire, or the Secretary-General of a weak and untried international organ?[8] Thus the advice of

[1] Roskill, ii. 73.

[2] [Maurice Hankey], The League of Nations. Sketch Plan of Organisation, 31 Mar. 1919, FO/608/242.

[3] Cecil to [Lloyd George], 4 Apr. 1919, File F/6/6/25, Lloyd George Papers, BLL.

[4] Hankey to Curzon, 4 Apr. 1919, Box 65, Folder Marked Letters 1919 H-L, Curzon Papers, IOL.

[5] Roskill, ii. 65–6.

[6] Lord Hankey, *The Supreme Control at the Paris Peace Conference 1919* (London: Allen and Unwin, 1963), pp. 103–4.

[7] Ibid., p. 104; Roskill, ii. 80.

[8] Private information.

Curzon, Esher, and Hurst, as well as Lloyd George's comments convinced Hankey to reject Cecil's offer. So despite the attractions of a high salary, a beautiful house on Lake Geneva, work that offered prospects for the furtherance of world peace, Hankey concluded that he 'could make a greater contribution to peace and security by continuing [his services] to the Supreme Council in Paris [as well as Secretary to the Cabinet] than in the superficially attractive post at Geneva'.[1] This decision dovetailed with Hankey's lifelong belief that the 'British Empire was a great force for peace and stability in the world', which no League of Nations or United Nations could possibly replace.[2]

Hankey conveyed his decision to Cecil on 18 April.[3] What Cecil's reply was, if any, is unknown. Hankey's rejection of the position after a two months delay could only have annoyed Cecil for it arrived at a most inopportune moment. The conference was coming to a close, and the need to appoint the Secretary-General if the League was to be organized and begin functioning was now unexpectedly a pressing question. One more loose end was added to all the others that had to be tied up before the peace conference could adjourn.

Fortunately, in the preceding weeks Colonel House and Cecil had developed a contingency plan should Hankey reject the offer. This plan envisaged a substitution of Drummond for Hankey.[4] House knew Drummond and had been impressed by him. They first met in 1915 when House officially visited London. They met again in 1917 in Washington following America's entrance into the war and later that same year when House visited London. Cecil undoubtedly agreed to Drummond's possible selection because like Hankey he also saw the political advantages that would accrue to London if a British candidate were selected. In addition, as Minister of Blockade and then Assistant Secretary of State for Foreign Affairs Cecil had come to know Drummond very well. Indeed, it was Drummond who suggested to Smuts that Cecil rather than Sir Walter Phillimore

[1] Hankey, *The Supreme Control at the Paris Peace Conference 1919*, p. 103.

[2] Roskill, i. 23, 276. See also, Lord Riddell, *Lord Riddell's Intimate Diary of the Peace Conference and After 1918–1923* (London: Gollancz, 1933), pp. 182–3, and also, Roskill, ii. 88.

[3] Roskill, ii. 79–80.

[4] House Diary, 28 Apr. 1919, p. 179, Edward M. House Papers, YUNH.

should be appointed as head of the League of Nations section of
the British delegation to the peace conference.[1] The time element
was of course an important factor. Drummond was readily
available since he was attached to the British delegation at the
peace conference and was a trained and experienced diplomat
who had acted as the liaison officer between the Foreign Office
and the Cabinet during the war.[2] All these factors help to explain
Drummond's selection.

Like Hankey, Drummond had also been involved in the early
cabinet discussions about the League, especially when Colonel
House visited London in 1917.[3] In fact, he had expressed himself
about international organization as early as June 1915 in a
memorandum dealing with the reduction of armaments.[4] By
January 1916 Drummond was in communication with Lord
Bryce. He was aware that a group led by Bryce and one led by
the former President, William Howard Taft,[5] were dealing with
the question of post-war international organization. Drummond
had been a successful private secretary to the Foreign Office's
Under-Secretaries, Lord Fitzmaurice and T. M. Wood (1906–
1908), to the Foreign Secretaries, Sir Edward Grey (1915–16)
and Balfour (1916–18), as well as to the Prime Minister, Herbert
Asquith (1912–15). In the Foreign Office Drummond had been
an unobtrusive official who had been marked for slow and steady
advancement.[6] Through his private secretaryships he made his
way up the Foreign Office hierarchy.[7] Moreover, during the
peace conference his familiarity with procedure and grasp of

---

[1] Drummond to [Smuts], 1 Dec. 1918, No. 88, Volume 19, Microfilm copy
of the Jan Christiaan Smuts Papers, CU.

[2] Lord Hankey, *The Supreme Command 1914–1918* (London: Allen and
Unwin, 1961), i. 184–5.

[3] G.T. 2667 E[ric] D[rummond], Proposed Formation of the League of
Nations to Secure the Maintenance of Future Peace, 15 Nov. 1917, CAB/24/32,
PRO.

[4] E[ric] D[rummond], An untitled memorandum dealing with the reduction
of armaments, 11 June 1915, Edward Grey Papers, FO/800/95.

[5] Bryce to Drummond, 17 Jan. 1916 and D[rummond] to Bryce, 18 Jan.
1916, Edward Grey Papers, FO/800/105.

[6] George Slocombe, *A Mirror to Geneva* (London: Jonathan Cape, 1937),
p. 79; Zara S. Steiner, *The Foreign Office and Foreign Policy, 1898–1914*
(Cambridge: Cambridge University Press, 1969), p. 121.

[7] Steiner, p. 121.

detail, combined with a marked detachment and sincerity had attracted attention and earned him a high reputation.[1]

Two days after Hankey rejected the offer the contingency plan was put into effect and within a week Drummond was selected for the position. On 20 April, Colonel House took up the matter with Balfour.[2] What was more natural than for Balfour to agree to the House–Cecil proposal since Drummond like Hankey had also suggested that he would like to be considered for the Secretary-Generalship.[3] This same day House mentioned to Miller that they now intended to have Drummond as Secretary-General. As instructed by House, Miller then wrote and reminded President Wilson of the need to appoint the Secretary-General.[4] Cecil likewise reminded Lloyd George. He thought it most important that an Englishman be selected and of those readily available Drummond would be the best man provided he accepted the offer. Could he assume, Cecil underlined in his scribbled note, that Lloyd George would approve of Drummond's selection? He pressed for an immediate reply. Cecil pointed out that there were only a few days left before the Covenant would be approved and Drummond would naturally want at least that amount of time to make up his mind. He emphasized with double underlining that perhaps Lloyd George could give him an oral reply.[5] The reply was undoubtedly in the affirmative, but when the offer was made Drummond hesitated to accept it, although as noted above he had suggested that he be considered for the post. He was very concerned about accepting the offer, Drummond admitted to Sir Ian Malcolm, Balfour's private secretary. He feared the task of organizing the League and thought that all things considered he would probably turn the offer down. Malcolm and Drummond then discussed substitutes and concluded that either Arthur Salter, a gifted civil

[1] Salter, 'James Eric Drummond', p. 314. See also, V. H. Rothwell, *British War Aims and Peace Diplomacy 1914–1918* (Oxford: Clarendon Press, 1971), pp. 163–4.

[2] House Diary, 20 Apr. 1919, p. 168, Edward M. House Papers, YUNH.

[3] Frank P. Walters, *A History of the League of Nations* (London: Oxford University Press, 1960), p. 75.

[4] David Hunter Miller, *My Diary at the Conference of Paris* (New York: Appeal, 1921), i. 261, 263 and viii. 457.

[5] Cecil to [Lloyd George], 21 Apr. [1919], File F/6/6/32, Lloyd George Papers, BLL.

servant and chairman during the war of the Allied Maritime Transport Council, or Geoffrey Dawson, the former editor of *The Times* of London, would be good replacements.[1] It appears that Henry Wickham Steed, then editor of *The Times*, was also mentioned.[2]

These men, however, were never considered for he 'was extremely lucky', Cecil later wrote, 'in persuading' Drummond to assume the Secretary-Generalship.[3] Drummond's change of mind probably occurred following discussions with his family.[4] When Malcolm heard that Drummond had accepted he was very surprised and made arrangements whereby Drummond during the period he served as Secretary-General did not surrender his position in the Foreign Office nor forfeit any retirement benefits he had earned.[5] Drummond's acceptance of the offer was conveyed to Miller by Cecil on 24 April. Arrangements were then made between Cecil and Miller to have Colonel House draft a resolution for the approval of the Allied leadership appointing Drummond as Secretary-General.[6] This was done by House several days later and forwarded to President Wilson. It was his understanding, House informed Wilson, that Lloyd George agreed to Drummond's appointment and that consequently only Clemenceau's approval was needed.[7] The approval of the three leaders soon followed on the morning of 28 April.[8] The confirmation of this decision by the plenary session of the peace conference that afternoon pleased House no end.[9]

Not everyone, however, was pleased with Drummond's appointment. The first to express openly his disapproval was James Ramsey MacDonald, one of the leaders of the British Labour Party. Drummond's appointment, he believed, almost

[1] Ian Malcolm Diary, 22 Apr. [1919], SRO-NRA. See also, Salter, *Memoirs of a Public Servant*, p. 147.

[2] Salter, *Memoirs of a Public Servant*, p. 147.

[3] Cecil, *All the Way*, p. 150.

[4] Ian Malcolm Diary, 22 and 26 Apr. [1919], SRO-NRA.

[5] Ian Malcolm Diary, 26 Apr., ibid.

[6] Miller, *My Diary at the Conference of Paris*, i. 273, 274.

[7] [House] to [Cecil], 26 Apr. 1919, Drawer 49, Folder 12, Edward M. House Papers, YUNH.

[8] *PRFRUS, The Paris Peace Conference 1919*, v. 315.

[9] His prior planning with Cecil, House wrote, and his subsequent moves illustrated how easy it was for the man with a plan of action to accomplish his purpose. House Diary, 28 Apr. 1919, p. 179, Edward M. House Papers, YUNH.

forbade anyone to have any hope in the League. Drummond was not the right man for the post since he had been 'brought up in the ways of Foreign Offices, trained in the methods of discredited diplomacy, with no Democratic vision and no conception of what Democracy means'. It was unreasonable to expect from Drummond 'any inspiration which would make the League anything more than it is now—the organ of the victors to dominate the world'.[1] MacDonald's later reservedness to the League might in part stem from the damage suffered by his ego in 1920 when after being invited to serve on the Labour Advisory Committee of the League of Nations Union his name was withdrawn from consideration because some members of the Union had raised objections.[2] His particular dislike for Drummond may be traced to the fact that his conversion to Roman Catholicism years before was neither forgiven nor forgotten by MacDonald who resented such action by a fellow Scot. Indeed, when Drummond in 1932 wanted to leave the League and return to the Foreign Office it was MacDonald, now Prime Minister, who blocked his appointment to Washington or Paris.[3] It was this religious factor which might also explain why MacDonald as Prime Minister in 1929 chose Sir Robert Vansittart over Drummond to be Permanent Under-Secretary of the Foreign Office, even though Hugh Dalton,[4] the Parliamentary Under-Secretary for Foreign Affairs, and Cecil,[5] deputy leader of the British delegation to the Assembly, were favourably disposed to Drummond's appointment to the position.

A more muted voice of disapproval was that of Sir Eyre Crowe, the powerful Assistant Under-Secretary of the Foreign Office. Crowe was contemptuous if not actually hostile to the

---

[1] J. Ramsay MacDonald, 'Fighting for a Peace to End Peace', *Forward* (Glasgow), 24 May 1919, p. 1.

[2] Interview with Noel-Baker, 24 July 1971; J. A. Thompson, 'The League of Nations and Promotion of the League Idea in Great Britain', *The Australian Journal of Politics and History*, XVIII, No. 1 (April 1972), p. 59 fn., and Earnest Bramsted, 'Apostles of Collective Security. The L.N.U. and its Functions', ibid., XIII, No. 3 (December 1967), p. 355.

[3] James Barros, *Betrayal from Within: Joseph Avenol, Secretary-General of the League of Nations, 1933–1940* (New Haven: Yale University Press, 1969), p. 3 fn. See also, Roskill, iii. 57.

[4] Dalton Diary, 8 July 1929, LSEPS.

[5] C[ecil] to M[urray], 14 Nov. 1929, Gilbert Murray Papers, BLOU.

League so that this must be kept in mind in evaluating his comment. Written a year after Drummond's appointment, Crowe felt that the selection of an Englishman for the position had been and would 'contribute to be a source of endless suspicion' both against the League and against Great Britain, especially in the United States, but likewise in France and in other countries.[1] Interestingly, as in the case of MacDonald, Crowe's hostility to Drummond's appointment may perhaps in part also be traced to the question of religion. Vansittart wrote later that Crowe 'hated Private Secretaries as others hate cats. He disliked especially Eric Drummond, once persistent in the function and a Roman Catholic with the ardours of a convert, while Crowe could never forget his [own] atheism. He would have it that Drummond—and therefore the whole genus—pushed private policies up backstairs'.[2] The question may be raised whether Vansittart, who was junior to Crowe in the Foreign Office, knew him well enough to make such a statement, but the circumstantial evidence would appear to substantiate Vansittart's comments.[3]

It might be asked why Drummond ever accepted the position,

[1] Minute by E[yre] C[rowe], 31 May [1920], FO/371/4313.

[2] Lord Vansittart, *The Mist Procession* (London: Hutchinson, 1958), p. 272. According to one student of the wartime Foreign Office Drummond's 'Catholic faith helped to account for his friendly attitude to the Poles'—a rare occasion when Drummond's faith appears to have affected his politics. Rothwell, pp. 56, 232.

[3] On private secretaries: writing to Lord Curzon in May 1922, Crowe denigrated the private secretary system which he felt, combined with the private-letter system, had led to the ruination of the Foreign Office. (Crowe to Curzon, 14 May 1922, Box 65, Folder Marked Letters 1922 A–C, Curzon Papers, IOL.) On Drummond's Roman Catholicism: though Crowe's two closest friends were Catholics, Tyrrell and the Portuguese Ambassador (see Lewis Chester, Stephen Fay, and Hugo Young, *The Zinoviev Letter* (London: Heinemann, 1967), p. 66), his own Foreign Office minutes on the question of the Vatican or Roman Catholicism are even more caustic than most of his minutes. To be religious as was Drummond or even to convert as he did, must have been incomprehensible to an atheist like Crowe. It is not customary, however, for anyone, let alone a confirmed atheist, to pen his religious prejudices in official government minutes. Vansittart and Crowe: it was Crowe who recommended to Curzon in August 1922 that Vansittart be assigned to the Paris embassy; his comments about Vansittart being of such a nature that it was obvious they knew each other very well. (Crowe to Curzon, 19 Aug. 1922, Box 65, Folder Marked Letters 1922 A–C, Curzon Papers, IOL.)

keeping in mind that there appears to have been some hostility to his appointment and considering that on the day before his name was confirmed by the plenary session of the peace conference, he was rather oppressed by the enormous task he had undertaken. Cecil hoped that he would be able to handle the job, but admitted that there was a danger. Civil servant types like Drummond, he thought, when suddenly forced to take personal initiatives and assume responsibility felt rather adrift without an official hierarchy and the machinery to back him up.[1] Gordon Auchincloss, a member of the American delegation, echoed somewhat similar fears. He thought that Drummond lacked sufficient 'executive ability' for the office. However, Auchincloss felt that Drummond might do provided he acquired a subordinate who had this ability.[2] Colonel House subsequently expressed analogous thoughts. He feared that Drummond was 'scarcely equal to the undertaking', and Cecil, on whom Drummond still leaned heavily for advice, was too erratic to be trusted. House did not dare leave Cecil and Drummond alone for any length of time and he felt it necessary to follow them to London to keep a check on them.[3]

Yet despite all this Drummond accepted the position. Actually several weeks before the offer was made to him Drummond had been inclined to resign unless within a year he could succeed Lord Hardinge as Permanent Under-Secretary of the Foreign Office. Malcolm begged Drummond to continue in the Foreign Office so that he could succeed Hardinge and thus establish a claim to the ambassadorship in Washington, which is what Drummond really wanted.[4] In fact, on 26 February Malcolm on Balfour's instructions had recommended Drummond along with others to Lloyd George for the Washington post.[5] Thus the prestige of the League appointment and its challenging nature were obvious considerations in Drummond's decision to leave the Foreign Office. The fact that he would be running his own

[1] Cecil Diary, 27 Apr. 1919, p. 136, Add. MS. 51131, Robert Cecil Papers, BL.

[2] Auchincloss Diary, 30 Apr. 1919, Gordon Auchincloss Papers, YUNH.

[3] House Diary, 10 June 1919, pp. 238–9, Edward M. House Papers, YUNH.

[4] Ian Malcolm Diary, 30 Mar. [1919], SRO-NRA.

[5] Malcolm to [Lloyd George], 26 Feb. 1919, File F/3/4/14, Lloyd George Papers, BLL.

show was probably even more important than the increased
financial remuneration.[1] Tension, as we have seen, within the
Foreign Office with Crowe, sharpened by Drummond's desire
for Hardinge's position which a year later was given to Crowe,
may have been an additional factor in deciding to accept the
Secretary-Generalship. Saying this, however, Drummond, as we
have noted, was taken as early as 1915 with the idea of some sort
of international organization after the war and unlike most
diplomats at Paris in 1919, especially on the British side, 'was
keenly interested in the idea of the League'.[2] It was probably this
interest plus being the chief executive officer of the League and
running his own show which largely explains Drummond's
acceptance of the offer.[3]

The French played no great role in Drummond's selection. It
was in no way fostered by Clemenceau. Therefore stories that the
French Prime Minister idly suggested Drummond as Secretary-
General must be dismissed as apocryphal.[4] So astute a practitioner
of statecraft as Clemenceau would be well acquainted with the
talents and experience of any British nominee. The French were
of course quite aware of the importance of even a depoliticized
Secretary-General. Therefore, there was an oral understanding
that Drummond's appointment was part of an arrangement
under which there would be a balance between British and
French interests, or, to put it another way, between British and
French representation, in the higher direction of the League and
the International Labour Organisation, the two important world
bodies established by the peace conference. In the League, the

[1] In 1919 Drummond was earning £1,500 a year (about $7,500). As minister
of a legation he could expect to earn £2,000 a year (about $10,000). As
Secretary-General his total remuneration would be over £10,000 a year (about
$50,000) which included a tax-free salary of £4,000 (about $20,000) and
£6,000 (about $30,000) for expenses, as well as a rent-free house. Considering
the lower living costs during this period it was a sizeable compensation.
Slocombe, p. 80.

[2] Walters, p. 75.

[3] Ambassador Thanassis Aghnides who rose up the ranks of the Secretariat
to become Under Secretary-General has noted that Drummond believed in the
League and very much desired its success. 'The Reminiscences of Thanassis
Aghnides' (typewritten manuscript), Oral History Collection, CUNY.

[4] Walters, p. 74. For the apocryphal stories see Slocombe, pp. 78–9, and
Arthur C. Temperley, *The Whispering Gallery of Europe* (London: Collins, 1938),
pp. 43–4.

Frenchman, Jean Monnet, would be Drummond's deputy, while in the International Labour Organisation, the Director would be the Frenchman, Albert Thomas, and his deputy would be the Englishman, Harold Butler. When Drummond and Thomas departed they would be succeeded by their respective deputies.[1]

Legally Drummond's tenure was in no way restricted. The annex to the Covenant appointing him placed no limit on how long he could serve as Secretary-General.[2] In the end, he served for fourteen years, the longest period that anyone held the office. When Drummond departed in 1933, the Paris understanding was executed and he was succeeded by his French deputy, Joseph Avenol, who had replaced Monnet in 1923. During the years that he served Drummond established traditions and precedents which were expanded by his successors. To a large extent the limitation that he placed upon his activities and his interpretation of both the Covenant and the Secretary-General's office largely reflected his prior training and experience as well as his own personality and value system.

[1] Barros, *Betrayal from Within*, pp. 1–14. See also, Edward J. Phelan, *Yes and Albert Thomas* (New York: Columbia University Press, 1949), pp. 25, 235–6.

[2] Cecil, *A Great Experiment*, p. 90; André Cagne, *Le Secrétariat General de la Société des Nations* (Paris: Jel, 1936), pp. 34–5.

II

JAMES ERIC DRUMMOND: ATTITUDES, APPROACHES, AND PERCEPTIONS

Realism's Restraint

James Eric Drummond was born in 1876 into one of the oldest families of Scotland.[1] Educated at Eton, he joined the Foreign Office in 1900 at a time when it was heavily staffed by fellow Etonians.[2] He was knighted in 1916 in recognition of his wartime service,[3] and in 1937 he became the sixteenth Earl of Perth upon the death of his childless half-brother.

His ancestry, his education, and his service in the Foreign Office undoubtedly made Drummond, as one associate noted, 'conscious of belonging to the ruling class in his own country. His reflexes were those of the civil servant, but tempered and modified by the psychology of one who "belongs". This psychology accounts for the measured temerity in which he indulged [during] the first years of the League's existence'.[4]

Though there is some truth in these remarks, Drummond's actions were also geared to the real world and based on his life experiences. Trained in the traditional secret diplomacy of the pre-1914 period[5] his Foreign Office experiences could only have

---

[1] *Burke's Genealogical and Heraldic History of the Peerage, Baronetage and Knightage* (99th edn.; London: Burke's Peerage, 1949), pp. 1574–5.

[2] Zara S. Steiner, *The Foreign Office and Foreign Policy, 1898–1914* (Cambridge: Cambridge University Press, 1969), pp. 217–21.

[3] *The Times* (London), 22 Dec. 1916, p. 8.

[4] *Proceedings of the Conference on Experience in International Administration, held in Washington on January 30, 1943, under the auspices of the Carnegie Endowment for International Peace* (Washington, D.C.: Carnegie Endowment for International Peace (roneographed), 1943), p. 9. Drummond, we are informed by a former associate, had 'préjugés aristocratiques' and these prejudices probably made him partial to certain countries to the detriment of certain other countries. Émile Giraud, 'Le Secrétariat des institutions internationales', *Académie de droit international. Recueil des cours*, Volume 79, No. 2 (1951), p. 417.

[5] The one characteristic that Drummond's former associates unanimously agree upon is that he was a 'diplomat' of the pre-1914 period. 'The Reminiscences of Thanassis Aghnides' (typewritten manuscript), 'The Reminiscences of Pablo de Azcárate y Florez' (typewritten manuscript), 'The

educated him to the paramount role and central importance of
the Great Powers in international politics, to the danger to peace
that their unbridled competition held for the world community,
and to the urgent necessity to accommodate and moderate this
competition in world politics. He was therefore, unlike other
well-meaning people, more restrained in his expectations of what
the League could accomplish in world politics and especially as
to what he in particular as Secretary-General could accomplish
in attempting to accommodate and moderate the conflicting
desires of states. That is not to say, however, that Drummond
viewed the League or the position of Secretary-General as
politically impotent or unimportant, but merely that in
peacefully resolving the conflicting desires of states or in
managing inter-state crises their roles were more marginal than
well-meaning people were either aware of or willing to admit.
This view largely dovetailed with his experience inasmuch as
Drummond as a civil servant was accustomed to viewing his role
as the executor not the originator of policy. It would be safe to
say, however, that during his Foreign Office service he had
discovered and learned of the power that can be exercised by the
civil servant through his ability to advise and thus influence the
policy maker. Indeed, it was this largely personal power that
would be his main manipulative instrument as Secretary-General
in managing political affairs. These attitudes, approaches, and
perceptions were in turn buttressed by certain personality traits
all of which go far in explaining Drummond's use of the office.

Finally, one has to keep in mind that the League in 1919 and
the powers of its Secretary-General were limited. Even more
important, the member states of the organization were, no less so
than states today, jealous of their sovereign rights and preroga-
tives. Unsolicited initiatives by the Secretary-General would
have been construed as interference and woe to any holder of the
office that forgot it. Moreover, the configuration of world politics
during the inter-war period did not allow the type of open
political initiatives that one generally associates with the
Secretary-General of the United Nations. True enough, the
official comments on the Covenant presented to Parliament in

Reminiscences of Branko Lukac' (typewritten manuscript), and 'The Reminiscences of Pablo de Azcárate y Florez, Édouard de Haller, and Van Asch van
Wijck' (typewritten manuscript), Oral History Collection, CUNY.

the summer of 1919 noted that the Secretariat had 'immense possibilities of usefulness, and a very wide field will be open for the energy and initiatives of the first Secretary-General'.[1] But in line with his attitudes and perceptions, Drummond never publicly showed any initiative. For example, he never addressed the Assembly's plenary session, and his comments in the Council, where he was entitled to sit, were no more than those of a 'secretary of a committee'.[2] He did this even though the rules of procedure allowed the Secretary-General to address the Assembly. Even the annual report to the Assembly, used so frequently by the United Nations Secretary-General to discuss and focus world opinion on major international problems, was under Drummond merely an enumeration of the League's activities for the previous year.[3]

After the Second World War with the example of the United Nations' Secretary-General as a comparison, Drummond insisted that public political activities on his part would have been out of the question. He rejected any comparison with the dynamic Albert Thomas. If Thomas had undertaken, Drummond considered, the type of public initiatives in the League that he had undertaken in the International Labour Organisation, he would have been forced to resign.[4]

Drummond may have been right. Thomas's public initiatives were undertaken in matters that were largely non-political in character. Indeed, when Drummond resigned in 1933 the Foreign Office wanted to replace him with another Englishman. It was interested in avoiding the oral agreement made at Paris in 1919. As politically inactive as Drummond appeared to be,

[1] *The Covenant of the League of Nations with a Commentary Thereon. Presented to Parliament by Command of His Majesty June 1919.* Miscellaneous No. 3 (1919), Cmd. 151 (London: H.M. Stationery Office, 1921), p. 16.

[2] *Proceedings of the Conference on Experience in International Administration*, p. 11.

[3] Stephen M. Schwebel, *The Secretary-General of the United Nations* (Cambridge: Harvard University Press, 1951), p. 6. See the criticism by Egon F. Ranshofen-Wertheimer, *The International Secretariat: A Great Experiment in International Administration* (Washington, D.C.: Carnegie Endowment for International Peace, 1945), pp. 38–9.

[4] Schwebel, pp. 3, 232 fn. 42, 271 fn. 79. On Thomas's energetic use of his office see Edward J. Phelan, *Yes and Albert Thomas* (New York: Columbia University Press, 1949); Bertus Willem Schaper, *Albert Thomas; trente ans de réformisme social* (Assen: Gorcum, 1959).

intrinsically the Foreign Office knew it was the Secretary-Generalship which was the more important political post.[1] Yet as guarded and discreet as he was Drummond was suspected in Geneva of playing 'too active a role'.[2] This made it even more difficult for him to act publicly and was clearly mirrored in the Assembly's early admonishments to the Secretariat to control its activities.[3]

In line with his cautious approach Drummond eschewed public acts or initiatives. He pointed out that not being a parliamentarian or a politician he was totally unaccustomed to making public speeches. Moreover, he did not believe that people were moved by public speeches or documents, whereas they were influenced by private talk. It was the Secretary-General's behind-the-scenes work, he maintained, which was more important. This type of approach, he explained, suited his temperament and prior experience.

The Covenant's limitations thus forced him, Drummond noted, to work behind the scenes, but that did not make his work any less effective. He felt that to have taken a public stand in a dispute would surely have detracted from his political influence.[4] Hence Drummond would not have thought of appealing to public opinion to defend the League's principles or to take a public stand on the great questions of the day. He would not have done it because, as an associate observed, Drummond thought that in making public statements he would have 'usurped a role which was not his'.[5] With this approach it would be safe to say that the new Wilsonian diplomacy of open agreements openly arrived at, seemingly personified in the League, was probably not to Drummond's liking; but it would also be safe to say that Drummond would have been content if the League could contribute in some small way to open agreements secretly

---

[1] James Barros, *Betrayal from Within: Joseph Avenol, Secretary-General of the League of Nations, 1933-1940* (New Haven: Yale University Press, 1969), p. 5.

[2] Hugh R. Wilson, *Diplomat Between Wars* (New York: Longmans, Green, 1941), p. 213.

[3] Felix Morley, *The Society of Nations* (Washington, D.C.: The Brookings Institution, 1932), pp. 322-3; Charles Howard-Ellis, *The Origin, Structure and Working of the League of Nations* (London: Allen and Unwin, 1928), pp. 197-8.

[4] Schwebel, p. 7. See also, Ernst Weizsäcker, *The Memoirs of Ernst von Weizsäcker*, trans. John Andrews (London: Gollancz, 1951), p. 75.

[5] Giraud, 'Le Secrétariat des institutions internationales', p. 420.

arrived at. This attitude might partially explain his opposition to the establishment of permanent missions in Geneva.[1] Drummond felt that the Secretariat should communicate directly with governments and not through intermediaries,[2] because he wanted to deal directly with the people who made policy not with their underlings.[3] Thus he prevailed upon London not to establish a permanent mission at Geneva.[4] When asked by the League's permanent delegates for closer liaison the most Drummond could offer was to set aside two afternoons a month at which time he would be at their disposal if they wished to see him.[5] It was not until after he had given public notice that he would resign that he was willing to give greater recognition to the permanent delegates established at Geneva.[6]

Complaints about Drummond's approach were raised from the very beginning by Raymond B. Fosdick, the American Under Secretary-General, who thought that he was too cautious,

---

[1] 'The Reminiscences of Thanassis Aghnides'; *Proceedings of the Exploratory Conference on the Experience of the League of Nations Secretariat, held in New York City on August 30, 1942, under the auspices of the Carnegie Endowment for International Peace* (Washington, D.C.: Carnegie Endowment for International Peace (roneographed), 1942), pp. 40, 45; Ranshofen-Wertheimer, pp. 193–4; Frank P. Walters, *A History of the League of Nations* (London: Oxford University Press, 1960), pp. 197–9.

[2] *Proceedings of the Exploratory Conference on the Experience of the League of Nations Secretariat*, p. 40.

[3] 'The Reminiscences of Thanassis Aghnides'.

[4] *Proceedings of the Exploratory Conference on the Experience of the League of Nations Secretariat*, p. 40; Ranshofen-Wertheimer, p. 194. Initially, Drummond's plan appears to have involved the British Minister in Bern acting as a permanent representative in between meetings of the Council, and requiring the establishment of a Geneva office. Drummond to Hankey, 2 Oct. 1920, and an attached note by Hankey, FO/371/5478.

[5] E[ric] D[rummond], Record of Interview, 19 Feb. 1924, General 1924: 40/34074/25596, LNA.

[6] Riddell (Geneva) to Skelton, 29 Nov. 1932, File 65Q, Box 265393, Department of External Affairs, PACRMB; Minutes of a Directors' Meeting, 2 Dec. 1932, LNA; Gilbert (Geneva) to the Secretary of State, No. 578, 2 May 1933, File 500.C001/802, RG 59, NA. Gilbert's report is partially reproduced in Arthur W. Rovine, *The First Fifty Years. The Secretaries-General in World Politics 1920–1970* (Leyden: Sijthoff, 1970), p. 48. See also, Walter A. Riddell, *World Security by Conference* (Toronto: Ryerson, 1947), p. 179, and Victor-Yves Ghébali, *Les Délégations permanentes auprès de la Société des Nations* (Bruxelles: Bruylant, 1971), pp. 97–103, 105–6, 107–8.

lacked strength and daring, and often wavered. Fosdick believed that Drummond was not the man for the slot since he was not enough of a leader and lacked the quality associated with leadership. He thought that once America joined the League Drummond should be replaced by someone who would be unafraid to be both bold and imaginative.[1]

Drummond's personality also contributed to his restrained use of the office. Though any composite of his personality is at best subjective there are certain consistent features commented upon by a number of persons who either observed him or worked with him. He was shy, it was said, and, as we have seen, frightened of speechmaking.[2] He was a person of 'considerable acumen' with the rare gift for conciliating divergent positions and in a modest and deprecating fashion offer a suggestion which would satisfy both sides and enable the work to be resumed.[3] He was assisted in this by certain personal qualities. Among these were a pleasant sense of humour which reflected the general poise of his temperament. Even more important he was not tempted 'to the dangers of the witty and memorable epigram'. In addition, Drummond did not have the kind of 'uncompromising precision of thought and language which sometimes handicaps a chairman or a negotiator who is seeking a solution through compromise'.[4] To the higher officials of the Secretariat he was always available for consultation and guidance even during the busiest periods.[5] To the large mass of the Secretariat, however, Drummond was considered distant and unapproachable which might in part be traced to his manner which was 'limp, melancholy and almost

---

[1] Fosdick to Gilchrist, 15 June 1920, File 1171, Raymond B. Fosdick Papers, PU.

[2] Schwebel, p. 5. See also, Drummond (Geneva) to Murray, 15 Oct. 1928, Gilbert Murray Papers, BLOU; Morley, p. 314; F. Yeats-Brown, 'The League of Nations. The Character of Sir Eric Drummond', *The Spectator*, 5 Jan. 1929, p. 14.

[3] Wilson, p. 213. See also, Lord Robert Cecil, *A Great Experiment* (London: Jonathan Cape, 1941), p. 90; Schwebel, p. 7.

[4] Lord Salter, 'James Eric Drummond', *DNB 1951–1960*, (London: Oxford University Press, 1971), p. 315.

[5] Ibid.; Lord Salter, *Memoirs of a Public Servant* (London: Faber and Faber, 1961), p. 148; 'The Reminiscences of Thanassis Aghnides', and 'The Reminiscences of Pablo de Azcárate y Florez'.

apologetic'. He gave the impression of just having come in from the moors and his whole appearance marked him as a Scot.[1]

He appears to have had common sense, prudence, tact, discretion, discernment, circumspection, resourcefulness, and a cautious unemotional nature.[2] Like any good Scot he was economical.[3] Yet what he seemingly lacked in imagination, in intuitive insight, in charismatic personality, and in spiritual commitment he more than possessed in administrative and organizational prowess.[4] One British observer described Drummond succinctly as 'Quite the right man in the right place, able, impartial, universally respected—adds to the prestige of G't Britain here. A very practical man but not without vision'.[5]

One can argue that as a converted and devout Roman Catholic Drummond's anti-communism largely flowed from his religion,[6]

---

[1] George Slocombe, *A Mirror to Geneva* (London: Jonathan Cape, 1937), pp. 333–4. See also, 'The Reminiscences of Pablo de Azcárate y Florez'.

[2] 'The Reminiscences of Thanassis Aghnides', 'The Reminiscences of Pablo de Azcárate y Florez', and 'The Reminiscences of Branko Lukac'. See also, Paul Hymans, *Mémoires* (Bruxelles: Solvay, 1958), i. 137–8; Arthur C. Temperley, *The Whispering Gallery of Europe* (London: Collins, 1938), pp. 44–5, 256; Morley, p. 314; Schwebel, p. 7; Walters, p. 77; Cecil, *A Great Experiment*, p. 90; Ranshofen-Wertheimer, pp. 48–9.

[3] Walters, p. 77.

[4] 'The Reminiscences of Thanassis Aghnides'; 'The Reminiscences of Pablo de Azcárate y Florez'; 'The Reminiscences of Branko Lukac'; 'The Reminiscences of Pablo de Azcárate y Florez, Édouard de Haller, and Van Asch van Wijck'; Slocombe, p. 85. See also, Temperley, pp. 44–5.

[5] Tennant to [Lloyd George], 12 Sept. 1922, File F/97/1/42, Lloyd George Papers, BLL.

[6] Does not the Soviet Union, Drummond wrote in January 1925, 'represent a system which is the exact antithesis of the League and all it stands for? Is not the Soviet ideal the establishment throughout the world of Soviet Republics with a headquarter Government at Moscow?' (Drummond to Strakosch, 5 Jan. 1925, MG, J1, Volume 114, Mackenzie King Papers, PAC.) During his Latin American tour in 1931 Drummond had an interview with Cuba's strong-man President Gerardo Machado y Morales. The President expressed the thought that the world's real danger was communism. He believed that nations should co-operate in order 'to combat the communist peril'. This was why, the President explained, he 'believed so strongly in the League'. Sir Eric replied that he agreed with the President on this point. Drummond thought that the world's 'two great antagonistic forces' were communism on the one hand, and the League on the other. It was obvious that these two forces were opposed to each other and though they temporarily coexisted, in the end a choice 'might have to be made between the two'. E[ric] D[rummond], Note by the Secretary-

but there is certainly no evidence to show that he attempted to obstruct Soviet Russia's admission to the League or its co-operation and association with the organization especially in disarmament questions. The evidence is very strongly to the contrary.[1] Drummond was too experienced a diplomat to want the League, or the United Nations for that matter, to be anything but a universal organization, no matter how much he found a particular government and its social and political philosophy objectionable.[2] Indeed, just before the end of the First World War, Drummond had expressed the thought that one had to 'if not on the ground of principle, at least on that of practicability, rule out the suggestion of [communism's] deliberate destruction by force'. He argued that some method had to be found to deal with it and advocated its confinement to those areas where it formed a vast majority of the population in the hope that it would be 'extinguished by its own fierceness'.[3] On the other

General on his Visit to Havana, 27–31 Jan. 1931, FO/371/15052. See also, Rovine, p. 47.

[1] K[err] to [Lloyd George], 26 May 1920 and the attached note by E[ric] D[rummond], same date, File F/90/1/9, Lloyd George Papers, BLL; Drummond to Cecil, 13 Feb. 1923, [Drummond] to Tufton, same date, and C[ecil] to Drummond, 16 Feb. 1923, Add. MS. 51110, Robert Cecil Papers, BL; Drummond to Strakosch, 5 Jan. 1925, MG 26, J1, Volume 114, Mackenzie King Papers, PAC; Drummond (Geneva) to Chamberlain, 19 Dec. 1925, FO/371/11068; [Cecil] to Chamberlain, 26 Nov. 1926, and the attached record of an interview by E[ric] D[rummond], 23 Nov. 1926, FO/371/11889; [Eric Drummond], Record of Interview, 28 Nov. 1926, FO/371/11890; [Eric] D[rummond], Note by the Secretary-General, 17 Feb. 1927, General 1927: 40/57540/57540, LNA; *ADAP 1918–1945*, B, i. Pt. II, p. 397 fn. and v. 342–4; Minutes of a Directors' Meeting, Thursday, 3 Mar. 1927, Council 1927: 27/57194/57194, LNA; *DBFP, 1919–1939*, IA, iv. 384–5; E[ric] D[rummond], Question of the Participation of the U.R.S.S. in the Preparatory Committee of the Disarmament Conference and in the Special Committee on Arbitration and Security. Note by the Secretary-General and E[ric] D[rummond], Record of Interview, 28 Nov. 1927, Disarmament 1927: 8/62451/62324, LNA; [Eric Drummond], Record of Conversation, 19 Apr. 1932, FO/371/15694; Drummond to Cadogan, 30 Apr. 1931, FO/371/15695; Russia, Komissiia po Izadaniiu Diplomaticheskikh Dokumentov, *Dokumenty vneshei politiki SSSR* (Moscow: State Publishing House, 1957–), ii–xvi. *passim*. See also, Chapter III, pp. 112–21.

[2] The Earl of Perth, 'San Francisco Hopes', *The Spectator*, 13 Apr. 1945, p. 330.

[3] E[ric] D[rummond], Memorandum, 20 Oct. 1918, Eric Drummond Papers, FO/800/329.

hand, attempts by the Communists to extend their sway beyond areas where they undoubtedly formed the great majority of the population were to be resisted by the Allies and the United States acting through the League. How could the Allies who had just defeated Germany, he rhetorically asked in December 1918, go to the peace conference with the aim of establishing a League of Nations which would protect small and weak states against aggression, while the embryonic nationalities of Finland, Poland, Esthonia, and elsewhere were being destroyed by external communist force, with no attempt made to protect them. Would not the peace conference forfeit the people's confidence?[1]

All things considered, however, Drummond rightly or wrongly probably feared the totalitarian Left far more than he feared the totalitarian Right. This was understandable if one kept in mind his social origins, his religiosity, and the impact that the Russian Revolution undoubtedly had on him as it had on others of his generation. The above in turn may partly help to explain his subsequent difficulties as British Ambassador in Mussolini's Rome,[2] and his sensitivity, as we shall see, to the Duce's desires during the period that Drummond served as Secretary-General. With all of this in mind an examination of Drummond's view of the League's problems and structure might be in order.

The American Problem

Like Hankey, Drummond realized that a League without the United States or lacking strong American support would be a badly crippled organization.[3] Thus from the moment he was appointed he had to contend with the problem of America's acceptance of the Covenant. When he expressed his fears Colonel

---

[1] [Drummond] to Grey, 30 Dec. 1918, ibid.

[2] Felix Gilbert, 'Two British Ambassadors: Perth and Henderson', in Gordon A. Craig and Felix Gilbert (eds.), *The Diplomats 1919–1939* (Princeton: Princeton University Press, 1953), pp. 537–54; Oliver Harvey, *The Diplomatic Diaries of Oliver Harvey 1937–1940*, ed. John Harvey (London: Collins, 1970), pp. 195, 239, 282.

[3] As early as 1916 Drummond observed that if it were true that the United States would not be willing to assume definite military obligations in any future League then 'the whole value of the scheme falls to the ground and it would not, I suppose, be worth pursuing'. Drummond to Spring Rice, 25 July 1916, Spring Rice Papers, FO/800/86.

House assured him that American support for the League 'would be forthcoming'.[1] As resistance to joining the League increased in the United States Drummond thought that Washington's adherence, even with sweeping reservations, was preferable to a League without the United States. He argued that the League's moral force which would be acquired by America's participation was essential to the success of the organization, and even in practical questions Drummond correctly feared that American absence would make the League's operation very difficult.[2] The Senate's open hostility to the Covenant likewise caused him to express his forebodings to Fosdick.[3] By mid-December 1919 he was willing to pay 'almost any price' to obtain the Covenant's ratification. He optimistically speculated that America might co-operate even if she did not ratify the Covenant. But he doubted whether under those conditions the 'League would ever be an international instrument of really first class importance' other than a centre for the handling of international subjects where conflict was not likely to arise. His hope was America's co-operating as a League member,[4] but this was not to be. 'The absence of the United States', Drummond wrote in 1945, 'left the League maimed from its inception'.[5] He publicly expressed this

[1] Eric Drummond, *The League of Nations* (Broadcast National Lecture No. 12; London: The British Broadcasting Corporation, 1933), p. 1.

[2] Drummond to Fosdick, 22 Nov. 1919, File 1919–20, Raymond B. Fosdick Papers, PU. See also, Minutes of a Directors' Meeting, 26 Nov. 1919, General 1919: 40/2196/854, LNA, and Terry L. Deibel, *Le Secrétariat de la Société des Nations et l'internationalisme américain, 1919–1924* (Genève: Dotation Carnegie, 1972), pp. 25–6.

[3] Drummond to Fosdick, 2 Dec. 1919, File 1919–20, Raymond B. Fosdick Papers, PU.

[4] Drummond to Fosdick, 15 Dec. 1919, ibid.; see also, Drummond to Kerr, 18 Dec. 1919, File GD40/17/56, Lothian Papers, SRO. In August 1920 Drummond opposed any American attempt to change the League by reconstituting it as a body dealing chiefly with international law and based on the Permanent Court of International Justice at The Hague. He considered that this attempt if successful 'would mean that the main object for which the League was found, i.e. the prevention of war in the future, would be thrown overboard, and we should go back to the system existing before 1914'. E[ric] D[rummond], Future of the League, 20 Aug. 1920, General 1920: 40/6218/6218, LNA.

[5] The Earl of Perth, 'San Francisco Hopes', p. 330.

view in 1933 when he departed from the League[1] and expressed
it privately during his tenure as Secretary-General. 'So long as
great and powerful States', he wrote to President Wilson in 1921,
in an obvious allusion to the United States as well as Germany
and Soviet Russia, 'remain outside, the League cannot, of course
be altogether what you and your collaborators at Paris intended
to create'.[2] The absence of the United States from the League
was one of Drummond's most important and persistent problems.
It haunted his every move and caused him to be sensitive to any
actions regarding Washington,[3] especially anything that might
raise the cry of European interference in American affairs, for
example, a visit by Cecil to the United States.[4] To avoid
difficulties, he attempted to answer American complaints against
the League by using third parties.[5] He made it a point to keep
London informed of Washington's attitudes toward the League[6]
as well as toward conferences sponsored by it which handled
technical matters but also had political importance and might
cause Anglo–American friction, for instance, the control of
opium.[7] Thus until the United States joined or closely co-

---

[1] Drummond, *The League of Nations*, p. 1. America's rejection of the Covenant
appears to have rankled Drummond. During the Second World War in a draft
article defending the original concept of the League he criticized America's
attitude. The Foreign Office, however, opposed the article's publication. It
feared the article would annoy Washington and be counter-productive at a
time when America was doing everything possible to assist in the struggle
against the Axis. See the correspondence in FO/371/26656, 31010, and 34512.

[2] Drummond (Geneva) to Wilson, 7 Sept. 1923, Folder Marked 5–7 Sept.,
Series 2, Box 223, Woodrow Wilson Papers, LC.

[3] E[ric] D[rummond], An untitled memorandum, 17 Jan. 1922, File
GD40/17/82, Lothian Papers, SRO; E[ric] D[rummond] to Ames, 15 Nov.
1922, Finance and Accounts 1922: 31/24754/24754, LNA; Drummond
(Geneva) to Cecil, 15 Mar. 1923, Add. MS. 51110, Robert Cecil Papers, BL.

[4] Drummond (Geneva) to Cecil, 15 Jan. and 15 Mar. 1923, Add. MS. 51110,
Robert Cecil Papers, BL.

[5] *The Times* (London), 23 May 1922, pp. 17–18; [Drummond] (Geneva) to
Grey, 26 May 1922, File F/42/7/14, Lloyd George Papers, BLL.

[6] Drummond (Geneva) to Waterhouse, 26 Nov. 1924 and the attached
memorandum, Volume 132, Stanley Baldwin Papers, CU; Drummond
(Geneva) to Cecil, 4 Mar. 1927 and the attached memorandum, Add. MS.
51111, Robert Cecil Papers, BL.

[7] Drummond (Geneva) to Cecil, 28 Nov. 1924, Add. MS. 51110, Robert
Cecil Papers, BL; Drummond (Geneva) to Waterhouse, 20 Dec. 1924 and the
attached memorandum, Volume 132, Stanley Baldwin Papers, CU.

operated with the League its coercive features would have to be downgraded and its conciliatory and mediatory functions accentuated. How could sanctions or other coercive measures be applied against an erring state, especially a powerful one, without the support or at least the passive acquiescence of one of the world's most powerful states?

Drummond had to grapple constantly with the fact that the problem of security was inexorably tied to America's membership or, at the very least, to Washington's very close co-operation with the League. An American commitment to the League was only partially realized by the Kellogg–Briand Pact of 1928 which outlawed war as an instrument of national policy and espoused the settlement of disputes by peaceful means. Because of the Pact's potential importance Drummond from the beginning became involved in the negotiations which led to its acceptance. The fact that the American Secretary of State was the treaty's co-author immensely pleased Drummond, for as early as January 1927 he had expressed the need of securing from the United States—a view he consistently held—that it 'would never aid, comfort, or abet the nation which commits the crime of aggressive war'. Such a declaration would greatly benefit the League and many of the difficulties regarding Article 16—dealing with economic and military sanctions against an aggressor—which appeared so important, especially in the disarmament field, would dissolve.[1]

When Frank B. Kellogg's proposals to France's Foreign Minister, Aristide Briand, were first broached Drummond naturally wanted them to dovetail with the Covenant. He was particularly interested in having the Americans led into the primary obligation which bound League members, namely, 'never to engage in war without at least a minimum period for arbitration, conciliation and reflection'. It appeared to Drummond that Kellogg's proposals presented an opportune moment to have the Americans concur with any League measures taken under Article 16. He felt that Paris could secure Washington's acknowledgement that war for the purpose of defending oneself was permissible. Once this acknowledgement was obtained it

[1] Drummond (Geneva) to Murray, 12 Jan. 1927, Gilbert Murray Papers, BLOU.

followed that defensive war could not be outlawed. Since defensive war was permitted it was only aggressive war to which Kellogg's proposals applied and once there was agreement that aggressive war should be outlawed, surely it would be very difficult to object to any measures taken under Article 16. Kellogg's proposals which spoke of war as an instrument of national policy echoed a phrase, he pointed out, previously used by Briand in order not to preclude a war being undertaken because of obligations under the Covenant. Drummond felt that the American proposals did not appear 'inconsistent with repressive or punitive action under the Covenant', though the proposals ruled out the wars permitted under certain conditions in Articles 12, 13, and 15 when the Council was divided and the due period had passed. But would this, he asked, be calamitous?

To include the League in the developing negotiations Drummond desired that the Great Powers be contacted for their views and that it might be useful during a Council session to have a personal exchange of opinions between the representatives concerned about the American proposals. He believed it was desirable for the Council's most important members to assume a common stance regarding the principles involved in a question which was of such vital interest to the League.[1]

A particular danger that Drummond wished to guard against in Kellogg's proposals was having a signatory of the Kellogg–Briand Pact breaking the Covenant by attacking a non-signatory of the Pact and one of the other signatories of the Pact feeling called upon to make war against the state that had broken the Covenant. Here was a possibility of a direct clash between the Pact and the Covenant that had to be avoided. There were other complications, for instance the Monroe Doctrine. On this sensitive question the Senate might insist on consenting to the Pact with a reservation that nothing prevented America from going to war in support of the Doctrine.[2] In co-operation with the Deputy Secretary-General, Avenol, Drummond prepared some points about the American proposals. Avenol then suggested to the Quai d'Orsay that Paris agree to circulate the Kellogg–Briand correspondence to the other powers for their consideration as had been proposed by Washington; and that in its reply to

[1] *DBFP, 1919–1939*, IA, iv. 531–2.
[2] Drummond (Geneva) to Tyrrell, 20 Feb. 1928, FO/371/12824.

Washington, Paris might state that it agreed with the principle of outlawing war and was ready to co-operate on this question. Added discussions would be necessary, however, especially on two points: exactly what was meant by the expression 'war' and how the obligations envisaged in Kellogg's proposed Pact should be squared, if necessary, with those of League members. Drummond had no idea what impact these suggestions would have in the Quai d'Orsay. He did agree with Avenol that it might be dangerous during the early stages in the negotiations 'to suggest to the Americans anything which might imply that sanctions against Pact-breakers should be discussed'.[1]

The point subsequently raised by the Foreign Office was why Drummond had not included the question of the Monroe Doctrine in Avenol's communication to the Quai d'Orsay. Drummond explained that if the Doctrine was specifically mentioned in Paris' reply to Washington it might result in alarming Senatorial and public opinion in the United States to such an extent that further negotiations would become far more difficult, and, indeed contribute to a disruption of the negotiations. It was for this reason that all reference to it had carefully been omitted.

Drummond pointed out that since the American proposals had contained no reservation regarding the Monroe Doctrine it would be unwise for any state to whom the proposals had been addressed to suggest that the United States should make a reservation which Washington initially had thought was unnecessary. Based on prior American actions he thought that the issue of the Monroe Doctrine would be raised. He did not see how it could be avoided, but thought it was better for the negotiations to have made some progress before such a delicate issue was broached. Drummond feared that the Americans might hold that the Monroe Doctrine was a matter of national policy. This contention would be strongly resisted by the Latin Americans who in fact were pressuring that reference to it in Article 21 of the Covenant be eliminated by amending this article. When asked about the Doctrine in Article 21, he responded that it could only equal the Doctrine's meaning at the

---

[1] Drummond (Geneva) to Cadogan, 1 Mar. 1928, Cadogan (Geneva) to Craigie, 2 Mar. 1928 and the attached note, FO/371/12790. See also, *DBFP, 1919–1939*, IA, iv. 585 fn.

time the Covenant came into force. He pointed out that a prior statement about the Doctrine by President Wilson could be considered as legally tenable and sensible, constituting for League members the Doctrine's definition, which excluded subsequent additions or extensions as outside the scope of the Covenant.[1]

In a matter involving a possible American commitment to the League Drummond was not particularly keen on having the negotiations in the League's behalf conducted solely by Briand and the French Government. He expressed these doubts to the Foreign Secretary, Sir Austen Chamberlain, pointing out that so much depended on Paris' answer to Kellogg's proposals that he could not think that other League members—a not too subtle hint to Chamberlain and the British Government—would disinterest themselves in this matter. Drummond was willing to admit that perhaps Kellogg's proposals had arrived at an inopportune and inconvenient moment, but he hoped they would be very seriously considered. The Geneva rumour that Chamberlain had expressed himself as hostile to Kellogg's proposals Drummond found particularly upsetting.[2] Though Chamberlain assured Drummond that he had expressed no opinion on Kellogg's proposals, he at the same time disapproved of any League intervention in the negotiations.[3]

Drummond's attempt to get the League involved in the negotiations was thus thwarted, but he nevertheless insisted that it was dangerous to have the French act unadvised as the League's sole spokesman in a matter that was of the greatest importance to the organization's future. He had to admit, however, that if France wanted to handle Kellogg's proposals on a bilateral basis, no one except the Americans could insist that others be included in the conversations.[4]

He was doing all he could, he explained to an American member of the Secretariat, to promote Kellogg's proposals as well as to discuss and clarify them.[5] He hoped Kellogg's proposals

[1] Drummond (Geneva) to Selby, 28 Mar. 1928, FO/371/12790.

[2] *DBFP, 1919–1939*, IA, iv. 584–5.

[3] Ibid., 585–6.

[4] Drummond (Geneva) to Chamberlain, 8 Mar. 1928, AC55/138, Austen Chamberlain Papers, UB. See *DBFP, 1919–1939*, IA, iv. 586 fn.

[5] Drummond (Geneva) to Bullard, 19 Mar. 1928, Arthur Bullard Papers, PU.

to outlaw war would help America realize the objects and the League's reasonableness more than anything else done previously. If American public opinion could be persuaded that the League's entire purpose was the preservation of peace and the abolition of war, politically a great step forward would have been made.[1] Yet he was prepared for the worst, he wrote to Cecil, if nothing developed in the Kellogg negotiations. He feared that a period of stagnation would follow, if not retrogression, in international affairs generally. If this proved true, Drummond did not think that anything better could be done for the League than just continuing as before.[2]

Unfortunately, the type of firm American commitment to the League that he wanted did not develop from the Kellogg–Briand negotiations. What he desired and what was possible based on the conflicting interests of the Great Powers were two different things. In the end his reaction reflected his general satisfaction with the Pact: there was no inconsistency, he believed, between Kellogg's proposals to outlaw war as an instrument of national policy and the Covenant. Though he had not convinced the French he pressed this personal opinion on all statesmen with whom he met. Drummond observed that League members were already bound not to resort to war against each other. Agreeing to Kellogg's proposals their obligations under the Covenant would commit them even more to the observance of the Pact. Moreover, they would be obligated because of the Covenant to take some sort of action against a League member violating the Pact.[3] When asked by Americans of his view of the Pact he replied that since the League's chief purpose was to 'establish peace, any progress in this sense, whether achieved by League means or outside the League', had to be sincerely welcomed by all who supported the organization. Personally he 'felt that the Kellogg Pact constituted a great advance for the maintenance of Peace'.[4]

[1] Drummond (Geneva) to Bullard, 23 Apr. 1928, ibid.
[2] Drummond (Geneva) to Cecil, 24 Apr. 1928, Add. MS. 51111, Robert Cecil Papers, BL.
[3] Wilson (Berne) to the Secretary of State, No. 47, 2 May 1928, File 711.4112 Anti-War/28, RG 59, NA. A paraphrased version can be found in *PRFRUS, 1928*, i. 48.
[4] Drummond (Geneva) to Cushendun, 23 Aug. 1928, FO/371/12799.

In a sense the Kellogg–Briand Pact was a disappointment to Drummond. By supporting the Pact he was not surrendering very much in his desire to avoid physical coercion through the League in the absence of American membership. The Pact was essentially a pious expression renouncing war in inter-state relations; non-aggression treaties and the Kellogg–Briand Pact in particular said nothing about the use of force which was not declared to be a legal state of war, nor did they deny the right of self-defence which essentially allowed each signatory to define her own actions. Finally, if the agreement was breached, as it subsequently was, aside from the state attacked what state would be willing to enforce the agreement unless her own interests were directly involved? Even more important, there was no real connection between the Kellogg–Briand Pact and the Covenant and, as we have seen, it was this connection that Drummond considered of the utmost importance.

Another reason to induce Washington to join the League, according to Drummond, was that it might cause certain Latin American states which were not members to join likewise. Chinese affairs could be treated more effectively, too, and it would reassure the present membership and silence the League's opponents everywhere. Despite American assurances that they were not hostile to the League, privately and semi-officially they discouraged Latin American applications. Unless Washington's co-operation was forthcoming Latin American membership would decline and the League would be left as a European and partly Asian and African organization. This development would destroy the initial hope that the League would be a 'universal instrument for human progress'. It was worth a high price to avoid this situation and to appease the Americans Drummond posed the possibility of abolishing Article 10—which guaranteed the territorial integrity of member states against aggression—and Article 16, and amending Article 15 which dealt with the peaceful settlement of disputes. In their place he would substitute a 'Council meeting or Conference to make recommendations and take decisions as regards each particular threat to peace'. This procedure would remove three-quarters of the League's present difficulties and Drummond undoubtedly thought it would make it more attractive to Washington. If no such arrangement was made he feared that the League ran 'a real danger of dwindling and becoming a minor factor in world affairs'.[1]

By December 1929 Drummond observed that unless Washington could be induced to announce, either directly by having the League amend the Covenant or indirectly by a public statement, that it would be prepared to confer with the Council when world peace was threatened, he feared that the position and indeed the very existence of the organization itself might be in jeopardy. Only the Kellogg–Briand Pact 'would remain, with all its lack of machinery and force, to take the League's place'. He looked 'upon such a possibility with dread'. Inasmuch as Philip Kerr (Lord Lothian), Secretary of the Rhodes Trust, was going to the United States with General Smuts, Drummond impressed upon him the 'great importance of the United States agreeing to some form of conference if world peace' was really threatened in violation of the Kellogg—Briand Pact.[2] As we shall see, Washington subsequently did not agree to any conference, but only to consult with Geneva when the Kellogg–Briand Pact was violated. It was no great concession and did nothing to solve Drummond's fundamental problem that without American membership or strong American support the League could never play the role in international affairs envisaged for it at Paris and this in turn greatly circumscribed what Drummond himself could do politically, especially behind the scenes. Like the mythical Sisyphus, Drummond was condemned to roll continually uphill a heavy stone only to have it topple back again—the heavy stone of America's non-membership.

The Security Question

Since the League could have only a marginal impact in accommodating and moderating the political competition between states, a situation aggravated by America's absence from the organization, Drummond unlike many others assumed a more evolutionary approach toward the League. Though he believed that the League's elimination of 'basic difficulties

---

[1] E[ric] D[rummond], An untitled letter or memorandum, 11 Dec. 1929, Drummond Folder, LNA.

[2] Drummond to Salter, 23 Dec. 1929, Add. MS. 51111, Robert Cecil Papers, BL.

between nations' would be commendable he did not believe that these difficulties could be 'tackled except by time'. If Geneva succeeded in solving superficial and passing questions a great deal would have been accomplished. He was willing to admit that the French might well be right that nearly all troubles stemmed from a feeling of political, military, financial, or economic insecurity.[1]

At the same time Drummond was not willing to agree that security necessarily led to armaments reduction and then to arbitration. This view no doubt reflected his Foreign Office experience: namely, that the desire for security merely mirrored the underlying political conflict of the international arena. It was only when nations felt safe from aggression and formed the habit of referring disputes to arbitration, he argued, that you would really get effective armaments reduction. Armaments constituted an enormous drain on state resources, but would a proportional reduction of armaments ever give security since there would invariably be a different standard for different countries, and some states would always be more powerful than others. Excessive armaments led 'to a warlike state of mind'. But since nations decided, at least in theory, their armaments according to national needs, it was only, he believed, by 'giving security and adopting the arbitration habit' that general armaments reduction could be obtained.[2]

In discussion with Russia's Foreign Minister, Maxim Litvinov, Drummond held to the view that over the long run, armaments were 'governed by whether or not a state felt itself to be secure'. What was necessary, therefore, was to create, as far as possible, a sense of peace following which the people themselves would insist that armaments should be reduced.[3]

Drummond hoped that the League could help create this atmosphere. This was important since no real progress in disarmament could be achieved especially with France, Europe's most powerfully armed and intransigent *status quo* state, unless it

[1] Drummond (Geneva) to Sweetser, 17 Aug. 1926, Box 31, Arthur Sweetser Papers, LC.
[2] Drummond (Geneva) to Cecil, 16 Apr. 1925, Add. MS. 51110, Robert Cecil Papers, BL.
[3] E[ric] D[rummond], Record of Interview, 27 Nov. 1927, Disarmament 1927: 8/62451/62324, LNA.

could be shown that there was substantial progress in the field of security. Though Drummond believed French public opinion was strongly pacific he also realized the obstacles that had to be overcome before France's extensive armaments could be curbed. These obstacles were a deep rooted fear of Germany and her greater population; a contempt for Italy and a distrust of Mussolini's regime; apprehension of an Italo–German agreement aimed against France; the matter of France's allies, especially Poland's relations with Germany and Yugoslavia's relations with Italy; and lastly, France's strong desire to maintain the peace settlement unimpaired.

Of course, the Locarno Pacts of 1925 establishing the Franco–Belgian–German frontiers should have given France a feeling of security *vis-à-vis* Germany. Yet despite what was said on the French side, Drummond did not believe French–German relations were really satisfactory. Germany thought that France wanted hegemony in Europe and this belief and her consequent dislike of France exposed itself clearly during unguarded moments. Unfortunately, France's military and nationalistic bodies were able to manipulate the deep-seated fears of French public opinion and use these fears in order to achieve a large military establishment.

Drummond had no illusions about French politicians. Because of the nature of French public opinion they professed peaceful intentions. They pronounced in favour of disarmament, provided security was proffered. Yet Drummond noticed that as soon as any approach to achieving real security was threatened, the French military bloc immediately decided that its position was being undermined and loudly declared that the security proposed was insufficient. They were supported in this attitude by France's eastern European allies who were very influential with the Parisian press.

Drummond optimistically believed that assuming his diagnosis of the problem was correct, the only method of defeating France's military and nationalistic circles was to give public opinion and those French statesmen who really believed in international co-operation—there were some—sufficient evidence and power to win over these extremist elements. The Locarno Pacts had proved useful in this respect and at one time it appeared that they might achieve this purpose. Unfortunately, this did not prove to be the case.[1] 'Unhappily, the logical French mind', Drummond noted, 'relies infinitely more on texts and declarations than on practical goodwill'. The French would never admit that Article 16 by itself gave them the security they needed unless and until there was some formal declaration from the Americans. They cited America's attitude toward the summer events of 1914, and to the fact that at one point it appeared almost possible that she would actually oppose the Allied powers because of the blockade measures they had instituted against American ships and commerce.[2]

There was only one way out of this dilemma according to Drummond and this required that London reassert its intention of strictly executing Article 16, and Washington declare that it was ready to consult with the League in the case of a threatened breach of the Kellogg–Briand Pact. These actions would show to the French populace that the security offered by Article 16 was so great that any fears it had were unwarranted. Once it was certain that the United States would consult with the League, then any blockade it instituted would be with the assent of the United States and be definitely effective. Thus not only French, but also British preoccupations would be met. Drummond desired therefore that Article 16 not be amended and awaited some sign from the Americans—a stance that was partially vindicated in May 1933 at the Disarmament Conference. Here, Norman Davis announced that Washington, if there was a substantive reduction of armaments, would consult with the League in a case where the Kellogg–Briand Pact was breached. In addition, Washington would do nothing to obstruct the League's action against an aggressor state if, following such consultation, it agreed with the action taken.[3] The problem of course was that the movement of military forces and the technology of modern war had increased greatly since 1914 and Drummond's proposed procedure had too many pitfalls to attract the French, as Davis's statement clearly showed. Moreover,

---

[1] Drummond (Geneva) to Cadogan, 24 Apr. 1930, FO/371/14958.

[2] Drummond (Geneva) to Cadogan, 30 Apr. 1930, ibid. For Drummond's attitude toward French naval rearmament see Drummond (Geneva) to Cecil, 25 Nov. 1929, Add. MS. 51111, Robert Cecil Papers, BL.

[3] Drummond (Geneva) to Cadogan, 24 Apr. 1930, FO/371/14958. For Davis's statement see Walters, p. 546.

France shared a contiguous border with her anti-*status quo* neighbour and what she needed in any confrontation with Germany was not a blockade assented to by the United States, which, as 1914–18 showed, had a military impact only with time, but immediate and massive assistance both in men and supplies. Until Drummond departed from the League the question of security remained omnipresent, especially after Japan's actions in Manchuria and China.

Bearing in mind Drummond's aversion to the League's coercive features in the absence of American membership, how could it contribute to solving the security dilemma and keeping the peace? Drummond noted that there were several unrecognized League features that could assist in this task. Since the question of prestige played so important a role in international relations the League's value 'as a "face-saving machinery" should not be under-estimated'.[1] In addition, the League, leaving aside everything else, was also 'an enormous safety-valve'—and cited its use by Berlin to protest Poland's treatment of the German minority in Upper Silesia.[2] Beyond this what other features did it possess? What could it be? What could it do? Drummond expounded his views in greater detail during the Corfu Incident of 1923—Mussolini's bombardment and occupation of the Greek island. According to Drummond the League's 'fundamental purpose' was, 'by the creation of permanent institutions and the building up of a system of *international cooperation*, permanently to maintain the peace of the world'. In the work which the League might 'undertake for the settlement of any international dispute' there were thus two different points that had to be kept in mind.

The first was the 'effects of the action that [was] taken on the actual dispute in question and its effects on the future efficacy of the League'. Hence in tackling a particular question the Council's task was 'not merely to secure a pacific settlement, but also to do what lies in its power to build up a *tradition and a practice* that will prevent dangerous disputes from developing in the future'. In establishing such tradition and practice there were again two points which were of prime importance. 'The first [was] the

[1] Eric Drummond, 'The League of Nations', *The Spectator*, 3 Nov. 1928, p. 639.
[2] Drummond (Geneva) to Murray, 26 Nov. 1930, Gilbert Murray Papers, BLOU.

moral authority of the Council and the Assembly of the League, the second [was] the creation of a general confidence that the clear and precise obligations of the Covenant will be loyally fulfilled by its members'.[1]

These comments were certainly no clarion call to use the League's coercive instruments to police the world. In fact, Drummond had emphasized the evolutionary approach from the beginning. When the Secretariat was being organized he had stressed the League's inevitability and felt that with the world's rapidly developing economic interdependence, time was running on the side of those who supported the organization. Sheer necessity, he believed, would bring about some form of world organization, even if the League experiment were bungled.[2]

This partly explains his emphasis on 'international cooperation' which tied in with his preference that states should settle their difficulties on a bilateral basis rather than with the assistance of third parties.[3] Drummond's comments clearly reflected both his own beliefs and experiences based on his service in the Foreign Office, as well as the realities of a League minus the United States; the comments of a former civil servant whose own country as a *status quo* power prior to the First World War had pursued a policy of international co-operation and had also over the centuries developed a constitutional system largely based on 'tradition and practice'. Was there a different way to develop the League in a heterogeneous world of sovereign states?

For Drummond the League and especially the Council were to be a type of consultative world parliament where heads of state or their foreign ministers could meet on short notice to discuss and co-ordinate their policies on important international questions. This idea was something that Drummond acquired from his former chief, Sir Edward Grey, who despite strenuous efforts in the summer of 1914 could not get the interested states, especially Germany and Austria-Hungary, to attend a conference

---

[1] Italics added. This memorandum is reproduced in James Barros, *The Corfu Incident of 1923: Mussolini and the League of Nations* (Princeton: Princeton University Press, 1965), pp. 317–20.

[2] Raymond B. Fosdick, *Letters on the League of Nations* (Princeton: Princeton University Press, 1966), p. 17; Raymond B. Fosdick, *Chronicle of a Generation* (New York: Harper, 1958), p. 193.

[3] Rovine, p. 47 fn.

to discuss the problems that had developed because of the assassination of the Austrian Archduke. Drummond maintained that Grey had failed 'because there was no machinery, no treaty obligation that the Powers should come to a conference if a political crisis arose, under pain of being branded as treaty violators and war-seekers if they refused to attend'. To Drummond the essential point in any international organization attempting to secure peace was a 'binding provision' that the member states would 'meet and discuss any serious political difficulties that may arise'.[1]

No similar service, Drummond maintained, was offered by the peace conference's Supreme Council. Its leadership was too preoccupied with domestic political matters to be able to meet immediately for foreign policy questions. If a single prime minister did not desire a meeting of the Supreme Council he could easily thwart any meeting and he was under no obligation either to attend or to delegate someone in his place. Because of Briand's delaying tactics the Supreme Council had not convened for a considerable period of time. The beauty of the Covenant was that it provided for meetings at short notice and members had to attend or otherwise lose their case by default. Moreover, the small states disliked the Supreme Council and were unwilling to accept its decisions. Being in the League, however, they were in a different situation. As members they regarded compliance to the League's requests 'as much more dignified than obedience to the commands of the Supreme Council'.

Naturally, in matters of the highest importance prime ministers would attend Council meetings, but such instances were few and far between. Initially it was difficult to say whether a particular question was, or was not, of the highest importance. He thought few people realized in 1914 that the Austrian Archduke's assassination would lead to war. If the question of the assassination had first come before the Council he did not believe that the prime ministers would have attended. As the question developed later they would have been only too eager to attend had a meeting of the Council been summoned.[2] The problem

---

[1] Drummond (Rome) to Mounsey, 11 Nov. 1935, FO/371/19688. See also, The Earl of Perth, 'San Francisco Hopes', p. 330.

[2] Drummond (Rome) to Sweetser, 2 Dec. 1921, Box 31, Arthur Sweetser Papers, LC. This letter is partially reproduced in Rovine, p. 44. As to
(*continued*)

with this whole approach of course was Drummond's faith in the ability of rational discussion to resolve conflict, a by-product of the nineteenth-century belief in the inevitability of progress, which was soon shattered at the conference tables of Geneva by the power competition of the Great Powers, and the irrational forces of ideology and nationalism unleashed by the First World War.

Nevertheless Drummond staunchly held to this position. In later years a proposal to reduce the annual Council meetings from four to three found him agreeing since he personally believed that the 'essential point' was for the foreign ministers to come to the Council and if this could 'only happen on the condition that the meetings are reduced to three a year, they must be so reduced'.[1] The possibility that Chamberlain, the Foreign Secretary, might not attend a particular Council session made Drummond apprehensive. It would create, he maintained, a 'serious precedent' if, because Chamberlain or his French and German counterparts 'could not attend a particular Meeting, the other two decided that it was not worth their while to do so'.[2] Obviously the whole rationale of the system would be undercut if high political personages either could not attend or abstained from Council meetings. After he had resigned from the League, and with the Manchurian crisis and the Sino-Japanese dispute under his belt, Drummond's thoughts on the question evolved further. He would like to see the Covenant, he wrote to Sir John Simon, the Foreign Secretary, 'formally detached' from the peace treaties and 'meetings of the Great Powers preceding meetings of the Council when important matters were on the agenda'.[3] On this question, at any rate, he appears to have come pretty close to a full circle.

Drummond's perception of the Council's pivotal role in the

Drummond's view that it would be a mistake for the Supreme Council to merge into the League Council until the peace-making task of the former was advanced and the Assembly had convened see Drummond to Kerr, 7 May 1920, and the attached untitled memorandum written by Drummond on 6 May 1920, File GD40/17/56, Lothian Papers, SRO.

[1] Drummond (Geneva) to Chamberlain, 19 Mar. 1927, AC54/160, Austen Chamberlain Papers, UB.

[2] Drummond (Geneva) to Chamberlain, 14 May 1928, AC55/139, ibid.

[3] Drummond (Rome) to Simon, No. 928, 1 Dec. 1933, FO/371/17395.

organization affected his views about other matters. For example, though he thought the establishment of conciliation committees desirable these committees could in no way short circuit a dispute first submitted to the Council. Bypassing the Council with these committees would deprive that organ of the 'possiblity of acting as [a] conciliator'. In fact, establishing these conciliation committees would require an amendment of the Covenant which he hesitated to do since the conciliation committees would both 'affect and change Article 11'. He was willing to admit that there was much to be said for the adoption of more treaties under which commissions of conciliation would be established. But it was Drummond's belief that these conciliation commissions were 'only likely to be successful among highly developed and pacific countries'.

Nor did Drummond like the idea of solemn declarations. League members, he argued, were already formally bound under Article 20 not to assume any obligations which were inconsistent with the Covenant. If any inconsistent obligations had been assumed, states had to take immediate steps to release themselves from these obligations. He opposed, however, the establishment of any authority which would judge whether or not a particular treaty was in line with the Covenant's provisions. If a state believed, Drummond maintained, that a particular treaty was not in conformity with the Covenant's provisions it would have the right to bring the matter to the Council's attention under Article 11 of the Covenant. Likewise on security pacts Drummond believed that the promise to give assistance to an attacked state ought to be made to the Council and recorded by it, and not be a matter of direct agreement between states themselves. Indeed, he thought it would be a 'mistake to try and lay down any final and definite criterion of an aggressor'.[1]

Within the higher echelon of the Secretariat Drummond made no secret of his guarded approach in the use of the League. As early as 1920 he admitted that it was his view that Article 10 could 'be cut out altogether, without damaging the Covenant in the slightest'.[2] This article was one of the most important articles

[1] E[ric] D[rummond] (London) to Sugimura, 30 Dec. 1927, Disarmament General 1928–32: 7A/1548/1548, LNA.
[2] Drummond (Geneva) to Sweetser, 19 June 1920, Box 31, Arthur Sweetser Papers, LC. See also, Deibel, p. 25.

of the Covenant and was included at President Wilson's insistence. Drummond recognized, however, that its abolition was impossible since its inclusion in the Covenant was one of the reasons why the small states were staunch supporters of the League. His desire therefore after he left the League was to amend Article 10 'by the addition of the words "inter se"'.[1] By this amendment the obligations under Article 10 would have been considerably narrowed obliging League members merely to guarantee the territory of member states against aggression by another member state. Drummond believed that the article gave 'an unfair prominence to the maintenance of the *status quo*'. Yet to do away with Article 10 without a tit for a tat would be unfair and as compensation he thought the scrapping of Article 19 would be in order. Under Article 19 the Assembly could advise the reconsideration by League members of treaties which had 'become inapplicable, and the consideration of international conditions whose continuance might endanger the peace of the world'. Drummond thought that scrapping Article 19 would raise no real problems, for Article 11 dealt with the question of war or the threat of war and of the right of member states to bring to the League's attention 'any circumstances affecting international relations which threaten to disturb international peace or the good understanding between nations upon which peace depends'. Therefore Article 11 really gave the '"have not" States the right to raise any questions affected by Article 19'.[2]

Less final were Drummond's views about Article 11 itself. An unofficial American proposal that a new world organization might be devised replacing the League but excluding Article 11 impelled him to note that this unofficial proposal was of some interest and more hopeful than usually was the case, '*though Article XI is the kernel of the Covenant as regards stopping war and I hope its spirit can be preserved*'.[3] However, his years of League experience left him with no illusions about Article 11. Its inadequacy, he pointed out after he resigned, was that any action under it required a unanimous Council decision. Council members,

[1] Drummond (Rome) to Simon, No. 928, 1 Dec. 1933, FO/371/17395.
[2] Drummond (Rome) to Mounsey, 11 Nov. 1935, FO/371/19688.
[3] Italics added. Drummond to Balfour, 30 July 1921 and the attached memorandum by Arthur Sweetser, Add. MS. 49749, Arthur Balfour Papers, BL.

however, according to Article 4 paragraph five of the Covenant, in the case of a dispute included the parties to the dispute in their discussions, regardless of whether they were regular Council members or not. The unanimity rule therefore gave to the disputing parties the right to block any action attempting to preserve peace proposed by the Council under Article 11 and thus placed 'a powerful weapon in the hands of a guilty State'.[1] Despite all this Drummond considered Article 11 the most valuable of all the Covenant's articles since its second paragraph permitted the 'ventilation of any grievance as a friendly right'. What beyond this right, he asked, was required?[2]

As to Article 16, his attitude in view of America's absence from the organization was a consistent one. When the Council threatened to institute a naval blockade of Greece following her invasion of Bulgaria in 1925 Drummond observed that 'theoretical discussion' stemming from intra-Secretariat memorandums dealing with the economic and legal questions involved in applying sanctions 'might be largely academic'. Each situation handled by the League where the question of sanctions was raised would 'present circumstances peculiar to itself', and accordingly would 'require special treatment'. If the League did act its action 'should always be based on specific articles of the Covenant'. In a perilous situation the use of the League's coercive weapons should be restricted to the economic one which was one of the Covenant's essential points. The League's founders, Drummond held, having the First World War in mind, 'intended to organize an economic barrier against future war'. Many people had supported the League's establishment with this attitude in mind. Though this feeling may have slightly subsided it seemed 'likely that under any serious danger of war it would again become very sharp'.[3]

By restricting the League's coercive weapon to the economic one Drummond ignored or shunned the possibility of physical coercion under Article 16 paragraph two of the Covenant.

---

[1] Drummond (Rome) to Simon, No. 958, 11 Dec. 1933, FO/371/17395.

[2] Drummond (Rome) to Mounsey, 11 Nov. 1935, FO/371/19688.

[3] For the intra-Secretariat memorandums and Drummond's observations see James Barros, *The League of Nations and the Great Powers: The Greek-Bulgarian Incident, 1925* (Oxford: Clarendon Press, 1970), pp. 126–38.

According to this paragraph the Council could recommend 'what effective military, naval or air forces' League members 'shall severally contribute to the armed forces to be used to protect the covenants of the League'. It would appear therefore that Drummond was willing to see the implementation of economic sanctions under Article 16 paragraph one. However, a close examination shows that this was not the case. First, he seemingly ignored the fact that even economic sanctions to be effective required a naval blockade of the erring state. The possibilities of a naval blockade either without the American navy or against it was one that Drummond did not wish to contemplate. The inevitable success of economic sanctions during the First World War—upon which Article 16 paragraph one was largely based—was due to the fact that the sanctions imposed against the Central Powers had been enforced by an Allied naval blockade led by the Royal Navy. Drummond was of course aware of this for when the question was raised in June 1920 of establishing a plan for implementing the League's economic weapon in the case of aggression, he was not very keen on establishing the permanent machinery needed and was likewise interested in avoiding any mention of the word blockade, which in his mind meant the inevitable use of the Royal Navy. He 'was not quite convinced', Drummond weakly argued, that the world's disturbed condition warranted the submission of any such plan to the Council and Assembly. The economic weapon presupposed the general resumption of financial and commercial relations between all states and this unfortunately was not the case at that time. He was willing to admit that there was an argument to be made that the mere establishment of the machinery for future emergencies would show that the League was in no way helpless, and that it intended when it was fully operative, to make every use of its powers. Also it could be argued that the Secretariat would be failing in its duties unless it arranged some scheme for the execution, should the need arise, of economic sanctions under Article 16.[1] The Council, however, did not agree with Drummond and proposed to the Assembly the establishment of an International Blockade Commission to study the questions, problems, principles, and the permanent

[1] E[ric] D[rummond], An untitled memorandum, Economic and Financial 1919: 10/1196/16, LNA.

machinery needed to implement the League's economic weapon.[1]

Some years later Drummond was more explicit. He did not want to see, he observed, any elaboration of Article 16 since he believed that it would result in a weakening of this key article of the Covenant.[2] After he resigned he was asked for his opinion several times by the Foreign Office. In the interim the League and Drummond had experienced the Manchurian crisis, the Sino–Japanese dispute, as well as Italy's attack on Ethiopia. Drummond replied that these actions proved that Article 16 could not be 'applied universally'. The automatic nature in the application of sanctions required some revision along regional lines. Personally, he wanted to see the complete elimination of Article 16.[3] Its mechanical sanctions, which were 'legally speaking applicable in every case', regardless of whether there did or did not exist 'extenuating circumstances', placed an 'intolerable burden' on League members—a burden which most members certainly could not handle. The disappearance of Article 16 would consequently require the amendment of Article 17 paragraph one which made Article 16 applicable to disputes between League members and non-members and also between non-member states provided they accepted the League's obligations for that particular dispute.[4] In substitution for Article 16 Drummond thought the League should rely on Article 3 paragraph three, and on Article 4 paragraph four, under which the Assembly and Council could respectively 'take any action either body may think fit for the preservation of the peace of the world'.[5]

He knew of course that if Articles 10 and 16 were scrapped *status quo* states would consider that the League had 'lost all political value for them'. However, Drummond did not believe that if it came to the crunch, these states would refuse to belong

[1] League of Nations, *Official Journal*, I (1920), pp. 305, 308–10.

[2] E[ric] D[rummond] (London) to Sugimura, 30 Dec. 1927, Disarmament General 1928–32: 7A/1548/1548, LNA.

[3] Drummond (Rome) to Simon, No. 928, 1 Dec. 1933, FO/371/17395.

[4] Drummond (Rome) to Mounsey, 11 Nov. 1935, FO/371/19688.

[5] Drummond (Rome) to Simon, No. 928, 1 Dec. 1933, FO/371/17395. 'Article 4 allows the Council to deal at its meetings with any matter within the sphere of action of the League or affecting the peace of the world. Almost enough in itself'. Drummond (Rome) to Mounsey, 11 Nov. 1935, FO/371/19688.

to an international organization containing the Great Powers, which would have as its function 'consultation in case of crisis and the potential power', if it thought fit, to impose any sanctions it might choose. In a flagrant case it might even use military measures under Article 11 or other coercive measures. Naturally, the Covenant's unanimity rule would have to be cancelled. As to the anti-*status quo* states they too would be satisfied. 'Equity would be the order of the day', Drummond thought, 'and with a universal League equity could hardly be resisted'.[1]

Keeping this restrained evolutionary approach in mind one must accept with reservations Drummond's comment in the early 1950s that things might have been different if he, like the Secretary-General of the United Nations, had had at his disposal an article similar to that of Article 99 of the Charter.[2] Though this article has been formally invoked only once—by Dag Hammarskjöld at the inception of the Congo crisis—one can perhaps argue that the mere threat to invoke it has been more effective than its actual application.[3] Nevertheless, under the League Drummond did have somewhat similar power bestowed upon him by two Assembly resolutions in the early 1920s dealing with Article 16 but chose to interpret these resolutions in a very narrow sense—which was in line with his attitude toward Article 16 and his general attitude toward the Covenant—correctly maintaining in later years that they were not amendments to the Covenant and thus carried less weight than Article 99 which was an integral part of the Charter.[4] In looking back at the League during these inter-war years one can only sympathize with Drummond who reminds us of the winter skater: carefully testing the ice here and there always aware that somewhere further on the ice is dangerously thin.

[1] Drummond (Rome) to Mounsey, 11 Nov. 1935, FO/371/19688.

[2] Schwebel, pp. 10–11, 17.

[3] Leland M. Goodrich, Edvard Hambro, Anne P. Simons, *Charter of the United Nations: Commentary and Documents* (3rd rev. edn.; New York: Columbia University Press, 1969), pp. 588–92.

[4] William E. Rappard, *The Quest for Security* (Cambridge: Harvard University Press, 1940), pp. 227, 237; Schwebel, pp. 230–1. Drummond was not interested in having his powers defined, noting that his obligations under Article 11—to call a meeting of the Council at the request of a member state—were not spelled out and believed it was wise not to do so 'to avoid any conceivable risk of delay'. Morley, p. 265.

Relations with London

When Drummond departed from the League he maintained that any linking of the Covenant and the Kellogg–Briand Pact leading to a common conference, required that each instrument preserve intact its own unique characteristics.[1] With Italy's invasion of Ethiopia Drummond held that the Kellogg–Briand Pact had proved of no use whatsoever. Indeed, it appeared to him that the Pact was overly favourable to the *status quo* nations. His desire was to introduce some of the Pact's wording in modified form into any amended Covenant, provided it would entice the United States into any new League.[2]

These thoughts by Drummond on the Kellogg–Briand Pact as well as his restrained attitude and general evolutionary outlook largely coincided with that of the British Government which, after the Senate rejected the Covenant, looked upon the League not as an instrument for coercion but as one for mediation and conciliation. The fact that Article 11 declared war or the threat of war anywhere as a matter of League concern gave London an important legal excuse for invoking the League's mediatory and conciliatory procedure whenever it found it in its interests to do so. The League was really an ideal instrument for the kind of mediatory procedures which traditionally had been relied upon by British Governments. Like Drummond, they also saw the League as an organ of discussion and consultation and as a meeting place where international disputes could be aired.[3]

The convergence of these two outlooks caused Drummond's former Secretariat associates to observe that he was 'known or believed to be, to some extent', a representative of his own government within the Secretariat, and that he was 'accustomed to consider' the British Foreign Secretary as his sole master. They were willing to admit that at certain moments this had its advantages because the League was a weak organization.[4] Drummond subsequently denied that he was anyone's agent in Geneva and asserted that his prime concern during these years

[1] Drummond, *The League of Nations*, p. 11.

[2] Drummond (Rome) to Mounsey, 11 Nov. 1935, FO/371/19688.

[3] Arnold Wolfers, *Britain and France between Two Wars* (New York: Harcourt, Brace, 1940), pp. 223–8, 321–64.

[4] *Proceedings of the Exploratory Conference on the Experience of the League of Nations Secretariat*, pp. 48–50, 65.

was to display his independence from London.[1] This view is shared by a very experienced American diplomat who had occasion to work closely with Drummond. He 'felt that Drummond regarded himself as non-political', and that all of his energy was directed toward making the League function and that when he intervened he seldom supported a British thesis, his comments being 'rather a contribution to a general agreement'.[2]

His associates' comments, however, were both unfair to Drummond as well as an oversimplification and a misreading of his relationship with successive British Governments and especially with the Foreign Office. His relationship with the Foreign Office, as we shall see, was intimate although he did not always agree with it, and he certainly endeavoured to maintain his contacts with 10 Downing Street, beginning with the Lloyd George government.[3] Indeed, Drummond continued during his Secretary-Generalship to have access to the Foreign Office's confidential reports.[4] Access to these reports, however, was secured only after some difficulty. Initially in July 1919 he asked Lord Curzon if the Secretariat could obtain from the Foreign Office political information dealing with events which were of special interest to the League, or of which the Council might be called upon to take cognizance. What Drummond had in mind was a summary of the Foreign Office's more important telegrams on questions of general interest and perhaps from time to time a copy of a dispatch. Inasmuch as the Secretariat, he observed, was

[1] Schwebel, p. 218.

[2] Wilson, p. 213. That Drummond was absolutely impartial and had no favourites is attested to by others. Fosdick to Gilchrist, 15 June 1920, File 1171, Raymond B. Fosdick Papers, PU; Tennant to [Lloyd George], 12 Sept. 1922, File F/97/1/42, Lloyd George Papers, BLL; Cecil, *A Great Experiment*, p. 90. In fact some Englishmen criticized Drummond for disregarding British interests in his zeal for League interests, by absenting himself, for example, from all League meetings dealing with the Mosul question involving Great Britain and Turkey. Viscount Kikujiro Ishii, *Diplomatic Commentaries*, ed. and trans. William R. Langdon (Baltimore: The Johns Hopkins Press, 1936), pp. 169, 179. See also, Schwebel, p. 7; F. Yeats-Brown, 'The League of Nations. The Character of Sir Eric Drummond', p. 14; H. Wilson Harris, 'The Creator of the League', *The Spectator*, 30 June 1933, p. 935.

[3] Hugh Dalton, *Memoirs: Call Back Yesterday* (London: Muller, 1953), i. 237; Drummond to [Lloyd George], 30 July 1921, File F/42/7/8, Lloyd George Papers, BLL.

[4] Barros, *Betrayal from Within*, p. 180 fn.

multinational the Foreign Office would have to exercise discretion in the selection of what was communicated.[1] He also made a similar appeal to Hankey, explaining that he wanted any contact between the Secretariat and the British Government to be effected through the Cabinet Secretariat (which Hankey of course directed) and not through the Foreign Office.[2] Considering the hostility to the League that existed in the Foreign Office and the access that Hankey had to Lloyd George and other cabinet officials, this was a shrewd move on Drummond's part—even if it proved unsuccessful.

Drummond, however, warned the higher officials of the Secretariat that in certain sensitive questions governments would not supply the full information they received which often was based on secret sources. In his mind, it would be sufficient if the Secretariat received from member states 'such summaries of current information' as would enable it to judge if a particular question was 'likely to become acute and to lead to a deterioration in international relations'. When it did the Secretariat should contact the concerned governments for all information regarding that particular problem and by this method it could secure 'adequate material to compile a reasoned case for presentation to the Council'. He deprecated any attempt to press for information from the Secretariat's own agents, like *ad hoc* commissions. The Secretariat had to remember they served a League of Nations and not any supranational body.[3]

As to his inquiry, Curzon informed Drummond that when he wanted papers it would be better if he asked for them 'informally'. When Drummond did this a year later, Lord Hardinge rejected his request on the grounds that he could not furnish confidential Foreign Office documents for the Secretariat's use. Drummond replied that he did not want documents containing the British Government's view or attitude. He explained he desired factual information to assist the Secretariat to compile an impartial summary of the facts and history leading to political questions submitted to the Council for its consideration. Obviously,

---

[1] Drummond to Curzon, 8 July 1919, FO/371/4310.
[2] E[ric] D[rummond] to Hankey, 28 July 1919, also E[ric] D[rummond] to Hankey, 29 July 1919, Political 1919: 11/506/506, LNA.
[3] E[ric] D[rummond] to Fosdick, Monnet, and Mantoux, 4 Oct. 1919, Political 1919: 11/1169/1169, LNA.

information drawn from various sources would make it possible to 'compile a more concise and complete statement'.[1] In time, however, an informal *ad hoc* arrangement was developed whereby Drummond was allowed to see the Foreign Office's secret and confidential documents, especially about questions that were of special interest to the League. This was done not because Drummond was considered by the Foreign Office to be their agent in Geneva, or because London was altruistic, but because it was considered to be in the interests of the British Government to have Drummond informed on a *continuing* basis of what British policy was. The Head of the League of Nations Department, Sir Alexander Cadogan, who supported this stance, noted that Drummond saw at Geneva the representatives—often the leading personalities—of every country in the world, and they freely discussed with him every conceivable question that might be of interest to their countries. Drummond's office therefore was in reality the 'clearing house' of Europe's political ideas. Other important members of the Secretariat were treated by their respective governments as if they were their diplomatic agents overseas. They were kept fully informed by their own governments and Cadogan did not doubt they were used—quite improperly—as diplomatic agents. The Foreign Office did not want to do this with Drummond. Though Drummond supplied London with a great deal of information it was always difficult to receive information without giving some in return. Tyrrell, now Permanent Under-Secretary, had no objection to keeping Drummond informed provided it could be done privately and informally as Cadogan had suggested. To this arrangement Chamberlain, as Foreign Secretary, gave his assent.[2]

Aside from this intimacy with the Foreign Office, Drummond also endeavoured to make the acquaintance of new governments at 10 Downing Street—witness his sojourn in January 1924 to meet MacDonald's recently elected Labour government[3] as well as his successful attempt to re-establish contact with Stanley

[1] Hardinge to Drummond, 7 July 1920 and E[ric] D[rummond] to Hardinge, 8 July 1920, Political 1920: 11/5526/468, LNA.

[2] Minutes by A[lexander] Cadogan, W[illiam] T[yrrell], and A[usten] C[hamberlain], 27 May 1927, FO/371/12685.

[3] Drummond (Geneva) to House, 1 Feb. 1924, Drawer 6, Folder 47, Edward M. House Papers, YUNH.

Baldwin's successor Conservative government later that year.[1]
Indeed, Drummond persuaded Baldwin to appoint Cecil, whom
he had first proposed to leave out of the government, as
Chancellor of the Duchy of Lancaster.[2] Cecil accepted on
Balfour's[3] advice only on the understanding that he would deal
with questions affecting the League.[4] Drummond had by this
action placed a friend within the Cabinet, a person dedicated to
the League and all that it stood for, and even more important,
someone who would undoubtedly do all in his power to see that
British policy was not merely friendly to the League, but that
London would actively use and co-operate closely with the
Geneva organization.

Drummond felt that the League's success, as long as Washington was not a member, would largely depend on the support that
the British Government working through the Foreign Office
would be willing to give it, along with the French and Japanese
Governments and those of the smaller powers. London's hostility
would destroy the League. At the least, its toleration would allow
the organization to survive. And who knew what might develop?
Washington might in time co-operate and collaborate with the
League, especially in non-political matters, or even join it.[5]

Politics is never static and it was conceivable that those in
America who had defeated the Covenant in the Senate might
weaken or even change their own attitude. Certainly, as Harding
was succeeded by Coolidge and Hoover, the attitude in
Washington toward the League perceptibly softened and became
more friendly and co-operative.[6] During these years for

[1] [Cecil], Memorandum of Conversation with the Prime Minister on
Monday, 10 Nov. 1924, Add. MS. 51081, Robert Cecil Papers, BL.

[2] Philip Noel-Baker, 'Edgar Algernon Robert Gascoyne Cecil', *DNB 1951–
1960* (London: Oxford University Press, 1970), p. 200.

[3] R[obert] C[ecil] to [Balfour], Saturday [8 Nov. 1924?], and A[rthur] J.
B[alfour], Memorandum of Conversation, 10 Nov. 1924, Folder 14, Arthur
Balfour Papers, SRO-NRA.

[4] Cecil to Baldwin, 10 Nov. 1924, Volume 43, Stanley Baldwin Papers, CU.

[5] Handwritten comments by Sir Eric Drummond (Lord Perth), 31 Jan.
1951, which were prepared and sent in response to questions posed by Stephen
M. Schwebel. These notes were kindly made available to the author by Mr.
Schwebel.

[6] For Drummond's views about the Coolidge and Hoover administrations
see Drummond (Geneva) to [Noel-] Baker, 25 Apr. 1924 and Drummond
(Geneva) to Parmoor, 6 May 1924, Add. MS. 51110, Robert Cecil Papers, BL.

(*continued*)

Drummond to have avoided using the excellent political contacts that he had in London and especially in the Foreign Office to ensure British support of the League would have been an act of folly.[1]

For example, the proposal in late 1919 that Great Britain should sever her connection with the League if America did not join since London would find it impossible to execute the obligations implied in the Covenant, caused Drummond to observe that it smacked of a return to England's 'old-time policy of isolation'. He cleverly contacted Kerr, a fellow Scot who was distantly related and was the director of Lloyd George's private secretariat which dabbled in foreign policy.[2] He observed to Kerr that Britain's post-war treaty commitments obligated her as far as possible to do everything in her power to see that these treaties were faithfully executed. London had therefore assumed wide obligations which might possibly involve the use of military force. These obligations were far more extensive than anything undertaken in the Covenant. Drummond cogently argued that the Covenant actually devolved the responsibility for maintaining these treaties on a far greater number of states than the actual signatories to these treaties and this fact made it less likely that Great Britain would be called upon to use her military forces. If the Americans joined the League so much the better. Even if they stayed out, was it not a wiser policy to try and get the peace settlement, to which London was formally committed, guaranteed by as many states as possible through the League?[3]

Drummond's thoughts on Britain's support of the League were best expressed to Balfour in 1921. Politically, Great Britain, he maintained, had never been a European state. Her main interests were extra-European. Drummond presumed that as far as

---

Also E[ric] D[rummond], Notes as Regards the Position of the US in Regard to the League of Nations, 12 Jan. 1929, Financial Administration 1928–32: 17/1157/1157, LNA, and Drummond (Geneva) to Bullard, 28 Jan. 1929, Arthur Bullard Papers, PU.

[1] Drummond believed in the League system, according to one of his former associates and he wished to obtain London's support for the Geneva organization. 'The Reminiscences of Thanassis Aghnides'.

[2] Gordon A. Craig, 'The British Foreign Office from Grey to Austen Chamberlain', in Craig and Gilbert, p. 19.

[3] Drummond to Kerr, 10 Dec. 1919, File GD40/17/56, Lothian Papers, SRO.

Europe was concerned London's policy should concentrate on maintaining the peace and on defending the balance of power in Europe. He felt that the League and the Covenant offered the 'best possible instrument for the execution of such a policy'. In order that she speak with great authority in European affairs while simultaneously avoiding any entanglement there, Britain, through her permanent seat on the Council, had an influential voice in settling European disputes which was matched, once they were fully examined, by none too onerous obligations under the Covenant. London's commitment was only one: namely, that if a state broke its solemn obligations under the Covenant, Great Britain would have to sever her financial and economic relations with that state. Even here there was a catch since it would be London which would judge whether the state in question had or had not broken these obligations.

Moreover, the Council's constitutional make-up offered a guarantee against European predominance by any state. If this danger arose, all the Council's other states would be brought together to oppose such a move. By recognizing these points Drummond believed that it 'would be agreed that the League was likely to be an extremely useful instrument for British policy as regards Europe in the future'.

Many people in England, while admitting to this, seemed to think that the best approach was to maintain the League with 'somewhat lukewarm support, but not to encourage its activities in present circumstances'. Though such an approach sounded very prudent, he doubted whether it was very practical. America's rejection of the League had been a great blow to the smaller states. If these states had the impression that the Great Powers only tolerated the League, Drummond thought that defections might develop, not necessarily by official withdrawals, but by not paying budget assessments, or not sending people to serve on League commissions and so on. This was a real danger, but it would be easily met if it were clear that London and Paris would support the League. Drummond was convinced that another and similar organization could not, at least for a long time, be established. If the League vanished, the Allied Powers would have to tackle something like a new German peace treaty since the League was so intertwined with the Versailles settlement.

Though he was willing to admit that Washington and a majority of the American electorate were opposed to the League, one had to keep in mind that several years previous eighty per cent of this same electorate were strongly in its favour. Perhaps Washington would like to see London leave the League or have it fail for want of support. When the American pro-League reaction inevitably came, there would be a bitter feeling against England's desertion since she was looked upon as one of the League's champions. This would be an unreasonable reaction, but, as Balfour had often said, the Americans were 'not always ruled by their intellect'.

Drummond was concerned whether Britain in the long run would not lose America's friendship by her failure to support the League. Amending the Covenant extensively was worthwhile provided American co-operation could be secured. One test, however, had to be applied to all schemes devised: namely, would it have prevented the outbreak of world war in 1914? He argued the necessity for the permanent type machinery that the League offered. Under the Covenant, disputes had to be submitted to the League and delay before war could commence was assured. Public opinion was given the time to make itself felt. None of Washington's schemes filled this condition. Drummond also communicated a copy of this letter to Lloyd George, reiterating some of the things he had said to Balfour. He attempted to reassure Lloyd George that the fact that there were small states sitting with equal rights with the Great Powers, particularly in the Council, had made for fair and reasonable solutions of the problems discussed. In fact, the Council unanimity rule removed the danger that an 'unpalatable decision' would be made against a great power—an obvious allusion to Great Britain—but if that state 'had an unreasonable case it would have to face the concentration of world-wide opinion against its attitude and this [was] a most prominent moral weapon, to which much force [was] given by the pressure of the small powers'.[1]

Drummond's comments probably had a greater impact on Balfour who was sympathetic to the League than on Lloyd George who was not known for his altruism. Indeed, Lloyd

---

[1] Drummond (Geneva) to Balfour, 29 June 1921, and Drummond to [Lloyd George], 30 July 1921, File F/42/7/8, Lloyd George Papers, BLL.

George subsequently commented that he was interested in replacing the League with a new association that would include Germany, Russia, and the United States. This comment attracted Drummond's attention not because he believed that the League and the Covenant were perfect, or that the Covenant could not be improved by amendment, but because he was convinced that the League's destruction would make the establishment of a new organization impossible. More than fifty states were League members, and if the League was scrapped many of these states, he feared, would refuse to pledge themselves to any new organization.

Unless the whole notion of an international association of nations was to be lost for many years to come, the line to follow was surely the development of the League and the amendment of the Covenant rather than the League's 'abolition in favour of some new and untried plan'. There were also many advantages in the retention of the present League. Its non-political success had been considerable—opium control, international health, and so on. Furthermore, many tasks under the peace treaties were assigned to the League, for example, the Saar and Danzig arrangements, duties concerning the protection of minorities. He considered the matter of such importance, he informed Kerr, that he intended to come to London to ascertain Lloyd George's real objections to the League as presently constituted. Drummond sincerely trusted that the Geneva organization would not become a British political football, as the effects of this on international co-operation might prove to be 'as disastrous as they have been in America'.[1]

Drummond's desire therefore to see the actions of the British Government mesh with those of the League helps to explain his desire to make the League's work better known to the Cabinet and Parliament[2] and his sensitivity to the coverage of League affairs given in the British press.[3] It also made him sensitive to

---

[1] Drummond (Geneva) to Kerr, 18 Jan. 1922, File GD40/17/82, Lothian Papers, SRO.

[2] Drummond to Cecil, 22 June 1923, Add. MS. 51110, Robert Cecil Papers, BL.

[3] Drummond (Geneva) to Cecil, 14 Mar. 1921 and Drummond (Geneva) to Cecil, 22 June 1923, Add. MS. 51110, Robert Cecil Papers, BL; Drummond to Kerr, 20 Oct. 1921, File GD40/17/82, Lothian Papers, SRO.

the rank and calibre of the British representative at Geneva.[1] Thus he succeeded in having Balfour maintained as the British representative at the Council to continue his work on the Austrian question,[2] extolled the excellence of Edward Wood (Lord Halifax) as President of the Council,[3] and likewise pointed out the inadequacies of Lord Parmoor as Britain's representative to the League,[4] a view shared by Cecil.[5]

During Drummond's Secretary-Generalship, however, the British Government on the whole gave the League less than full support. Although at some times London's attitude toward the League was one of active collaboration, at others it was merely one of toleration. A complete and open abandonment of the League, at least during Drummond's tenure, was never contemplated for it would have been unacceptable to the majority of the British electorate. How far London meshed its policy with the League naturally often depended on the type of government sitting at 10 Downing Street, the question at issue, and the exigencies of international politics.

The Myth of the Secretariat

Drummond's memorandum of 31 May 1919, discussing the establishment of an international secretariat, has done much to perpetuate the myth of the impartial, non-political international civil service.[6] That this international secretariat would in any way be analogous to the civil service of national governments, that it would be non-political and remove itself from influencing

[1] Drummond to Hankey, 6 Oct. 1919, File 1919–20, Raymond B. Fosdick Papers, PU. Also Drummond to Fisher, 17 Oct. 1921, File F/25/2/33, Lloyd George Papers, BLL.

[2] Drummond to [Bonar Law], 16 Dec. 1922, File 111/16/85, Bonar Law Papers, BLL; Sydney H. Zebel, *Balfour: A Political Biography* (Cambridge: Cambridge University Press, 1973), p. 279.

[3] Drummond to [Bonar Law], 27 Apr. 1923, File 114/4/4, Bonar Law Papers, BLL.

[4] Drummond to Cecil, 27 June 1924, Add. MS. 51110, Robert Cecil Papers, BL.

[5] C[ecil] to Murray, 8 Mar. 1924, Gilbert Murray Papers, BLOU. See also, J. A. Thompson, 'The League of Nations Union and Promotion of the League Idea in Great Britain', *The Australian Journal of Politics and History*, XVIII, No. 1 (April 1972), p. 59.

[6] E[ric] D[rummond], Memorandum, 31 May 1919, FO/608/242.

the policy process, that individuals would be chosen for their intelligence or talents rather than for their nationality, and be loyal only to the world organization was probably never envisaged by Drummond when he wrote the memorandum. He was too much of a realist to believe that the bureaucratic apparatus with which he was most familiar—that of the British civil service and the Foreign Office in particular—could ever really be developed by the Secretariat. As homogeneous as was the League's membership (mostly European and Latin American) the Secretariat did not contain within itself the characteristics and values generally associated with the Weberian bureaucratic model of which the British civil service and the Foreign Office were excellent examples.[1] Indeed, from the very beginning Drummond readily admitted all this. Writing to the classicist and League advocate, Gilbert Murray, in September 1919 Drummond thought that an overemphasis on the Council made people lose sight of the Assembly which surely resembled Parliament, and from which the Council or Cabinet derived its power. The Secretariat should in his mind, Drummond noted, be the 'Civil Service through which decisions of Parliament and the Cabinet are carried out. *The analogy cannot of course be carried too far*', but was not the future's main hope in the Assembly?[2]

Aside from what he conceded to Murray, Drummond in subsequent years, by both his actions and his admissions, clearly

[1] See the excellent article by David A. Kay, 'Secondment in the United Nations Secretariat: An Alternative View', *International Organization*, XX, No. 1 (Winter 1966), pp. 63–75.

[2] Italics added. Drummond to Murray, 18 Sept. 1919, Gilbert Murray Papers, BLOU. The practical restriction on the Assembly's ability to expand its powers and activities was the unanimity rule. The adoption of 'voeux', however, in which the Assembly expressed its desires by a simple majority vote was welcomed by Drummond who saw 'practical advantages' in this procedure. He believed that it was very desirable that the Assembly's resolutions should on their own be binding. The most serious danger to this approach was the previous attitude of the French Government that Assembly resolutions were not binding unless they were incorporated in a formal treaty. He thought this French view was wrong and was pleased that it was being rejected. On the other hand, voeux removed the difficulty that when a country objected to an Assembly proposal it had, under the unanimity rule, the power to destroy the proposal. The 'voeux' avoided this problem by allowing an Assembly majority 'to come to an agreement for common action, even where a small number of members dissented'. Minutes of a Directors' Meeting, 10 Aug. 1922, LNA.

showed that he did not subscribe to the concept of a non-political international secretariat. This idea was an illusion perpetuated by the unknowing and by well-meaning League supporters, an illusion that still lingers on and does nothing to help understand the role that an international secretariat plays in the problem of crisis management or conflict–resolution under the aegis of an international organization. For Drummond the notion of non-involvement in the policy process was in practice hopefully to be confined to the lower reaches of the Secretariat. Though he chided his associates 'to do nothing which could be taken as a handle by critics of the League',[1] and talked of his 'anxiety ... that the members of the Secretariat were inclined to take up rather too much the attitude of acting as representatives of their individual national Governments',[2] Drummond himself in making appointments to the Secretariat did in fact carefully differentiate between those which 'might be called political appointments', and those called 'administrative posts'.[3] As with its successor, the United Nations Secretariat, the League Secretariat's higher and more important positions were reserved as political conduits between the Geneva organization and important member states. The persons selected to fill these particular positions were chosen with this consideration uppermost in everyone's mind, rather than on the individual's intrinsic qualifications.

This was something that Drummond admitted to in private. Nationals of the Great Powers, he divulged to his closest associates in 1925, holding senior positions in the Secretariat were obliged 'to keep in close touch with their Governments because it was a fact that these Governments exercised a great influence in international politics'. But it was incorrect to state that these same officials should or even attempted to ensure the success of their own government's point of view in the Secretariat. This was maintained in a book by William E. Rappard, the former Director of the Mandates Section, who wrote that these senior British, French, and Italian Secretariat officials were duty bound '"de faire prévaloir" the views of their respective Governments

[1] Minutes of a Directors' Meeting, 29 Apr. 1921, LNA.
[2] Minutes of a Directors' Meeting, 30 Mar. 1922, LNA.
[3] Secret Meeting of the Council of the League of Nations, 13 Jan. 1922, Council 1928–32: 14/9887/2385, LNA.

in the Secretariat'.[1] Thus seemingly non-political in their actions these individuals were—like Drummond—politically active in private and often with great effect.

What were the mechanics of selecting candidates for the Secretariat? First, Drummond indicated the nationality in which he would prefer to find a candidate. The best persons were then sought, sometimes narrowing it down to two or three candidates of that particular nationality. Next, if Drummond thought it necessary, the League representative of the country in question would be confidentially contacted to ascertain if the candidate's government had any objections to his appointment. If objections were raised, if the government contacted presented valid reasons, Drummond had to accept them since he could not afford to jeopardize his relations with that government.[2] It certainly was a realistic and perhaps even a rational procedure keeping in mind that every nation knew the political gains or advantages that could accrue by having one's own nationals, but ones acceptable to the government, within the Secretariat. This explains the pressures on Drummond even from the earliest days to make available Secretariat positions, especially at the senior level, to the nationals of permanent Council members or to the nationals of Council members who had hopes of permanent membership, as in the case of Spain and Brazil.[3] The whole procedure, however, was in no way even remotely analogous to anything that occurred within national governments which desired to develop impartial non-political civil services on the lines of the Weberian bureaucratic model.

With some countries, however, this procedure was not an *ad hoc* arrangement and was also slightly different in certain important respects. In the case of Canada, it was a regularized procedure based on an agreement drawn up by Drummond and the Canadian Government. Interestingly, the agreement was arranged in early 1920 by the Canadian, Sir Herbert Ames, who held the sensitive post of League Treasurer. According to the agreement, when an important post was to be filled and the desire was to appoint a Canadian, a communication would be

[1] Minutes of a Directors' Meeting, 3 June 1925, LNA.

[2] 'The Reminiscences of Pablo de Azcárate y Florez'.

[3] Secret Meeting of the Council of the League of Nations, 13 Jan. 1922, Council 1928–32: 14/9887/2385, LNA.

addressed to the Canadian Prime Minister or to the Acting Prime Minister and a 'nomination requested'. Ames, knowing the Canadian situation, was to 'keep in personal touch' with the Department of External Affairs in order to advise in advance of any forthcoming appointments and to furnish the special data regarding conditions and also suggestions as to possible persons 'showing the type of Canadian required'. As League Treasurer, Ames of course was in an excellent position to furnish this information. Ames's communications were to be regarded as unofficial but copies were to be sent to the Canadian High Commission in London. As to minor appointments, or to staffing League commissions, they could be made by Drummond communicating directly with the Canadian national involved. 'Excellent', Drummond wrote, in regard to this arrangement. The arrangement was also approved by the Colonial Office in London.[1] In the years that immediately followed Drummond appears to have kept to the arrangement made.[2]

In later years when the political configuration both inside and especially outside the League had changed and Ames had departed from the Secretariat, the arrangement was executed less often and only with some difficulty.[3] Germany by this time had joined the League and obviously her demands for Secretariat representation, which, as we shall see, Drummond was very quick to fill,[4] as well as Italy's desires for greater representation befitting what she considered to be her due as a great power, made Drummond more sensitive to pressures from Berlin and Rome and less amenable to Ottawa's desires.

The Canadian case, however, should not be looked upon as some sort of devious or special arrangement merely because Canada was a member of the British Empire. It was probably no different from other arrangements that were devised. Any

[1] H[erbert] B. Ames, Memorandum for the Secretary-General, 14 Feb. 1920, Ames to Perley, 16 Feb. 1920 and Ames to Rowell, 16 Feb. 1920, File P9/P29, MG 25, A2, Volume 156, PAC. For the arrangement with Germany see Chapter IV, pp. 179–83, 191–92.

[2] Drummond to Perley, 4 Aug. 1921, File P9/92, MG 25, A2, Volume 156, PAC.

[3] [Walter A. Riddell], Interview with the Secretary-General, 25 Mar. 1929, [Walter A. Riddell], Interview with the Secretary-General, 21 Jan. 1930, Walter A. Riddell Papers, YUT. See also *DCER*, iv. 595–6.

[4] Minutes of a Directors' Meeting, 3 Mar. 1926, LNA.

differences that did exist were undoubtedly in form and not in substance; some of these arrangements, for example, were unquestionably oral. It would be safe to say that the one similarity that exemplified all these agreements was that the more powerful the state the greater was the deference shown to it by Drummond in accepting its nominations, in consulting it, and in accepting and acting upon its advice and recommendations.

However, despite Drummond's attitude that the lower reaches of the Secretariat were not to get involved in the policy process, this often did not prove to be the case.[1] Even at the middle and lower levels of the Secretariat political activities were visible. These activities were attempts generally to foster or propagate what might be called a pro-League policy, as though the Secretariat could make policy on its own and ignore the dictates of the Council and Assembly, which were the League's policy-making organs and reflected the desires of the organization's membership.

From the beginning, unsolicited or unilateral political moves by Drummond or the Secretariat caused immediate annoyance in British official circles. A memorandum by Drummond criticizing the draft constitution for the Free City of Danzig and proposing alterations and generally advising as to the course that the Council should adopt, caused Crowe to minute that the Foreign Office again found that in this important question Drummond was performing the role of 'political adviser' to the Council. 'One would have expected that such functions would be discharged', he commented, 'not by the Secretary[-General] but by a committee or subcommittee of the Council itself'.[2]

Drummond attempted to discuss the question of his political initiatives quite frankly with Chamberlain, the Foreign Secretary, in the summer of 1927. Because of a misunderstanding that had developed over the selection of the Assembly's President, Drummond conceded that it was not the task of the Secretariat to promote candidates. However, when a government representative asked the Secretary-General for suggestions as to who would be a suitable Assembly President, Drummond held that it was both 'right and proper for him to give an honest opinion based on what he believes to be the best for the League'.

[1] Minutes of a Directors' Meeting, 30 Mar. 1922, LNA.
[2] Minute by E[yre] A. C[rowe], 28 Oct. [1920], FO/371/5408.

Furthermore, if he and his associates were international civil servants, whose only interest was promoting the League's welfare, 'may not our advice and our views concerning League interest be worth having, and [was] not any Member of the League entitled to ask for them'.[1]

But Drummond by these words raised more questions than he answered. Where was the dividing line between views solicited and those freely given? In addition, how far down the Secretariat hierarchy could advice and views be solicited and given? Lastly, was not Drummond avoiding an even more difficult question? Any political advice is largely subjective and the person giving it is in turn consciously or unconsciously guided, no matter how impartial he attempts to be, by his own value system which has been nurtured since childhood. In an international civil service this leads to difficulties and Drummond was aware of it. He tried to grapple with it, first, by being a 'very loyal servant of the League itself' and secondly, by trying 'to inspire his Staff with the same strict loyalty and independence of national prejudice'.[2] People past their formative years, however, do not readily relinquish values already acquired.

By the late 1920s the focus of attention had switched and it was now the Secretariat rather than Drummond which was exposed to criticism. Writing to Tyrrell, Lord Onslow, the leader of the British delegation to the Assembly, noted that there had always been 'criticism of the Secretariat for their political tendencies', and he thought that this criticism was 'not misdirected'. Personally, it seemed to him as though a large part of the Secretariat—he excepted those at the top—were 'active propagandists of a "League Policy"'. First, it appeared to Onslow that the Secretariat were the servants of the League and 'not its directors'. Second, if the Secretariat continued in this manner a 'serious blow' would be 'struck at their own credit'. He did not know that much could be done to stop this political activity or whether Drummond himself could counteract it, but anything that could be done should be done to help the League's real interests. To this dispatch Cadogan minuted that Lord Onslow

[1] Drummond (Geneva) to Chamberlain, 17 Aug. 1927, Austen Chamberlain Papers, FO/800/261.

[2] [Chamberlain] to Birkenhead, 18 May 1925, Austen Chamberlain Papers, FO/800/258.

was right and that the Secretariat's political tendencies were 'reaching a pitch where something will have to be done about it'. Cadogan had collected evidence from varied sources, some of which he had permission to use, and he proposed to present it, urging Drummond to do something 'to avoid the necessity of a public scandal'. If there was no improvement in the Secretariat's behaviour then Cadogan thought a 'regular fuss' might have to be made. This was a difficult matter and Drummond's position somewhat delicate. Cadogan was sure, however, that Drummond would do everything possible and it was best to wait to see what he could do.[1]

A year later the Secretariat was again a topic of discussion. It was ominously raised by the central office of the ruling Conservative Party. This time Vansittart was requested to speak to Drummond. It was feared that because of the Secretariat's activities the League might become the subject matter of party controversy in Great Britain. This situation could be avoided by focusing the Secretariat's attention on the League's main task which was to help settle international disputes, and by skirting any detailed examination of League policy upon which there might be different view points and opportunities for sharp disagreement.

For example, the Secretariat had in the past been embarrassed by attempting to force upon London a premature disarmament policy which had alarmed some of Europe's smaller powers into thinking that they were in danger of losing Great Britain's support. The suspicions of these states had been aroused. Thus the League's work 'in producing a conciliatory atmosphere and advancing negotiations had been seriously embarrassed'—a view that emanated from the Foreign Office.[2]

To the discerning observer the politics of it all was obvious from the very beginning. The two initial Under Secretaries-General appointed were an American to handle essentially administrative matters, and a Frenchman to handle political matters.[3] The fact that the American, Fosdick, had been a

---

[1] Onslow to Tyrrell, 25 Sept. 1927, and the attached minute by A[lexander] Cadogan, 11 Oct. 1927, FO/371/12686.

[2] Pembroke Wicks to Vansittart, 18 Oct. 1928, Volume 132, Stanley Baldwin Papers, CU.

[3] Fosdick, *Letters on the League of Nations*, p. 3.

student of Woodrow Wilson at Princeton University undoubtedly enhanced his qualifications. The appointments of the Italian Dionisio Anzilotti, and the Japanese Inazo Nitobe were negotiated through their respective governments. Indeed, in the case of Nitobe the objection was raised that his appointment would have to be of the same grade as that of the others for 'it would create a very unfortunate impression if Japan of the five powers was put on a grade lower than the other four powers'.[1] To this pressure Drummond succumbed.[2]

In the years that followed (1922–6), when the post of an Under Secretary-General fell vacant a person of the same nationality was appointed to the position and the nationals of smaller powers were consistently excluded from higher Secretariat posts.[3] Within his own office Drummond made no attempt to practise the multinational secretariat that he preached. All his immediate assistants were British or from the Dominions. Likewise, Avenol had only French assistants. This practice of having only one's own nationals—'national islands', they have been called, 'playing national politics'—repeated itself in the offices of all the Under Secretaries-General and other high Secretariat officials.[4]

Drummond's attitude on the question is best shown by his not raising any objections when Mussolini's government decreed that Italians must first obtain Rome's permission before accepting employment in the Secretariat and by his not admonishing some of its Italian members, especially the Under Secretary-General, Marchese Giacomo Paulucci de Calboli Barone, for their blatant pro-Fascist antics.[5]

---

[1] Auchincloss to Drummond, 21 June 1919, Drawer 6, Folder 48, Edward M. House Papers, YUNH. The Italians pressed Anzilotti on Drummond, who in turn asked the British Ambassador in Rome to inform him 'privately' of Anzilotti's 'reputation and character'. The Italian Foreign Minister when contacted by the British Ambassador of course supported Anzilotti's appointment. Drummond to Rodd, 21 June 1919 and Rodd (Rome) to Russell for Drummond, 26 June 1919, Correspondence Respecting the League of Nations, FO/800/400.

[2] Drummond to Auchincloss, 25 June 1919, Drawer 6, Folder 48, Edward M. House Papers, YUNH.

[3] Ranshofen-Wertheimer, p. 62.

[4] Ibid., p. 60. See also, Rovine, pp. 37 fn., 110, 112 fn.

[5] Ranshofen-Wertheimer, pp. 249–52, 408; Morley, p. 301; Rovine, p. 38. See also, Walters, p. 234.

And so it went through the echelons of the Secretariat. The next level of officials were the Directors of the Secretariat's important functional sections, dealing with political questions, mandates, and so on. They too were parcelled out with the nationality factor uppermost in everyone's mind, though there were exceptions to the nationality rule based on political considerations and expediency. Drummond himself admitted in a 1923 Directors' Meeting that although technically the Secretariat could not have any policy of its own, he did recognize that individual Directors actually did exercise substantial influence on opinion within their own countries in League matters.[1] Drummond's awareness of this influence is indicated by the initial appointments to fill these important posts. George Louis Beer, an American who had first proposed the mandates system, was appointed Director of the Mandates Section, even though Drummond had desired an Englishman for the position.[2] His replacement was Rappard, a Swiss, a necessary selection since Switzerland like the United States was not involved in the mandates system which automatically excluded an Englishman, a Frenchman, a Japanese, or a Belgian. England was represented by Salter, who was made Director of the Economic and Financial Section, and Dame Rachel Crowdy, who was made Director of the Social Affairs Section.[3] Interestingly, when Dame Rachel Crowdy was being considered for the directorship of this section Drummond 'demurred', claiming that there were already too many British nationals in the Secretariat. He suggested that an attempt be made to get a Scandinavian for the position 'because he wanted a wider geographical distribution of personnel of the Secretariat'. Only after the search for a Scandinavian had proved fruitless did Drummond consent to Crowdy's appointment.[4]

Italy was represented by Bernardo Attolico who was made Director of the Communications Section. The important Political Section was given to a Frenchman, Paul Mantoux, while a fellow

[1] Rovine, p. 48.

[2] Drummond to Kerr, 20 May 1919, File GD40/17/75, Lothian Papers, SRO; Beer Diary, 23 May 1919, pp. 97, 119, 121, 129, George Louis Beer Diary, James T. Shotwell Papers, CUNY.

[3] Walters, pp. 78–9.

[4] Raymond B. Fosdick, *The League and the United Nations After Fifty Years. The Six Secretaries-General* (privately printed, 1972), p. 24.

countryman, Pierre Comert, was made Director of the Press and Information Section. It was only the Legal and Administrative Commissions Sections that were held by nationals of states neutral during the war. But it would have been awkward if the former had been given to a national of the wartime coalition since the cry could have been raised that interpretations of legal questions raised by the peace treaties and given to the League to decide were being made by the very persons who had won the war. Similarly, the Director of the Administrative Commissions Section, responsible also for the question of the protection of minorities, could have been appointed only from a country neutral during the war. Finally, as we have seen, Ames of Canada was appointed to the post of Treasurer.[1]

Initially, the American Secretariat officials were Drummond's most important associates.[2] Through them Drummond attempted to establish and maintain his links with the American Government and people in order to facilitate the Senate's acceptance of the Covenant by attempting to explain what the League was and also by projecting a more favourable image of the organization than the jaundiced one that had developed.[3] The Senate's hostility to the Covenant and the resignation of Fosdick in early 1920,[4] which Drummond tried to head off, moved him to write that even if the Senate rejected the Covenant, he hoped that Americans would continue to co-operate on the Secretariat.[5] Why not? Americans in the Secretariat, like Arthur Bullard for example, who served in the Press and Information Section, could be useful and convenient conduits with influential fellow countrymen.[6] This was the reasoning he used to keep Arthur

[1] Walters, pp. 78–9. For the different considerations and difficulties that affected the appointment of directors of sections during this early period see the interesting letter from Gilchrist to Fosdick, 7 Feb. 1920, File 1919–20, Raymond B. Fosdick Papers, PU.

[2] These officials were: Fosdick, Under Secretary-General; Beer, Director of the Mandates Section; Arthur Sweetser, Press and Information Section; Manley O. Hudson, Legal Section; and Huntington Gilchrist was assigned to Fosdick.

[3] Rovine, pp. 60–3; Fosdick, *Letters on the League of Nations, passim.*

[4] Fosdick, *Letters on the League of Nations,* pp. 102–4.

[5] Drummond (London) to Fosdick, 2 Dec. 1919, File 1919–20, Raymond B. Fosdick Papers, PU. See also, *DBFP, 1919–1939,* I, v. 1044 fn.

[6] See Drummond (Geneva) to Bullard, 17 Dec. 1927, Arthur Bullard Papers, PU.

Sweetser as a member of the Press and Information Section. He would be, Drummond maintained, using the supposed arguments of Comert, the Director of the Section, the 'liaison with [the] League to Enforce Peace and American Public Opinion'—the former a pro-League organization.[1] In the years that followed, Sweetser was the main contact man for the League with Washington and with the American diplomatic missions in Switzerland,[2] though his unbridled enthusiasm for the League was often counter-productive.

Drummond's most damaging admission about the political nature of the Secretariat was made in the early 1950s. In 1929 the Assembly decided, on the initiative of the British Foreign Secretary, Arthur Henderson, to institute a thorough examination of the secretariats of the League, the International Labour Organisation, and the Permanent Court of International Justice at The Hague. Henderson took this initiative without consulting Drummond, who thought that 'his position had been rendered very difficult' by this action. Drummond felt that the initiative had caused 'a great stir' in Geneva and would propel the smaller states in this question to lose 'all sense of realities'. They believed that London was leading them and that they could defy the other Great Powers who were, he maintained, the League's 'real backbone'. To undertake this study a Committee of Inquiry was established which became known as the Committee of Thirteen. The committee's long report was not unanimous: the majority minimizing the Secretariat's political role in League affairs, while a contrary view was assumed in a minority report penned by the German and Italian members of the committee. The minority report pointed out that the Secretary-General by the very nature of his duties could not avoid involvement in substantive issues. 'The political influence of the Secretariat, and especially of its principal officers', the minority claimed, was, 'in fact, enormous and it would be a mistake to close our eyes to this fact'. Therefore, the Secretariat's organization was an important question. Accordingly, the minority report proposed that the

---

[1] Gilchrist for Drummond to Sweetser, 2 Feb. 1920, File 1919–20, Raymond B. Fosdick Papers, PU.

[2] Walters, pp. 348–9; Joseph C. Grew, *Turbulent Era*, ed. Walter Johnson (Boston: Houghton Mifflin, 1952), pp. 457, 458, 460–1, 463, 609. See also, Deibel, *passim*.

number of Under Secretaries-General not be increased and the extra posts given to non-permanent Council members. States had to realize that the Under Secretary-Generalship held by a national of a state with permanent Council representation was 'not a constitutional rule or privilege', but practicable since 'the nationals of countries with general interests are, by their capacity to serve as liaison agents, specially qualified to discharge the duties of Under Secretary-General'. They proposed that a governing board be established consisting of the Under Secretaries-General and chaired by the Secretary-General. They would discuss all questions, actions to be taken in the execution of Council and Assembly decisions, examine the draft agendas of League organs, and so on. It would also be attended by Directors of Sections when questions touching their sections were discussed. Another possibility was the establishment of an Under Secretaries-General committee which would be informed of all political questions and give its opinion to the Secretary-General on all political matters. If it desired the committee would have the right to express its opinion, before any measures were taken by the Secretary-General, in matters involving important political issues or principles. In addition, the minority report proposed that the Directors of Sections instead of being directly responsible to the Secretary-General would be grouped under different Under Secretaries-General.[1]

Drummond's compromise counter-proposal tendered to Cecil in the spring of 1930 was to increase the Under Secretaries-General to seven which, including the Secretary-General and the Deputy Secretary-General, would be nine senior positions, plus eight Directors of Sections, making seventeen senior positions in the Secretariat. He erroneously thought that the fears expressed in the minority report would be largely absorbed by his plan since there would always be a national of each of the Council's permanent members among the top senior positions, and League members who were always non-permanent Council members 'would have the certainty of more or less adequate

---

[1] Dalton, i. 224; League of Nations, *Official Journal*, Special Supplement No. 88, pp. 313–15. For the work of the Committee of Thirteen see Howard B. Calderwood, *The Higher Direction of the League Secretariat* (Dallas: Southern Methodist University, 1937).

representation in the higher ranks of the Secretariat'.[1] The president of the Committee of Thirteen for tactical reasons suggested to Drummond that his proposal had a better chance of success if it was put forward as a last minute compromise, and to this Drummond agreed.[2]

In late August Drummond made known to the permanent Canadian representative in Geneva his strong opposition to the minority report.[3] During this same period he attempted to influence through the Foreign Office both the selection of the specific Assembly committee which would consider the Committee of Thirteen's report as well as who would be chairman of the Assembly committee chosen. He wanted the report to be considered by the Assembly's Fourth Committee which dealt with budget and financial questions—which proved to be the case—rather than by the First Committee which dealt with constitutional and legal questions and where the Italians and the Germans thought they had greater influence.[4] In the end, Count Carton de Wiart of Belgium was made chairman of the Assembly's Fourth Committee. During the consideration of the committee's report Drummond felt impelled to intervene in the discussions. It was one of those rare occasions when he spoke up and he argued against the acceptance of the minority recommendations on the grounds that they would affect the Secretariat's efficiency, would be a burden to him personally as well as to the staff, and were superfluous since all interested parties within the Secretariat were already consulted on all important matters. 'If I had not devoted ten years of my life to this administration', Drummond concluded, 'I would not have ventured to take sides on this question'.[5]

To have remained silent, to have admitted to the minority report's contentions, or to have even agreed to accept its recommendations would have undermined Drummond's whole

[1] Drummond (Geneva) to Cecil, 8 May 1930 and E[ric] D[rummond], An untitled memorandum, 3 May 1930, Add. MS. 51112, Robert Cecil Papers, BL.

[2] E[ric] D[rummond], Record of Interview, 7 May 1930, ibid.

[3] [Walter A. Riddell], Interview with Sir Eric Drummond, 29 Aug. 1930, Walter A. Riddell Papers, YUT.

[4] Drummond (Geneva) to Cadogan, 28 Aug. 1930 and Drummond (Geneva) to Cecil, 1 Sept. 1930, Add. MS. 51112, Robert Cecil Papers, BL.

[5] League of Nations, *Official Journal*, Special Supplement No. 88, p. 153.

position and, as one student of the Secretary-General's office has written, 'would have shaken the League to its foundations'.[1] So he argued against the minority report's recommendations. Twenty-odd years after the event, however, Drummond felt no such constraints: 'I am afraid', he said, 'that the judgment of the minority was entirely right'.[2] He was certainly more candid than those, before or since, who have disingenuously insisted on the non-political character and civil service nature of international secretariats.[3]

[1] Schwebel, p. 10.

[2] Ibid.

[3] After Drummond's departure from the League one anti-Hitlerite German observer in Geneva wrote that everyone at the Secretariat regarded 'himself as his country's representative rather than as the League's official. His behaviour in the Secretariat is so designed as to ensure that his government will give him a good post as soon as he leaves. Most members of the Secretariat belong to their country's diplomatic service and look on their time with the League as just another posting. ... This personnel policy is quite enough to explain the League's failure. The only neutrals and really international officials are those Germans, Russians and Italians who are not Nazis, Communists or Fascists and have broken their links with their home governments without leaving the Secretariat. ...' Michael Balfour and Julian Fisby, *Helmuth von Moltke, A Leader Against Hitler* (London: Macmillan, 1972), pp. 65–6.

III

DRUMMOND IN POWER, 1919–1920

Establishing the League

The world Drummond faced in 1919 was in disarray. Aside from the obvious political unrest of victors and vanquished, there was also civil, ideological, social, and economic turmoil. The problems were innumerable. Drummond's immediate task, therefore, was to organize the Secretariat quickly so that the League could begin to function and assist or contribute to a solution of some of these problems and to return the world community as quickly as possible to a normal state. His initial problem was the question of sufficient financial credit to run the League. In view of the mounting opposition against the League in America Drummond wisely attempted to secure such financial credit from the British Treasury. Despite his contacts in London his approaches were resisted particularly by the Treasury which reflected to a certain extent the suspicion against the League to be found in some government circles as well as the primary desire to curb government expenditure. In the end, an advance was secured, but it was insufficient and unsatisfactory; Drummond called the Treasury's attitude 'parsimonious'.[1] In the months that followed Drummond used his contacts with both Hankey and the Foreign Office to get the League around some tight financial corners.[2]

Naturally, Drummond's most persistent problem during his first year in office was America's ratification of the Covenant. His

---

[1] Cecil to Balfour, 10 May 1919, Drummond to [Balfour], 12 May 1919, Tilley to The Secretary to the Treasury, 16 May 1919, Heath to [Curzon], 20 May 1919, Tyrrell to The Secretary to the Treasury, 27 May 1919, Curzon to Balfour, 27 May 1919, Heath to [Curzon], 3 June 1919, [Curzon] to Drummond, 11 June 1919 and two letters Drummond to Graham, 21 June 1919, FO/371/4310 and FO/608/243.

[2] Drummond to Hankey, 30 Sept. 1920 and Drummond to Montgomery, 4 Oct. 1920, FO/371/5477. Financially, the International Labour Organisation was dependent on the League. The League's early financial difficulties naturally affected that organization and had some amusing repercussions. See Edward J. Phelan, *Yes and Albert Thomas* (New York: Columbia University Press, 1949), pp. 46–8, 98–101.

ability to influence and affect this event was minimal. Yet Drummond's thoughts and actions on the question of American ratification and all the other issues that flowed from it reflected his hopes, anxieties, and apprehensions about the success of the organization. Closely tied with American acceptance of the Covenant were a number of important questions that had to be considered immediately by the Council, but preferably by a Council containing American representation.

One such question was Spain's and Switzerland's admissions to the League as well as those of several Latin American states. Transferring the League from London, where it was initially established, to Geneva was another question, along with convening the Council's first meeting as soon as the Versailles Treaty was operative. There was also the matter of the Council's agenda. A wide agenda handling matters beyond those arising out of the peace settlement brought up the question of publicity. Further agenda items, according to Drummond, might be the establishment of the Permanent Court of International Justice at The Hague and moves toward disarmament 'for the sake of public opinion'. In addition, the Council would have to establish the date of the Assembly's first meeting.[1]

To Drummond the birth of the League was even more important than America's ratification of the Covenant. The League's establishment might inevitably be followed by Washington's acceptance of the organization. Correspondingly, he could not allow America's rejection of the Covenant to lead to the organization's demise and he therefore correctly argued that American participation was not legally speaking absolutely indispensable to bring the League into being, and its birth was not dependent on the will of one signatory.[2] At the same time he wanted to do nothing that would assist the anti-League elements in America, and their increasing opposition to America's joining the League prompted Drummond in August 1919 to suspend all

---

[1] Minutes of a Directors' Meeting, 13 Aug. 1919, General 1919: 40/854/854, LNA. Also Minutes of a Directors' Meeting, 20 Aug. 1919, General 1919: 40/855/854, LNA.

[2] E[ric] D[rummond], Memorandum, 25 Aug. 1919, Organization: Council 1919: 27/887/193, LNA. See also, *PRFRUS, 1920*, i. 4–6.

further Secretariat appointments in order to avoid giving them ammunition.[1]

Optimistic reports in September[2] that the Senate might consent to the Covenant could only have increased Drummond's confidence that in the end all would go well. Accordingly he contacted Kerr to impress on him the kind of important questions from the League's point of view that Clemenceau intended to raise at a forthcoming Paris meeting with Lloyd George and Colonel House.[3] Doubtlessly secure about the future Drummond attended this Paris meeting.[4] In his desire to see the organization established and functioning as quickly as possible, Drummond set out an extended and detailed agenda for the Assembly's first session. The agenda was compiled on the supposition that the Assembly would convene six to seven weeks after the Senate's consent to the Covenant and that the agenda items if tackled would keep the Assembly busy for some time.[5]

By early October the confidence of September began to wane as it became clearer that there was formidable Senate opposition to the Covenant. Drummond's sensitivity about American ratification is reflected in his comment that if an American representative could not be present during the Council's first meeting the only subject that should be discussed was the selection of the Saar delimitation commission. This particular meeting ought probably to be held in Paris, and with an absence of publicity—a view subsequently shared by the Foreign Office. On the other hand, the presence of an American representative— obviously a more auspicious occasion—should lead to a London meeting lasting several days. To this London meeting the fullest publicity should be given. As to the Assembly's first meeting

[1] Minutes of a Directors' Meeting, 27 Aug. 1919, General 1919: 40/908/854, LNA.

[2] Minutes of a Directors' Meeting, 3 Sept. 1919, General: 40/1005/854, LNA; and Minutes of a Directors' Meeting, 10 Sept. 1919, General 1919: 40/1114/854, LNA. See also *PRFRUS, 1920*, i. 6–7.

[3] Drummond to Kerr, 10 and 11 Sept. 1919, File GD40/17/55, Lothian Papers, SRO.

[4] Minutes of a Directors' Meeting, 24 Sept. 1919, General 1919: 40/1252/854, LNA.

[5] Drummond to Kerr, 16 Sept. 1919, File GD40/17/55, Lothian Papers, SRO; [Drummond] to Hankey, 16 Sept. 1919, General 1919: 40/1215/1215, LNA.

Drummond hoped that President Wilson would decide to summon it in Washington as soon as this was practicable after America's ratification of the treaty.[1] Drummond's own preference was that an American be appointed as chairman of the Saar Governing Commission and he justified a Council meeting in London on the grounds that this was the Secretariat's temporary headquarters.[2]

The Senate's initial rejection of the Versailles Treaty in November caused Drummond during December and January 1920 to look into the possibilities of having the reservations raised by Senator Henry Cabot Lodge of Massachusetts accepted by Great Britain and France provided this would facilitate the Senate's consent to the treaty and America's entrance into the organization.[3] It was to no avail. In this question Drummond could do no more than King Canute, for Drummond like Canute was contending with forces more powerful than himself or his office. Canute confronted the tides of the sea while Drummond had to confront the tide of American and especially Senatorial isolationism. By early January 1920, France, Great Britain, Italy, and Japan had ratified the treaty and thus accepted the Covenant. Therefore it was decided that the Council's first meeting should be held in Paris on 16 January. In accordance with Article 5 paragraph three of the Covenant President Wilson had no choice but to convene such a meeting even though the Senate had not yet consented to the treaty.[4]

As desired by Drummond the Council's first meeting dealt only with the appointment of the Saar delimitation commission,[5]

---

[1] Minutes of a Directors' Meeting and the attached memorandum by Drummond, 1 Oct. 1919, General 1919: 40/1329/854, LNA. See also, *DBFP, 1919–1939*, I, v. 741, 759–60 and fnn.

[2] Drummond to Fosdick, 4 Oct. 1919, File 1919–20, Raymond B. Fosdick Papers, PU.

[3] Drummond to Kerr, 18 Dec. 1919, File GD40/17/56, Lothian Papers, SRO; Drummond to Fosdick, 2 Jan. 1920, and Drummond to Fosdick, 8 Jan. 1920, File 1919–20, Raymond B. Fosdick Papers, PU. See also, *DBFP, 1919–1939*, I, v. 1065.

[4] *PRFRUS, 1920*, i. 9–10.

[5] Drummond to Nicolson, 12 Nov. 1919, File 1919–20, Raymond B. Fosdick Papers, PU. League of Nations, Council, *Minutes of the First Meeting of the Council of the League of Nations Held in Paris, January 16, 1920*, pp. 2–7; League of Nations, *Official Journal*, I (1920), pp. 19, 24–5.

but contrary to his earlier wish the meeting was publicized[1]—it being felt that if the League did not arrange any publicity its opponents would do so. This would have been an unfortunate move as America's absence and a limited agenda would have made it possible for the League's opponents to intimate that the organization was dead from its inception. Therefore, publicity was necessary in order to explain the League's real state of affairs from the standpoint of those interested in the organization's welfare.[2] On the first day of the meeting, despite the 'surprised and doubtful' look of its members, the Council president, Léon Bourgeois of France, invited Drummond to take a seat at the Council table.[3] This precedent was continued in the years to come and was expanded to include Drummond's presence at the Council's secret meetings. Indeed, at these secret meetings it was usually Drummond himself who kept the minutes.[4] During these early sessions, however, Drummond had not yet established the basis of trust and confidence that was to mark in later years his relationship with Council members. Throughout these early Council sessions, therefore, Drummond was excluded from the room whenever appointments other than ones for the Secretariat were being considered.[5]

Drummond was pleased with the Paris session. When consulted by Lord Curzon about his prospective Council speech Drummond was able to get the Foreign Secretary 'to lay special stress on one or two points' which he thought might assist the pro-League

[1] Minutes of a Directors' Meeting, 8 Jan. 1920, General 1920: 40/2696/854, LNA.

[2] [Drummond] to Harrison, 21 Nov. 1919, Huntington Gilchrist Papers, LC.

[3] Frank P. Walters, *A History of the League of Nations* (London: Oxford University Press, 1960), p. 86. See also, League of Nations, Council, *Minutes of the First Meeting of the Council of the League of Nations Held in Paris, January 16, 1920*, p. 2; League of Nations, *Official Journal*, I (1920), p. 18.

[4] See the secret meetings of the Council of the League of Nations in Council 1928–32: 14/9887/2385, LNA. Drummond would probably have partially agreed with Crowe in thinking 'the craze for publicity to be ill-considered. Publicity leads inevitably to oratorical speeches, and real business suffers ... any general rule regarding the publication of all resolutions and minutes of proceedings is dangerous. The proper course is to decide at the end of each [Council] meeting what should and what should not be published'. Minute by E[yre] A. C[rowe], 10 Feb. [1921], FO/371/7053.

[5] Walters, pp. 86–8.

struggle going on in the United States.[1] After the Paris session
ended it was decided to hold in London, as Drummond desired,
the Council's second session which was scheduled for about mid-
February.[2]

On 19 March 1920, the Senate again refused to consent to
ratification of the Versailles Treaty. Since this action assured no
American representation in the League, at least in the immediate
future, the question that Drummond now had to contend with
was where the permanent seat of the organization would be
established. In this politically important question the French
from the beginning had desired Paris or Versailles and, if this
was not possible, then Brussels, a proposal which was supported
by the Belgian Government. However, neither President Wilson
nor Cecil supported the idea of situating the League in one of the
Allied capitals. On the contrary, they desired that the League be
established in a country neutral during the war and thus opted
for Geneva. They believed that if the League was established in
an Allied capital then the organization would merely appear to
be an Allied coalition founded on the hatreds generated by the
World War.[3]

Within the Secretariat, Monnet, doubtlessly reflecting the
feelings of the Quai d'Orsay, pressed for Brussels. He argued that
Brussels was more accessible than Geneva. Like President Wilson
and Cecil, however, Drummond was partial to Geneva 'because
of its neutral position, and from what may be called the *spiritual*
side of the League'. Monnet's alternate scheme was that at an
early Council meeting, with an American representative present,
the choice of Geneva as the League's site should be confirmed
and arrangements made to erect suitable buildings. Until these
buildings were ready—probably two years—the League's
headquarters should be near Brussels. Drummond was more

[1] Drummond to Fosdick, 19 Jan. 1920, File 1919–20, Raymond B. Fosdick
Papers, PU. For Lord Curzon's speech see League of Nations, Council, *Minutes
of the First Meeting of the Council of the League of Nations Held in Paris, January 16,
1920*, pp. 4–5; League of Nations, *Official Journal*, I (1920), pp. 20–2.

[2] *PRFRUS, 1920*, i. 10.

[3] William E. Rappard, *Uniting Europe* (New Haven: Yale University Press,
1930), pp. 229–40; Egon F. Ranshofen-Wertheimer, *The International Secretariat:
A Great Experiment in International Administration* (Washington, D.C.: Carnegie
Endowment for International Peace, 1945), pp. 410–13; Paul Hymans,
Mémoires (Bruxelles: Solvay, 1958), i. 305, 402; Walters, pp. 36–7.

receptive to this alternate scheme since it offered all the advantages of both Geneva and Brussels. During the early years, he noted, when the League would of necessity be rather dependent on the western powers, close contact could be kept with these powers and the practice established of conferences held through the medium of the Secretariat. As the states of central and eastern Europe were again stable and strong, the League would move eastwards to Geneva to contend with new developments. For the next two years, however, Drummond thought it clear that European politics would be largely centred around Paris, London, and Berlin. He was not sure whether Cecil would approve of this arrangement, but he was sure that Monnet's scheme would be good for both the Secretariat's work and the League. In line with this Drummond attempted to ascertain through Fosdick what thoughts Colonel House might have on the question. Though he hated having to support Monnet's scheme, he could not see how he could do otherwise.[1]

This was in the autumn of 1919, but as resistance in the Senate to the Covenant increased, Drummond began to have doubts. On 26 November, a week after the Senate rebuffed the Versailles Treaty for the first time, he hoped that in the question of Brussels over Geneva no decision would be taken until the American attitude toward the Covenant was known. He rightly feared that the proposal to transfer the League's site from neutral Switzerland to Belgium might be used by the Senate's anti-League faction to vindicate their arguments that the organization was an association of the victorious powers.[2] By early December Drummond's resistance to the unofficial French campaign weakened. He argued that Monnet's scheme of a temporary headquarters near Brussels 'would stimulate the infant life of the League', while the use of Geneva 'might lead to [the League's] atrophy'. After several years at Brussels the 'League would either become an important and recognized factor in international political life, or it [would] fail on its political side'. If the League was a failure

---

[1] Drummond to Fosdick, 4 Oct. 1919, File 1919–20, Raymond B. Fosdick Papers, PU.

[2] Drummond to Curzon, 26 Nov. 1919, Box 65, Folder Marked Letters 1919, H–L, Curzon Papers, IOL. Also Drummond to Fosdick, 28 Nov. 1919, File 1919–20, Raymond B. Fosdick Papers, PU, and *DBFP, 1919–1939*, I, v. 853, 890.

where it established itself would make little difference.[1] Of course, if the United States joined the League and insisted that all important political questions be discussed in the Council, then Drummond would not hesitate to urge that the organization be established as soon as possible at Geneva. This was because it was essential for the other powers to secure America's co-operation and to work through the channel offered by the Council. He warned that if America failed to join the League the situation would be far different.[2] The League would have to rely on the western states and Geneva 'would probably be ignored' with the prime ministers meeting in London and Paris.[3]

The Senate's refusal in March 1920 to consent to the ratification of the Versailles Treaty renewed pressure to reconsider Brussels as the seat of the organization. Brussels to the French meant a League more anti-German in its orientation. To Drummond the capital of Belgium meant, now that the Americans had rejected the organization, a city more likely to attract the top political leadership of the western states whose support he rightly considered indispensable to launch the world organization successfully. Two months after the Senate's decision, on 19 May, the Council adopted a unanimous resolution requesting that President Wilson convoke the Assembly's first session in Brussels. For Wilson to have acceded to this request would have seriously undermined the possibility of establishing the League in Geneva since Article 3 paragraph two of the Covenant spoke of the Assembly meeting 'at the Seat of the League'. With no American representation on the Council and the first session of the Assembly convened at Brussels the Council might have established Brussels as the seat of the League since, under Article 7 paragraph two of the Covenant, the Council could at any time fix the seat of the organization.

The Swiss, fearful that the League might be established in Brussels, informed President Wilson of their apprehensions. This

---

[1] E[ric] D[rummond] to Ames, 8 Dec. 1919, General 1919: 40/2147/527, LNA.

[2] Drummond to Fosdick, 15 Dec. 1919, File 1919–20, Raymond B. Fosdick Papers, PU. See also, Minutes of a Directors' Meeting, 17 Dec. 1919, General 1919: 40/2495/854, LNA.

[3] Minutes of a Directors' Meeting, 17 Dec. 1919, General 1919: 40/2495/854, LNA.

increased Wilson's own fears that his wishes of establishing the
League in neutral Switzerland might be ignored by the Council.
Accordingly, the American Ambassador in London, John W.
Davis, was instructed to discuss the matter with Drummond.
Drummond was now caught between the opposing views of the
Council, largely influenced by France and Belgium on one side,
and President Wilson on the other. Keeping in mind the immense
influence that Paris had now acquired in the League because of
Washington's rejection of the organization the French pressure
on Drummond can be well imagined.[1]

In his interview with Drummond, Davis pointed out that
although President Wilson wished to avoid any controversy he
was strongly partial to Geneva as the Assembly's first meeting
place. Wilson felt that it was his right to convoke the first meeting
at any place he saw fit, but it would be awkward if he did so in
opposition to the desires of several of the Council's more
important members. Drummond frankly replied that he did not
believe that the present situation could be maintained. It was
well known in Paris that President Wilson intended to convene
the first meeting in Washington and that accordingly the point
about the necessity of holding this meeting in Geneva really
vanished. Moreover, it would be a bold step for Wilson under
present conditions to convene the Assembly at one city when the
Council had unanimously expressed a wish that it should be
convened in another. Drummond then spoke about Brussels'
accessibility and better communications facilities. He explained
that this point had not been raised for fear that it might arouse
Wilson's suspicions that the change of the League's seat from
Geneva to Brussels might be in contemplation. To appease
President Wilson Drummond agreed to insert a sentence in his
message to Wilson assuring him that the question of changing
the League's seat had never been raised at any Council meeting.[2]
Drummond's added sentence was factually correct, but obviously
formal and informal discussions on this point had been going on
outside the Council.[3]

---

[1] Ranshofen-Wertheimer, pp. 413–14. See also, Rappard, *Uniting Europe*,
pp. 241–2 and League of Nations, *Official Journal*, I (1920), p. 127.

[2] [Eric Drummond], Record of Conversation, 2 July 1920, Huntington
Gilchrist Papers, LC; Ranshofen-Wertheimer, p. 414.

[3] Phelan, pp. 77, 79.

Wilson's fears, however, were unrelieved and several days later Drummond was informed that under the powers given President Wilson in Article 5 of the Covenant and in compliance with the Council's May request, the President was convoking the Assembly's first session in the city of Geneva for 15 November. Drummond pointed out to Davis that the phrase, in compliance with the Council's request, was misleading since the Council had requested a meeting in Brussels. Washington informed Davis that the phrase was to be construed as a reference only to the Council's request that the President convoke a meeting of the Assembly upon the assumption that only the President in accordance with Article 5 of the Covenant could determine where the first session should be convened. The text therefore was amended to make this point clearer.[1] Wilson also acquired support from Thomas, who pointed out to the Governing Body of the International Labour Organisation that any move to Brussels would make even more difficult Germany's future participation in the Labour organization. The Governing Body agreed and decided to establish the Labour organization's seat in Geneva.[2] Although Drummond still proposed a return of the League to London after the Assembly session,[3] faced by Wilson's and Thomas's moves, the Council in early August 1920 resolved to install the organization at Geneva as quickly as possible since this would lead to a unification of its work and to financial saving.[4] The League was now fully established.

Though Drummond had feared any confrontation with the French over this issue he came to appreciate Geneva's value. When the Austrian representative, Emerich von Pflügl, proposed that the League be transferred to Vienna,[5] a proposal which the Austrian Government does not appear to have strongly supported,[6] Drummond was cool to the idea. Certain countries,

---

[1] *PRFRUS, 1920*, i. 10–12. See also, Rappard, *Uniting Europe*, pp. 242–3.

[2] Phelan, pp. 77–81; Ranshofen-Wertheimer, p. 414.

[3] Rappard, *Uniting Europe*, p. 243.

[4] Ranshofen-Wertheimer, p. 414. See also, League of Nations, Council, *Minutes of the Eighth Session of the Council of the League of Nations Held in San Sebastian, July 30–August 5, 1920*, pp. 53, 209; League of Nations, *Official Journal*, I (1920), p. 327.

[5] [Eric Drummond], Record of Interview, 19 Dec. 1927, FO/371/13385. See also, *DDI*, 7, v. 633–4.

[6] E[ric] D[rummond], Record of Interview, 26 Jan. 1928, FO/371/13385.

he pointed out to Cadogan, favoured such a move because they held that any transfer to Vienna would prevent for many years to come any possible *Anschluss* between Germany and Austria. He did not himself think that either the League's presence or absence from the Austrian capital would 'ultimately have any final or decisive result' on this question. In Drummond's mind such a transfer would be disadvantageous to the League. It would find itself situated in a capital city where there were all kinds of intrigue. The League would probably be placed in the centre of the present danger zone. But he thought that quite often finer preventive work could be done from outside the zone rather than in it, simply because from outside one could consider matters dispassionately. Also it would be undesirable to have the Secretariat in Vienna 'since obviously they would be much more influenced by their national Governments as they would be in constant communication with their Ministers in the capital'. There would likewise be lost the goodwill of Geneva's name which had been built up during the preceding years and was something of an asset in the League's publicity. Personally, Drummond admitted that he would prefer to reside in Vienna, but he was absolutely convinced that from the League's point of view Geneva or some other Swiss city was far and away the best site for the League.[1] Pflügl's proposal, however, went no further for Chamberlain informed Drummond that he was 'inflexibly opposed to any such idea'.[2]

Danzig and the Saar

Even before the Secretariat was fully organized Drummond attempted to tackle some of the enormous problems generated by the World War and especially those questions which directly or indirectly touched the League and emanated from the peace settlement. Of particular importance were the questions of Danzig and the Saar which affected Germany's relationship with the League as well as with France and Poland. Drummond's tack was to have the League assume its responsibilities in these two areas as quickly as possible and to make sure that in doing so

[1] Drummond (Geneva) to Cadogan, 19 Dec. 1927, ibid.
[2] Villiers to Drummond, 3 Jan. 1928, ibid.

nothing occurred which might contribute in any way to the already strained relations that existed between the victorious French and Poles on one side and the vanquished Germans on the other.

In mid-July 1919 Drummond raised the question with Balfour whether the intended promotion of General Richard Haking, the Allied commander in Danzig, to provisional administrator with the possibility of appointment as High Commissioner by the Council might not be a serious mistake. General Haking, he argued, might be and very probably was the best man for this temporary post at a period when the situation was difficult and military prestige and perhaps military knowledge were of prime value. However, the duties to be entrusted to the Danzig High Commissioner appointed by the Council surely required qualifications of a far different nature. The High Commissioner, Drummond noted, was to help in drawing up a constitution for the Free City. He was to advise on difficult administrative problems. In other words, the High Commissioner had to be a 'statesman'.

This was not a task for which a soldier was especially well fitted. He also doubted the expediency of appointing an Englishman as High Commissioner. In fact, the appointment of an Englishman as High Commissioner would make it difficult to resist the French claim to the chairmanship of the Saar Governing Commission. To accept this claim would, in his opinion, be bad for France, for the Allied powers, and for the League. The chairmanship of this commission was, he believed, being viewed by the neutral states as a test: was the League to be an alliance to hold Germany in her place, or was it a sincere attempt at universal equity. The choice of chairman of the Saar Governing Commission was of the greatest importance and Drummond very much hoped that the Council would, with France's agreement, select an American for the post.

Would it not be easier for the French, he queried, to yield on this point if a neutral were chosen as Danzig's High Commissioner. Drummond's suggestion was that the Swedish Social Democratic leader, Karl Hjalmar Branting, be appointed. He was a man of great political knowledge, whom Germans, Danzigers, and Poles alike could trust and respect and whose decisions would carry weight. If Branting refused, and no other pre-eminent neutral was available, then an Englishman—perhaps even a soldier—might be selected.[1]

What Drummond desired was not to be had. At the end of October 1919 Drummond supported as practical the arrangement to have the Allied administrator appointed by the Council as High Commissioner until the treaty between Danzig and Poland had been ratified and the Free City's constitution had come into force. Drummond thought that the advantages of this arrangement were so great that despite the fact that it was desirable in theory to differentiate between what was done by the League and what was done by the Allied powers, the wisest policy was to adopt it. Of course, it did not necessarily follow that the Allied administrator and provisional High Commissioner should be the permanent High Commissioner. However, the period during which he administered Danzig on behalf of the Allies would give a good indication of his qualifications to be the permanent High Commissioner.[2]

In early February 1920, Sir Reginald Tower, a senior member of the British diplomatic service, arrived in Danzig to be the administrator for the Allied and Associated Powers.[3] Some days later on 11 February, the Belgian Paul Hymans, presented his Rapporteur's report to the Council on Danzig recommending that Tower also be High Commissioner. To this the Council agreed unanimously.[4] Tower served as High Commissioner until late 1920 and was then succeeded by General Haking who served until 1923.

Though Drummond had not succeeded in getting a neutral appointed as High Commissioner thus influencing, as we shall soon see, the selection of the chairman of the Saar Governing Commission, he nevertheless worked closely with Tower in trying to keep the potentially explosive Danzig situation under control. He supported Tower's endeavours, for example, to have

---

[1] Drummond to Balfour, 17 July 1919, Arthur Balfour Papers, FO/800/217.

[2] E[ric] D[rummond], Note on Danzig, 31 Oct. [1919], Administrative Commissions: Danzig 1919: 4/1872/4, LNA.

[3] Christoph M. Kimmich, *The Free City: Danzig and German Foreign Policy, 1919–1934* (New Haven: Yale University Press, 1968), p. 23.

[4] League of Nations, Council, *Minutes of the Second Meeting of the Second Session of the Council of the League of Nations Held in London, February 11, 1920*, pp. 9, 16; League of Nations, *Official Journal*, I (1920), pp. 53–5.

the Poles exclude the name of Heinrich Sahm, Danzig's
Oberbürgermeister, from the list of war criminals to be handed over
for trial. Drummond emphasized to Lord Derby, the ambassador
in Paris, the difficult situation foreseen by Tower, and pointed
out how undesirable it would be from the League's point of view
if Tower, who needed to be in the closest collaboration with the
Danzigers, should be forced to take any personal action against
Sahm. If Sahm's name could not be removed, Drummond noted,
from the list of those whose trial was being demanded, was it
possible to have Sahm arrested not by Tower, but by General
Haking's troops in Danzig?[1] Derby's unsatisfactory reply was
that Drummond should refer the matter to the Foreign Office.[2]
Whether Drummond approached the Foreign Office is not
known. He did something better, however, and that was to
contact the powerfully placed Kerr. As it appeared likely, he
informed Kerr, that the question of the war criminals' list might
come up for discussion during Allied meetings in London, he
thought he ought to bring the problem to his attention. Though
Drummond's anxieties were warranted, his impact on this
question appears to have been nil, for Sahm's name was removed
from the list of war criminals by the Polish Foreign Minister
acting on his own, who understood the difficulties that Sahm's
arrest would pose for Tower and the popularity that he had with
the Danzigers.[3]

Drummond's interests in Danzig continued during the
remainder of 1920. In April he pointed out to John D. Gregory,
the Head of the Foreign Office's Northern Department, that
although the League was not involved in Danzig's administration,
it was nevertheless indirectly affected by what occurred there
since the Free City was to come under the League's protection.
Gregory's admission that the Allies had not commenced
consideration of the treaty which under the Versailles settlement
had to be negotiated between Poland and Danzig, caused
Drummond to suggest that the Allies might establish a small and

---

[1] [Drummond] to Derby, [14] Feb. 1920, File GD40/17/56, Lothian Papers,
SRO. See also, *DBFP, 1919–1939*, I, xi. 229.
[2] Derby to Drummond, 18 Feb. 1920, File GD40/17/56, Lothian Papers,
SRO.
[3] Drummond to Kerr, 23 Feb. 1920, ibid., and *DBFP, 1919–1939*, I, xi. 229
and fn., 238–9 and fn.

special commission to meet the Polish Government's representatives in Danzig in an attempt to conclude the required draft treaty. By doing this the commission could hear evidence from Tower and also investigate questions of fact in Danzig itself. Favourably impressed by Drummond's idea Gregory stated that he would tender proposals along these lines.[1] This exchange is interesting for it shows Drummond's cautious use of his office to implant ideas and propose methods of settling or tackling a particularly vexing problem through a third party without Drummond himself being identified as the originator of the idea or being involved in any way with the question at hand. In this case, however, his idea never came to fruition.[2]

By late September Danzig was again a topic of discussion, this time with Tower, the High Commissioner. Among the subjects discussed were Tower's resignation as soon as the draft treaty between Poland and Danzig stipulated in the Versailles settlement was signed. As to the next High Commissioner Lord Derby felt that he should also be the proposed chairman of Danzig's Port and Waterways Board which would be equally composed of Poles and Danzigers with a neutral chairman. Tower's information was that Derby already had someone in mind who could handle both positions. If this was so, Drummond informed Derby, he would be grateful if this person's name could be given to him privately since with Derby's interest in the matter a recommendation from him would be of some value.[3]

Though Derby pressed his view that the High Commissioner

---

[1] E[ric] D[rummond], An untitled memorandum, 28 Apr. 1920, Administrative Commissions: Danzig 1920: 4/4068/4068, LNA.

[2] Another example is Drummond's frustrated bid during the peace conference to have a clause added, in revising certain prior treaties as well as a contemplated African arms and liquor convention, so that a dispute between parties to these conventions relating to their application which could not be settled by negotiation be submitted to arbitration until the proposed Permanent Court of International Justice was established. Drummond pointed out that as Secretary-General he had 'no standing whatever in a matter of this kind, and that any suggestions' which he made and which were approved of had to appear as coming from others 'as it would be very bad for me to appear in such a connexion'. Drummond to Strachey, 18 Sept. 1919, Treaties 1919: 17/780/780, LNA.

[3] [Drummond] to Derby, 29 Sept. 1920, Administrative Commissions: Danzig 1920: 4/7166/4, LNA.

should also be the chairman of the proposed Port and Waterways Board, he noted that it was a plan that might not succeed. Though he did have someone in mind who might be fitted for the chairmanship of the board, this person was not interested in being High Commissioner.[1] Derby's plan to have Tower's successor assume the two posts never materialized. Drummond's actions in this question, however, are interesting for, in approving an interim provisional High Commissioner on 10 December 1920 following Tower's resignation, the Council selected Bernardo Attolico, the Italian Director of the Secretariat's Communications and Transit Section. It can be safely assumed that Attolico's appointment could not have been made without consulting Drummond. Indeed, it might have been Drummond who proposed Attolico for the post. It can be cogently argued that this was an attempt on Drummond's part to implement independently and indirectly what Derby had desired, since Attolico's functional post in the Secretariat made him well qualified to follow the activities and deliberations of the Port and Waterways Board. Keeping in mind Drummond's aversion to General Haking's appointment as High Commissioner, it might have been Drummond's hope that Attolico's provisional appointment might at some future point be changed to a permanent one and tied to the chairmanship of the Port and Waterways Board. This would have had the added advantage of an Italian High Commissioner, thus assuaging Rome which felt that Italy was underrepresented in League assignments. Any such plan was, of course, aborted on 17 December 1920, a week after Attolico had been selected, by the Council's appointment of General Haking as High Commissioner.[2]

Because it involved the League and emanated from the peace settlement the important Saar question also attracted Drummond's attention. In late July 1919 Drummond asked his old Foreign Office friend, Sir George Clerk, to send him the Saar Basin report presented to the Supreme Council some days before by the committee supervising the execution of the peace treaty with Germany. He pointed out to Clerk the great assistance that

[1] Derby to Drummond, 1 Oct. 1920, ibid.
[2] League of Nations, Council, *Minutes of the Eleventh Session of the Council of the League of Nations Held in Geneva, November 14–December 18, 1920*, p. 37; League of Nations, *Official Journal*, II (1921), pp. 13, 166.

would be rendered if, when the Council dealt with questions like the Saar and Danzig as soon as the Versailles Treaty came into force, all information about the Supreme Council's discussions, including the pertinent documentation, could automatically be forwarded to the Secretariat. If this was not possible the Secretariat would at any rate be pleased to receive as much information as could be given.[1]

This request to Clerk is an excellent example of Drummond's use of old friendships and political contacts to acquire information for himself and the Secretariat. Clerk did not disappoint him and Drummond soon received a copy of the report. Drummond did not know whether the report's recommendation, that any Supreme Council decision about the Saar should follow discussions with the League's Secretary-General, would be executed. Thus he conveyed to Clerk for Balfour's information his unofficial views on the Saar question, a question already examined by the Secretariat, especially in its legal aspects.

Drummond explained that the Secretariat's scheme envisaged that either at its first or second session the Council could proceed to the selection of three of the five members of the Saar delimitation commission, and he observed, 'we have names ready for the purpose'. He then queried whether the report's suggestion of a separate agreement with Germany over the Saar was not dangerous. Eager to protect the League, he pointed out that if a separate agreement failed the position of the Great Powers, as well as that of the organization, would be greatly weakened. If it succeeded it would replace what had been decided by the Versailles Treaty to be a League function. Clerk knew as well as he did the impression that this would create with the smaller states.

Drummond sincerely hoped that it would be decided to allow the Council to function as stipulated in the Versailles Treaty. He felt sure that the Council ought, if possible, to undertake the duties assigned to it under the treaty, and in no way lay itself open to the charge, now current, that it was 'purely an instrument of the Allied and Associated Powers'.[2]

---

[1] E[ric] D[rummond] to Clerk, 29 July 1919, Administrative Commissions 1919: 2/521/453, LNA.
[2] E[ric] D[rummond] to Clerk, 8 Aug. 1919, Drummond Folder, LNA.

As we have seen, at its first session in January 1920 the Council chose three of the five members of the Saar delimitation commission. It is unclear, however, whether the three military officers selected (an Englishman, a Japanese, and a Belgian, the latter replaced by a Brazilian) were the three that Drummond admitted the Secretariat had in mind.[1] The selection of the Saar's five-member Governing Commission was reserved for the Council's second session. Eight days before the Council convened, however, the French Ambassador in London, Aimé de Fleuriau, called on Drummond to discuss with him unofficially the important question of who would be the commission's chairman. Drummond, as we have seen, wished to avoid a French chairman by appointing an American to the post. Fleuriau explained that his Prime Minister, Alexandre Millerand, placed the greatest importance on selecting a French chairman. Drummond demurred. Fleuriau argued that the Saar's position was closely tied with that of Alsace-Lorraine which had been returned to France under the Versailles Treaty. For the commission to be successful, it would be necessary that the closest contact be established with the administration in Alsace-Lorraine. Fleuriau's strong stance and the knowledge that an Englishman rather than a neutral would be Danzig's High Commissioner left Drummond with few acceptable options. Faced by what was an obvious Anglo–French trade-off, a British High Commissioner in Danzig for a French chairman of the Saar Governing Commission, Drummond had to give in. His observation that he had not expressed to Fleuriau any opinion on the question which he felt did not rest with the Secretariat was certainly a disingenuous statement considering that he had already expressed his opinion on the matter to Balfour months before.[2]

It is obvious that the interview with Fleuriau regarding the commission's chairman, and Drummond's inability to get a neutral appointed as Danzig's High Commissioner had helped bend the Secretary-General to Paris' will. The events that followed became, to quote Alice in Wonderland, 'curiouser and curiouser'. At the Council on 13 February 1920 the Greek

[1] League of Nations, *Official Journal*, I (1920), pp. 24–5, 52.
[2] Eric Drummond, Saar Basin Governing Commission, 3 Feb. 1920, File 1919–20, Raymond B. Fosdick Papers, PU.

representative, Demetrios Caclamanos, presented his Rapporteur's report on the Saar Governing Commission. It recommended that the French member of the commission be appointed its chairman. Caclamanos justified this appointment on the grounds that the Saar's economic development and its general prosperity largely depended on the assistance that France might give to the region. Therefore the Saarlanders' welfare and the necessity to maintain order required close collaboration between France, which under the Versailles Treaty controlled an important part of the region's economic life, and the Saar Governing Commission which the Council entrusted with the area's administration. The Council agreed and appointed the French member, Victor Rault, the commission's chairman. On the previous day the Council had accepted Hymans's proposal that Tower be Danzig's High Commissioner.[1] The Council's selection of Rault was less than wise. A French chairman and the commission's composition weighted it in France's favour.[2]

What role did Drummond play in influencing Caclamanos's and Hymans's reports? One cannot ignore his initial comments about Danzig and the Saar and then his acquiescence to Paris' pressure that a Frenchman be chairman of the Saar Governing Commission. Years later Drummond admitted that the Council's Rapporteur 'usually was entirely dependent upon the Secretariat. He was generally the national of a small state [as were Caclamanos and Hymans] amenable to the Secretariat's suggestions. We were always proposing solutions to him. He could adopt them or reject them. When the proposals came forward they were his'.[3] There is reasonable suspicion, therefore, that Drummond despite what he wanted played no small role in having the Council accept the Anglo–French trade-off on Danzig and the Saar. In view, however, of his inability to get a neutral selected as Danzig's High Commissioner and France's increased

---

[1] League of Nations, Council, *Minutes of the Fourth Meeting of the Second Session of the Council of the League of Nations Held in London, February 12, 1920*, pp. 3–5; League of Nations, *Official Journal*, I (1920), pp. 45–50, 53–5.

[2] Laing Gray Cowan, *France and the Saar, 1680–1948* (New York: Columbia University Press, 1950), pp. 121–3; Frank M. Russell, *The Saar: Battleground and Pawn* (Stanford: Stanford University Press, 1951), pp. 29–32, 51.

[3] Quoted in Stephen M. Schwebel, *The Secretary-General of the United Nations* (Cambridge: Harvard University Press, 1952), p. 253 fn. 11.

influence in the League following America's rejection of the Covenant, Drummond had little room for manœuvre and correspondingly little choice in the matter.

Mandates and Humanitarian Endeavours

Since the Covenant's mandates system was one of the League's unique features Drummond's initial moves were to see that the system was implemented as quickly as possible. Thus the refusal of the French Colonial Minister to attend the meetings of the Allied Commission established by the Supreme Council to formulate the different types of mandates left Drummond uneasy. He pointed out to Balfour in early August 1919 that the minister argued that Paris considered it premature to discuss the mandates designated as 'A' mandates unless and until the Supreme Council decided to confer such mandates. He also maintained that no decision had been reached whether or not any former Turkish territory would come under the mandates system. This did not square, Drummond noted, with the Versailles Treaty which clearly stated that certain formerly Turkish areas should be administered as 'A' mandates. Drummond thought that Paris did not wish any discussion of the 'general principles' of the 'A' mandates until it knew the exact areas over which it would be the mandatory power. It would then attempt to whittle the mandate down to suit itself and it might even hope by extended delays to establish such a tight hold on the administration of the area in question that it would be most difficult to superimpose over these areas the mandatory system envisaged in Article 22 of the Covenant.

The League's and Britain's interests appeared to lie in the opposite direction, and Drummond believed that they should insist on the commission's immediate discussion of the terms of the 'A' mandates. This would establish the general principles which would be difficult for France or any other state to reverse. Such a step would be wise and also in the interests of the indigenous peoples, especially perhaps the Zionists in Palestine— a pointed remark considering Balfour's wartime declaration and his role as champion of the Zionist cause in British official circles.

A difficulty, however, had also arisen regarding the 'B' and 'C' mandates. From the League's point of view it was of the greatest importance that the mandates' scope should be defined by the Council. Drummond hoped that the Supreme Council would be able to place the actual terms which they recommended for the mandates before the Council. Of course, the selection of specific mandates clearly rested with the Allied powers since all the former German colonies would by the peace settlement's terms pass into their possession. Drummond trusted that it might be found possible to publish the 'B' and 'C' mandates at present formulated.[1]

What actions Balfour took are unknown. It would appear, however, that Drummond's appeal had only a limited success. Although the commission did agree on the terms for the 'A', 'B', and 'C' mandates, France and Japan raised certain objections, and the applicability of the draft terms for the 'A' mandate could not be determined until peace was concluded with Turkey. In the end, the draft terms for the 'A' mandates were abandoned because of divergent Allied views.[2]

The more serious question that Drummond had to contend with was Washington's attitude toward the mandates system which was complicated by the fact that it had rejected the Covenant. Initially, Washington insisted that the open-door doctrine had to be adhered to in all the mandated areas which it then expanded to include American approval of the mandates' terms as well as the conferring of mandates on Germany's former colonies.[3] No doubt to avoid a confrontation with Washington, Drummond supported a French proposal that the Council was not in a position to define the mandates' terms until the question of their actual disposition had been settled with the United States. Simultaneously, Drummond impressed upon Balfour that the mandates question exceeded in popular interest any other American foreign policy matter. Informed sources maintained that the Harding administration intended to treat this question as a test of Europe's friendliness and if it noted America's protests Washington would agree to closer co-operation with Europe, something that was obviously to London's advantage. If no notice

---

[1] E[ric] D[rummond] to Balfour, 7 Aug. 1919, File GD40/17/75, Lothian Papers, SRO.
[2] Quincy Wright, *Mandates Under the League of Nations* (Chicago: University of Chicago Press, 1930), p. 47.
[3] Ibid., pp. 48–53.

was taken of Washington's claim, however, the United States was likely to lapse again into isolation, this time with full popular support.

In the mandates question not only must the actual territories themselves be taken into account, but also the fact that any action might seriously affect Anglo–American relations. Drummond thought risky and counter-productive the suggestion that through pressure London might line up the other Council members against the American position. He believed that America's main point regarding the Mesopotamian (Iraq) mandate was the oilfields. He suggested that the oilfields question be negotiated directly between the two countries. The popular notion in America that Mesopotamia was a country of limitless and untapped resources and a very valuable addition to the British Empire would not be altered by speech-making. What might change it would be a definite offer by London that it would share the mandate with Washington. Washington could hardly impute selfish motives to such an offer, though he did not anticipate that there was any probability whatever of its acceptance. Drummond was certain that to ignore the United States would lead to 'continuous American interference and objections'.[1] Balfour was swayed by Drummond's arguments and conveyed his letter to Curzon as well as to Winston Churchill, the Colonial Secretary.[2]

Some weeks later Drummond returned to the question, this time pressuring H. A. L. Fisher, Balfour's replacement on the Council, with the great importance for London to begin immediate negotiations with Washington. Drummond explained that he had discussed the mandates question with Butler Wright of the American Embassy, who had recommended that if Lord Curzon broached the question orally with the ambassador, George Harvey, explaining its urgency, that Harvey would do everything possible to have the points at issue settled in Washington. Wright thought that this would be far superior to any exchange of notes and did not believe that the State Department wanted through delay to cause Great Britain difficulties in either Mesopotamia or Palestine.[3] The result of all

[1] [Drummond] (Geneva) to Balfour, 2 June 1921, FO/371/7050.
[2] Balfour to [Curzon], 3 June 1921, ibid.
[3] Drummond (Geneva) to Fisher, 23 June 1921, ibid.

this appears to have been a postponement of any discussion of the mandates question by the Council since the United States did not accept its invitation to attend a June meeting. This was then followed by a Council decision that the mandatory powers might communicate to the United States texts of the proposed mandates.[1] By February 1922 the negotiations had progressed to the point where the Council was in a position to deal with the question of the 'B' mandates. From information that Drummond had received, it appeared that the French were engaged in activities in Togoland and the Cameroons which were contrary to the terms of these 'B' mandates, but until the League formally approved these mandates, he was powerless to do anything. Accordingly, he contacted his old Foreign Office friend, Charles Tufton, to see if at the Council's April meeting the 'B' mandates could be dealt with.[2] Delays in the negotiations with the Americans ensued and it was only in August that all the 'B' mandates were confirmed by the Council.[3]

Drummond also tackled, with some success, the question of the Permanent Mandates Commission. There was no doubt that in the public's mind, he observed, the Permanent Mandates Commission was tied to a group of experts, though there was nothing in the Covenant warranting such an assumption. He agreed that the mandates commission should be restricted to thirty-six members representing the Council's nine states, each of whom should appoint four members, two of these official and two unofficial. The commission was to meet annually to consider the mandatory powers' reports and to advise the Council regarding these reports.

Drummond, however, did not think it was practicable that the mandates commission's permanent core should consist of members drawn from the Secretariat's Mandates, Political, and Minority Sections. Although the Secretariat was international it did not seem fair to Drummond that any one of its members should be placed in a position where he would be in direct opposition to his government's official representatives. This might develop if members of the Secretariat attended and voted as members of the mandates commission. His suggestion was that

[1] Wright, pp. 54–5 and p. 55 fn.
[2] Tufton to Villiers, 20 Feb. 1922, FO/371/8323.
[3] Wright, p. 56.

the Director of the Mandates Section be the secretary to the mandates commission and that all the commission's preparatory work and agenda tasks be handled by this section.

To deal with urgent matters when the commission was not sitting Drummond proposed the division of the commission into two sub-committees. One of these sub-committees would deal with 'A' mandates and the other with 'B' and 'C' mandates. Should something develop the Director of the Mandates Section would bring it to the attention of the Council, recommending which of the two sub-committees should convene. The Council would then decide the issue, and if need be, give the Director the necessary guidance.

Finally, Drummond thought that on matters of importance it was inadvisable for the Secretariat's Mandates Section to make reports to the Council. Such a procedure might produce an 'invidious and difficult' situation, since it had to be kept in mind that the Council members would be 'representing the same national interests as the members of the Mandates Commission'. Drummond saw no reason why confidential information could not be conveyed by the Mandates Section to the mandates commission for discussions at the commission's meetings. Of course, it was not necessary that this confidential information should be included in the commission's published reports.[1]

What Drummond desired and what was possible were not necessarily the same. When the British representative at the Council in late 1920 proposed that the mandates commission, to save expenses, be composed of only five members Drummond demurred. He argued that since the mandatory powers would have to be represented at commission meetings there would be no financial savings. Moreover, a small commission would enlarge the individual responsibilities of the members of the commission and increase their difficulties in criticizing a great power. The compromise finally proposed by Drummond and accepted by the Council was for a nine-member commission of which five would be nationals from non-mandatory states. The resolution adopted by the Council on 1 December 1920 also stipulated that the members of the commission were to be

[1] E[ric] D[rummond], Note on Mr. Beer's Memorandum on the Mandatory Commission and the Mandatory Section of the International Secretariat, 21 Nov. [1919], Box 152, Alfred Milner Papers, NCO.

appointed by the Council and selected for their expert qualifications. Members during their service on the commission were to hold no government office. The annual report of the mandatory power, as Drummond desired, was to be examined by the commission which would then report to the Council. Some of Drummond's other suggestions were adopted in practice about the relationship between the commission, the Secretariat, and especially its Mandates Section.[1]

Aside from these incursions into the mandates question Drummond also attempted to influence the establishment of a mandate in eastern Galicia and the internationalization of Constantinople (Istanbul) under the League's protection. The establishment of the former was an attempt on his part to remove one of the biggest obstacles to any Polish–Ukranian co-operation and to help calm passions in an area seething with political unrest; and his activities over the latter were likewise an attempt to remove from contention a city whose possession contributed to inter-Allied tensions.

A visit to London in October 1919 by the Polish Prime Minister and world-renowned pianist, Ignace Paderewski, to impress upon Lloyd George his views regarding eastern Galicia caused Drummond to raise the possibility of a mandate over the area. With its capital at Lwow (Lemberg) the area, he noted to Kerr, was being bitterly disputed by Poland and the Ukraine. The Allies had hesitated to assign eastern Galicia to Poland since its population was predominantly Ukrainian, although the capital city of Lwow was Polish. The Secretariat's proposed solution to this problem was that there should be a Polish mandate for eastern Galicia. Naturally, the mandate's terms would have to be carefully spelled out, but they would ensure that as long as Poland treated the local population in a decent manner, Warsaw would remain in control of the area. The mandate's duration would entirely depend on Polish good government. Such a solution would be in the interests of all concerned, although he did not know if Paderewski would consent to it. He was inclined to think Paderewski would reject it—at least initially—pleading that it would be unsatisfactory to his Polish opponents. At the same time, Drummond thought the

[1] Wright, pp. 86, 91, 136–7, 139–41, 164, 184, 622–3.

proposal a 'just and reasonable' one which warranted 'very careful consideration'. Of course, he took his customary cautious tack. Kerr would realize, Drummond emphasized, that this was an unofficial probe, 'as of course we have no *locus standi* in the matter at all'.[1]

Kerr agreed, but thought that the mandate should be for ten years, at the end of which time the question should be reconsidered by the League. It was also important to make clear that eastern Galicia was not incorporated into Poland under the League's authority. To do so would place the League in a difficult situation in the future and lead to a violent agitation which would be the only alternative open to the indigenous population. Moreover, no provision should be afforded for premature agitation prior to the expiration of the ten-year term. If the Ukrainians knew that the question was unsettled they would acquiesce to Polish rule, provided it was indeed reasonably decent; the Poles would be motivated to govern well in order to secure the people's consent and the League's for the permanent incorporation of eastern Galicia into Poland. The ten-year term would allow the League, after suitable investigation and tests, to incorporate the area into Poland, to give it independence, to continue the mandate arrangement, or to transfer the area to the Ukraine.[2]

Drummond thought it would be a mistake to restrict any mandate for eastern Galicia to ten years. The very nature of a mandate implied that the administration by the mandatory state was not a permanent arrangement. A fixed period would lead to unrest in the area. The indigenous population would agitate to be set free. The Polish reaction might be to deport or terrorize their leadership.

Drummond also thought that a mandate without a set term would allow the Council or Assembly under the 'general spirit of the Covenant', to determine the mandate's duration when at any particular moment it became clear that the indigenous population was fully capable of governing itself. Poland would of course be entitled under Article 4 paragraph five of the Covenant to sit at any Council meeting when such a decision was made. To avoid

---

[1] Drummond to Kerr, 11 Oct. 1919, File GD40/17/55, Lothian Papers, SRO.
[2] Kerr to Drummond, 13 Oct. 1919, ibid.

a Polish veto it was thus desirable to insert into the terms of the mandate a clause that the mandate would be terminated by a unanimous Council decision and that Poland would consent to accept such a decision. Without such a clause, one would have to rely only on the moral pressure which might be eventually exercised by other powers.[1]

Drummond pressed the matter with Kerr when informed that the British experts at the peace conference dealing with the question were upset by the Foreign Office's uncompromising instructions that a set time period should be stated in the terms of the eastern Galician mandate. At the end of the fixed period the wishes of the indigenous population would be ascertained. The experts were to argue this point regardless of whether the mandate proposed for eastern Galicia was rejected or accepted. They had pointed out, and Drummond thought with some force, that this approach would certainly be defeated since it was opposed by both the French and the Americans. The net result would be to create Polish enmity toward Great Britain. Therefore, Drummond again urged his proposal as the best solution. It covered the situation and made possible an independent eastern Galicia at an earlier period than if there was a fixed time limit. He queried Kerr if there was any chance of getting the matter reconsidered.[2]

Lloyd George, however, resolved that he would not move from the position he had taken. He felt that Drummond's proposal was 'still tantamount to annexation' because it implied that the peace conference approved Polish rule over eastern Galicia until Council unanimity could be got in favour of effecting a change in the area. Yet this unanimity probably would never be obtained unless the Galician situation was so critical that it involved the risk of war. Lloyd George's view was that the eastern Galician arrangement was itself a compromise. He had always been against it. He did not believe that one could resolve the problem until the Russian situation was far clearer than it was at present. Lloyd George was prepared to agree to a Polish mandate for ten years in order to resolve the question. Kerr shared this view and pointed out to Drummond that people

---

[1] Drummond to Kerr, 16 Oct. 1919, ibid.
[2] Drummond to Kerr, 31 Oct. 1919, ibid.

did not realize that Russia was only temporarily crippled. It was really madness to attempt a final solution of the question which profoundly affected Russia until that country and her peoples were in a position to express some opinion.[1]

Drummond had successfully sowed the idea for a Polish mandate over eastern Galicia. However, on the question of whether the mandate should be unspecified or a fixed time period Drummond was rebuffed. The Supreme Council's decision in late November 1919 was to award Poland a twenty-five year mandate and, when the mandate expired, the League was to reconsider the question again. The Poles objected to the arrangement, the Allies were not prepared to press the matter, and finally in late December the scheme for a mandate was quietly buried on the initiative of the French.[2]

About this time Drummond also attempted to internationalize Constantinople. The possibilities of a mandate for the Turkish capital were virtually nil once the Americans had rejected such a proposal.[3] By mid-December 1919 Drummond heard that the French had made proposals regarding Constantinople and that London's decision was to remove the Sultan from the city which would then be occupied and administered by France, Great Britain, and Italy. To effect this expulsion of the Turks from Europe with the least disturbance to Muslim feelings in India and elsewhere Drummond proposed to Kerr that Constantinople and adequate territory around it should be made a Free City and placed under the League's protection. It could then be governed like the Saar by a five-member commission. Two of these, Drummond suggested, should be Muslims. If it was necessary, it could be stipulated that the other members of the commission should be from France, Great Britain, and Italy.

Since India and Persia (Iran) were League members, it could with some justice be said that they shared equally with other members in the protection and administration of Constantinople. They could speak up on behalf of Muslim opinion. There was an additional point: in looking into the future when Russia had recovered, Drummond queried, 'would it not be better for her to

[1] Kerr to Drummond, 3 Nov. 1919, ibid.
[2] Harold Temperley (ed.), *A History of the Peace Conference of Paris* (London: Frowde and Hodder and Stoughton, 1924), vi. 274.
[3] Ibid., 26–8.

find Constantinople under the protection of most of the nations of the world than under that of three Powers?'[1]

A memorandum by Erik Colban, the Norwegian Director of the Secretariat's Administrative Commissions Section, suggesting that the Council should have a free hand in choosing the commission for Constantinople, caused Drummond to scribble an explanation. He agreed in theory with Colban, and divulged that the only reason why he had suggested French, British, and Italian members for the commission was that he 'was afraid that from what was happening without some such proposal there would be little chance of the whole plan being accepted'. In view of this he 'thought it more prudent to suffer a small evil than risk rejection'.[2]

To drum up support for his proposal Drummond also contacted Lord Curzon[3] as well as Balfour whom he hoped might think that his Constantinople plan was not without merit.[4] Some days later Drummond had second thoughts about the matter and again wrote to Lord Curzon explaining that it had occurred to him that the proposal which he had put forward for a Free City or State for Constantinople might lead to considerable difficulties because of the city's polyglot population. Accordingly, he wanted to withdraw that particular part of his proposal and substitute the phrase that Constantinople should be made an international territory under the League's protection. This might, Drummond thought, be considered a development of the lower Danubian river plan under which the lower Danube was governed by a commission which flew its own flag.[5]

Fearful that his proposal might be rejected Drummond went out of his way to suppress any information that might raise doubts about its feasibility. When he sent Kerr and also Lord Curzon a memorandum by Dr. Joost Adrian van Hamel, the Dutch Director of the Secretariat's Legal Section, dealing with

[1] Drummond to Kerr, 13 Dec. 1919, File GD40/17/56, Lothian Papers, SRO.

[2] A note by E[ric] D[rummond] about Colban's memorandum, 16 Dec. 1919, Political 1919: 11/2432/2432, LNA.

[3] Drummond to Curzon, 13 Dec. 1919, ibid.

[4] E[ric] D[rummond] to Balfour, 13 Dec. 1919, ibid.

[5] Drummond to Curzon, 16 Dec. 1919, File GD40/17/56, Lothian Papers, SRO.

the legal aspects of the Constantinople question,[1] Drummond had the Secretariat delete from the document Van Hamel's discussions of the New Hebrides in the south-west Pacific. These islands, Drummond noted, were an Anglo–French condominium and the 'system followed there has not been in any way a success'. He did 'not think it would be wise to suggest any possible analogy between the system followed there and that to be followed in Constantinople'.[2] He pressed Kerr about his Constantinople proposal in late December[3] and registered the last word on the matter to Kerr in a missive on 30 December 1919. The rumour had reached him, he explained, that it was proposed to have an international commission for Constantinople, appointed by the powers and responsible to them, but under the League's protection. Unless the League had some sort of authority over the commission—for example, having the commission report to the League annually—Drummond did not think that this was a viable proposal. If because of conflicting national interests in the commission the proposed system failed, the responsibility and blame would be placed on the League, under whose minimal protection the commission functioned. The League would be placed in an invidious position which no one would assume in private life. Had Article 24 of the Covenant been overlooked, Drummond asked? This article established that all commissions regulating matters of international concern should be placed under the League's direction. Of course, he concluded, it might be that he was 'writing on an entirely wrong hypothesis' in which case he asked forgiveness.[4]

His hypothesis was incorrect and his endeavours came to naught. The victors do not appear to have suggested the removal of the Sultan from Constantinople. To have done so would not have served their interests for the Sultan and his government were pliable tools for the execution of Allied policy in Turkey. At the same time the idea of removing the Turks from Europe was not pressed. Several months later in mid-February 1920 the

[1] Drummond to Kerr, 18 Dec. 1919, ibid.

[2] A note by Drummond about Dr. van Hamel's memorandum, Political 1919: 11/2432/2432, LNA.

[3] Drummond to Kerr, 27 Dec. 1919, File GD40/17/56, Lothian Papers, SRO.

[4] Drummond to Kerr, 30 Dec. 1919, ibid.

British High Commissioner in Constantinople announced that he had been instructed to state that the Allies had decided to allow Turkey to retain the city—a small remuneration, no doubt, for the Sultan's collaboration. The only move that the Allies undertook was in March when they dispatched a strong military force into Constantinople to expel the nationalist followers of Mustafa Kemal Atatürk.[1]

Drummond also tackled during his first year humanitarian questions whose solution would contribute to returning the world to a normal state and lessen the anguish of the war's aftermath. In early June 1920 he pleaded with Hankey on behalf of the Norwegian explorer Fridtjof Nansen, who had been appointed by the Council to investigate the problems connected with the repatriation of prisoners of war, for additional naval transports to be supplied by the Admiralty to move repatriated prisoners from Baltic ports to Swinemünde in German Pomerania.[2] Simultaneously, Drummond asked Balfour to use his 'great influence' with the British Government on Nansen's behalf. 'It would be rather sad', he observed, 'if the League failed in a question for which it has assumed a certain responsibility'. Would Balfour find it possible to place Nansen's request for naval transport before the First Lord of the Admiralty and have him nominate someone to discuss the details of the problem with the Secretariat—a successful plea which led to the release of three German ships.[3] Drummond returned to the subject in July. He emphasized that the ships released by the Reparations Commission to Germany for the purposes of prisoner repatriation should be allowed to continue until late October. He apologized to Balfour for this request in addition to his previous request that Great Britain appropriate additional funds to the International Committee for Relief Credits. Any change in present shipping arrangements, he observed, would lead to dislocation in prisoner

---

[1] Temperley, vi. 27–8.

[2] [Drummond] to [Hankey], 1 June 1920, General 1920: 40/4582/2792, LNA.

[3] E[ric] D[rummond] to Balfour, 2 June 1920, Internal Administration Buildings and Furniture, 1933–40: 18B/40565/37845, LNA; and League of Nations, Council, *Minutes of the Sixth Session of the Council of the League of Nations Held in London, June 14–16, 1920*, p. 11.

repatriation and contribute to a very serious overcrowding in the prisoner-of-war camps at the ports of embarkation, with a possible stoppage of train service from Soviet Central Asia to the embarkation ports. The alternative was to use ships with British crews, but this he dismissed as undesirable for several reasons. He thanked Balfour for his previous assistance with the Chancellor of the Exchequer on the matter of relief credits and hoped that he would give his new request similar consideration.[1]

From the available evidence it is unclear whether the German ships released by the Reparations Commission continued in service until late October 1920 as Drummond desired. What is clear is that the British contribution to the International Committee for Relief Credits was by far the largest contribution made by any state; a contribution no doubt due to Drummond's promptings.[2]

Drummond's other humanitarian endeavour during this period involved the Armenians. This was triggered in March 1920 when Lord Bryce asked whether Drummond thought it possible for the League to take over and administer Armenia. Understandably, in so delicate and emotive an issue Drummond assumed a careful tack. He doubted whether such a plan would be successful, if no great power would assume the responsibility for Armenia. However, he thought it might be possible to get some lesser power to do so, provided the costs of the mandate were borne by the League. Bryce's suggestion that the United States pay any mandate deficit that might occur Drummond dismissed as an optimistic proposal.[3]

That Bryce's probe was merely part of a larger offensive became apparent when Lord Curzon inquired on behalf of the Supreme Council whether the League would be prepared to accept the protection of an independent Armenian state. From Curzon's communication as well as that of the peace conference's Armenian delegation it was obvious that the League was being pressed to accept an Armenian mandate in accordance with

[1] E[ric] D[rummond] to Balfour, 7 July 1920, Prisoners of War 1919: 42/5341/5213, LNA.

[2] League of Nations, *Official Journal*, II (1921), pp. 124–30.

[3] Drummond to [Kerr], 11 Mar. 1920, File GD40/17/56, Lothian Papers, SRO.

Article 22 of the Covenant.[1] Clearly, the Supreme Council wanted to unload the Armenian question on the League; and to the Armenians themselves, the League appeared as their last hope.

Perhaps fearful of the French reaction, Drummond wondered whether Monnet and Bourgeois realized the strong emotion that the Armenian question generated in England not only in official or educated circles. Indeed, this emotive feeling, he pointed out to Monnet, went back to the Bulgarian atrocities of 1876, and was very pronounced in non-conformist and labour circles, who were, Drummond observed, strong League supporters. If the League, therefore, refused to assume any responsibility regarding the future of Armenia or minority protection in Turkey, he feared that British public opinion would very much lose its belief in the League's efficacy.

Though Drummond thought that the League ought to issue a statement that it was prepared to undertake this responsibility, it should do so only under conditions that would ensure the likelihood of its success. The Supreme Council might refuse to give the assurances which the Council should, in his view, require. If this occurred, the entire blame would fall on the Supreme Council and not on the League.

Drummond also tried to assure Monnet about Curzon being the British representative at the Council should the Turkish and Armenian questions come up for discussion. He pointed out that there was a danger in believing that the Council consisted 'in an *assembly of certain men*', while, as a matter of fact, according to the Covenant's terms, it consisted of the '*representatives of certain states*'. True, when these representatives sat in the Council, they were supposed to view things more broadly than their own narrow national interests. Yet it had to be kept in mind that these Council representatives were primarily agents of their own governments. Drummond, however, felt no difficulty about Curzon's being the British representative at any Council meeting—obviously not Monnet's attitude who reflected French opinion which distrusted Curzon. Indeed, Drummond thought that Curzon was not likely to be unreasonable toward any conditions which the Council might wish to formulate. No doubt with France in mind,

[1] League of Nations, *Official Journal*, I (1920), pp. 81, 85.

Drummond noted that Council decisions required unanimity and an objector would, he hoped, be required to explain his negative vote. The Armenian decision, he warned, could not be postponed for very long.

When Comert, who aside from Monnet was one of Drummond's main contacts with the French Government, pointed out to him the objections that Frenchmen had to Curzon as the British representative if and when the Armenian question was discussed Drummond succumbed. He would make every effort, he informed Monnet, to have Fisher appointed as the British representative to the Council. He warned that this would not be easy to arrange.

As to the substantive problems of any League involvement in the Armenian question, Drummond noted that he and Colonel Pierre Chardigny of the French army, who was to command the Council's international force to oversee the Vilna plebiscite, had both come to the conclusion that the Armenian question was, in essence, a purely financial one. Chardigny thought that large sums of money would be required for reconstruction and for the long-term stationing of troops in Armenia. If this was true, Drummond saw no possibility of raising millions each year for Armenian purposes from League members. He also did not think it was right to request it, and he greatly doubted whether the Allies would be willing to guarantee a loan on the scale required. The Armenians told him that they wanted from the League about £200,000 ($1m.) annually to balance their budget, but Colonel Chardigny talked of six to ten million pounds sterling ($30m. to $50m.).

Drummond proposed, therefore, to have Mantoux contact the Supreme Council's experts so that a balance sheet of projected expenditures and revenues could be prepared in consultation with the Armenian delegation to the peace conference. Unless the funds could be found, Drummond thought 'it would be quite useless for the League to undertake the protection of the country', since it would be assuming responsibility for an Armenian state which was bankrupt from the very beginning—and this to his mind was 'an impossible proposition'.[1]

---

[1] Three letters from E[ric] D[rummond] to Monnet, 22 Mar. 1920, Minority Questions 1920: 41/3542/807, LNA.

His stance on this question was confirmed to him following a discussion with J. H. Thomas, an important Labour M.P. whose views on the subject were valuable for the insights they gave into both labour and non-conformists attitudes. Thomas had made it very clear, Drummond informed Monnet, that it would be a serious mistake for the Council to refuse in an offhand manner to assume any responsibility for Armenia's future. Such an action would quickly destroy to a large extent labour and non-conformist beliefs in the League. On the other hand, Thomas had been equally clear that it would be a cardinal mistake for the League to assume responsibility for an Armenian mandate unless it was well provided with the means to carry out any such assignment. Thomas's point was that the League's future was too important to allow the taking of any risks. He concluded that the Council should express its great sympathy with the notion of the League's offering protection to Armenia. It should state that it would be very willing to do what it could to help provide certain needed guarantees to be given by the Supreme Council and that these guarantees would be of such a nature that they would ensure that the League could assume the protection itself or that they would attract a smaller power to assume the task. If the Supreme Council, however, stated that it was unable to render such guarantees the League would express its regrets, but the onus would be on the Supreme Council and not the League.

Thomas's ideas so coincided with his own, Drummond observed, that Monnet might be inclined to think that he had inspired them. He assured his French deputy that this was not so. He had said virtually nothing during the discussion and these were Thomas's own opinions. Thomas had, however, emphasized that the Armenian question had captured the attention of British public opinion.[1]

If Drummond's comments to Monnet were an attempt to round up Paris' support for an Armenian mandate by the League they were unsuccessful. Remotely situated, militarily and materially weak, racked by internal dissensions, at odds with the other Transcaucasian Republics of Georgia and Azerbaijan, surrounded and squeezed in by Turkey and Soviet Russia, both of whom were clearly hostile states, the possibilities and burdens,

[1] E[ric] D[rummond] to Monnet, 23 Mar. 1920, ibid.

both financial and political, of a League mandate for Armenia were far from attractive. It was these reasons that foreclosed the type of assurances from the Supreme Council that Drummond wanted. Correspondingly, the League, not to mention Drummond, wanted to side-step the issue of an Armenian mandate, but to do so blatantly or in an offhanded manner would only have caused a loss of faith in the organization by those who looked to it as the hope of the future.

Undoubtedly, because of Drummond's endeavours, Fisher was the British representative at the Council meeting of 11 April which discussed the issue. The Council's reply to the Supreme Council on Armenia's future was delivered by Fisher, though the reply itself had been drafted by Balfour.[1] The reply cleverly argued that mandates under Article 22 of the Covenant were to be accepted by states and not by the League *per se*. The League's task was merely to supervise the execution of the mandate and not to assume mandates itself. The Council also realized the organization's own limitations: it was not a state, it had no army, it had no independent finances, its impact on public opinion in Asia Minor would be far less than in Europe. Its conclusion was that Armenia's future could be best assured if a League member or some other power—an allusion to the United States—could be found willing to accept an Armenian mandate. This would require that the interested state be assured by the Supreme Council on questions of finances, military assistance, and so on.[2] Taking the Council's hint the Supreme Council quickly offered the mandate to the United States and President Wilson submitted the offer to Congress for approval which rejected it by large majorities in both Houses.[3] No one wanted to assume the responsibility for the mandate. The Armenians were left to their fate.

The War's Aftermath

Drummond's guarded activities and initiatives during his first year continued in questions blatantly political and involving either the threat to use force or its actual use between states, some

---

[1] Walters, p. 109.
[2] League of Nations, *Official Journal*, I (1920), pp. 81–2, 85–7.
[3] Walters, p. 109.

of whom were League members. To remove or lessen the possibility of armed clashes, Drummond attempted to calm political passions and resolve the question through the peaceful settlement procedures offered by the League. His actions therefore entailed varying initiatives and actions. One question where the use of force was an omnipresent threat was Sweden's claim to the Aland Islands lying off Finland's coast. Overwhelmingly the islanders who considered themselves to be Swedish in race, language, and culture, had expressed a desire for union with Sweden.

Drummond's initial reaction had been that when the issue came before the Council the Secretariat would have to have ready a plan providing for the islands' temporary occupation. Because of the conflicting claims, he thought that an arrangement for governing the area along the lines envisaged for Danzig might prove to be the best way of handling things in the island group. This arrangement as a possible solution to the problem was rejected by the islanders. When Lord Curzon finally brought the question to the League's attention Drummond advised the Finns that it would be an error on their part to refuse to discuss the matter before the League on the grounds that it was a domestic question. This claim, under Article 15 paragraph eight of the Covenant, might be raised, Drummond argued, but it should be presented in a manner so that if it was rejected by the Council, Finland would be prepared to have the question discussed and dealt with by the Council.

To resolve the whole question Drummond proposed in late June 1920 to both Curzon and the Directors of the Secretariat sections that the Council should submit the issue to binding arbitration—a proposal that he had made to the Finns earlier that month. If this procedure was unacceptable to both sides the alternative could be a Council commission of inquiry with recommendations by the commission on how the question should be settled. According to Drummond, the commission would attempt to solve the question by mediation, and secure a settlement between Sweden and Finland. Objections to his proposal by his Secretariat colleagues caused Drummond to modify it to one in which the Council would merely appoint a commission which would proceed to the islands, its three members being drawn from countries which had no interest in the question. The proposal was well received in the Foreign Office and was reflected in the position paper that was drawn up on the question and circulated within the government. It was a carbon copy of Drummond's proposal though his contribution was neither acknowledged nor was his name mentioned. However, before Drummond's proposed three-man Council commission could even be selected the Finns raised the objection of domestic jurisdiction. In line with Drummond's advice, however, they raised the issue in a moderate manner and when their objection was rejected continued to recognize the Council's authority and defended their country's interests before that body.

In the discussions leading to the establishment of the Council's commission Drummond again showed the same guarded initiatives. He pressed the opinion that the commission should contain British and French representatives. His own preference was his former wartime chief, Herbert Asquith, and France's former Colonial Minister, Étienne Clémentel. Neither London nor Paris desired to be involved in this vexing matter and in the end the commission that was formed contained no British or French representation. Drummond's role in containing this question and in producing a settlement that would be acceptable to all sides continued down to the very end. When the commission recommended the retention of the islands by Finland it was around Drummond's own dinner table that Monnet, Fisher, and Gabriel Hanotaux, France's Council representative, discussed the procedures that would be followed in the Council in devising a settlement for the Aland question—and reached agreement.[1]

Given a choice of war or a settlement devised by the Council, Sweden and Finland chose the latter. Drummond, however, by his proposals and actions behind the scenes and without jeopardizing his position with any of the parties to the conflict, had played an active and important role in helping to solve peacefully what was a potentially dangerous dispute.

Conflicts raging in eastern Europe, however, were not as amenable to peaceful settlement as the Aland Islands question. This was especially true in Soviet Russia where the war's

[1] James Barros, *The Aland Islands Question: Its Settlement by the League of Nations* (New Haven: Yale University Press, 1968), pp. 179, 211, 239, 261–6, 302–3, 326.

aftermath had brought with it undeclared wars against neighbouring states, revolts, and civil strifes, as well as social, economic, and political chaos.

Russian events had attracted Drummond's attention from the beginning but differences of opinion on how this problem and its threat to peace should be tackled had left him undecided on what approach he should assume. Some argued for Council action on the grounds that if the League avoided the question it would stultify as an organization and be viewed as an unimportant and valueless mechanism in vital international questions. Others argued that the possibility of failure was so great that wisdom dictated that the problem be dealt with by the Allies since it would be very difficult to secure any policy consensus among the powers in the League. Even if a policy consensus could be achieved within a League context any decision would be most unpopular among large segments of public opinion and success would be unlikely.

Drummond originally had strongly favoured the latter approach, but with time began to believe that it would be in the Council's interest to tackle the Russian problem. How it would do this was another matter. The only step that Drummond thought the Council could usefully take would be to set up a representative commission to be sent to Russia to ascertain whatever facts it could (since reliable information as to what was happening in Russia was absent) and then report back.[1]

Initially, the possibilities of implementing this scheme were nil. The Allies during 1919 were deeply involved in supporting the counter-revolutionary armies of Admiral Alexander Kolchak, as well as those of Generals Nikolai Yudenich and Anton Denikin. Moreover, it was only by February 1920 that the Versailles Treaty was ratified, the League established, the Council convened, the counter-revolutionary armies defeated, the Allied blockade lifted, and suggestions made to re-open trade with Soviet Russia.[2] In this new atmosphere the Supreme Council wanted to dispatch a mission to Russia, an idea that appears to have been Lloyd George's. It would be safe to say that this was

[1] Drummond to Fosdick, 19 Nov. 1919, File 1919–20, Raymond B. Fosdick Papers, PU.
[2] Walters, pp. 94–5.

Drummond's idea (keeping in mind that Drummond appears to have expressed it first and that passing ideas to Lloyd George through Kerr was Drummond's established policy) which events had now made acceptable to Lloyd George and the Supreme Council. Within the International Labour Organisation's Governing Body a similar proposal had been broached in January 1920 by the Polish representative but a decision had been postponed until its next meeting scheduled in March.[1]

Pressured by the International Labour Organisation the Supreme Council referred to the Council the question of sending to Russia a commission of inquiry. The Council unanimously agreed to this on 13 March and informed the Russians of its decision to do so 'in order to obtain impartial and reliable information on the conditions now prevailing' in their country. The Council queried whether they would extend entry to the commission ensuring it free movement, communication, investigation, and protection during its stay in Soviet Russia.[2] Moscow's long silence, however, caused Drummond to think that it might be desirable to have another Council meeting in connection with the commission since he feared that Russian quiescence might portend an argumentative response to its communication.[3] Drummond was needlessly apprehensive. Indeed, the first reply of 22 March did not reject the Council's overtures,[4] and interviews given by the Foreign Minister, Georgii Chicherin, and his chief assistant, Litvinov, gave hope that a favourable reply might be forthcoming.[5]

Whatever bridge-building Drummond hoped to achieve by his scheme it came to naught. The Polish attack against Russia in late April destroyed any prospects of a positive reply. Despite this and hoping that perhaps something might be salvaged, Drummond some days after the attack contacted Moscow, pointing out that the matter would again be dealt with at the

---

[1] Phelan, pp. 50–3.

[2] League of Nations, Council, *Minutes of the Third Session of the Council of the League of Nations Held in Paris, March 12–13, 1920*, pp. 2–11, 13–15, 21–7; League of Nations, *Official Journal*, I (1920), pp. 61–2, 64–6.

[3] E[ric] D[rummond] to Monnet, 22 Mar. 1920, Minority Questions 1920: 41/3542/807, LNA.

[4] League of Nations, *Official Journal*, I (1920), p. 99.

[5] Walters, p. 95.

Council's meeting on 14 May and that the Secretariat appreciated a reply to the Council's earlier communication.[1]

Drummond's response, however, to the Polish attack against Russia and what should be the League's reaction was less than pessimistic. His doubts 'on what grounds the League could interfere' were realistic in view of the situation that had now developed in eastern Europe between Poland, her western supporters, and Russia. Soviet Russia, he dubiously argued, had not been diplomatically recognized, so that the League could not call on the two parties to submit the conflict to the organization. His more telling observations, however, were that the League could not exercise any control over Moscow and that if the question was to be brought before the League it had to be brought there by some member of the organization. Drummond sarcastically noted that though they 'frequently heard complaints that the League of Nations did not act, no Member [of the League] seemed ready to set its machinery in motion'.[2] In August when the Russian counter-offensive toward Warsaw had commenced and there was pressure to use the League's machinery against Moscow he continued to hold to these views. He believed that the League might be placed in a 'false position' if it now intervened; that it would have been better if in the beginning the question had been brought before the League when Russia 'was protesting its anxiety for peace and before the Polish Army had made headway in its advance towards Moscow'.[3]

What followed the Polish attack on Russia was something of an anti-climax. Replying on 13 May, Moscow welcomed the Council's decision to establish a commission of inquiry. It could not help note, however, that though Poland was a League member and had violated Russian territory, her action had not been opposed by the organization. Indeed, Poland had even received support from other League members. Nevertheless, the authorities were willing to allow the commission to enter Russia and give it all the rights requested. This would be done provided that the commission did not contain either persons antagonistic

[1] League of Nations, *Official Journal*, I (1920), p. 99.
[2] Minutes of a Directors' Meeting, 5 May 1920, General 1920: 40/4199/854, LNA.
[3] Minutes of a Directors' Meeting, 18 Aug. 1920, General 1920: 40/6195/854, LNA.

to Moscow or persons from nations that supported Poland in her actions against Soviet Russia—a not unreasonable request. The Council replied that the Russian answer was tantamount to a refusal. It maintained that the League was a separate entity and Moscow's attempt to differentiate between acceptable and unacceptable representation was unwarranted since League agents represented no particular state, but only the League itself. This message provoked Chicherin to more or less reiterate Moscow's stance.[1] Thus Drummond's attempt to establish some sort of contact or working relationship with an isolated Moscow and perhaps bring Soviet Russia back into the family of nations had been stymied.

The question does not appear to have been raised again until 18 June when Drummond was unofficially approached by the Polish Minister in London, Prince Eustachy Sapieha. The gist of Sapieha's comments was an attempt to have the League assume some ironclad guarantee that eastern Poland and its inhabitants would be defended against Russian aggression and oppression. If the League assumed such a guarantee it would have obviously been placed as a buffer between the Poles and the Russians. Sapieha knew of course that in view of the League's rejection of an Armenian mandate that no such guarantee would be forthcoming. Accordingly, he argued whether it was reasonable to press his country to withdraw her forces from the disputed areas and submit her fate to the decision of the organization. Moreover, would not such a withdrawal place the League in an extremely difficult position?

Though Drummond agreed that it was impossible for the League to administer and protect the areas in question, he maintained that this did not really appear to him to touch the main issue which was peace between Poland and Soviet Russia. This could be effected in only two ways. The first was for the Poles to ask the League to mediate the dispute. The result would be peace negotiations between the two sides in the Council's presence and under its auspices. The second way to effect peace

---

[1] League of Nations, Council, *Minutes of the Fifth Session of the Council of the League of Nations Held in Rome, May 14–19, 1920*, pp. 7, 112–21; League of Nations, Council, *Minutes of the Sixth Session of the Council of the League of Nations Held in London, June 14–16, 1920*, pp. 47–9; League of Nations, *Official Journal*, I (1920), pp. 149–51, 219–20.

was for the Poles to attempt to negotiate a peace settlement directly with the Russians. In this endeavour they should make the offer to refer to the Council's mediation or decision any points on which there was disagreement. Personally Drummond preferred the latter method. If the Poles offered this League reference and it was rejected by the Russians, public sympathy would swing more to the Poles than it was presently.[1] Drummond's advice was never accepted. Equally unsuccessful was an Allied proposal in July for an armistice. During the summer and autumn of 1920 the fighting swayed back and forth. Finally after both sides had exhausted themselves they signed at Riga, Latvia, two treaties (October 1920 and March 1921) which brought an end to the hostilities and established a definitive Polish–Russian frontier.

Though the Polish–Russian conflict was never appealed to the League this was not true in the case of the Russian bombardment on 18 May 1920 of the Persian port of Enzeli (Pahlevi) on the southern shores of the Caspian Sea. The Russian action was ostensibly carried out for the purpose of taking over the ships abandoned in Enzeli by the defeated counter-revolutionary General Denikin. What occurred in Enzeli caused the Persian Foreign Minister, Prince Firuz Mirza Nosret-ed-Dowleh, to bring the question to the League's attention under Article 11 of the Covenant.[2] Since Persia was an area of British influence London was naturally sensitive to events there, but the Cabinet doubted that the Russian action was a serious invasion, an attempt to quarrel with Great Britain, or a prelude to an invasion. Because Lord Curzon desired more information he proposed to discuss the incident with Prince Firuz when he arrived in London. In the interim the British Minister in Teheran was asked to dissuade the Persians from assuming a pessimistic attitude which was not warranted by the situation that had so far developed.[3]

Since Prince Firuz's message did not spell out which paragraph

[1] E[ric] D[rummond], An Unofficial Conversation with the Polish Minister, 19 June 1920, Political 1920: 11/4993/4192, LNA.

[2] League of Nations, Council, *Minutes of the Sixth Session of the Council of the League of Nations Held in London, June 14–16, 1920*, p. 25; League of Nations, *Official Journal*, I (1920), pp. 215–16.

[3] *DBFP, 1919–1939*, I, xiii. 492.

of Article 11 he was invoking, Drummond took no immediate
steps to convene the Council as was required under paragraph
one of that article. At the same time he did not point out to Firuz
the mistake he had made. In his reply on 26 May, a week after
he had received Firuz's message, Drummond merely noted that
he had sent a copy of his message to the Council and League
members. It was not until 31 May that Firuz realized his error
and requested Drummond to summon a Council meeting under
Article 11 paragraph one of the Covenant.[1] It would be safe to
assume that Drummond's delaying tactics were largely influenced by Curzon's attitude that further information was needed
before any moves were made.

Personally Drummond believed that Firuz's move was clearly
covered by Article 11 of the Covenant. The fact that the question
had been brought to the Council's notice by a member of the
organization indicated that an early meeting of the Council was
called for. Drummond therefore intended on 26 May—the day
he informed Firuz that he had circulated his message to the
League's membership—to contact the Council's President, Italy's
Tommaso Tittoni, requesting whether he would authorize the
Secretary-General to summon in ten days a Council meeting in
London. Assuming the Council convened, the question placed
before that body would be what action, if any, the Council could
effectively take. Drummond noted that Article 17 paragraph
one of the Covenant allowed a non-member state such as Soviet
Russia to be invited to accept the obligations of League
membership for the purpose of a particular dispute upon such
conditions as the Council might set. The Council therefore might
invite Moscow to its deliberations under this procedure. This
would not necessitate any recognition of the Soviet authorities as
the government of Russia, but would only recognize that they
were the country's *de facto* government and that a dispute had
arisen between them and the Persians. The condition the Council
might lay down in its invitation would be that Russian troops
should evacuate all Persian territory pending a settlement of the
dispute.

[1] League of Nations, Council, *Minutes of the Sixth Session of the Council of the
League of Nations Held in London, June 14–16, 1920*, pp. 27–9; League of Nations,
Official Journal, I (1920), pp. 215–17; Nasrollah Saifpour Fatemi, *Diplomatic
History of Persia 1917–1923* (New York: Russell F. Moore Co., 1952), p. 207.

What Drummond envisaged was a Russian acceptance of the invitation provided the Council also dealt with the Polish–Russian dispute. With the Polish military offensive slowing down, it appeared to Drummond desirable on both political and ethical grounds that the Council should agree to arbitrate this dispute, provided Moscow was willing likewise to submit the Persian dispute to its decision.

If this occurred the entire Russian question really would come up for League settlement. The ultimate and probable result of this would be the recognition of the Soviet authorities as the government of Russia. The only two alternatives to the present Moscow government were anarchy and reaction. The former would delay the restoration of Europe's political and economic well-being; the latter would undoubtedly result in a renewed Russian imperialism which would attempt to regain the frontiers of the Czarist Empire. The Soviet authorities had also a political disadvantage in that they professed that they did not desire to govern any peoples that were not ethnographically Russian. It therefore appeared that only through the recognition of the Soviet authorities as the government of Russia could peace with Moscow be secured along with independence for the newly created states that bordered Russia. The Council's proposed commission, Drummond thought, would probably have led to the recognition of the Soviet authorities as the government of Russia, but that was not now likely to occur. The present Persian–Russian dispute, however, offered a possible opportunity of achieving the same goal by another route, and did not, any more than the Council's proposed commission, invoke separate negotiations between individual national governments and the Russian authorities.[1]

In transmitting to Lloyd George Drummond's thoughts on the matter Kerr observed that there was much to be said for them.

---

[1] E[ric] D[rummond], Note, 26 May 1920, File F/90/1/9, Lloyd George Papers, BLL. As to Article 17, Drummond subsequently thought it 'somewhat desirable that a certain distinction should be drawn between the rights of Members and Non-Members of the League'. If non-members of the League were allowed exactly the same privileges as League members, 'there would be', Drummond argued, 'very little inducement for nations now outside to join the League'. E[ric] D[rummond], An untitled and undated memorandum, General 1922: 40/21466/21466, LNA.

Now that a Russian trade delegation had arrived in England, Kerr believed that a move might be made to settle the problems of eastern Europe. Drummond had told him confidentially that Bourgeois was in favour of recognizing the government in Moscow. This was significant because in the struggle over reparations between Raymond Poincaré, the former President of the Republic and his supporters on one side, and Millerand and Bourgeois on the other, it was Drummond's impression that Millerand would win out in the end. In a postscript to his note Kerr scribbled that he had 'just seen from the Bolshie intercepts that the Bolsheviks seem to contemplate withdrawing from Enzeli on their own account. If they do', he correctly concluded, 'Drummond's scheme can't come off'.[1]

Indeed, it did not. By cracking the Russian code Lord Curzon was now aware that the descent on Enzeli was no forerunner of greater Russian involvement in Persian affairs. Moreover, the Russians and Persians, following Teheran's protest to Moscow over the bombardment of Enzeli, had established amiable contacts to negotiate a settlement of the question. Lastly, the French were wary that the Council's possible application in this question of Article 17 of the Covenant might ultimately lead to recognition of the Soviet authorities as the government of Russia—as desired by Drummond—something which Paris wished to avoid. The Quai d'Orsay did not believe that reference of the question to the League could in any way be productive. It also could not see what action the League could undertake which would influence Moscow. The French attitude was that Prince

---

[1] P[hilip] H. K[err] to [Lloyd George], 26 May 1920, File F/90/1/9, Lloyd George Papers, BLL. Drummond's successes in Persian affairs were spotty. In 1919 he argued that the Anglo–Persian agreement need not be registered with the Secretariat as required under Article 18 of the Covenant since the Versailles Treaty was unratified and the Covenant inoperative. He recommended an exchange of notes arranging that the agreement should not come into force until it was approved by a majority of the Council. Lord Curzon's communication to the British Minister in Teheran shows clearly that he based his policy on Drummond's advice. *DBFP, 1919–1939*, I, iv. 1155 and fn. pp. 1155–6. In 1921, desirous of having the Permanent Court of International Justice's protocol accepted by as many states as possible, Drummond suggested that the British representatives in Liberia and Persia be instructed to recommend the protocol's ratification. The Foreign Office, however, rejected the suggestion. Drummond (Geneva) to Spicer, 19 May, 1921, FO/371/7034.

Firuz's message to the League had been a great mistake, an attitude that was also shared by Curzon.[1] Though Firuz's reference to the League was the first received under Articles 10 and 11 of the Covenant the Anglo–French consensus was to side-step the whole question. When the Council met publicly in London in mid-June to discuss the issue under the Presidency of Lord Curzon, it was decided with Prince Firuz's grudging consent to take no action on the Persian appeal, but to await the results of the Russian–Persian negotiations then in progress.[2] Subsequent talks between the two parties brought the incident to a close.[3] Again, as in the Polish–Russian dispute, events external to the League setting had undercut Drummond's attempt to establish some sort of rapport with the Soviet authorities in Moscow.

During this period there were other conflicts in which Poland was involved that attracted Drummond's attention. The peaceful settlement of these disputes, aside from the Polish–Russian conflict, was absolutely necessary if peace and, especially, the return of eastern Europe to a normal state was to be achieved. In the case of the conflicting claims of Poland and Czechoslovakia over Teschen, a rich mining district, as well as the areas of Spis and Orava, historic, economic, and ethnic considerations were involved, though the populations of these areas were very mixed and included a sizeable German minority. Clashes in January 1919 had caused an armistice line to be drawn defining the Czech and Polish zones in Teschen. The peace conference's advice was that the question be settled through bilateral negotiations. Its continuance, however, caused the Supreme Council to decide in September 1919 that a plebiscite was the only way to settle the questions, but tensions in Teschen, Spis, and Orava made any plebiscite difficult and this led in turn to increasing friction between Warsaw and Prague.[4]

---

[1] *DBFP, 1919–1939*, I, xiii. 498–9, 503–4, and fnn.; League of Nations, Council, *Minutes of the Sixth Session of the Council of the League of Nations Held in London, June 14–16, 1920*, pp. 37–9.

[2] League of Nations, Council, *Minutes of the Sixth Session of the Council of the League of Nations Held in London, June 14–16, 1920*, pp. 3–9, 17, 18, 41; League of Nations, *Official Journal*, I (1920), pp. 214, 217–18.

[3] *DBFP, 1919–1939*, I, xiii. 615, 645–64, 718, 740–1 and fnn.

[4] Temperley, iv. 348–61, 364–7.

It was in this atmosphere that Eduard Beneš, the Czech Foreign Minister, called on Drummond on 1 June 1920. In an obvious attempt to use the League's machinery to buttress the Czech position, Beneš explained that he intended to ask Drummond that the League send a commission of inquiry to Teschen to investigate and publicly report on the various accusations made by both sides. Drummond observed that there might be some difficulty in this since there was an Allied commission already in Teschen. Beneš replied that this commission was not in a position to make any public announcements since it would immediately be accused of supporting one side over another. This accusation could hardly be made against a League commission. Drummond thought it would be wiser if Beneš in his request made direct reference to Article 11 paragraph two and Article 15 of the Covenant. Reference to these articles, he noted, would enable the League to take the necessary action at an early date.[1]

In line with Drummond's advice Beneš's appeal to the Council dated 31 May requested League intervention under these two articles of the Covenant and the establishment of a commission of inquiry.[2] Drummond's opinion was that the Teschen question was outside the province of the Versailles Treaty and also beyond the Supreme Council's effective jurisdiction. Teschen was a warlike situation and he 'believed that the League would have to act—carefully of course—despite the presence of an Interallied Commission in the Teschen district'. The Allied commission was of course in an awkward position for if it expressed its views or opinions it would be interpreted as an attempt to influence the outcome of the proposed plebiscite. Accordingly, Drummond 'could not see any great danger in sending a League Commission of enquiry to look into this situation'.[3] Drummond then made arrangements with the Secretariat on how the question would be

---

[1] E[ric] D[rummond], An untitled memorandum, 1 June 1920, Political 1920: 11/4580/2040, LNA.

[2] League of Nations, Council, *Minutes of the Sixth Session of the Council of the League of Nations Held in London, June 14–16, 1920*, pp. 59–63.

[3] Minutes of a Directors' Meeting, 2 June 1920, General 1920: 40/4653/854, LNA.

tackled,[1] but before he could implement these arrangements the whole question took a sudden and unexpected turn.

This was provoked by Beneš's previous suggestion to Crowe to refer the question to the arbitration of King Albert of the Belgians. Kerr's observation that this constituted a severe blow to the League was unacceptable to Crowe who argued that it rested on a misunderstanding of the Covenant. In fact, though Crowe had heard that Beneš had contacted the League, the Foreign Office, he noted, 'had no official information of this, as we are never informed of what goes on in the League, until "post festum"'.[2] Obviously, in Drummond's scheme of things, any confrontation with the all-powerful Crowe was to be avoided. Drummond's own withdrawal from the question soon followed. He questioned, he told his associates, whether the Teschen dispute was a 'subject which the Council could properly take up'—a reversal of his previous position. He had ascertained, he informed them, that the Ambassadors' Conference had suggested to both sides—no mention that it was Beneš's suggestion—that they should accept the assistance of King Albert. If Poland and Czechoslovakia did this, it seemed to Drummond useless for the League to involve itself with discovering who was at fault. When it was proposed to write to Beneš or that the Secretariat should communicate with him on this matter, Drummond held that it would be better to wait. No one knew what would result from the offer and even the fact that King Albert had been mentioned was unknown to the general public.[3]

Beneš's appeal of 31 May was discussed informally by the Council at its mid-June meeting. Since the question had been referred to King Albert for arbitration, Drummond was instructed to draft a reply to Beneš pointing out that pending the king's decision it did not seem expedient for the Council to intervene in the matter.[4] Beneš's actions had obviously embar-

---

[1] E[ric] D[rummond], Memorandum on Czech–Polish Relations over Teschen, 4 June 1920, Political 1920: 11/4580/2040, LNA.

[2] *DBFP, 1919–1939*, I, x. 681–5 and fnn.

[3] Minutes of a Directors' Meeting, 9 June 1920, General 1920: 40/4793/854, LNA.

[4] League of Nations, Council, *Minutes of the Sixth Session of the Council of the League of Nations Held in London, June 14–16, 1920*, p. 15.

rassed Drummond and his letter to him conveying the Council's decision had a tint of annoyance to it.[1]

In the end neither the proposed arbitration by King Albert nor the League's commission of inquiry was implemented. Whether the commission of inquiry would have helped in solving the dispute to the satisfaction of both parties is a moot question. Following a Czech–Polish agreement to suspend the Supreme Council's proposed plebiscite, the Ambassadors' Conference imposed on both sides a partition of the area.[2] It was a partition that was ill received, especially in Poland, and was an irritant in Czech–Polish relations during the inter-war years not to be resolved until Poland annexed the Teschen area following the Munich settlement in September 1938.

Equally vexing as the Teschen question was the Polish–Lithuanian dispute over Vilna. Unlike Teschen, however, the League became directly involved in Vilna though Drummond's success in this bitter quarrel was minimal. Vilna was claimed by the Lithuanians as their historic capital though the Lithuanian element within Vilna was only a small percentage of the population. Clashes between Polish and Lithuanian forces in the early autumn of 1920 led the Poles to appeal to the Council, a somewhat incongruous move considering that they had not appealed for its intervention during the fighting against the Russians. The Allies, eager to avoid further conflicts in eastern Europe and to placate France's Polish ally, quickly placed Warsaw's appeal on the Council's agenda. In mid-September an agreement was hammered out that included a Polish promise not to attack the Lithuanians; a Lithuanian promise not to assist the Russians; the establishment of a demarcation line between the two military forces which both governments promised to respect; and lastly, the Council's dispatch of a military commission to guard against any violation of the demarcation line and to ensure that both sides executed their engagements.[3]

Soon after Drummond was approached by the Lithuanian chargé d'affaires in London, Count Alfred Tyszkiewicz, who insisted on quick League action and expressed apprehensions

---

[1] Drummond to Beneš, 16 June 1920, Political 1920: 11/4916/2040, LNA.

[2] Temperley, iv. 361–7.

[3] Alfred Erich Senn, *The Great Powers Lithuania and the Vilna Question 1920–1928* (Leiden: Brill, 1966), pp. 27–46; Walters, pp. 105–7.

about further Polish occupation of Lithuanian territory, especially of Vilna. Assurances by Drummond that the League was greatly interested in the question did not satisfy the Lithuanians for later that day Tyszkiewicz requested that in accordance with Articles 11 and 17 of the Covenant the Council be immediately convoked to consider the situation created by Poland's invasion of Lithuania. Drummond's reply several days later attempted to spell out the steps that the Council had already taken and to show that it was prepared to convene immediately if this proved necessary.[1]

The Lithuanian fears, however, were justified. Though Drummond's actions appear sluggish, even Lord Curzon was slow during this period despite the fact that he had learned from a 'reliable source'—a euphemism for a controlled British intelligence source—that the Poles were contemplating the possibilities of a further advance to Vilna. It was only after additional information was received from 'reliable sources' in Warsaw as well as from the British mission there that Curzon took energetic steps in collaboration with the French to prevent a Polish descent on the city. But it was too late. Polish troops largely composed of men from the Vilna district occupied the city on 9 October.[2]

The British then proposed that an Inter-Allied Conference convene to discuss and settle all territorial questions connected with the boundaries of states, like Lithuania, which had formerly been part of the Russian Empire. Though the Lithuanians were willing to attend such a conference, they stipulated that this did not mean that the Vilna question should be removed from the League's consideration. Drummond saw no inconsistency between this proposal and the general principles which the League followed. It was not the League's function, he noted to Augustinas Voldemaras, the Council's Lithuanian representative, to determine definitively the boundaries of states which had come into being as a result of the war. The organization's main purpose was to stop fighting between such states, though the League, he believed, would always be prepared to offer its good offices for the purpose of definitively determining frontier lines. If Poland

[1] League of Nations, *Official Journal*, Special Supplement No. 4, pp. 77–9.
[2] *DBFP, 1919–1939*, I, xi. 574, 577–81, 583–8, 592.

and Lithuania decided on a provisional arrangement of the frontiers the final arrangement could in Drummond's view be left to an Inter-Allied Conference.[1]

Drummond's thoughts on how to solve the dispute centred on the one point in the Vilna question on which all sides agreed: that the people in the disputed area should 'decide their own fate'—a procedure to which Drummond was very partial. Would not, he queried, the Council's wisest policy be to say to the Poles and the Lithuanians that it was prepared to execute these expressed desires, and to ask whether they would submit themselves to any conditions which the Council might set in order that the inhabitants might be consulted in as 'impartial a manner as possible?' If one side refused, they would place themselves completely in the wrong and be condemned for it by the Assembly when it convened.

If there was an acceptance, the Council would doubtlessly be able to formulate the conditions which would lead to a truly impartial plebiscite. Personally, Drummond believed that the Council should confine itself to an approach of this type and not attempt to impose conditions on Warsaw which might prove to be an endless source for argument and likely to incite Polish public opinion.[2]

What had merely been Drummond's thoughts on 25 October soon transformed themselves into a Council resolution, accepted by the Poles and the Lithuanians. The plan was for the League to organize a plebiscite and the forces in Vilna to be replaced by an international force acting under the Council's orders.[3] As in the Danzig question Hymans, the Belgian, was Rapporteur, but the presence of Balfour, as British representative to the Council,

[1] E[ric] D[rummond], Record of Interview, 24 Oct. 1920, Political 1920: 11/7835/6596, LNA.

[2] E[ric] D[rummond], An untitled memorandum, 25 Oct. 1920, Political 1920: 11/7842/6596, LNA. The 'Principle that nationality should govern territory [was] accepted absolutely' by Drummond in a letter in March 1919. E[ric] [Drummond] to [Kerr], 25 Mar. 1919, File GD40/17/61, Lothian Papers, SRO.

[3] League of Nations, Council, *Minutes of the Tenth Session of the Council of the League of Nations Held in Brussels, October 20–28, 1920*, pp. 39–43, 47–51, 59, 280–282; League of Nations, *Official Journal*, Special Supplement No. 4, pp. 134–43, 146–7.

easily explains the conduit used by Drummond to convey his idea into the Council's bosom.

The Council's action, however, brought no end to the fighting. Unsatiated with their occupation of Vilna and the surrounding area, the Polish forces strove to capture Lithuania's temporary capital at Kaunas (Kovno) and the remainder of the country.[1] It was in this setting that Voldemaras again called on Drummond on the morning of 1 November. From the tenor of his remarks it was clear that the Lithuanians feared that the Poles would not keep their word if they lost the plebiscite. He also raised the Polish agreement with the Allies in July at Spa renouncing Vilna. Drummond's response was that the League was in no way responsible for the Spa agreement. He pointed out that the League could not organize a plebiscite to decide Vilna's future and then, if the vote was in favour of Poland, allow Lithuania to invoke the Spa agreement. As to forcing Warsaw to observe the plebiscite agreement Drummond noted that there were specific sanctions at the League's disposal mentioned in the Covenant: referral of the question to the Assembly; a nation's expulsion from the League; a naval blockade; and lastly, the use of force. In addition, the Council had the general power to do anything it deemed wise to safeguard world peace. These enumerated powers, he noted, merely explained the powers that the League possessed, but their use depended on circumstances.[2]

From the thrust of Voldemaras's other remarks it was clear that the Lithuanians approached with apprehension any impartial plebiscite in the Vilna region. Being a small minority of the total population their chances of an electoral success were very slim. They also argued, with some justification, that during the period that the Polish forces had been in occupation of Vilna, pressure had been exerted and propaganda used to ensure a vote favourable to Poland. The proposed plebiscite was never held.[3]

Drummond's attempt to have a plebiscite decide the issue had failed. Like Teschen and so many other questions originating from the war the Vilna dispute was not resolved by the League.

---

[1] Walters, pp. 140–1.
[2] E[ric] D[rummond], Record of Interview, 1 Nov. 1920, Political 1920: 11/7823/6596, LNA.
[3] Walters, pp. 140–3; Senn, 54–62.

In the years that followed Drummond was to pay particular attention to the Vilna question and use whenever possible his influence and his position as Secretary-General to bring the parties together, to maintain at levels acceptable to the international community the seething tensions between the two parties, and do whatever he could to make sure that the bitter Polish–Lithuanian feelings over Vilna did not erupt into armed conflict which might in turn lead to greater complications in eastern Europe and to a destabilization of the whole area.[1] It was a thankless task, compounded by Polish acts of bad faith and unreasoning Lithuanian obstinacy. It was only in late 1927 that the Council finally succeeded in ending the state of war between Poland and Lithuania, but even this act did not erase the bitter hostility that remained. Finally, in 1938 Lithuania under Polish duress agreed to establish regular diplomatic relations with Warsaw.[2]

During this first year and a half, as we have seen, Drummond developed a number of techniques to assist him in attempting to resolve conflicts and manage crises. These techniques were used in different mixes depending on the question at issue, the parties involved, and the role that Drummond thought he or the Secretariat could play in tackling the issue at hand. These techniques ran the gamut. At one end were the techniques that required political involvement only in a tangential way, the unofficial and the official confidential requests for information, for example. Next came the techniques that required greater political involvement, the unofficial and official confidential conversations and interviews in which schemes, proposals, requests, and ideas were proffered to see what might be the reaction of the parties and what counter-proposals might be offered. Finally came initiatives undertaken by Drummond either directly or indirectly through third parties, sometimes members of the Secretariat or the representatives of League members, proposing in a very concrete manner how a particular question should be handled. Drummond's moves in helping to establish the League and the mandates system, in humanitarian endeavours, in political questions like Danzig and the Saar, in

[1] The sources are too numerous to be cited, but they are mostly to be found in the political files of the League of Nations archives for the years 1921–8.

[2] Walters, pp. 398–400.

conflicts like the Aland Islands, the Polish–Russian fighting, Russia's action in Persia, the Teschen and Vilna questions, as well as his attempt to establish some sort of rapport between Moscow and the League, show in varying ways the different mixes and use of these techniques.

During his office, Drummond refined and expanded these techniques and used them with increasing frequency. The disadvantage that he initially faced, that he was known only to a very small group of people in and around the League, disappeared as the years went by. Through his long tenure as Secretary-General, more and more statesmen coming to Geneva made Drummond's acquaintance, and his great discretion and careful use of his office and of the confidential information given to him established confidence in his judgement and advice and increased his influence—especially among small states[1]—something enjoyed by very few men in Geneva during this period.

His circles of contacts expanded not only in Geneva, but in the capitals beyond, especially in the British Government. Aside from his acquaintance with the statesmen coming to Geneva, his trips to member states helped in this regard as did his association with their representatives on the Council and Assembly, many of whom were to rise to important policy-making positions within their own governments. Within the British Government, men who had been of his rank when he left government service to assume the Secretary-Generalship moved up the bureaucratic ladder, and the friendships and mutual respect that had developed in the offices at Whitehall proved important and stood Drummond in good stead throughout the 1920s and the early 1930s. Men who had been Drummond's juniors in the Foreign Office, Sir Alexander Cadogan is one, also moved up the bureaucratic ladder. However, unlike some of their seniors in the Foreign Office, who looked upon the League with a jaundiced eye, Crowe for example, they were willing within certain limits to work in co-operation with the world organization and saw in the League system certain advantages in helping implement British foreign policy desires and maintaining peace.[2] These attitudes in turn helped Drummond immeasurably in executing

---

[1] Schwebel, p. 172.
[2] Sir Alexander Cadogan, *The Diaries of Sir Alexander Cadogan 1938–1945*, ed. David Dilks (London: Cassell, 1971), pp. 4–5.

his own task in Geneva. Clearly, one of the most important British foreign policy objectives during the early 1920s was the establishment of normal relations with Germany which required Berlin's admission to the League. It goes without saying that any such policy objective had advantages for the League—keeping in mind Drummond's philosophy that an international organization like the League, to be really successful, had to strive for universality. Germany was, along with the United States and Soviet Russia, one of the important stones missing from the League system of security, peaceful settlement of disputes, and international co-operation that Drummond hoped would be a constructive force in world politics. Drummond's role, therefore, in German affairs during his tenure as Secretary-General was in no way a static one and it is to these actions that we now turn.

IV

THE GERMAN QUESTION

From Versailles to Upper Silesia

No matter which way Drummond turned, he encountered the German problem. In France it meant German disarmament and French security, the reoccupation of Alsace-Lorraine, and the desire for extensive war reparations as well as control of the Saar; in Belgium it meant a rectification of the frontier in Eupen and Malmedy; in Denmark it involved a plebiscite in Schleswig. In eastern Europe the problems of Upper Silesia, Danzig, and Memel were far more bitter because the medley of peoples intermixing in the border areas greatly complicated the task of drawing the frontiers. Any union of Germany and Austria was forbidden by Article 80 of the Versailles Treaty. The German question was for the Secretary-General a veritable witch's cauldron.

Initially, Drummond's task was to see that the League executed whatever obligations touching Germany it had under the Versailles Treaty, but in a manner that would not embitter relations with Berlin. He wanted to normalize the League's relations with Germany not only to help lessen Europe's tensions, but also as a first step in expediting her entrance into the League. Drummond thought he and the Secretariat could play this role and thus make the League better reflect Europe's power relations which would not be the case unless Germany was a member. In devising formulas or rendering advice expediting Germany's admission Drummond had to be sure that he did not aggravate his relations with France. One of course should not overemphasize Drummond's actions. Often they were on the question's periphery and sometimes in its centre. Once Germany entered the League, however, Drummond's actions shifted, attempting to assist in accommodating and moderating through the organization her political desires, which if unresolved, might exacerbate her anti-*status quo* policies, especially in eastern Europe and the Baltic. As in the matter of Germany's admission to the League the greatest caution had to be exercised. Many of these issues in eastern

Europe revolved around Poland and Czechoslovakia which were allied to France and Drummond's assumption of any stance in these matters that could be construed as pro-German would obviously lead to strains in his relations with Paris, Warsaw, and Prague. He was forced to walk a very tight line; if either side believed that he was partial he would have compromised his position, and any bridge-building role that he could have played—a not unimportant consideration in view of the deep mistrust that pervaded French–German relations and the fact that few individuals inspired any confidence in either camp.

Drummond's first recorded interest in German affairs was his request to Clerk in July 1919 for information on the execution of the Versailles Treaty in relation to Belgium and the Saar.[1] In particular, he wanted the League's role clarified in Germany's execution of the treaty. Could the Allies, he asked the Foreign Office in October 1919, directly pressure Germany and if need be take coercive measures against her? Did questions like these have to be dealt with through the Council to which Germany would almost certainly appeal, and to which she would probably have to be invited under the conditions outlined in Article 17 of the Covenant? Would the Allies be able to take any coercive measures against Germany and what might these measures be when the matter in question was being referred to the Council? These problems, he pointed out, the Secretariat was very reluctant to tackle. Indeed, it was not at present the Secretariat's business to do so.[2] It was obvious from these comments that Drummond did not want the League involved in coercing Germany to implement the Versailles settlement.

During late 1919 and early 1920, as we have seen, Drummond was involved in the affairs of Danzig and the Saar.[3] It was not until April 1920, however, that he was again enmeshed in German affairs. Fearing a communist insurrection in the Ruhr, Berlin dispatched, without Allied authorization, a military force into the area to suppress the rebels. Unlike the British, the French opposed this move, correctly pointing out that it was in violation

[1] E[ric] D[rummond] to Clerk, 29 July 1919, Administrative Commissions 1919: 2/421/453, LNA.
[2] Extract from a letter Drummond to Campbell, 16 Oct. 1919, FO/371/4310.
[3] See Chapter III, pp. 85–94.

of the peace settlement, and countered by occupying the cities of Frankfurt and Darmstadt.

Since the French were on firm legal ground, Drummond's position was delicate. Attempts to involve the League would have proved both difficult and dangerous. France considered this issue of the highest strategic and political importance and made it clear that the occupation of the two cities would terminate only when German forces evacuated the Ruhr. Paris would brook no League interference with Germany's strict execution of the Versailles Treaty.[1]

Drummond accordingly had to trim his sails for any confrontation with the French would have been impolitic. He therefore argued that if the question was raised, either the French would say it was one for the League, but that they had had no time to bring it before the Council, or that it would be raised under Article 11 and come immediately before the Council. Personally, he believed that the question was one which, going by the Covenant's strict terms, should have been brought before the League initially, but at the present time it was far better not to raise the question. The Council's discussion of the French occupation, he noted, 'under present conditions might involve grave danger'. The only consolation that Drummond could offer for the League's inaction and the criticism levelled at it, was the suggestion that Germany's case was so feeble that she could not get any League member to press it before the Council. He held to this position throughout the French occupation and optimistically argued that in several months' time the issue would dissolve once Germany became a League member; that the opinion would develop that the Council assented to the idea that military occupation of territory under certain circumstances was allowed by the Covenant. He correctly thought that no Council member would propose an examination of this question as no one did.[2] The reciprocal withdrawal of troops from the Ruhr in mid-May brought the incident to a close. Since no further difficulties developed, Drummond's surveillance of German

---

[1] Frank P. Walters, *A History of the League of Nations* (London: Oxford University Press, 1960), p. 116.

[2] Minutes of a Directors' Meeting, 14 Apr. 1920, General 1920: 40/3866/854, LNA; Minutes of a Directors' Meeting, 5 May 1920, General 1920: 40/4199/854, LNA.

events soon led in August to the equally important but less dramatic question, namely, Germany's admission to the League.

Because France opposed Germany's early admission Drummond's problem was to convey his thoughts on the matter in such a way that Paris' ire would not be raised. For this purpose Monnet was his conduit. His transmission to the Quai d'Orsay of Drummond's thoughts could only be construed as the Secretary-General's unofficial and informal observations. During conversations with both the President of Switzerland and the Swedish Crown Prince, Drummond noted to Monnet, it had been strongly voiced that the one issue which interested their countries was the question of Germany's admission to the League at the first Assembly session. To emphasize the point Drummond also noted that the American member of the Secretariat's Legal Section, Hudson, considered that the treatment of this question would largely influence Washington's future policy regarding its entrance into the League. In fact, certain influential circles in Holland considered withdrawing from the League if Germany was not admitted.

From these conversations Drummond was almost certain that Germany's admission would be raised at the coming Assembly session, either by Germany or some previously neutral state on her behalf. Therefore, unless the Secretariat prepared the ground, Drummond very much feared the situation which might arise. They might find that a split existed on this question in the Assembly with results which would be very injurious to the League. Drummond thought that the Secretariat should have some set policy line, but to frame this line it was essential to know—and here was the key point—the attitude on this subject in French governmental and parliamentary circles. Monnet knew his own view which was that the execution of the Versailles Treaty could be 'better controlled' with Germany in the League rather than outside it. Drummond feared that this approach might not be favoured in French political circles. Perhaps Monnet might think it advisable to discuss the question informally with Bourgeois, or with such people as he thought wise, and ascertain what was France's position on Germany's admission to the League.[1] Because of Monnet's excellent contacts

[1] Drummond to Monnet, 21 Aug. 1920, Admissions to the League 1920: 28/6426/1032, LNA. See also, E[ric] D[rummond], Future of the League, 20 Aug. 1920, General 1920: 40/6218/6218, LNA.

Drummond's probe was a clever move. When Drummond himself was approached by Balfour and asked for his views about the question he freely gave them. Almost instinctively he also contacted the strategically-placed Hankey and conveyed to him the same information he had given Balfour.[1]

Drummond's endeavours to secure Germany's admission to the League were optimistic in the extreme. Six more years passed before this was achieved. The difficulties that lay ahead must have become very clear to him at the Assembly session in November. In Paris it was announced that Germany's admission would be immediately followed by France's withdrawal. Comments welcoming Austria's admission and expressing the hope that Germany's would quickly follow, drew from the French representative 'a stormy rejoinder' reminding those present of the losses suffered by France and the Allies in defeating Germany's aggression. It was not empty rhetoric as some thought at the time.[2] It expressed an attitude held by many Frenchmen and shared by most of the political leadership. It was a real obstacle that had to be overcome by any Secretary-General interested in bringing Germany into the League and woe to him if he ignored or forgot it.

That the time was not ripe for Germany's admission was brought home to Drummond in March 1921. Disagreement over reparation payments caused the Allies to occupy the cities of Düsseldorf, Duisburg, and Ruhrort, as well as other towns. This legally questionable action moved Germany to appeal to the League claiming that the Allies had contravened the Versailles Treaty. As a non-member of the League Germany invoked Article 17 and requested the Council to commence the procedures for peaceful settlement provided for in the Covenant in order to have the Allies abandon immediately their coercive measures. In this question the Germans accepted the obligations of League membership. Drummond acknowledged receipt of the message and informed Berlin that he would circulate it to the Council's members and would also send it to all other League members for their information.[3]

The German appeal provoked no comments from any League member. Certain members of the Secretariat, and many

---

[1] Drummond to Hankey, 8 Oct. 1920, Treaties 1919: 17/7284/1740, LNA.

[2] Walters, pp. 116, 124.

[3] League of Nations, *Official Journal*, II (1921), pp. 265–9.

newspapers, thought that Drummond should formally place the question on the Council's agenda and request a special meeting to consider it. Unlike the United Nations' Secretary-General, Drummond, as we have seen, did not have at his disposal an article analogous to Article 99 of the Charter. More important, he knew that if he exceeded his powers in this question French resentment 'would be such as to make his position untenable'. That he would have to tread carefully had been made very clear to Drummond only days before when he had behind the scenes called the Council's attention to a Panamanian–Costa Rican dispute which appeared as though it might lead to hostilities. When this move became known it brought down on him the wrath of the isolationist contingent in the American Senate who charged that the Monroe Doctrine was being 'endangered by the improper act of an official of a moribund organization'.[1]

The Secretariat's attitude was best expressed by the Italian Under Secretary-General, Anzilotti. He argued that though the request of any League member under Article 11 only concerned the Secretary-General's duty to summon a Council meeting, the Council itself had the right to take the initiative in all cases dealing with Article 17.

Drummond's comments reflected his predicament. He could not agree with this thesis, noting that Article 11 was divided into two paragraphs both of which were completely different in their application. The first paragraph applied to war or the threat of war and if any League member invoked it he had to act. Regarding the second paragraph, he had only to communicate the request to Assembly and Council members and each body had to decide for itself. The Council was no more than its members and except in certain well-defined situations it acted only on the request of a League member. The Council's President, Drummond maintained, could not convene any special Council meeting except as a national representative. Accordingly, the comments of the Council's Brazilian president that it could not intervene in the question except at the request of a member state were accurate.[2] With the Great Powers unwilling to act and the small powers afraid to act the League and Drummond remained

[1] Walters, p. 137. See Chapter V, pp. 250–52.
[2] Anzilotti to the Secretary-General, 21 Mar. 1921 and Drummond's attached note, Political 1921: 11/11715/11624, LNA.

passive throughout this episode. Naturally, Germany felt frustrated and her public opinion viewed the League with greater hostility.[1]

Before 1921 ended, however, Drummond was again involved with the German question. This time the area of conflict was in the east and involved the partitioning of Upper Silesia. The Supreme Council was unable to decide the question, with Poland's claims upheld by France and Germany's by Great Britain and Italy. Fearful that continual disagreement might lead to a rupture in Anglo-French relations the Supreme Council agreed to submit the question to the League Council. The Council's rejection therefore of the prior offer of an Armenian mandate had not destroyed, at least for the Supreme Council, the League's usefulness as an organ for settling a question that affected vital Allied interests. Therefore, it was important to Drummond that the Council settle the question in a manner satisfactory to all concerned and enhance the League's position and reputation in Allied circles thus leading to closer collaboration with the Geneva organization.

To implement this desire Drummond attempted to suggest the procedure that should be followed in settling the question. In a memorandum to Balfour Drummond envisaged Polish and German representation at the Council to give information if necessary. He also thought that the Council's Rapporteur should be Spain's representative, José Martin Quiñones de León. Most important, he contemplated the appointment of an impartial three-man commission to recommend the frontier line in Upper Silesia.[2]

Complications, however, developed. Quiñones de León declined to act as the Rapporteur on instructions from Madrid. After examining various options Drummond concluded that the only procedure to adopt was to have the Council's President, Japan's Viscount Kikujiro Ishii, present the preliminary report on the Upper Silesian question. On his own initiative Drummond

[1] Walters, p. 137.

[2] Drummond to Balfour, 15 Aug. 1921, and two memorandums entitled Suggested Procedure of the Council of the League as a Result of the Resolution passed by the Supreme Council with Regard to Upper Silesia, one of which is dated 13 Aug. 1921, Add. MS. 49749, Arthur Balfour Papers, BL.

stated that he was positive that such a step would be accepted by Balfour and believed that the French would also agree.

Though this *ad hoc* procedure got the Council out of an immediate embarrassment, Quiñones de León's refusal made it necessary to take a different procedural tack from that which Drummond contemplated. Excluding Council members whose countries were also represented on the Supreme Council, Drummond noted that those who might be considered as a possible Rapporteur were: Quiñones de León who had refused; Hymans who Lord Curzon had stated was unacceptable to London; Gastao da Cunha of Brazil who could not possibly act alone because of his personality; and lastly, Wellington Koo of China whose appointment would be ridiculed in the French press and who would have little influence because China was weak.

Drummond therefore thought that the plan to have a single Rapporteur had to be abandoned as well as the idea of a League commission which was strongly resisted in Paris, especially by the League's best supporters. The alternative plan proposed was that the four Council members whose states were not represented on the Supreme Council should form a Rapporteurs' committee and present a report on the question. Drummond thought the president of the committee should be Da Cunha. The committee would of course be authorized to obtain expert assistance in no way associated with the League.

By appointing such a Rapporteurs' committee Drummond believed the same result would have been reached as had been previously hoped for under the rejected three-man League commission, and the fact that the four interested parties in the Council stood aside would be completely understood. In fact this type of committee was one of the schemes broached by Lord Curzon to Viscount Ishii, and Drummond assumed that the Foreign Office could have no possible objections to the proposed committee. He believed that it was the best way out of the Council's present difficulties and trusted that Balfour would give it his 'full and unqualified approval'.[1]

[1] Drummond to Balfour, 23 Aug. 1921, ibid. Fortuitously, Drummond's proposed scheme was somewhat similar to one raised in the Foreign Office a week before. In the Foreign Office scheme, however, it was proposed that only Koo, Hymans, and Quiñones de León, should form the committee. An

Though we have no record of Balfour's reply it must have
been affirmative. Following his talk with Drummond and after
receiving Tokyo's permission Ishii agreed to present the
preliminary report on the question.[1] As to Quiñones de León,
Anglo-French pressure caused Madrid to instruct him to serve
on the Rapporteurs' committee though it declined to allow him
to serve as its president.[2] Finally, at its meeting of 1 September,
the Council appointed Koo, Hymans, Quiñones de León, and Da
Cunha as members of the Rapporteurs' committee.[3] Drummond
could only have been pleased with what he had accomplished.

Working in secret and assisted by a small group from the
Secretariat and several outside advisers, the Rapporteurs'
committee presented its report to the Council on 12 October. It
recommended that Germany be awarded two-thirds of the
territory, while Poland be given the greater share of the area's
mineral wealth and industrial plants. The Council accepted both
the report and its recommendations without discussion and
forwarded them to the Supreme Council. Unfortunately for
Drummond, this complex matter continued. Neither the make-
up of the committee, the procedure it followed, nor the
committee's recommendations were acceptable to certain non-
governmental and governmental circles in London.

Comments by the *Daily Chronicle* moved Drummond to write
to Kerr who had assumed the paper's political directorship. He
pointed out that the Supreme Council's question to the League
was not who was to get the territory—as implied by a leader in
the *Daily Chronicle*—but where to trace the frontier line in Upper
Silesia in accordance with the Versailles Treaty's provisions.
Drummond felt that the League Council gave the Supreme
Council's submission on Upper Silesia the only response possible
in its acceptance of the recommendations proffered by the

alternative committee was one composed of Koo, Quiñones de León, and Da
Cunha. *DBFP, 1919–1939*, I, xvi. 327–8 and fnn.

[1] Viscount Kikujiro Ishii, *Diplomatic Commentaries*, ed. and trans. William R.
Langdon (Baltimore: The Johns Hopkins Press, 1936), pp. 155–6. For Ishii's
report see League of Nations, Council, *Minutes of the Extraordinary Session of the
Council of the League of Nations Held in Geneva, August 29 to October 12, 1921*, pp. 7–
10; League of Nations, *Official Journal*, II (1921), pp. 1220–3.

[2] *DBFP, 1919–1939*, I, xvi. 334 and fn.

[3] League of Nations, Council, *Minutes of the Extraordinary Session of the Council
of the League of Nations Held in Geneva, August 29 to October 12, 1921*, p. 4; Walters,
p. 153.

Rapporteurs' committee. As to the suggestion that the proper method would have been the appointment of a three-man commission of impartiality and reputation taking evidence in public and on the spot, Drummond noted that this idea had occurred to many in the League when reference of the question to the organization was first raised. However, there were some obvious objections to it. First, securing such a three-man commission would have been very difficult keeping in mind that Great Britain, France, and other states had either supported one side or the other. Drummond doubted whether under these conditions the League could have secured the services of any European. The fact that Quiñones de León was not allowed to act as the lone Rapporteur shows how difficult the selection of a three-man commission would have been. Even if such a commission had been secured, the suggestion that they should have proceeded to Upper Silesia and taken public evidence would not have proved practical, and would only have led to delay and to renewed violence and ill-feeling in the area. There was also an additional objection to be offered. Had the League established this commission, it would have been quickly and truthfully argued that the Council had shirked its responsibilities by simply passing them on to three arbitrators, a procedure which the Supreme Council might well have followed had it wished to do so.

Drummond believed that the method adopted was the correct one, namely, that the preparatory work should be done by the representatives of the Council's four disinterested powers, but the final responsibility for the recommendations offered should be equally assumed by the representatives of the Council's four Allied powers whose states were also represented on the Supreme Council. Kerr could see from this, Drummond observed, that he did not consider the solution arrived at as in any way ideal, but if it was not, the fault did not rest with the League, but with the Versailles Treaty. Given the treaty's provisions Drummond did not believe that any better settlement could have been recommended.[1]

Kerr agreed with Drummond about the *Chronicle*'s stance on the merits of the question, but disagreed with him about the

[1] Drummond (Geneva) to Kerr, 20 Oct. 1921, File GD40/17/82, Lothian Papers, SRO.

League's procedure which he felt inspired no confidence.[1] Drummond responded that his original idea had been a commission similar to that appointed for the Aland Islands question, but he was very quickly convinced that this procedure could not be implemented for reasons that he had previously mentioned. Drummond realized that there was a great deal of propaganda directed against the League and especially against the Council's decision about Upper Silesia and for that purpose, certain interested individuals had not hesitated to concoct stories about the experts who had advised the Rapporteurs' committee. These experts had never been asked for their opinions as to where the frontier line should be drawn in the area. Their task was to make recommendations providing for the continuance of Upper Silesia's economic life regardless of where the frontier line might be drawn.

On the question of taking evidence, it was true that the British, French, and Italian experts who had been involved in the Supreme Council's discussions had not been heard by the Rapporteurs' committee. It was the Council's desire to separate itself from the atmosphere created by these discussions since to do otherwise the deadlock which paralysed the Supreme Council would repeat itself. Conversely, the outside experts attached to the Rapporteurs' committee did take evidence from Polish and German Silesian employers and workers.

Sometimes it appeared to Drummond that British opinion had forgotten the events that preceded the reference of the question to the League. The Supreme Council discussions had reached a point where it seemed that the question was likely to cause a breach in Anglo-French relations, which in his mind would have caused incalculable damage to European peace for many years to come. If no decision was reached, the area would have to be held under Allied occupation. The uncertainty would continue. Both sides preferred an immediate decision, even a bad one, to this state of uncertainty. It was in this situation that the question was given to the League and recommendations made six weeks later. Drummond was willing to admit that the League's recommendations had not been popular in various quarters. The desires of none of the countries directly concerned had been

---

[1] [Kerr] to Drummond, 17 Nov. 1921, ibid.

satisfied. At the same time he knew that the League's decision was motivated neither by opportunism nor expediency, but by the belief that it was just according to the provisions of the Versailles Treaty. Within a short span of time the Upper Silesian decision, he believed, would remove a factor which had been disturbing Europe's economic and political life; it would allow Anglo-French relations once more to become harmonious. For all these reasons he was convinced that the League's work had been good and could be well defended.[1] Drummond had cogently argued his case. Kerr does not appear to have responded.

The governmental complaint was raised by Hankey who like Kerr objected to the procedure used to handle the question.[2] Thanks to oral messages from Hankey conveyed through a third party Drummond was aware of his criticism even before it arrived. Drummond thought that the best way to explain to Hankey the difficulties that had developed in the Upper Silesian question was to send him the extract of his first message to Kerr. In forwarding to Lloyd George Drummond's covering letter and the extract of the message written to Kerr on 20 October, Hankey scribbled across the top of Drummond's letter that it was 'not a very convincing document'.[3]

The actual arrival of Hankey's criticism moved Drummond to supply further details about the League's procedure in the Upper Silesian question. He defended the Rapporteurs' committee and divulged that he had taken part in every discussion of the committee and that the four representatives throughout attempted to treat the question solely according to the Versailles Treaty's provisions. The two men who had counted most were Hymans and Quiñones de León, and both of these men had been scrupulously impartial. He felt sure that the French never attempted in any manner whatsoever to put pressure on either of them. In fact Drummond knew that it was Berlin which made overtures in Madrid in an attempt to have instructions given to Quiñones de León to assume a pro-German stance. He maintained

[1] Drummond (Geneva) to Kerr, 21 Nov. 1921, ibid.

[2] Hankey to Drummond, 21 Oct. 1921, File F/25/2/35, Lloyd George Papers, BLL.

[3] Drummond (Geneva) to Hankey, 24 Oct. 1921, and the extract from Drummond's letter to Kerr, 20 Oct. 1921, File F/25/2/36, ibid.

that the League's decision was not a compromise, but that the Rapporteurs' committee had commenced its examination of the question in relation to the Versailles Treaty and developed its solution to the question according to that treaty.

There was, Drummond explained, his own position in this whole question. Because Balfour was not given any experts by London, Drummond himself 'was placed in the extraordinarily difficult situation of having to some extent to work for Mr. Balfour, and to advise him on certain points as they arose'. This really was an unfair position for him to be placed in, and Drummond felt he could not have done this if he had not believed that the recommendations arrived at were absolutely just. The one objection that perhaps could have been raised was that the Poles, by the way in which the frontier line was drawn, received twenty thousand more people than had voted for them in the March plebiscite and, correspondingly, the Germans twenty thousand less. Drummond admitted that he had 'endeavoured to get this rectified to some extent', but the only support he received was from the Council's Italian representative, while Balfour had been opposed. There was no doubt in his mind that although Poland had been treated slightly better than Germany (if one looked at the March plebiscite figures) the economic clauses of the settlement gave Berlin considerable advantages, so that all things considered the Germans were slightly ahead.

To have the largest group of influential people in London understand what occurred in this question, Drummond enclosed several copies of his letter to Hankey, deleting, however, the paragraphs dealing with his own activities in the question. He would be pleased if Hankey would pass them around, he concluded, and wished that Lloyd George had time to look at his letter. Hankey took the hint and passed the full letter to Lloyd George. The letter, however, had had its impact for, unlike the note that Hankey had written on Drummond's first letter, his second note was more understanding: 'This letter from Drummond', he observed to Lloyd George, 'is very interesting and throws a good deal of light in the Silesian business'.[1]

---

[1] Drummond (Geneva) to Hankey, 29 Oct. 1921, File F/25/2/39, ibid. See also, Stephen Roskill, *Hankey: Man of Secrets* (London: Collins, 1972), ii. 234. In settling the Upper Silesian question, wrote an Italian member of the Secretariat's Political Section, thanks were due to the technicians: Drummond,

(*continued*)

London's complaints about how the question had been handled had obviously made Drummond overly sensitive to any attack on, or lack of appreciation of, the League's work. Sweetser's failure to give the League due credit for its work during the previous three years caused Drummond to ask him if he had forgotten what it had accomplished politically. Its settlement of the Aland Islands question had probably prevented a war. Its intervention in Vilna, although no settlement was achieved, had stopped the fighting. Its solution for Upper Silesia was achieved despite the fact that the question had almost created a rupture in Anglo–French relations. Albania had been constituted as a state and her frontiers defined and acknowledged by other states owing to the Covenant's strength, and a threatened Yugoslavian attack had been prevented. There was Nansen's success over the repatriation of prisoners of war and Russian refugees. The League's epidemic commission had helped to stave off a severe outbreak of typhus in Europe. The League had also strengthened the provisions against the traffic in opium and the white slave trade. In land disarmament—the League's weakest point he admitted—progress had been slowly made.[1] This small outburst is one of those very rare occasions when Drummond exposed his frustration with what was an exhausting and difficult task. His difficulties in the German question must have been especially nerve-racking.

Germany's Admission to the League

The events of 1919–21 made it clear to Drummond that the German question was inextricably tied to disarmament which was impossible to accomplish as long as France harboured feelings of insecurity toward Germany. Accordingly, in December 1921, he attempted to implant an idea in Lloyd George's mind on how this disarmament–security knot might be cut so as to lead to closer French–German relations and perhaps to Germany's admission to the League. Had Lloyd George thought, he queried, of the 'possibility of having some sort of general

Mantoux, and especially Monnet. Daniele Varè, *Laughing Diplomat* (London: John Murray, 1938), p. 199.

[1] Drummond (Geneva) to Sweetser, 25 Nov. 1921, Box 31, Arthur Sweetser Papers, LC.

European guarantee of territorial integrity—something on the lines of the Pacific Agreement, only applying to Europe?' The details of such an agreement required careful study, but if it was feasible, it would 'make it much easier for France, who is still haunted by an extraordinary fear of Germany to agree to a reduction of her land forces'.

As to the nature of a general European disarmament plan, Drummond thought that the Assembly's Temporary Mixed Commission on Disarmament might work on it immediately. Even if the French would not agree to any disarmament measures, he thought it would be useful to have a set plan, so that when the moment arrived it would be implemented. Not only was France maintaining an army beyond her means, but so were Poland and Yugoslavia.[1] Drummond's plan with modifications would be agreed to at Locarno in October 1925, but for the moment, he was thinking quicker than the powers directly concerned.

Drummond returned to the question following Lloyd George's remark during the Cannes Conference (6–13 January 1922) that he desired to see an association of nations which would include the United States, Germany, and Soviet Russia. Their absence from the League, Lloyd George maintained, explained its weakness. Though their association with the League was desirable it was no easy task, and some of the blame for their absence, Drummond noted to Kerr, hoping no doubt that his comments would end up on Lloyd George's desk, fell on the Allied powers. Not only was the United States, he observed, unlikely to become a League member in its present form, but it was also improbable that she would join any international association until European political conditions were in a more settled state. The United States might co-operate in humanitarian endeavours, but this would be about as far as she would go at the present time.

Until now Germany's admission to the League depended on what France's attitude would be regarding such an application. There was little doubt that if Berlin applied for admission at the next Assembly session, it would be given. However, Germany had not been encouraged by the Allied powers to make any such

[1] Drummond to Lloyd George, 17 Dec. 1921, File F/42/7/13, Lloyd George Papers, BLL.

application, nor had she taken steps to arrange that an application for admission would be favourably received. If London approached Paris and urged Germany's admission, and proposed to Berlin that it should apply, Drummond was sure that Germany would then be willing to enter the League.

According to the peace settlement, Drummond noted, the League had to deal with matters which were of great interest to Germany, for example, the Saar, Danzig, and so on. Germany would want a say on how these matters were handled, and would probably also expect to be admitted as a permanent Council member. Whether permanent membership should be granted required discussion among the Allied powers represented on the Council. What applied to Germany also applied to Russia but that was complicated by the fact that Moscow had to receive *de jure* diplomatic recognition, which if given would doubtlessly lead to Russia's admission to the League. The admission of these three states would make the League a complete world organization. Indeed, Germany's early admission and then Russia's would make it most difficult, Drummond believed, for the United States to refuse at the very least to co-operate with the League.[1]

In a visit to London about six weeks after he made these observations Drummond took 'every opportunity ... of urging the importance' of Germany's admission into the League. If the forthcoming Genoa Conference, he noted to his Secretariat colleagues, resulted in the League's being given the economic reconstruction question, it would be an inducement to Germany to join the organization. It would also make it possible for any government that desired to do so to express its wish to see Germany in the League. Drummond hoped that the question would surface without any difficulty, but if it did not, 'the Secretariat must see that it did come up'.[2]

Drummond set himself two tasks for the Genoa Conference. The first was to ensure that the conference would not create new organs which would duplicate the League's technical organizations. Rather that they should entrust to these technical organizations whatever action in the social and economic fields that the conference might decide on. The second was to see that

[1] E[ric] D[rummond], An untitled memorandum, 17 Jan. 1922, File GD40/17/82, Lothian Papers, SRO.
[2] Minutes of a Directors' Meeting, 3 Mar. 1922, LNA.

the conference's effect be to 'bring Germany and Russia into closer contact with the League, and if possible into actual membership'.[1] As a League member Germany would of course partake in the work entrusted to the League by the Genoa Conference. In the interim until she was admitted to the League, she should be represented on all League committees and other organs which would deal with the work of the forthcoming conference. What Drummond proposed regarding Germany would also apply with regard to Soviet Russia if steps were taken to admit her into the League.[2] Toward these ends Drummond attempted to 'influence the attitude of the principal governments in their own capitals', and sent to the conference some of the Secretariat's ablest men to follow its proceedings,[3] and perhaps to lobby.

Before the Genoa Conference convened, Walter Simons, Germany's former Foreign Minister, explained to Drummond that Berlin perhaps feared to make an application for membership because of the conditions for admission that might be set. Drummond presumed that if the Assembly asked Germany whether she adhered to the Versailles Treaty and intended to fulfil her treaty obligations, the reply would be in the affirmative. Personally he believed that it would be far better to raise the question of Germany's application 'unofficially at Genoa, where it could come up automatically', if, as he thought likely, certain decisions by the Genoa Conference would be entrusted to the League for execution. He assured Simons that he felt very certain that an application by Berlin would be favourably received by London, and that Paris would not oppose Germany's admission at the forthcoming Assembly session provided that in the interim everything went well.[4]

Drummond's endeavours during this period unfortunately failed. The Genoa Conference did convene as scheduled in April, but Germany alienated herself further from the Anglo–French by signing on 16 April a treaty with Soviet Russia at Rapallo under which both states renounced reparations. This agreement,

[1] Walters, p. 166.

[2] Minutes of a Directors' Meeting, 30 Mar. 1922, LNA.

[3] Walters, p. 166.

[4] E[ric] D[rummond], An untitled memorandum, 16 Mar. 1922, Drummond Folder, LNA.

rightly or wrongly, was viewed by the Allies as an incipient Russo–German alliance aimed at them and the acrimonious exchanges between Germany and the Allies were followed by the withdrawal of the German delegation from the conference.

Though Drummond could only have been discouraged by the turn of events, it did not stop him in June from sketching for Balfour and Cecil his thoughts about the Council's future composition. He pointed out that the question of an increase in the Council's membership was certain to be an issue at the next Assembly session, and there appeared to be two approaches to the question. One idea was that the Council's membership should remain static, but that if Germany was admitted as a permanent Council member, an additional non-permanent Council member should be selected. It was felt that this non-permanent member should probably be chosen from among the Latin American states who would then have two non-permanent Council seats. Spain, however, claimed that she was the Council's only neutral member. She strongly held that if Germany was admitted as a permanent Council member she also should be made a permanent member. Drummond did not believe that Spain's claim was well founded—a point that he had made almost a year previously to Balfour. It was a claim that would inevitably lead to difficulties with Brazil, and conceivably with Belgium. He doubted that if Germany was admitted as a permanent Council member Spain would depart from the League, as she had hinted she might do, unless she were placed on an equal footing with Germany.

The second idea was to enlarge the Council in order to provide for European regional representation. In this way purely European matters could be treated initially by what would be a sub-committee of European states. This policy at first glance appeared attractive, but there were obvious dangers. Drummond feared that it might lead to the establishment of regional arrangements for Latin America and also perhaps for the Far East. The whole scheme warranted careful investigation before any favourable decision was arrived at. If the idea was adopted the Council's composition would probably be from fifteen to twenty members meeting twice a year, with the Assembly perhaps meeting every second year. Drummond was undecided as to which was the better plan, but his inclination was that circumstances would drive everyone to accept the second scheme.

He was willing to concede that purely European affairs could be dealt with initially in a more satisfactory manner by a kind of sub-council of European states with an appeal possible, if necessary, to a larger and more universal organ.[1]

Drummond conveyed this same memorandum to Crowe, pointing out that perhaps the best plan to follow at the forthcoming Assembly session was to secure Germany's admission as a permanent Council member, and at the same time add two more non-permanent members to that body. This would increase the Council's membership to eleven, five permanent (Great Britain, France, Italy, Japan, and Germany) and six non-permanent. Drummond believed that the larger number of non-permanent members could probably be rationalized on the grounds that under the Covenant a permanent Council seat always had to be held in reserve for the United States if she decided to enter the League. A Foreign Office minute on Drummond's memorandum noted that the Allies were disposed to giving Germany a Council seat but were against giving her a permanent seat immediately. It was also thought that Drummond was correct in his analysis about Spain and Brazil. Yet despite his view there was much to be said for leaving the Council's composition unchanged for one more year and selecting Germany only for one of the Council's non-permanent seats.[2]

Within a week Drummond again contacted Balfour to explain that Lord D'Abernon, the ambassador in Berlin, appeared to think that there would be little difficulty in securing Germany's application for admission, provided London made it clear that it approved, and that it promised to support Berlin's candidacy as a non-permanent Council member. D'Abernon was, Drummond thought, rightly apprehensive that London should not be placed in a position whereby it could only proceed in the German question in direct opposition to the French. D'Abernon suggested that the wiser policy might be to say to the French Prime Minister, Poincaré, that London had decided that Germany had to be admitted at the next Assembly session and that it intended

---

[1] Drummond to Cecil, 12 June 1922, and the attached memorandum, Add. MS. 51110, Robert Cecil Papers, BL. See also, Drummond to Balfour, 30 July 1921, Add. MS. 49749, Arthur Balfour Papers, BL.

[2] Drummond to Crowe, 13 June 1922, and the attached memorandum as well as an undated, unsigned, and typed minute, FO/371/8330.

to act along these lines, but would naturally be pleased in Paris' co-operation, which it hoped would be forthcoming since it was certainly in France's own interest to do this. Drummond thought it unnecessary to develop D'Abernon's thesis further but it seemed to him to have some force.[1]

Though Drummond had attempted to use his influence in London, aware that it was more accommodating on this issue than Paris, he was also aware that it was Paris' attitude that was crucial and here the situation was very delicate and largely depended on the outcome of the reparations discussions going on in London as well as on Germany's own attitude. Drummond was most unwilling to have French–German difficulties, and the friction that they produced between France and Great Britain, transferred from Allied counsels to the heart of the League. This he felt might prove to be disastrous. If, on the other hand, a settlement of the reparations and other German questions could be reached between London and Paris there would be little difficulty in securing France's consent to Germany's admission to the League. Germany's application was likewise a problem. Though Great Britain had taken public action—the Cabinet had publicly expressed itself as partial to Germany's admission— it had to be recognized that the League was unpopular in Germany. It had been placed in the role of a scapegoat. Also Drummond did not know whether the German Government could resist additional criticism. In this case, too, much would depend on what transpired during the London discussions.[2]

These London discussions, however, proved inconclusive as did the follow-up talks of December and those in early January 1923. The Assembly at its 1922 September session was not willing to wait for a settlement of the German question among the Allies and Berlin's admission to the League before any increase could be made in the Council's non-permanent membership. Moreover, the jump in the League's membership from forty-two to fifty-two also contributed to the pressure to increase the Council's non-permanent membership. The British and the French understood this, for under the leadership of Balfour and Bourgeois—and in

[1] Drummond to Balfour, 17 June 1922, Correspondence Respecting the League of Nations, FO/800/400.

[2] Drummond to Fosdick, 10 Aug. 1922, File 9027, Raymond B. Fosdick Papers, PU.

line with Drummond's advice—two new non-permanent seats were created to which Sweden and Uruguay were elected.[1] Thus Latin America's representation in the Council increased to two as Uruguay joined Brazil as a non-permanent member.

If there were any doubts about this decision they must have been immediately dispelled in January 1923 when French and Belgian troops occupied the Ruhr on grounds that Germany had defaulted in her reparations payments. The German question now appeared further from settlement than ever before. To Paris and Brussels the Ruhr occupation, which was diplomatically supported by Rome, was not the kind of question that they would allow to come before the League under any conditions. Direct involvement by Drummond in this crisis would have been political suicide. As in the French occupation in April 1920 and the Anglo–French occupation in March 1921, Drummond said nothing publicly.

This is not to say, however, that Drummond was inactive or that he did not attempt to draw London's attention toward certain proposals that might settle the question. The Ruhr occupation had divided the Allies, and Drummond observed to Cecil in May that any discussion at the Council would likewise divide its members and he 'did not think this would be a very edifying spectacle for the world at large'. On the other hand, he thought that France was more desirous for a settlement than she had been in the past. It was Drummond's understanding that the scheme being proposed by the Parisian daily, *Le Temps*, was semi-official and that though most of the French Government favoured it, Poincaré was still undecided. Under this scheme Germany would assume the responsibility for the French internal loan spent on war devastated areas, as well as the interests from the loan. The French would offer their own guarantee for the service of Germany's debt as a collateral security. Drummond believed the proposed scheme had 'many political advantages' and hoped that London would see its way to giving support to any proposal along these lines that might be tendered.[2]

Drummond returned to the question in July when he conveyed to Cecil information about the French attitude on reparations

[1] Walters, pp. 237–8.
[2] A memorandum to Cecil, Conversation with Sir Eric Drummond, 23 May 1923, Add. MS. 51110, Robert Cecil Papers, BL.

transmitted to him by Comert who had been to Paris. The gist of the French proposal was that Great Britain forego immediate repayment of her American debt from the sums owed her by France, Italy, and Germany—the latter from reparations. Drummond hoped that perhaps something along these lines might be arranged. When Drummond asked Comert what the French attitude toward the Ruhr occupation might be, he replied that if an arrangement of the reparations question were devised, France, although she would not withdraw completely from the Ruhr, would be prepared to leave only a token force. Drummond observed that this did not appear 'to give sufficient security' that France would refrain in the future from moving any troops into Germany. He believed that there had to be some sort of future guarantee, perhaps that no additional forces would enter Germany unless the Allies agreed unanimously that Germany had deliberately broken her treaty commitments. Comert believed that such a concession was possible. Opinion was nervous in Paris. More and more people were realizing the essential nature of the Anglo–French entente, and that Poincaré had to be reasonable and attempt to settle the reparations–Ruhr questions with London. Drummond thought he might get additional information on his way through Paris. If he did, he would pass it along when he arrived in London. Cecil certainly had his permission to convey to Lloyd George all this information.

He ended with a word of caution. From what Comert had said it appeared to Drummond that, according to French opinion, if there was a settlement of the reparations question Germany's admission to the League would present no problem. If, on the other hand, there was no settlement, and Germany applied for membership under British pressure, the present French attitude was that Germany's admission would be followed by France's withdrawal from the League. Drummond had responded that this 'meant definitely tearing up the Treaty of Versailles, but Comert replied that if England and France were actually in antagonism, the Treaty of Versailles would in any case practically vanish'.[1] Comert was right. In this question, however, the Ruhr occupation continued since no British–French–German consensus could be reached on reparations payments until the

[1] Drummond (Geneva) to Cecil, 11 July 1923, ibid.

Dawes plan in 1924 tied Germany's payments to her prosperity and ability to pay.

The Saar, Danzig, and Memel

Drummond's difficulties during this period were compounded by other matters emanating from the peace settlement which further complicated the German question. They were the Saar, the Free City of Danzig, and the port city of Memel in the Baltic. The Saar was an irritant in French–German relations; Danzig involved Poland, an ally of France and Memel involved Lithuania which events in Vilna had shown was beholden to no one.

In the case of the Saar, tensions generated by the Ruhr occupation had led to a miners' strike and widespread unemployment. Fearing the situation might get out of control, the chairman of the Saar Governing Commission, Rault, requested that the French garrison be doubled and issued a decree for the maintenance of public order. The decree was objected to as an infringement of civil liberties. The German press was in an uproar. Questions in the House of Commons led the government to state that it would demand a full inquiry into the conduct of the governing commission.[1] Drummond's desire was to avoid any inquiry, let alone a British inquiry. There was enough Anglo–French tension over the Ruhr without having to add the Saar. A British inquiry, he observed, that reported to the League about an international adminstration for which many nations were responsible could not be agreed to because of the precedent that it would set.

Even an international inquiry would create problems. The objection would be raised that the members of the governing commission were impartial administrators and that London had agreed to their appointment by the League; therefore, it was impossible to appoint an international body to investigate the proceedings of an international commission unanimously appointed by the Council itself. These objections, Drummond warned, would be raised by the French and supported by others because to dispatch a commission of inquiry would imply that the Council had originally erred and not chosen impartial men.

[1] Walters, pp. 240–2.

He regretted that he did not know beforehand what London would propose since he feared that the scheme would not ameliorate the present situation.

Drummond desired to be kept informed of London's moves because if time could be gained, he would attempt, though he was unsure of success, to have Rault modify his public order decree; if it could be modified the main stumbling block would be avoided for the foreseeable future.[1] The way out of this impasse that Drummond envisaged was an inquiry conducted by one or two Council members. This kind of proposal would be hard for the French to oppose, though likewise it would be difficult to find a Council member who would take on the assignment. Any inquiry by the Secretariat was of course out of the question.[2] The compromise that Drummond pressed for was a British promise to drop the idea for an inquiry and a French promise to have Rault withdraw his decree and to remove at the first opportunity the pro-French members of the governing commission.[3]

In this Drummond appears to have succeeded. Rault withdrew the decree. In the Council Cecil did not press the idea of an inquiry but proposed instead that it interview in public the whole governing commission so that they could give an account of their stewardship. This was subsequently done. In the future the chairmanship of the governing commission was held by a Canadian and then by an Englishman.[4] By 1924 the pro-French members had all left the governing commission.[5]

The second matter was Danzig which as we have seen had engaged Drummond's attention during 1919–20. By the spring of 1923 the Free City was being subjected to Polish economic pressure and fears of a Polish military descent on the city did nothing to assuage the apprehensions of the Danzigers;[6] it contributed to strained German–Polish relations not to mention

[1] Drummond (Geneva) to Tufton, 11 May 1923, FO/371/8762.

[2] Drummond (Geneva) to Tufton, 14 May 1923, ibid.

[3] A memorandum to Cecil, Conversation with Sir Eric Drummond, 23 May 1923, Add. MS. 51110, Robert Cecil Papers, BL.

[4] Walters, pp. 242–3.

[5] Laing Gray Cowan, *France and the Saar, 1680–1948* (New York: Columbia University Press, 1950), pp. 132, 143 fn.

[6] Christoph M. Kimmich, *The Free City: Danzig and German Foreign Policy, 1919–1934* (New Haven: Yale University Press, 1968), pp. 56–60.

German–French relations too. In an attempt to calm this tense situation Drummond along with Mantoux arrived in Warsaw in June. He interviewed the Prime Minister, the Foreign Minister, and other top Polish officials. During these interviews, which acted as a catharsis for the Poles, there was an outpouring of complaints, real or imagined, against Danzig and the Danzigers.[1]

Drummond's impression was that Poland was still very bitter toward Great Britain. Poland appeared to feel that England had been the principal obstacle to her territorial expansion. Drummond's criticism was that the Poles wanted everything immediately and were not content to let things develop which, in time, would surely give them everything they hoped for.[2] In his opinion the only solution to Polish complaints over Danzig was to alter the Versailles Treaty. The Poles could not get what they required under the present arrangements stipulated in the treaty. Indeed, no one could get anything through the Danzig bottleneck into Poland without extended delays.[3]

In Danzig Drummond interviewed the High Commissioner and the top officials of the city's administration. His suggestion to the Danzigers was the same he had given to the Poles: if they had any complaints to present them to the High Commissioner who would convey them to the Secretariat who would in turn pass them on to the Council. Until the Council met the Danzigers should vigorously strive to avoid further friction with the Poles since the present situation was acute and any action that increased friction was to be avoided. Drummond's general impression was that the Danzigers would execute the provisions of the peace settlement but not go one inch beyond. Unfortunately, both sides were devoid of goodwill and every minor official tended to make the situation as difficult as possible.[4] Though Drummond sympathized with Poland on some points, it appeared to him that Warsaw had a very weak legal case.[5]

[1] The record of these conversations dated 3–5 June 1923, can be found in FO/371/9326.

[2] [Eric Drummond], An untitled memorandum, 5 June 1923, ibid.

[3] Leeper (Warsaw) to Selby, 6 June 1923, ibid.

[4] The record of these conversations dated 8 June 1923, can be found in FO/371/9326. See also, Heinrich Sahm, *Erinnerungen aus Meinen Danziger Jahren 1919–1930* (Marburg/Lahn: Bahr, 1958), pp. 83–4; Heinrich Sprenger, *Heinrich Sahm Kommunalpolitiker und Staatsmann* (Koln: Grote, 1969), p. 98.

[5] Drummond (Prague) to Gregory, 10 June 1923, FO/371/9326.

Drummond's visit was not only well-timed but also well-received, the British Minister in Warsaw reported to the Foreign Office. It increased Poland's interest in the League. It was important to do this during the present controversy over Danzig since it would divert Poland from acting independently to secure what she considered she had a right to and would dispose her to take her case to the League.[1] Somewhat similar information was sent by the British Consul in Danzig who noted that a 'Calming effect' had been produced by Drummond's visit.[2] By showing the flag and reaffirming the League's responsibilities in Danzig as well as its desire to see Polish rights protected, Drummond had helped to pour some oil on troubled waters to ease German–Polish–Danzig tensions in particular and German–French tensions in general. Drummond's actions in Danzig, however, could only be stopgap measures. It was in the relevant capitals, especially in London and Paris, that a solution to the Danzig question could be devised.

The same could be said for the port city of Memel in the Baltic which under the Versailles Treaty was to be given to Lithuania. Its transfer, however, was delayed because of the Polish–Lithuanian fighting as well as the Polish–French belief that Memel might better serve their interests as a Free City like Danzig. Doubtful of Memel's transfer the Lithuanians in January 1923 occupied the port as well as its hinterland area. Protests were lodged and attempts were made by the Allies to reach an agreement with the Lithuanians as to Memel's future status and the treatment of its German dwellers. The Ambassadors' Conference acting for the Allies drew up a draft convention which stipulated that Poland would share in Memel's administration and its commerce would enjoy privileges equal to those of Lithuania herself. Though Lithuania accepted much of the draft convention it was these clauses which she specifically rejected. A deadlock ensued and finally in September 1923 the Ambassadors' Conference decided to transfer the whole question to the Council.[3]

Drummond, as one might expect, was not pleased by this

[1] Muller (Warsaw) to Curzon, No. 263, 11 June 1923, ibid.
[2] H.M. Consul (Danzig) to the Foreign Office, No. 12, 11 June 1923, and Fry (Danzig) to Curzon, No. 32, 13 June 1923, ibid.
[3] Walters, p. 303.

referral which merely reflected divergent Allied policies. He therefore attempted to have the Allies and especially the Anglo–French co-ordinate their actions in the Council. The position that the Allies had got themselves into, he observed to Cecil, was most involved. The Ambassadors' Conference had erred in thinking that the Lithuanian acceptance in principle of the draft convention should be considered as an acceptance in detail. The Lithuanians contended that their acceptance in principle did not cover specific points in the scheme devised by the Ambassadors' Conference and requested an appeal to the World Court. Drummond was willing to admit that under the peace settlement the Allies completely controlled Memel's disposition, but unfortunately they seemed to have in their communications committed themselves to the proposition that Lithuania had the right to be consulted. It seemed to Drummond therefore that it would be most difficult for the League to refuse Lithuania's request for a reference to the World Court. The question was studded with difficulties and he trusted that Cecil would have time to examine it most carefully before the Council's next meeting.[1]

When the expected Allied Anglo–French co-ordination did not materialize, however, Drummond again returned to the question and used his friendship with Cecil to warn him of Mantoux's information that it would be hard to persuade the French to adopt the idea of a commission which was divorced from the Council—a procedure which would get the League off the hook. Drummond thought it was of great importance that the four Great Powers concerned should agree on a similar line of action. He suggested that it would be wise for Cecil to discuss the matter with the French and the Italians before the Council convened and see whether they could not come to a consensus. Drummond presumed that the Great Powers had little direct interest in the question. What they desired was a settlement which would be acceptable to both sides. Naturally, France would represent Poland's point of view, and if the procedural method devised was acceptable, Drummond did not think anybody else would raise objections. The chief problem was that

[1] Drummond (Geneva) to Cecil, 15 Oct. 1923, Add. MS. 51110, Robert Cecil, BL.

although the question had been referred under Article 11 of the Covenant, no indication had been given as to what exactly the Ambassadors' Conference expected from the Council.[1]

Drummond's advice appears to have been heeded, for the Council's decision was to entrust the question to a special commission composed of states which were not directly involved in the problem and chaired by Norman Davis of the United States. The compromise devised by Davis's three-man commission protected the rights of Memel's German population; the efficiency of Memel as Lithuania's principal port; and Poland's equal right with others to use the port. This arrangement was accepted by the Allies and Lithuania and, although Poland protested, she made no attempt to block the decision.[2] Drummond attempted to assist Davis's commission behind the scenes by having the actions of the Ambassadors' Conference mesh with those of the Council[3] and by attempting to have London apply pressure on Lithuania[4] to accept the commission's compromise scheme. His efforts to solve the question quickly and peacefully were, at least for the moment, successful. Memel, however, was like Danzig, Teschen, and Vilna—one of Europe's running sores during the inter-war period. Lithuania's rule over Memel led to unending tension with Germany which was not resolved until Memel was occupied by German troops in March 1939.[5]

The Road to Locarno

The thaw that commenced in French–German relations in April 1924 once the Dawes plan was presented caused Drummond to return to the question of Germany's admission to the League. From time to time he conveyed to the secretary to Ramsay MacDonald, the new Prime Minister, information which he

---

[1] Drummond (Geneva) to Cecil, 4 Dec. 1923, ibid.

[2] Walters, p. 304.

[3] Two letters from Drummond (Geneva) to Cadogan, 4 Feb. 1924, H. M. Consul (Geneva) to Cadogan, No. 3, 4 Feb. 1924, and Drummond (Geneva) to Cadogan, 8 Feb. 1924, FO/371/10360; Drummond (Geneva) to Parmoor, 9 Feb. 1924, Add. MS. 51110, Robert Cecil Papers, BL; Drummond (Geneva) to Parmoor, 18 Feb. 1924, FO/371/10360.

[4] Drummond (Geneva) to Cadogan, 4 Feb. 1924, and H. M. Consul (Geneva) to Parmoor, No. 4, 3 Mar. 1924, FO/371/10360.

[5] Walters, p. 305.

thought might interest MacDonald because of the different slant it gave to what was occurring in Europe from the information usually conveyed through the Foreign Office. MacDonald's comment that he was anxious that the League be associated in any general settlement that might be devised caused Drummond to think over the League's possible role in any such settlement. Accordingly, he offered his observations and included the question of inter-Allied debts since he felt that no final settlement could be reached, even on reparations, until that problem as well as that of French security was resolved.[1]

His comments on inter-Allied debts and reparations, however, were merely preliminary to the memorandum's main point which was the problem of French security. Drummond noted that France had concluded or was endeavouring to conclude, defensive treaties with a number of European states. These treaties did not appear to be contrary to the Covenant's general terms. Assuming that Germany violated Articles 16 or 17 of the Covenant—according to whether she was or was not a League member—and the Council recommended that the governments concerned should take effective military action, the states with whom France had defensive treaties would of course be bound to act. Would it be feasible, Drummond queried, for London to give Paris an assurance that in this case Great Britain would agree in advance to take military action too? Naturally, in practice, this would be very safe since Great Britain as a permanent Council member would be able to veto any such recommendation if she disapproved. Yet this proposal would probably go a long way toward satisfying France and conceivably might be accepted in lieu of any special treaty arrangement. There appeared to be in theory no objection to giving a similar assurance to Germany, if and when she entered the League. If this British assurance were combined with the Rhineland's neutralization and demilitarization and perhaps a League guarantee for the Ruhr, it was not improbable that successful talks might be concluded on some such proposal.[2] Drummond's query was of course optimistic in the extreme. No prior

[1] Drummond (Geneva) to Waterhouse, 29 Apr. 1924, File 1/116 (1924), MacDonald Papers, PRO.
[2] E[ric] D[rummond], Notes on the Questions of Reparations, Inter-Allied Debts, and French Security, 28 Apr. 1924, ibid.

commitment to any state, despite Drummond's cogent arguments, was still established British policy during this period.

For Drummond the settlement of Europe's outstanding political questions like reparations, French–German relations, and Soviet Russia must of necessity take place outside the League's framework. He hoped, however, that if and when these questions were settled, the League's apparatus would be utilized for supervisory purposes, especially as regards reparations and French–German relations.[1] Of course he never lost sight of the great difficulties posed to Germany's admission, not only by France and Belgium, but also by Brazil and Spain who wanted permanent Council seats. Nevertheless, it was his belief that once Germany was admitted she was almost certain to be elected as a non-permanent Council member and remain in that position until she became the Council's fifth permanent member. He thought this procedure would meet in substance Germany's desire to be given a permanent Council seat when she was admitted to the League.[2]

It was these arguments that Drummond used in early June when he discussed in Berlin Germany's admission with Baron Ago von Maltzan, the Foreign Ministry's influential State Secretary. Supported by D'Abernon, Drummond strongly pressed Maltzan on the advantages that would accrue to Germany by becoming a League member. As to Germany's claim to a permanent Council seat Drummond explained the difficulties and observed that much was being asked of France and Belgium—not only to admit Germany as a member, but simultaneously to give her a permanent seat. Then on this question Brazil and Spain, too, posed problems. As Maltzan knew, Drummond noted, Germany's selection as a permanent Council member required that body's unanimity and he did not think that this could be obtained. Personally, Drummond did not consider that the question of prestige was involved. Once selected to sit on the Council, Germany would almost certainly continue to be a member of that body until she was elected to a permanent seat. Drummond asked whether, if private Council discussions on Germany's admission took place and the Council were

[1] Drummond (Geneva) to Parmoor, 6 May 1924, Add. MS. 51110, Robert Cecil Papers, BL.

[2] Eric Drummond, Record of Conversation, 29 May 1924, FO/371/10568.

unanimously in favour of it, this would prove useful from the point of view of propaganda. Maltzan thought it would, but cautioned that it would raise the question of Council membership. If the Allies agreed to push Germany's admission, but disagreed to her election to a permanent seat, they should avoid stating whether Council membership should be either permanent or non-permanent.[1] From Maltzan's comments it was obvious that for Germany admission to the League could not be separated from immediate and permanent Council membership.

This German stance was reaffirmed by Bernhard von Bülow, the Director of the Foreign Ministry's League of Nations Department. When Drummond repeated what he had told Maltzan, Bülow replied that it would only make things difficult since it was held in Germany that only by securing a permanent Council seat would she be certain of fair treatment. The German people would never admit that their admission would be on probation, or as a second-rate power.

Drummond responded that this was an odd position to assume since Germany had great interest in many subjects aired by the League. These interests would undoubtedly increase if, as he thought likely, the League were asked to secure a guarantee between France and Germany and also to take control under Article 213 of the Versailles Treaty by which Germany agreed to give every assistance in any investigation which the Council deemed necessary. Bülow was ready to agree. However, the German public, he pointed out, thought that the Allies' object in trying to get Germany into the League was to treat her as an inferior. The German people after their experience were most suspicious. Drummond had to keep this in mind.

Drummond's impression after this discussion was that the whole question really depended on France's attitude. If Paris really desired Berlin's admission to the League and made things as easy as possible for it to happen, he thought that Germany might enter by September. On the other hand, if Paris required assurances and promises which German public opinion thought were humiliating, he feared that the difficulties might prove insurmountable. Drummond preferred that Germany's application for admission should be the result of a realization that the

[1] [Eric Drummond], Record of Berlin Conversation, 5 June 1924, File 1/201 (1924), Macdonald Papers, PRO.

League was involved now, and probably would be increasingly involved, with questions of security and control, matters which were of the greatest interest to Germany. Because of this it would be to Germany's advantage to become a League member, particularly if the Allies made it clear that they would like to see her elected to a non-permanent Council seat. Drummond was sure that if the Germans were convinced of a change in the French attitude things would be far easier all round.[1]

In conveying the record of these conversations to MacDonald, Drummond feared that they showed that there would be great difficulty in effecting Germany's admission at the upcoming Assembly session, though these difficulties were not insurmountable. Drummond observed that he would also give copies of these conversations to the Council representative, Lord Parmoor, but since no French Government had yet been formed following the recent elections, he thought it would be somewhat dangerous to discuss the question at the Council though conversations between its members might be useful.[2]

Unfortunately, these Berlin conversations appear to have made no impression on Parmoor, for his comments in the press that there would be no difficulty in giving Germany a permanent Council seat upset Drummond a great deal. Even if France and Belgium agreed, which Drummond wrote to Cecil he thought unlikely, Spain and Brazil would almost certainly voice objections, unless they too were simultaneously given a permanent Council seat. Moreover, he doubted whether a permanent seat for Germany at the present time was wise. Bülow during their talk had implied that in certain matters of importance to Germany, like the Saar and so on, which under the Versailles Treaty must be decided by a Council majority, she desired to be sure of a permanent seat, so as to be able when these matters were discussed to threaten to obstruct the Council's work on other issues. Drummond knew that it was most difficult for Cecil to do anything, but thought he ought to tell him what was happening since he himself was powerless—a hint to Cecil to do something.[3]

Frustrated by events, in late August Drummond also tried to

---

[1] E[ric] D[rummond], Record of Berlin Conversation, 5 June 1924, ibid.

[2] Drummond (Geneva) to MacDonald, 7 June 1924, ibid.

[3] Drummond (Geneva) to Cecil, 27 June 1924, Add. MS. 51110, Robert Cecil Papers, BL.

contribute to the question of European security, no doubt with the hope that it would expedite Germany's admission. By this point MacDonald had rejected the Draft Treaty of Mutual Assistance which obligated the signatories to support each other from any aggressor named by the Council, and discussions had commenced on what was to be the Geneva Protocol. This was an agreement which declared war an international crime and proposed to facilitate the Covenant's system for the pacific settlement of disputes and the reduction of armaments. It called for compulsory arbitration, and regional military action against an aggressor state, and was to take effect when general armaments reduction had been agreed to.

In an attempt to integrate the Covenant into these discussions Drummond hoped that, in the consideration of any security question, Article 12, which provided a definite obligation that League members would not resort to war until after the expiration of a given period, would not be lost sight of. It seemed to him, he observed to Sir Walford Selby of the Foreign Office now acting as MacDonald's private secretary, that it might well be that an extension of Article 12, tied to some sort of sanctions when violated such as those stipulated in Article 16, might provide the best solution to the security and disarmament questions. The latter, Drummond believed, would follow once the security question was resolved.[1]

Several days later Drummond communicated to Selby a memorandum which he wanted to give to MacDonald. Developed by Drummond and others in the Secretariat it offered some concrete ideas on the best way to achieve security and disarmament. Drummond thought that the basis of any such scheme had to be the Covenant since that instrument already went a long way in the direction of security. He hoped that some of the ideas presented in the memorandum might be developed at the forthcoming Assembly session, and noted that since an American had had a large share in drafting it—probably Sweetser—the phrases used were of a nature that would have special attraction for an American audience. The scheme had adopted some of the best ideas proposed by the Americans, Professor James T. Shotwell and General Tasker Bliss, and also

---

[1] Drummond (Geneva) to Selby, 22 Aug. 1924, FO/371/10569.

from the Draft Treaty of Mutual Assistance. He thought the great advantage of the proposed plan was that it would require a new convention. Different parts could also be accepted by different countries without injuring the scheme as a whole.[1]

At the Assembly's September session the Geneva Protocol, after some intense negotiations, was hammered out. A close examination of the protocol shows that some of the ideas in Drummond's memorandum influenced the drafting of its final clauses.[2] The fall of MacDonald's government, however, and its replacement by a Conservative government under Baldwin in November 1924, with Austen Chamberlain as Foreign Secretary, sealed the protocol's fate although it was not until March 1925 that London officially rejected it. Drummond quickly established contact with Chamberlain, a process made easier by Sir Austen's unsolicited invitation that Drummond write to him privately about any matters which he thought might interest him.[3] This close relationship which became very friendly did not deter Drummond from disagreeing with Chamberlain's qualms about the protocol's efficacy. Its rejection was a setback in Drummond's struggle to get Germany into the League. He believed that the advantages that accrued to Great Britain from the protocol, especially in securing that future Franco–German disputes would be settled by arbitration, far exceeded London's difficulties of referring certain questions to arbitration. It was a matter of deciding where the balance lay. The same went for the protocol's application in Latin America. Practically the whole of that continent was in the League and in the case of a conflict the League would call on the Latin American states themselves to deal with the aggressor state, a system which ensured that there would be no infringement of the Monroe Doctrine.[4]

The question of security and Germany's admission was further complicated on 12 December when Berlin asked Drummond if

[1] Drummond (Geneva) to Selby, 25 Aug. 1924, ibid.

[2] For the protocol's text see, Philip J. Noel-Baker, *The Geneva Protocol for the Pacific Settlement of International Disputes* (London: King & Son, 1925), pp. 215–224.

[3] Drummond (Geneva) to Chamberlain, 24 Nov. 1924, AC51/104, Austen Chamberlain Papers, UB.

[4] Drummond (Geneva) to Cecil, 15 Dec. 1924, Add. MS. 51110, Robert Cecil Papers, BL. See also, Drummond to Strakosch, 5 Jan. 1925, MG 26, J1, Volume 114, Mackenzie King Papers, PAC.

and when it entered the League it could be excused from the obligations under Article 16 because it was virtually disarmed under the Versailles Treaty.[1] It was perhaps an attempt to avoid any future implementation of sanctions against Soviet Russia, and in view of the fact that the other vanquished and disarmed states (Austria, Bulgaria, and Hungary) had made no such demand when they entered the League, and even Switzerland had agreed to share in the application of economic sanctions, it was a request that Drummond did not sympathize with. As he wrote some weeks later on 5 January 1925, Germany, 'if properly handled', and he thought she had to be with 'firmness and courtesy', would join the League before many months had passed. On the other hand, he himself did not 'believe in the policy of over-entreatment and too great concessions' when it came to negotiating with Germany on her admission.[2]

Personally, Drummond was very doubtful about what lay behind the German note though several theories had been advanced to explain it.[3] Nevertheless, the whole question of Article 16 and Berlin's reference to it bothered Drummond for in mid-February he admitted to Cecil that he had been thinking about it, especially since it was also very much in the minds of Baldwin and Chamberlain. Drummond felt that some method ought to be found allowing them to make clear the British position with regard to Article 16. As Cecil knew, Drummond himself thought any formal declaration unnecessary, since he believed it to be 'generally assumed that economic and financial sanctions could not be applied without American consent and co-operation'. Though he did not say it, Drummond was obviously interested in some sort of British declaration about Article 16 that might assist him in his negotiations with the Germans over this same article. Would it be possible, he queried, to raise the question at the next Assembly session? He did not mean this in a formal sense. When Chamberlain was talking about security and the Geneva Protocol, he might, Drummond

[1] League of Nations, *Official Journal*, VI (1925), pp. 323–6.

[2] Drummond to Strakosch, 5 Jan. 1925, MG 26, J 1, Volume 114, Mackenzie King Papers, PAC. See also, Drummond (Geneva) to Cecil, 22 Jan. 1925, Add. MS. 51110, Robert Cecil Papers, BL.

[3] E[ric] D[rummond], Record of an Interview, 22 Jan. 1925, Minutes of a Directors' Meeting, 22 Jan. 1925, LNA.

thought, very easily make a statement that, naturally, it had 'always been understood that financial and economic sanctions' under Article 16 'could hardly be applied unless with the consent and co-operation of any great economic and financial Power outside the League'. Should such a situation arise the Council would obviously attempt to obtain this co-operation. If it did not obtain this co-operation, the position would have to be reconsidered. There would be a 'grave risk' that the application of economic and financial sanctions might fail with the result that the state breaking the Covenant might receive the very political support which the Covenant meant to deny it. He wanted Cecil to think about it and perhaps speak with Chamberlain, and let him know that he had contacted him about the question. Drummond was certain that this was a better approach than to place any explanation into a document, where naturally it would attract wide attention and its ultimate motives viewed with suspicion.[1]

To get a personal feel for the situation, Drummond, following a visit to Finland and the Baltic States, stopped off in Berlin on 2 March on his return to Geneva. He first called on Carl von Schubert who had replaced Maltzan as State Secretary. Discussing the note of 12 December Schubert thought that the question of Germany sending troops to aid a League member was of no practical importance. Nor was his country completely unwilling to take part in economic and financial sanctions under Article 16. The real difficulty was the passage of foreign troops through Germany. Berlin was unwilling to risk the possibility that war might be declared by the country against whom the troops were being sent, and, furthermore, the passage of French troops would almost certainly give rise to incidents and therefore was not a practical proposal. However, there were other outstanding questions, Schubert observed, like the establishment in the Rhineland of a permanent control organization and the Saar problem.[2] The attitude of 'Schubert was satisfactory', Lord D'Abernon wrote in 1930, 'in the sense that he thought some arrangement could be made regarding Article XVI on the basis

---

[1] Drummond to Cecil, 13 Feb. 1925, Add. MS. 51110, Robert Cecil Papers, BL.

[2] Minutes of a Directors' Meeting, 5 Mar. 1925, LNA.

that the League recognized "ultra posse nemo obligatur"' (no one is obligated to do more than he can).[1]

A conversation that followed with the German Foreign Minister, Gustav Stresemann, was even less productive. Like Schubert, Stresemann feared that Germany might be attacked by any state which defied the Covenant. Drummond pointed out Germany's position might be easier in such a situation if she were a League member since there was the possibility of outside assistance. His attempt to remove any misgivings about Article 16 caused Stresemann to remark that the League had to discover a way of freeing Germany from the obligations of this article which under present conditions it could not assume. When Drummond responded that the League could not have different types of member states, Stresemann rejoined that unfortunately there were different types of nations in the world community. When he pointed out that Switzerland had been exempted from Article 16, Drummond explained that Switzerland had agreed to partake in economic sanctions. Stresemann held that to exclude another state from economic intercourse with sixty million Germans would be a warlike act. Drummond maintained that the League did not expect a member state to do the impossible.[2]

The discussion had obviously produced nothing. Drummond's general impression was that Stresemann did not really desire Germany's admission, and therefore was not inclined to make things easier. Influential German circles feared that if Germany entered the League, she would be treated as an inferior, and were also apprehensive of a serious break with Soviet Russia. Drummond's view was that Germany feared alienating Soviet Russia because she was Berlin's only support and would lose it once Germany entered the League.[3]

He was very disappointed, Drummond informed Lord D'Abernon, with Stresemann's attitude, especially his insistence that Germany be excused from the obligations of Article 16.

[1] Edgar Vincent D'Abernon, *An Ambassador of Peace* (London: Hodder and Stoughton, 1930), iii. 146–7.
[2] Minutes of a Directors' Meeting, 5 Mar. 1925, LNA; Gustav Stresemann, *Gustav Stresemann, His Diaries, Letters, and Papers*, ed. and trans. Eric Sutton (London: Macmillan, 1937), ii. 69; D'Abernon, iii. 147.
[3] Minutes of a Directors' Meeting, 5 Mar. 1925, LNA.

Drummond did not honestly think that it was possible to give in on this point without destroying the whole League system. He was willing to admit that the Assembly's 1921 interpretative resolution on Article 16 might be used in Germany's favour. This seemed to him the most that could be done to meet the German demand. Whether a formula might be found on the passage of foreign troops through Germany, to assist a state attacked, Drummond failed to see it.

It appeared to Drummond that Germany's demands regarding admission had progressively increased. First, she asked to be treated like any other Great Power. When this could be obtained, she then asked for special treatment. If this was based on the notion that the League could not really go on existing unless Germany was admitted it was completely fallacious. The League, Drummond maintained, was growing stronger each month and could well continue to increase in strength whether Germany was or was not a League member. This did not mean that he was not very keen to see her join. Her membership was the best, 'if not indeed the only method of securing *general* European peace and associating Germany once again in world activities'. He doubted, however, whether the League ought to pay the very high price which Germany now requested.

Drummond held that it was more in Germany's interest than in the League's that she join the organization. In the end Berlin would be forced to enter if it wished again to take its proper place in European affairs. Germany's theory was that if she could secure one concession, she could secure many more. If this was so, there was a point when this had to be checked, and Stresemann had to keep in mind that there were those who would be pleased to see Germany outside the League. These people had been willing, or had been forced, to make concessions so that Berlin would be treated on the same basis as the other Great Powers. However, they would not be unhappy if, because of her demands over Article 16, Germany's application for admission failed. There was time before the next Assembly session and discussions at the March Council session would give a clearer picture of the whole situation.[1] Drummond's comments appear to have had

---

[1] [Drummond] (Geneva) to [D'Abernon], 5 Mar. 1925, Add. MS. 51110, Robert Cecil Papers, BL.

some impact for Lord D'Abernon subsequently warned a surprised Stresemann 'that the view prevailing at Geneva and in western capitals' was that though Germany previously had asked for equality, it now demanded a privileged position in the League—something akin to a 'specially reduced subscription on entering a club'.[1]

The German question, catalysed by the note of 12 December, was coming to a head and Drummond knew it. He relayed to Hymans his misgivings about Germany's wish to enter the League, but pointed out that it was highly desirable that she accept the Covenant since she would then be bound by Article 10 which guaranteed the political independence and territorial integrity of League members. This was, of course, an important consideration for a small state contiguous to Germany, such as Belgium. On the question of security, Drummond explained to Hymans that since London's attitude was fixed it was useless to seek its adhesion to a tripartite pact. If a British guarantee was wanted it was necessary to adhere to the five-power pact suggested by Germany on 9 February—the origins of the Locarno agreements. Such a pact had advantages for Poland and did not involve the abandonment of the French–Polish alliance. If a failure was registered on this occasion Drummond warned that no further opportunities would be offered.[2]

These comments show that Drummond was aware that London had decided to reject the Geneva Protocol, a decision soon communicated by Chamberlain to the Council. In explaining London's reasons for rejecting the protocol Chamberlain observed that the best means for achieving security and disarmament was to supplement the Covenant 'by making special arrangements in order to meet special needs'. Defensive in character and framed in the Covenant's spirit they could be best attained by tying together through treaties the nations immediately concerned whose disagreements might lead to renewed conflict.[3]

The first step in this process was the Council's reply to the note of 12 December. Initially, the desire had been to send a provisional reply. If pressed by Berlin the questions raised in the

---

[1] D'Abernon, iii. 147.

[2] *DDB 1920–1940*, ii. 130.

[3] League of Nations, *Official Journal*, VI (1925), pp. 446–50.

note were to be 'authoritatively answered only' by the Assembly. The Secretariat, however, surely influenced by Drummond if one keeps in mind his prior remarks, urged that if a reply was postponed until the Assembly convened the Germans might be offended. Also the Assembly itself might be unable to come to a final vote on Germany's admission.[1] Eager to close the whole question the Council accordingly replied on 14 March to the note of 12 December. Its reply was friendly in tone and pointed out that though the Covenant involved 'equal rights and equal obligations', under Article 16 the Council could only recommend the use of armed forces and it would be for Germany to decide to what extent she was in a position to comply with this recommendation. As to economic sanctions the League members themselves decided what steps were to be taken, and by her Assembly and Council membership Germany would of course have a voice in deciding the application of Article 16.[2]

To his Secretariat colleagues Drummond optimistically noted that the effect of the British rejection of the Geneva Protocol would probably be lessened by the fact that the Council's reply to the note of 12 December amounted to a reaffirmation of the importance of the obligations under Article 16. Since this reply to the Germans had been agreed to and approved by Chamberlain it might, in a way, be considered as more important than the British declaration rejecting the Geneva Protocol.[3] Drummond appeared pleased by the Council's ability to mesh the obligations of Article 16 with Germany's desire to avoid these very obligations. He believed that the Council's reply could not have been any better, and its friendly tone, he informed Lord D'Abernon, should help remove Germany's fears about her possible isolation if she lost Russia's support. If a formal German request could now be secured asking for admission, the whole issue could be considered virtually settled since there was no doubt that a unanimous Assembly vote in favour of Germany's admission would follow. Such a request would make the present security negotiations far easier. However, he pointed out that the problem had become one which could not, at least for the time

[1] Walters, p. 281.
[2] League of Nations, *Official Journal*, VI (1925), pp. 490–1.
[3] Minutes of a Directors' Meeting, 18 Mar. 1925, LNA.

being, be treated at Geneva. It had to be dealt with by negotiations among the principal European capitals concerned.[1]

As the exchanges leading to the Locarno agreement continued through the autumn of 1925 Drummond attempted to make sure that volatile European questions like Danzig[2] and Memel[3] did not flare up and upset the unfolding negotiations. When asked by Cecil in April for suggestions on Germany's admission Drummond sent him copies of his correspondence with Lord D'Abernon. He thought that he had nothing further to add, except that it was not really possible to let other questions simmer until Germany entered the League. Everyone shared the view, he noted, that Germany's admission was inextricably tied up with proposals for a security pact in which Germany would participate, and which would include the evacuation of the Cologne zone and the right of investigation into the Rhine's demilitarized zone. Drummond doubted that there was any chance of Germany's admission unless it formed 'part of a general settlement of all these matters'. He had never been sure of the reasons that had led Germany to propose her Rhineland security pact, and was somewhat suspicious that it had been done in order to keep Russia's friendship by making no commitments regarding Germany's eastern frontiers, and by avoiding an unconditional entrance into the League. Russia rightly felt that Germany's unconditional entrance would cause a fundamental reorientation in her foreign policy. It was for this very reason that Drummond hoped that Germany's admission would be made one of the proposed pact's cardinal points. Of course, prospects would be much brighter if Field Marshal Paul von Hindenburg lost the presidency of the Weimar Republic in the coming election. He also thought that Stresemann was a first-class opportunist. Though apprehensive Drummond concluded that for the moment there was really nothing to be done, except to see how things developed in Germany and also in France.[4]

[1] [Drummond] (Geneva) to [D'Abernon], 27 Mar. 1925, Add. MS. 51110, Robert Cecil Papers, BL.
[2] E[ric] D[rummond], Record of Interview, 24 Apr. 1925, Disarmament 1924: 8/39570/39570, LNA.
[3] E[ric] D[rummond], Record of Conversation, 5 Oct. 1925, Political 1925: 11/46918/15971, LNA.
[4] Drummond (Geneva) to Cecil, 16 Apr. 1925, Add. MS. 51110, Robert Cecil Papers, BL.

While Drummond watched and waited in the wings he gave some thought to the distribution of the Council's permanent seats which Germany's admission would obviously effect. One possibility he envisaged, he told Cadogan in May, was to give the Latin American 'ABC' powers (Argentina, Brazil, and Chile) a permanent seat between them on the Council. The Latin Americans contended that because of their wealth and population these states were entitled to such a seat. He admitted that as regards the League such a move would help things generally in Latin America. A counter-argument was that the Council's permanent seats had only been given to great powers on the ground that they were interested in everything that occurred in the world and that the admission of this group would lead to demands for similar treatment from other groups like the Little Entente—Czechoslovakia, Rumania, and Yugoslavia—and the Scandanavian states. On the whole Drummond thought that the arguments against the scheme were stronger. If this were so the situation might be handled by some sort of Council declaration that one of the ABC powers 'could always be elected as a nonpermanent' member.

Chamberlain rejected the proposal. He pointed out that, privately, Drummond had admitted that for the present the re-election of the Council's non-permanent members was desirable. If Germany was admitted to the League it would help smooth things along if the other Council members were unchanged. Chamberlain thought there was 'much force in this'.[1]

Since the negotiations with Germany were still continuing in June Drummond made arrangements with Beneš that the coming Assembly session would avoid dealing with matters of security and arbitration.[2] With this potential problem solved Drummond reverted to the question of the Council's permanent membership. He warned Chamberlain, following a conversation with Quiñones de León, that, although Spain would not oppose Germany's admission, Germany's acquisition of a permanent Council seat would cause Madrid likewise to demand a permanent seat. If this was not given or if she was elected as a non-permanent member

---

[1] Drummond (London) to Cadogan, 14 May 1925 and the attached minute by A[usten] C[hamberlain], 26 May [1925], FO/371/11070.

[2] E[ric] D[rummond], Record of Conversation, 12 June 1925, Austen Chamberlain Papers, FO/800/258.

Quiñones de León had instructions to withdraw from both the Council and the Assembly. Drummond feared that this action would harm the League because of Spain's unusual position, particularly her relationship with the Latin Americans. Faced with such a possibility Drummond drew back from his previously stated belief that a Spanish claim to a permanent seat was ill-founded. Spain was a special case, he argued, and it might be possible to give her a permanent seat without creating embarrassing precedents since she had never been considered either a great power or a small power. He had to admit, however, that it was odious to yield to anything that in any way appeared to be blackmail.

As to the question of the ABC powers Drummond now offered Chamberlain a slightly altered version of his previous scheme. He thought it might be possible to introduce an Assembly recommendation that it was desirable that two Council seats 'should always be held by Latin America, and of these one should be held in rotation by the ABC countries'. He admitted that the recommendation would not be binding but it would, he believed, be well received in Latin America. Aside from the possible opposition of the ABC powers to Spain's desire for a permanent seat, Drummond presumed that the only other possible opposition could come from Belgium and possibly Poland. These states, however, had never belonged to the Great Powers. Drummond hoped that when he came to London Chamberlain would allow him to discuss the question with him.[1] In view of the subsequent difficulties that developed, Chamberlain would have been well advised to take heed of Drummond's comments and advice.

During the following months Drummond appears to have made no further probes, clearly waiting to see how the negotiations would develop. He was too much of a realist to believe that his involvement in a political discussion of so high an international order would have been anything less than impolitic. On 13 October Drummond must have known that the negotiations would be successful when Chamberlain from Locarno asked him for information on the quickest procedure

---

[1] Drummond (Paris) to Chamberlain, 27 June 1925, AC52/331, Austen Chamberlain Papers, UB.

that could be followed if Germany in the near future applied for admission to the League.[1]

In his reply Drummond went into considerable detail on the administrative and procedural questions that Chamberlain had raised. He emphasized that a permanent Council seat for Germany would almost inevitably raise the question of seats for Spain and Brazil and probably also for Poland. If France and Great Britain agreed Spain and Germany could simultaneously be given permanent seats which would raise no difficulties although France would be bound to press the Polish claim. He reiterated, however, that Spain had always been considered a special case.[2]

On 16 October, two days after Drummond's reply, the Locarno agreements were signed and a new Europe appeared in the offing. Sitting in Geneva Drummond could only have been pleased with how things had developed. If he could have foreseen the difficulties that still lay ahead before Germany was admitted, largely because his warnings and advice had been disregarded, he would only have shuddered. The first hurdle presented itself within days when Greek troops following a border skirmish advanced deep into Bulgaria. The possibility that another Balkan crisis might develop, as in the summer of 1914, and undermine the achievements at Locarno by dividing the Great Powers caused them—including Germany—to co-operate and to co-ordinate their pressures on both sides but especially on the Greeks through the League. Their first requirement was a cease-fire and an immediate return to the *status quo ante*. In this the Great Powers were assisted in every possible way by Drummond. Fortuitously, his aim and those of the powers to maintain undisturbed the Locarno agreements converged. Indeed, even before the powers consulted and before the Bulgarian appeal reached Geneva, Drummond through various members of the Secretariat conveyed his apprehensions to the Greek chargé d'affaires in Bern about what was occurring on the frontier.

When this proved ineffective Drummond took the initiative and asked that Chamberlain himself attend the Council meeting called to handle the crisis because of the question's great

[1] Chamberlain (Locarno) to H.M. Consul in Geneva for Sir Eric Drummond, 13 Oct. 1925, FO/371/11071.
[2] Drummond (Geneva) to Chamberlain, 14 Oct. 1925, ibid.

importance from the League's point of view. The Greek invasion was a serious challenge to the League, he argued, and the organization's members would watch with the greatest interest whether the League's machinery could function adequately and with dispatch. Chamberlain's presence would add immensely to the value of any Council decision, and would have a profound impact on the Balkan situation in general. As Drummond desired, Chamberlain attended the Council's meetings, but the decision to do so had been made before Drummond's message arrived. When the Council considered in a secret session the possible application of Article 16 against Greece, Drummond was present and contributed to the discussion.[1] Though the possibility of invoking Article 16 against Greece was seriously considered, this proved unnecessary for the Greeks withdrew from Bulgaria. The League's peaceful solution of this incident was one of its most notable political successes during the inter-war period, but this was due to a unique combination of factors which were not repeated in the years that followed.

A Permanent Council Seat

Further negotiations among the Locarno powers and internal German political considerations despite Drummond's prodding of Berlin,[2] delayed until February 1926 the formal request for admission to the League.[3] On 3 February, before Germany's request was made, Drummond returned to the question of the distribution of the Council's permanent seats. Everyone appeared to agree, he noted to Chamberlain, that Spain should be given a permanent seat—an allusion clearly to the Cabinet's decision of November 1925 to support Madrid's candidature. However, there were the immediate problems of Poland and Brazil. As to Poland, if it was in everyone's interest that she should be given a permanent seat, it seemed to him that this should be done simultaneously with the offer of a permanent seat to Germany.

He noted that Poland's geographical location appeared to make her presence in the Council desirable for years to come.

---

[1] James Barros, *The League of Nations and the Great Powers: The Greek-Bulgarian Incident, 1925* (Oxford: Clarendon Press, 1970), pp. 24–6, 43–4, 78–9.

[2] *ADAP 1918–1945*, ser. B, i. Pt. I, p. 174.

[3] Walters, p. 316.

Initially, he had thought that a three-year seat for Poland as a replacement for Spain would be sufficient, but it was very unlikely that the settlement of all outstanding questions between Poland and Germany would occur within that period. He did not feel that it would be right for Berlin to use this restricted membership—which he feared would be done if Poland was merely a non-permanent member—against Warsaw since it would place Poland in three years' time in a less advantageous position *vis-à-vis* Germany. There was also the Assembly's insistence on the rotation of the Council's non-permanent seats. Drummond felt that if the Assembly would reject this principle, which he believed it would not, Poland might be re-elected for another three-year period. If this could be done the case for a permanent Polish seat would disappear. Of course, the Covenant provided that a state affected by the Council's consideration of a question became a Council member during discussion of the question. Theoretically, this provision protected Poland even after her non-permanent seat had to be relinquished. In practice it was not and could not be quite the same thing.

Doubtlessly, a great and even dangerous outcry would be heard in Germany that Poland had been given a permanent seat in an attempt to neutralize her influence in the Council. The answer to this was that since unanimity was required for Council decisions, Germany's influence could in no way be diminished. Drummond feared, however, that Poland's election to a permanent seat would not be favourably received in many British circles and in the Dominions, and even perhaps in the United States.

The advantages and disadvantages were neatly balanced, but all things considered Drummond was inclined to share Chamberlain's view that Poland should be elected to a permanent seat provided that the necessary Council unanimity could be secured for such a recommendation to the next Assembly—a major qualification. Then Drummond's warning: Brazil might make a favourable Council vote conditional on her acquisition of a permanent seat, and Sweden, acting on her own initiative or under German influence, might refuse the plan for a permanent Polish seat. A failure would have very unhappy results, for the odium attached to the proposal would have to be incurred while no corresponding advantages would be secured. Drummond concluded that the wisdom of initiating the proposal depended on whether or not it would be accepted by the Council and the Assembly. He wondered if the French—who were Poland's main supporter for a permanent seat—were in a position to ascertain this, and to shape their policy accordingly. Clearly, this was a hint that pressing Poland's claim was less than wise. If Drummond was opposed to a permanent Polish seat, Anglo-French support of Warsaw had made him too cautious to express it openly.

The same did not apply to Brazil's claim for a permanent seat which was not supported by anyone. If she acquired a permanent seat this would greatly offend Argentina and Chile, both of whom felt strongly that they be treated equally; nor would it be especially popular among other Latin American states who desired that three Council seats be available to them one of which would always be filled from among the ABC powers. Drummond thought this was about the most Brazil could expect although her representative was more optimistic than Rio de Janeiro. Since the Council had recently appointed a Brazilian to a high Secretariat post this in itself would give Brazil considerable satisfaction. It would be a mistake in regard to other Latin American states to allow Brazil to monopolize the League's good things.

Drummond suggested that the Council's four permanent seats be increased to seven by the inclusion of Germany, Poland, and Spain. In addition, one non-permanent seat should be created making seven in all, three of which would be reserved for Latin America, one for Asia, and three for Europe. This would allow for the representation of the Little Entente, Scandinavia, Holland, and Switzerland, as well as one other state outside these groups.

If and when Soviet Russia and the United States joined the League the permanent seats would be increased to nine. At that time an increase in the non-permanent seats might be considered. Though Council membership would be sixteen or seventeen Drummond saw no objection to this since once one had twelve members, whether one had fifteen, sixteen, or seventeen was not very important. He admitted that work would have to be done through Council committees, but this was already becoming the practice. The main argument against an increase in the Council's membership would be that its strength would render the

Assembly less important, an argument he dismissed as invalid since in any case one would have to envisage a Council of not less than fifteen.[1]

From Drummond's comments it was obvious that he was warning of the difficulties that lay ahead if the Polish candidature was pressed. The trade-off, however, was Chamberlain's support of Spain's candidature, first broached by Drummond in June 1925, provided that at the very least Drummond would raise no difficulties about Poland's candidature. This candidature had been forced on Chamberlain by the French who surrendered to the anti-German forces of the Right, as well as to Polish pressures apprehensive over the fact that the Locarno agreements guaranteed only the sanctity of the Franco–Belgian–German frontiers. When opposition to Poland's candidature was voiced by Cecil, Chamberlain attempted to convince him by conveying Drummond's letter, a move which proved unsuccessful.[2]

Though permanent seats for Poland and Spain complicated Germany's admission, Drummond raised no difficulties to the Polish candidature. Perhaps he correctly perceived that the Germans themselves would raise objections to this candidature and would only grudgingly accept the Spanish one since there were no outstanding political problems between Berlin and Madrid. Nevertheless, Drummond as before cautioned Chamberlain of the obstacles that existed to the Polish candidature. On 12 February and on the following day he relayed to him the record of his conversations with the Council's Swedish and Belgian representatives which showed that both countries were opposed to any permanent seat being given to any state other than Germany.[3] As non-permanent members a negative vote by either of these states would thwart the giving of permanent seats to Poland and Spain.

Several days after these conversations Drummond journeyed

---

[1] Drummond (Geneva) to Chamberlain, 3 Feb. 1926, AC53/243, Austen Chamberlain Papers, UB.

[2] David Carlton, 'Great Britain and the League Council Crisis of 1926', *The Historical Journal*, XI, No. 2 (1968), pp. 355–6; Walters, pp. 317–18.

[3] Drummond (Geneva) to Chamberlain, 12 Feb. 1926, E[ric] D[rummond], Record of Interview, 12 Feb. 1926, Drummond (Geneva) to Chamberlain, 13 Feb. 1926, [Eric Drummond], Record of Conversation, 13 Feb. 1926, AC53/246–8, Austen Chamberlain Papers, UB.

to Berlin, a mission arranged through Lord D'Abernon,[1] to gauge the German situation and to explain the steps being taken in view of the Council's decision to meet on 8 March to deal with Germany's admission to the League. He first interviewed Schubert who complained about any attempt to increase the Council's permanent membership, and Poland's candidature in particular. Drummond replied that he appreciated this feeling and, undoubtedly to assuage Schubert, noted as accurate the report that Sweden, except for Germany, would oppose any increase in the Council's permanent members. He pointed out, however, that no one could be prevented from proposing another League member to a permanent Council seat. The proposal's acceptance naturally depended on the position assumed by the different Council members. Drummond held this required a unanimous Council recommendation to the Assembly. He feigned no knowledge of London's attitude regarding this question. His own personal view was that Spain had the best chance of being elected as a permanent member.

The next matter they tackled was German representation on the Secretariat. Drummond was willing to accept a list of names offered by Schubert and consider them for possible appointment though he noted that he could not pledge himself regarding any particular persons. He wanted it to be understood that in appointing Germans to the Secretariat he wanted to be as helpful as possible—a point he had made to Cecil months before. On the other hand, there were limits beyond which he could not go; for example, he could not ask the Assembly to create posts which could not be justified administratively. Drummond agreed, however, despite a prior Assembly decision to reduce the number of Under Secretaries-General, to ask the Assembly to increase the present number by one. He envisaged that the earliest that a German Under Secretary-General could be appointed was in early 1927. In the interim he thought he could get Assembly approval for the appointment to responsible Secretariat posts of six Germans. Drummond noted the difficulties that he faced since long-time members thought they were underrepresented in the Secretariat. He reiterated that he was moved by the best of intentions and that he had gone as far as he could in making

---

[1] *ADAP 1918–1945*, ser. B, i. Pt. I, pp. 17, 228.

proposals which he thought had any chance of being accepted by the Assembly.[1]

Drummond continued his talks with Stresemann and affirmed that the Secretariat wanted Germany's admission to be as quick and as simple as possible, but correctly pointed out that certain matters were beyond its competence. As to the question of permanent Council seats Drummond responded that he did not think that London was committed to Poland's claim. Nor did he think it wise that Stresemann formally declare in the Reichstag that Berlin would consider that it had been disloyally treated if at the coming Council meeting further permanent seats were created in addition to the one created for Germany. Such a statement might have the reverse effect to that anticipated since it would be said that Germany was attempting to dictate to the League even before she was a member of the organization. On the question of Secretariat appointments Drummond explained that he never formally consulted European governments about them though naturally he would make sure that if a German Under Secretary-General was appointed he would be acceptable to Berlin. He thought that Stresemann might rely on him to make satisfactory arrangements.[2] Drummond, Lord D'Abernon informed Chamberlain, considered that his two conversations had been 'quite satisfactory'.[3]

The next day, 16 February, the conversations continued. This talk between Drummond, Schubert, and Bülow largely dealt with appointments to the Secretariat. Pressed for an early appointment of a German Under Secretary-General, Drummond bent to the pressure and promised to explain to the Assembly that the new post would be filled by a German and, because of the 'exceptional circumstances', to ask the Assembly that the

[1] E[ric] D[rummond], Record of Conversation between Sir E. Drummond and Herr von Schubert, 15 Feb. 1926, FO/371/11263. For Schubert's version of this conversation with Drummond see Microfilm of the German Foreign Ministry Archives, 4586/E179806–807, NA. Minor Secretariat posts would not satisfy the Germans, Drummond had noted to Cecil in November 1925. 'Surely it is much wiser to give them a post right inside [the Secretariat] so as to secure their collaboration and satisfy, as far as may be possible, their exigencies'. Drummond to Cecil, 28 Nov. 1925, Add. MS. 51110, Robert Cecil Papers, BL.

[2] E[ric] D[rummond], Record of Conversation between Sir E. Drummond and Herr Stresemann, 15 Feb. 1926, FO/371/11263.

[3] *DBFP, 1919–1939*, IA, i. 435.

appointment might be made as quickly as possible thus allowing the new Under Secretary-General to acquire some experience of the Secretariat's workings.

It was at this point that Drummond offered his formula by which German candidates would be appointed to the Secretariat. They were to be told that all appointments were primarily a matter for the Secretary-General and referred to Drummond. Privately, Stresemann was to give Drummond a list of candidates who had special qualifications. In the case of applications already received by Drummond, Stresemann should forward a list of names drawing his attention to any person that seemed particularly suitable. Regarding the Under Secretary-Generalship, no appointment would be made without previous consultations and an agreement between Drummond and Berlin as to the best candidate. Until the Under Secretary-General was appointed Drummond would let Stresemann know privately the names of the Germans he proposed to appoint to the Secretariat so that Stresemann might have the opportunity to object to any particular candidate should he desire to do so. If any objection was raised, Stresemann would inform Drummond of the reasons and they would discuss the matter before any further action was taken.

They then examined the various Secretariat Sections (Political, Social and Opium, Press and Information, Legal, Economic and Financial, Health, and Transit) to which Drummond thought German appointments might be possible. When asked if it was possible to have Germans in the Minorities and Mandates Sections, Drummond demurred. He pointed out that the former section was composed of persons whose countries had no special interest in minority questions, and the appointment of a German, Drummond argued, would almost immediately destroy confidence in the section's impartiality. As for the Mandates Section he thought that the time was not opportune for appointing a German to it. To these comments no objections were raised.[1]

Later that same day Drummond had a talk with Chancellor Hans Luther. More or less the same ground was covered in this conversation as in the others, and Luther's comment that

---

[1] E[ric] D[rummond], Note by Sir E. Drummond recording a conversation with Herr von Schubert and Herr von Buelow, 16 Feb. 1926, FO/371/11263.

Drummond's visit had been of 'considerable value and help'[1] indicated his satisfaction with the way the discussion had gone. The attitude expressed in the Foreign Office when the record of these conversations reached London was not far different from that expressed by Luther.[2]

Before departing for Geneva Drummond had a final interview with Stresemann on the morning of 17 February. The gist of this talk was that Germany would withdraw her application for admission if France pressed Poland's candidature. When Drummond reiterated Sweden's opposition to any increase in permanent seats, Stresemann, who was visibly moved, responded that he feared that if this was so Stockholm would be pressured to give way, and he could not rely on its opposition.

Stresemann then disclosed that he accepted Drummond's procedure regarding appointments to the Secretariat, and raised the possibility of an appointment to the Mandates Commission. Drummond explained that commission members did not represent their governments but were selected because of their personal knowledge regarding colonial questions. He advised Stresemann not to raise the matter too soon. Stresemann's final words expressed his pleasure over Drummond's visit which he thought 'had been most useful in establishing closer collaboration between the German Government and the secretariat, and he hoped that that collaboration might have fruitful results in the future'.[3] Lord D'Abernon was also pleased by Drummond's visit. 'Everything appears to have passed off well', he wrote in his diary, 'for Drummond is a man who raises no unnecessary difficulties'.[4] Drummond likewise was pleased. The visit exceeded his expectations, he informed Sweetser, and he thought that the Germans once they became League members were 'determined to do their level best to collaborate fully with us'[5]—an observation he repeated to his Secretariat colleagues some days later.[6]

[1] E[ric] D[rummond], Record of Conversation between Sir E. Drummond and Dr. Luther, 16 Feb. 1926, ibid. See also, *DBFP, 1919–1939*, IA, i. 438.

[2] *DBFP, 1919–1939*, IA, i. 438–9 fn.

[3] E[ric] D[rummond], Record of Interview, 17 Feb. 1926, FO/371/11263. See also, *DBFP, 1919–1939*, IA, i. 449.

[4] D'Abernon, iii. 224. Also [D'Abernon] to Chamberlain, 17 Feb. 1926, Add. MS. 48929, Edgar Vincent D'Abernon Papers, BL.

[5] Drummond (Geneva) to Sweetser, 20 Feb. 1926, Box 31, Arthur Sweetser Papers, LC.

[6] Minutes of a Directors' Meeting, 3 Mar. 1926, LNA.

By his visit Drummond had helped remove whatever apprehensions Berlin may have had about his personal attitude toward Germany's admission as well as toward the important question of Secretariat appointments. Spain's decision, however, that she might be relied upon not to oppose Germany's admission as a permanent member, though she would not agree to becoming a permanent member after Germany had already been admitted, complicated the situation that Drummond faced. In no way could Spain's acquisition of a permanent seat, Quiñones de León explained, be dependent on Germany's vote, even if it was certain that this vote would be favourable to Spain's candidature. Indeed, if refused a permanent seat Spain would withdraw from the Council. Drummond observed that the Spanish threat to leave the League might have a very regrettable effect.[1] As requested by Quiñones de León Drummond quickly brought this new Spanish tack to Chamberlain's attention.[2]

The new turn of events that had developed made Drummond apprehensive, but he still thought things might right themselves. He believed that the whole affair had been 'abominably handled'[3]—a not unfair comment considering that all his prior warnings had gone unheeded. To avoid the impasse that had developed, Drummond proposed to Chamberlain that two Council proposals be simultaneously presented to the Special Assembly which had convened: one, that Germany be admitted as a permanent member, and two, that Spain be admitted as a permanent member on 1 January 1927, that is from the date when Spain's present term as a non-permanent member expired. The last proposal would be the creation of a new non-permanent seat as of 1 January 1927.

Germany would thus receive the satisfaction of being the only permanent member admitted in the March Council session. Spain would get satisfaction because she would become a permanent member when her present non-permanent seat expired and thus would sit continuously on the Council. Drummond did not believe that Spain would reject such a proposal. Poland which would suffer most by this scheme would feel her chances of election to a non-permanent seat would be

---

[1] E[ric] D[rummond], Record of Interview, 21 Feb. 1926, FO/371/11264.

[2] Drummond to Chamberlain, 23 Feb. 1926, ibid.

[3] Drummond (Geneva) to Sweetser, 3 Mar. 1926, Box 31, Arthur Sweetser Papers, LC.

more or less secure if Spain vacated her non-permanent seat in January 1927 and an additional non-permanent seat were created. The Latin Americans (and China) would also be satisfied by the notion of an additional non-permanent seat which would give them added opportunity of being elected to the Council. Sweden might likewise be persuaded to accept such a scheme since it did not involve any alteration of the Council beyond Germany's admission at the Council meeting scheduled to convene in a few days. Drummond had no idea whether anyone concerned was ready to accept such a scheme, but as Chamberlain would soon be discussing the question with those concerned he wanted to present the proposal.[1]

During this period Drummond 'appeared worried' and admitted that the 'situation was very grave'.[2] Unfortunately, it is difficult to gauge the full impact of Drummond's communication to Chamberlain. It more or less dovetailed with the Cabinet instructions issued to Chamberlain. It is undoubtedly these instructions which explain why Chamberlain during the negotiations among the Locarno powers at Geneva pressed for a permanent seat for Spain and a non-permanent seat for Poland.[3] As the negotiations unfolded Drummond conveyed to Chamberlain whatever information he received throwing light on Spain's position.[4] Likewise he informed Chamberlain of Beneš's proposed solution to Germany's objections over establishing a new non-permanent seat for Poland. Germany would accept Sweden's offer to vacate her own non-permanent seat in Poland's behalf provided that another non-permanent seat was vacated to which a neutral state like Sweden would be appointed. Beneš's scheme was that Czechoslovakia, like Sweden, would resign her non-permanent seat provided this was not objected to by the other members of the Little Entente.[5] Though this compromise was finally arranged, Poland and Holland replacing Sweden and

---

[1] Drummond (Geneva) to Chamberlain, 4 Mar. 1926, AC53/250, Austen Chamberlain Papers, UB.

[2] Riddell (Geneva) to Skelton, 5 Mar. 1926, File 65C, Box 265281, Department of External Affairs, PACRMB.

[3] *DBFP, 1919–1939*, IA, i. 498–500 and fn.

[4] Drummond to Chamberlain, 6 Mar. 1926, AC53/252, Austen Chamberlain Papers, UB.

[5] Drummond to Chamberlain, 13 Mar. 1926, AC53/251, ibid. See also, Carlton, 'Great Britain and the League Council Crisis of 1926', p. 360.

Czechoslovakia, Spanish and Brazilian objections soon made any definitive settlement of the question of Germany's admission impossible. Madrid maintained that if Spain was denied a permanent seat she would withdraw from the League though she would in no way obstruct Germany's acquisition of a permanent seat. Brazil declared that she would veto any permanent seat for Germany unless she received one at the same time.[1] Resilient as always, Drummond proposed that Germany and Poland should be appointed to the non-permanent seats vacated by Sweden and Czechoslovakia. This would make it possible for Germany to become a Council member immediately. Germany could then acquire a permanent seat in September at which point he presumed Brazil would be removed as a non-permanent Council member.[2] This proposal, however, got nowhere. Faced with certain failure in view of the Brazilian veto it was decided to postpone until September any action on the German application. Moreover, the Council decided to establish a committee to study the entire question of membership and the method of their election.[3]

Cecil proffered the Canadian proposal that 'something like semi-permanent seats might be created' by the committee. Under this arrangement the holders of these seats could be re-elected once their term had expired. Drummond felt it important that, excluding the Council's permanent members, the Assembly should have the right to terminate, either by a two-thirds or a three-quarters majority, any of the Council's non-permanent seats, including those of a semi-permanent character. He agreed with Cecil that the Council's permanent membership should only be increased by Germany's admission and that three semi-permanent seats should be created to be held from three to five years with re-election possible once the mandate expired.

Where he disagreed with Cecil was that these semi-permanent seats should be justified on the grounds that there existed a category of powers who were between the great and small powers. Drummond felt that such a distinction was dangerous. It created a new category of powers and, in addition, it might

[1] Walters, p. 320.
[2] Drummond (Geneva) to Cecil, 15 Mar. 1926, Add. MS. 51111, Robert Cecil Papers, BL.
[3] Walters, p. 321.

mean that those powers initially selected would for all practical purposes be chosen forever. At any rate Drummond recommended that Spain and Poland be assigned to these semi-permanent seats. As to the third semi-permanent seat Drummond favoured giving it to China. His information was that her re-election to the Council would produce a good impression in China and be of considerable assistance against the Chinese communists. Furthermore, the day would certainly come when the League would be called upon to deal more so than before with Asian questions, and China's presence in the Council would be advantageous. Though it was in a chaotic state China was so vast a country and her co-operation with Geneva of such importance that he felt it would be wise to maintain the Middle Kingdom within the organization's orbit.

Drummond also accepted Cecil's proposal to leave unaltered the Council's six non-permanent seats. He believed, however, that Cecil would have to recommend that three of these seats be given to Latin America in order to gain its support since it comprised a third of the League's membership. He supposed that the rest would be given to the Scandinavian–Dutch group, one to the Little Entente, and one somewhere else. As to the Latin American seats, he considered that Cecil should attempt to arrange that the Latin Americans themselves make recommendations involving their distribution, though things would be easier if they acquiesced to a permanent seat for the ABC powers.

Concerning the possibility raised by Cecil of group representation in the Council, Drummond divulged that he was frightened of extending the system. Had it not a special danger, he queried, namely, that when an important question arose the representative sitting for the group would say that he must consult the group's individual members. True, the system with Beneš and the Little Entente had worked fairly well, but even Beneš sometimes found himself in difficulties by the very fact that he was their Council spokesman.[1]

---

[1] *DCER*, iv. 603–7; Drummond (Geneva) to Murray, 29 Mar. 1926, Gilbert Murray Papers, BLOU; Drummond (Geneva) to Cecil, 24 Apr. 1926, and two letters Drummond (Geneva) to Cecil, 4 May 1926, Add. MS. 51111, Robert Cecil Papers, BL; also [Eric Drummond], Record of Interview, 30 Apr. 1926, Add. MS. 51098, Robert Cecil Papers, BL. In a discussion with the Yugoslav Foreign Minister, Momcilo Ninčić, Drummond pointed out that there were

To facilitate Cecil's task on the committee and to make sure that the compromise offered would be accepted by Spain Drummond contacted Chamberlain. He pointed out that Comert had the impression following a talk with Quiñones de León that Spain's withdrawal from the League might be prevented by a direct appeal either to King Alfonso or to his Prime Minister, Primo de Rivera.

It seemed probable, Drummond noted to Chamberlain, that such a British appeal might be more likely to succeed than any other appeal since it might flatter Spanish pride which underlay the present difficulty. He did not know how this suggestion dovetailed with present policy that Cecil should come to the committee with no prior commitments. Drummond thought, however, that an appeal to Spain to collaborate with Cecil on the committee in order to discover a way out of the present impasse hardly seemed objectionable.[1] Though Chamberlain and Cecil saw no objection in making this appeal[2] it was not made until after the committee had met in May and the three new semi-permanent seats were proposed, one of which was obviously earmarked for Spain. The appeal, however, proved unsuccessful and Spain gave notice in September that she would withdraw from the League.[3]

The discussions in the Committee on the Composition of the Council produced a plan that largely followed the ideas developed between Cecil and Drummond: the Council's membership would be increased from ten to fourteen; Germany would be a permanent member; non-permanent members were to be increased from six to nine. These three new seats were to have a three-year mandate; a non-permanent member was in principle not immediately eligible for re-election once the mandate had expired. This rule, however, might be waived by

two more objections to group representation in the Council. First, it was very difficult to pinpoint such groupings. The second objection was that a system of group representation would remove all the control that the Assembly had in selecting the Council's non-permanent members. E[ric] D[rummond], An untitled memorandum, 24 May 1926, Drummond Folder, LNA.

[1] Drummond (Geneva) to Chamberlain, 24 Apr. 1926, FO/371/11894.

[2] Minute by A[usten] C[hamberlain] to Cecil, 26 Apr. [1926] and a minute by R[obert] C[ecil], ibid.

[3] *DBFP, 1919–1939*, IA, ii. 13–14, 28–9, 55–7, 67–71 and fnn. See also, Walters, pp. 324–5.

a two-thirds vote of the Assembly and no limit was placed on how many times a state might be re-elected to a semi-permanent seat. In practice, of course, a state could expect to retain this semi-permanent seat for an indefinite period. Of the nine non-permanent seats three were reserved for Latin America and their selection was unofficially to be decided at a separate Latin American caucus. The remaining non-permanent seats were reserved for Asia, the Little Entente, the European ex-neutrals, one for the British Dominions and one of the semi-permanent variety for Poland.[1]

Any hopes generated in Drummond after conversations with Julio Barbosa Carneiro, the Brazilian delegation's economic expert, that Brazil might resign from the Council but remain in the League and accept a permanent seat for Germany[2] soon disappeared during the Council's June meeting. His country, the Brazilian representative announced, was immediately resigning from the Council and would soon resign from the League.[3] Drummond feared that this step would make it very difficult to arrange any compromise with Madrid. Spain would feel that Brazil which had prevented her from securing a permanent seat was now no longer an obstacle. Madrid therefore might attempt once more to accomplish its aim. Although, he informed Cecil, he had always wanted a permanent seat for Spain, Drummond felt personally that any such move was now impossible, even if it were practicable which he did not think it was. To give way to Spain would make the League appear very weak and susceptible to threats. The one possibility that Drummond envisaged which might be helpful in keeping Spain in the League was 'for some démarche to be made by the Vatican'.[4] Drummond was clutching

---

[1] Walters, pp. 323–4, 335. Though it was the Assembly that selected the Council's non-permanent members Drummond was often consulted on this question and had no qualms about discussing with London what states might be appointed to the Council and for how long a period of time. See [Eric Drummond], Record of Interview with M. Titulesco, 8 June 1926, FO/371/11896; Drummond (Geneva) to Cecil, 11 Sept. 1926, Add. MS. 51111, Robert Cecil Papers, BL.

[2] [Eric Drummond], Record of Conversation with Barbosa Carneiro, 29 May 1926, Austen Chamberlain Papers, FO/800/259.

[3] Walters, p. 324.

[4] Drummond (Geneva) to Cecil, 14 June 1926, Add. MS. 51111, Robert Cecil Papers, BL.

at straws and he must have known it. When his proposal was forwarded by Cecil to Chamberlain[1] it caused the Foreign Secretary to minute that though he was interested he was also alarmed for Geneva appeared to be less well informed than London. Drummond's 'advice must not be received', he wrote, 'as a Delphic oracle'. Chamberlain did not believe that the Vatican could or would help London in this matter.[2]

During the early summer Drummond continued to be somewhat optimistic about keeping both Brazil and especially Spain in the League.[3] In the case of Spain Drummond proposed to Chamberlain that concessions be made to Madrid, including that her mandate for the semi-permanent seat be good for five years, and stipulating re-eligibility as well as a number of other concessions. Simultaneously, King Alfonso should be pressed on the matter during his forthcoming London visit. Drummond thought that the proposal could be explained on the grounds that because of European and world political considerations it was not possible for London to support Spain's claim to a permanent seat. On the other hand, London was most anxious to treat Spain's case as exceptional which explained its proposal to create specific Council seats with long-term mandates carrying re-eligibility.[4]

Though this proposal also got nowhere Drummond's optimism about keeping Spain in the League did not dissolve until mid-August when Madrid requested a new meeting of the Committee on the Composition of the Council. It astonished Drummond how Spain persisted in the illusion that numerous states when it came to a final vote would not dare oppose her on the question of a permanent seat. He feared, he correctly observed to Cadogan, that Spain would not discuss the formula for a semi-permanent seat unless the Council rejected her request for a permanent seat. Once it was turned down and only then would

[1] Henty to Selby, 16 June 1926, Austen Chamberlain Papers, FO/800/259.
[2] Minute by A[usten] C[hamberlain], 16 June 1926, ibid.
[3] Drummond (Geneva) to Cecil, 24 June 1926, Add. MS. 51111, Robert Cecil Papers, BL; Drummond (Paris) to Chamberlain, 2 July 1926, AC53/255, Austen Chamberlain Papers, UB; Drummond (Paris) to Tyrrell, 2 July 1926, FO/371/11896.
[4] Drummond to Chamberlain, 2 July 1926, AC53/256, Austen Chamberlain Papers, UB.

she consider alternatives. Madrid apparently believed that the committee was more hostile to her than the Council was likely to be and accordingly preferred discussion of her claim in the Council.[1]

Whatever Spain hoped to achieve by this move never materialized. The compromise plan framed by the Committee on the Composition of the Council was quickly accepted by the Assembly, although Holland and the Scandinavian countries had misgivings over the Council's increased membership. Brazil's absence and Spain's acquiescence to the plan finally made it possible on 8 September formally to admit Germany to the League and as a permanent Council member. Since the Council's reorganization did not give Madrid a permanent seat Spain several days later followed Brazil and withdrew from the League.[2] Under Article I paragraph three of the Covenant, however, two years would have to elapse before Spain's and Brazil's withdrawals took effect. During these two years Drummond worked energetically to keep both of them in the League. His endeavours in this direction appear to have commenced as early as November 1926 and continued unabated until Spain decided to rescind her withdrawal notice in March 1928—a decision expedited by the successful French–Spanish negotiations over the question of Tangier.[3]

Germany in the League

Drummond's endeavours to expedite Germany's admission were, as we have seen, a largely peripheral operation since the fundamental political questions involved were far beyond the

[1] Drummond (Geneva) to Cadogan, 17 Aug. 1926, FO/371/11898.

[2] Walters, pp. 325–6.

[3] Drummond (Geneva) to Cadogan, 12 Nov. 1926, and [Eric Drummond], Record of Conversation, 12 Nov. 1926, FO/371/11899; Drummond (Geneva) to Cadogan, 21 June 1927 and the enclosed note, FO/371/12683; E[ric] D[rummond], Record of Interview, 19 Nov. 1927, Austen Chamberlain Papers, FO/800/261; Drummond (Geneva) to [Chamberlain], 14 Jan. 1928, AC55/129, and Drummond (Geneva) to [Chamberlain], 9 Feb. 1928, AC55/135, Austen Chamberlain Papers, UB; [Eric Drummond], Record of Conversation, 12 Feb. 1928, Drummond (Geneva) to Chamberlain, 27 Feb. 1928, E[ric] D[rummond] to Quiñones de León, 27 Feb. 1928, FO/371/13395; *DBFP, 1919–1939*, IA, iv. 191–2, 236–7, 295–6, 302; Walters, pp. 388–9.

effective control or even the influence of the Secretary-General. At the same time, one cannot dismiss as completely ineffective his constant comments, warnings, and advice, which in the case of restructuring the Council's membership, appear to have had some impact, especially on British policy makers. On the other hand, matters that were within Drummond's own control or influence, for example, German Secretariat appointments, were dealt with expeditiously to assure Germany that certainly within the Secretariat everything possible would be done to smooth her entrance into the League.

With Germany now in the League, Drummond showed Berlin the same deference and sensitivity to its interests as he had shown London and Paris. This was no obsequious act on his part, but a recognition that Germany was a world power with vast industrial and human potential, despite her virtual disarmament under the Versailles Treaty. The League's survival and Drummond's ability to influence and accommodate Berlin's actions in the organization depended on the organization's utility to Berlin within the total context of world politics and especially the objectives of German foreign policy. A Secretary-General apathetic or, even worse, unfriendly to the Germans would have quickly destroyed the development of any meaningful relationship between Geneva and Berlin. Drummond's constant problem was to strike a proper balance between recognition of Germany's position in world politics and the support or accommodation of her stance on various issues that came before the League. It was a balancing act that was difficult in the extreme and filled with pitfalls.

As soon as Germany was in the League the question was raised of her representation on various League bodies. Of special interest was representation on the Mandates Commission, first raised by Stresemann during Drummond's February visit to Berlin. The issue, at least from Drummond's side, was not the unwarranted nature of the request, but the suitability of the German that would be proposed. His suitability, he made clear to Berlin, depended on his personality, whether he was of broad and liberal views, had a knowledge of the technical aspects of colonial questions, and would use his appointment for political purposes. Personally, Drummond was partial to the selection of a German on the grounds that it would strengthen Stresemann's position in Germany. His recommendation to the Germans was to broach the question in an informal manner and to press for an appointment when a vacancy arose in the commission. This advice was followed. Since no vacancy developed, the Council in September 1927 increased the commission's membership by one and appointed a former member of the German colonial service as a member of the commission.[1] Less complicated was the recruitment, with Berlin's approval, of Germans into the Secretariat and the appointment of Albert Dufour-Feronce as Under Secretary-General. Like other Secretariat officials the Germans were a conduit between Geneva and their own government and in the case of Dufour-Feronce, who had served as counsellor of the London embassy, it would be safe to say that he considered himself as nothing other than an agent of the Wilhelmstrasse seconded to the Secretariat's upper echelon.[2]

Recruitment was of course a simple problem for Drummond to handle when compared with questions which Germany considered of the highest political importance. This was brought home to Drummond with some force when Schubert complained in June 1928 that the appointment of Poland's Foreign Minister as Rapporteur in the Albanian–Greek question dealing with Albanian property and the Albanian minority in Greece had been received in Germany with very great dismay. According to Schubert his country expected to have greater attention paid to her interests. His protest was an obvious attempt to isolate Poland

[1] Drummond (Geneva) to Cadogan, 9 Nov. 1926, E[ric] D[rummond], An untitled memorandum, 9 Nov. 1926, Drummond (Geneva) to Cadogan, 11 Nov. 1926, E[ric] D[rummond], Record of Conversation, 11 Nov. 1926, FO/371/11877; *ADAP 1919–1945*, ser. B, i. Pt. II, pp. 445–6 and fnn.; Drummond (Berlin) to Tyrrell, 28 Nov. 1926, E[ric] D[rummond], Record of Interview, 28 Nov. 1926, FO/371/11877; Drummond (Berlin) to Selby, 28 Nov. 1926, FO/371/11332; extract of a note from Drummond to Cadogan, 12 Aug. 1927, FO/371/12681.

[2] See a revealing letter from Dufour-Feronce to Bülow, 27 June 1927, Microfilm of the German Foreign Ministry Archives, K2342/K666781–782, NA. Drummond also kept the Germans in mind for appointments to temporary political bodies, witness his suggestion in August 1929, subsequently ignored, that a German be included in the proposed Liberian Slavery Commission. E[ric] D[rummond], Record of Conversation, 26 Aug. 1929, Mandates Slavery 1928–32: 6B/14697/14352, LNA.

within the League system since the Albanian–Greek question was not an issue in which German interests were directly involved. Nevertheless, Drummond did not reject this interference in League affairs. On the contrary, he apologized and promised 'to keep German interests at heart', admitting that he had committed a serious mistake in thinking a Pole was a suitable Rapporteur merely because he was acceptable to Paris and Rome.[1]

This episode made it inevitable that months later Drummond would spring into action when the Canadian representative gave notice that he intended to submit suggestions to reform the Council's procedure for the protection of minorities—the rawest nerve in German–Polish relations. Drummond was cool to the plan since he believed that it would be impossible to convince states with minority treaties to consent to any direct information being given to the petitioner. He thought the only way around this problem in order to avoid jurisdictional disputes between the Council and the Assembly was to publish once or twice a year and circulate to Council members for their information a document listing the petitions received with a concise indication of how each petition was treated. Since this Council document would be public the petitioner would be able to ascertain what had occurred regarding his petition. There was also the added advantage of showing to the general public that the Council's Committee of Three which handled minority petitions took its duties seriously. Likewise it would help to remove the impression that minority petitions were as a rule shelved. Drummond concluded that the procedure actually in use was probably the best that could be devised under the circumstances. He feared that if more was attempted there might be a revolt of states having minority treaties and it had to be remembered that these treaties could be amended or even abolished by a majority vote of the Council. If the Canadian representative confined himself merely to this proposal Drummond thought that there would be no great difficulties, but if he went further afield he feared a situation would develop where Canada would find that Germany was her main supporter and this, he noted, would entail

[1] Harald von Riekhoff, *German–Polish Relations, 1918–1933* (Baltimore: The Johns Hopkins Press, 1971), p. 130.

'awkward consequences'.[1] Discussions with the Polish representative brought home to Drummond the dangers that existed in
this question and the possible German–Polish clash that might
develop.[2] He sought Cadogan's assistance, and warned the
Canadian delegation of the problems that were involved since
the suggested reform was criticized both by the present Director
of the Secretariat's Minorities Section and by his predecessor
whom Drummond had consulted.[3]

Drummond's suggestion for reform turned on the belief that
greater publicity was needed to dissipate the wrong impressions
that had developed in the public's mind about the Council's
handling of minority petitions. He therefore also supported the
line that the Council's Committee of Three confidentially inform
the Council of its decision on each minority petition by
communicating the petition, along with a copy of the letter of
reply which was always sent to the representative of the
concerned state. The Committee of Three should likewise be
enlarged to take into account the increase in the Council's
membership that had occurred. Drummond emphasized that the
practice of securing concessions from the concerned states by
informal and unpublished negotiations should not be undermined. The concerned state also had to be protected from the
propaganda effect produced by the publication of numerous
petitions which, even if accompanied by adequate governmental
replies, undoubtedly contributed to spreading the impression
that the state in question mistreated its minorities. Lastly, he
hoped that any changes finally made in the minorities procedure
would in no way destroy the possibility at an early stage of
unofficial Secretariat action. Drummond pointed out that in
certain serious cases the Secretariat had found it possible,

---

[1] Drummond (Geneva) to Cadogan, 10 Jan. 1928 [*sic*], FO/371/14122;
E[ric] D[rummond] to Vannier [*sic*], 10 Jan. 1929, and E[ric] D[rummond] to
Vannier [*sic*], 4 Feb. 1929, FO/371/14123. See also, Nicolae Titulescu, *Documente
Diplomatice*, ed. George Macovescu (Bucureşti: Editura Politică, 1967), pp. 270,
303–4.
[2] E[ric] D[rummond], Record of Conversation, 6 Feb. 1929, E[ric]
D[rummond], Record of Conversation, 7 Feb. 1929, and E[ric] D[rummond],
Record of Telephone Conversation, 8 Feb. 1929, FO/371/14123.
[3] Drummond to Cadogan, 25 Feb. 1929, Drummond (Geneva) to Cadogan,
26 Feb. 1929, ibid.; Drummond (Geneva) to Cadogan, 16 Apr. 1929,
FO/371/14124.

privately, to draw the governments' attention to the seriousness of the accusation made and that the charges made did not seem without foundation. By doing so the Secretariat had put an end to the abuse or effected a change for the better, even before the Committee of Three was faced with the petition.[1]

At the Council's session of June 1929 almost all of the changes that Drummond proposed and supported were accepted. These changes, as well as those proposed by the Rapporteur, had the effect of giving 'greater publicity to the action of the Committee of Three'—exactly what Drummond had wanted. The Canadian representative declared that he was satisfied and Stresemann thought that the changes made 'were an important improvement' to the minority procedure.[2] For the moment Drummond's work on this issue had averted a serious clash between Germany and Poland, not to mention a wider clash between states bound by the minority treaties and those other states whose fellow kinsmen lived under an alien flag and were entitled to the protection of these very treaties.

Danzig, however, was Drummond's most persistent problem. His actions in this question were geared to preserving the status of the Free City, maintaining a grip on the situation so that calm would prevail, and keeping the Germans and Poles apart in order to avoid any deterioration in their relations which might lead to an armed clash. The fact that Poland was France's ally complicated the task, for any actions by Drummond considered pro-German would lead to Warsaw's appeal to Paris and corresponding pressure on Drummond either directly by the Quai d'Orsay or indirectly through the Foreign Office. It was, to put it mildly, a delicate situation.

In June 1927 the Danzigers, assisted and supported by the Germans, maintained that the Westerplatte promontory, awarded to Poland by the Council in March 1924 as a site on which it could store munitions, was still subject to Danzig's

---

[1] E[ric] D[rummond], Note by the Secretary-General, 16 Apr. 1929, FO/371/14124.

[2] Walters, pp. 402–11; Riekhoff, pp. 223–5; League of Nations, *Official Journal*, X (1929), pp. 1005–6; Pablo de Azcárate, *La Société des Nations et la protection des minorités* (Genève: Dotation Carnegie, 1969), pp. 61–2, 70–1. See also, Richard Veatch, *Canada and the League of Nations* (Toronto: University of Toronto Press, 1975), pp. 101–14.

jurisdiction and had to be accessible to its officials. Drummond, who in 1923 when the munitions issue had been raised had supported the Free City's position, now assumed a less friendly stance. The Danzigers and the Germans by their action had obviously produced a situation that could seriously strain German–Polish relations. Accordingly, he supported the Rapporteur's recommendation and the Council's decision to postpone consideration of the question until its next session, hoping no doubt that in the interval some sort of compromise could be hammered out. But he made it clear to Dufour-Feronce that he was annoyed, and observed that after a long respite from questions about Danzig the Council was once again being forced to handle the Free City's problems.[1]

In September at Stresemann's suggestion it was agreed that the Danzigers' charges be examined by a jurists' committee. Their report supported the Danzigers' contentions and though the Poles pressed for an advisory opinion by the World Court, they agreed to resolve the issue by direct negotiations guided by the jurists' report. These negotiations produced an agreement under which Poland granted the Danzig police access to the Westerplatte at all times for the purposes of verifying the safety precautions being taken at the munitions depot.[2] While these negotiations unfolded Drummond in March 1928 continued his unfriendly attitude toward the Danzigers, this time on the World Court's advisory opinion dealing with the jurisdiction of Danzig's courts. He attempted to obstruct their use of the Council in this question which he perhaps feared might contribute to a further heightening of German–Polish tension over the Free City.[3] Likewise in December he desired to avoid any Council involvement in the plebiscite to be held in Danzig to amend the Free City's constitution.[4]

The year 1929 brought further difficulties. The Free City's High Commissioner, Van Hamel, the former Director of the Secretariat's Legal Section, wanted to communicate to the Council, before relinquishing his post, a report giving his views

[1] Sahm, pp. 90–1, 132; Sprenger, pp. 160–3; Kimmich, p. 99.

[2] Sprenger, pp. 163–5; Kimmich, pp. 99–100.

[3] Sahm, p. 138.

[4] E[ric] D[rummond] to Aguirre and Rosting, 5 Dec. 1928, Administrative Commissions Danzig 1928–32: 2B/4394/4394, LNA.

on the political situation in Danzig, and the Polish corridor. Since Berlin considered Hamel anti-German and had privately objected to his selection, and Drummond had admitted to the Germans that he considered him a person of mediocre talents, any such report would have produced an immediate and violent German reaction. This was to be avoided and, accordingly, Drummond doubted whether the report should be communicated to the Council because he felt that it went outside the scope of Hamel's office. Hamel could of course communicate the report to the Council's members on his own initiative, but in this case the Secretariat could not be responsible for his action. Drummond's strong advice to Hamel was not to insist on circulating the report and he had grave doubts as to whether he could under the Covenant communicate it to the Council. If, however, Hamel insisted that the report be communicated on the grounds that it fell within his competence as High Commissioner, Drummond would communicate it to the Council together with the letters that they had exchanged on the question. Faced with this possibility Hamel backed off. Though he was convinced that the report fell within his competence, he left it up to Drummond whether to present or suppress the report. The report was never published, but the Hamel–Drummond exchange was no secret, for it soon became known to the Germans. Their decision was to take no action, but certainly the exchange could only have strengthened Drummond's image in the Wilhemstrasse.[1]

No sooner was this problem solved than others developed. Danzig's desire to join the International Labour Organisation was one such problem.[2] Another was Danzig's complaint that

[1] Kimmich, pp. 96–8; *ADAP 1918–1945*, ser. B, ii. Pt. I, pp. 8–9; E[ric] D[rummond], Note by the Secretary-General, 27 Feb. 1929, E[ric] D[rummond], Note by the Secretary-General, 9 and 21 Mar. 1929, Administrative Commissions Danzig 1928–32: 2B/10458/2339, LNA; Sprenger, p. 185; Sahm, p. 149.

[2] E[ric] D[rummond], Record of Conversation, 23 Aug. 1929, E[ric] D[rummond], Record of Conversation, 26 Aug. 1929, E[ric] D[rummond], Record of Conversation, 24 Oct. 1929, E[ric] D[rummond], Note by the Secretary-General, 1 Feb. 1930, E[ric] D[rummond], Record of Conversation, 5 Mar. 1930, E[ric] D[rummond], Record of Conversation, 26 Mar. 1930, E[ric] D[rummond], Record of Interview, 7 May 1930, E[ric] D[rummond], Note by the Secretary-General, 9 May 1930, E[ric] D[rummond], Record of Interview, 28 May 1930, Administrative Commissions Danzig 1928–32:
(continued)

when the Secretariat communicated documents to non-member states, or invited these states to conferences sponsored by the League, no consideration was given as to whether the Free City should be included among the non-member states of the League.[1] Fortunately, Drummond was able to handle both of these essentially technical but political questions and by doing so remove them as a potential cause of increased friction in German–Polish relations, since both questions turned on the complex legal and political relationships between Poland and Danzig established by the Versailles Treaty.

The world financial crisis and the severe trade slump in 1930 led to the construction on the coast of the Polish corridor of the competing port of Gdynia (Gdingen) which exacerbated the Free City's depressed economic conditions. In line with a decision made by the High Commissioner, Haking, in the early 1920s, the Danzigers, who had discussed the issue with the Germans beforehand, contended that the Poles were obligated to make full use of the Free City despite other ports that Warsaw might in the future open on the Baltic Sea. Berlin saw in this protest a welcome way to bring the Polish corridor question before the world. It also sought to prevent the Poles from using the Free City's economic distress to bring Danzig into closer relations with Poland thus depriving Germany of the enclave's loyalty.

Drummond naturally opposed the complaint, since a public airing of the Free City's demand would have contributed to greater German–Polish tension, and so argued with Sahm, now the President of Danzig's Senate, as well as with Dufour-Feronce. Germany would also be considered as the instigator of the complaint and be accused of wanting to reopen the question of the Polish corridor. Berlin, he maintained, should use its influence with Danzig to have the question shelved. Drummond thought the moment to make this complaint was poorly chosen—an allusion to the intended withdrawal ahead of schedule of Allied

---

2B/12404/12404, LNA; E[ric] D[rummond], Note by the Secretary-General, 13 Dec. 1929, Legal Court of International Justice 1928–32: 3C/11139/5242, LNA.

[1] E[ric] D[rummond] to Aguirre, 6 Sept. 1929, E[ric] D[rummond], Untitled Memorandum, 12 Oct. 1929, E[ric] D[rummond], Note by the Secretary-General, 18 Oct. 1929, Administrative Commissions Danzig 1928–32: 2B/14521/14521, LNA.

troops from the Rhineland as a concession to Germany for adopting the Young Plan in reparation payments. Germany's Foreign Minister, Julius Curtius, however, refused to have the complaint postponed and so informed Drummond.[1] The question dragged on for several years, contributing to the strained relations between Warsaw and Berlin and it was not until the autumn of 1933 that a broad agreement was reached.

In early October 1930 it was Poland's turn to raise the question when Drummond was approached by the Polish representative, Francois Sokal, with an *aide-mémoire* which related to passages in the High Commissioner's report concerning German and Polish nationalistic manifestations in the Free City. Essentially, it was a request from Poland as a Council member that the High Commissioner should be asked to expand this portion of his report suggesting methods to prohibit effectively such nationalistic manifestations.

Drummond observed that he did not think that as Secretary-General he could communicate such a document to the High Commissioner—an obvious attempt to divorce himself from this matter. The *aide-mémoire*, he argued, was written by Poland as a Council member, and the correct procedure would be to circulate it to all members and to place the question on the Council's agenda for the next meeting. He took the same position he had assumed in the question of Hamel's report and did not think it was within the High Commissioner's competence to make suggestions having to do with Danzig's internal affairs. The High Commissioner could use his personal influence in such matters, but officially they appeared to be outside his competence unless the Free City's constitution was threatened.

Drummond suggested that Sokal write him a semi-official letter noting that Warsaw had been most interested in these passages in the report and that his government was unclear as to what Polish nationalist manifestations were referred to and it doubted anyway whether these manifestations had decreased as the report suggested. In concluding the letter there could be a statement that Warsaw would be grateful if in his next report the High Commissioner would deal more fully with the whole subject. He could quite properly, Drummond noted, equally pass

---

[1] Kimmich, pp. 109–13; Sahm, p. 164; Sprenger, pp. 198–9.

on semi-officially this letter to the High Commissioner who would then have to decide whether or not to satisfy Poland's request. Convinced by these arguments Sokal promised to prepare a letter along the lines that Drummond had indicated.[1] Drummond had by this proposal very neatly turned aside what could have been an embarrassing Polish demand.

Concurrently, Drummond also had to face the troublesome question of the next president of the Saar Governing Commission. Curtius explained that the state of German public opinion made impossible the appointment of the commission's Saarlander member, Bartholomaus Kossmann, as the commission's president. If appointed Kossmann would be unable to accept the presidency and public opinion would be strongly opposed to his selection as it was generally held in Germany that the Saar ought to be returned before 1935. The appointment of Kossmann would give the impression that this could not occur and that the *status quo* would continue until that date. Drummond observed that in view of Germany's opinion no pressure would be exercised in Kossmann's behalf. He thought it remarkable how things change. Some years before the theory had been, and Stresemann had supported it, that the commission's president for the first five years should be French, followed for the next five years by a neutral and then a German for the last five years. Curtius smiled and said that naturally changes occurred, but it was quite clear that German public opinion was opposed to Kossmann's nomination as the commission's president.[2]

To avoid the difficulties that would arise by Kossmann's selection, Drummond called upon the commission's incumbent president, Sir Ernest Wilton, to continue in office. Without informing Wilton of Curtius's visit, Drummond argued that his departure would raise very difficult questions about the commission's presidency and future composition. Europe at the present moment was in such a state, he noted, 'that to add inflammable fuel to the existing smoke might have far-reaching results'. He was acceptable to everyone and Drummond wondered whether knowing this Wilton would not think the

[1] E[ric] D[rummond], Record of Conversation, 3 Oct. 1930, Administrative Commissions Danzig 1928–32: 2B/12952/12952, LNA.

[2] E[ric] D[rummond], Record of Conversation, 3 Oct. 1930, Saar Basin 1928–32: 2C/24709/949, LNA.

matter over and 'help the cause of international cooperation'. He honestly assured Wilton that he was not exaggerating and if Wilton was ready to continue Drummond believed he would be doing a great service to Franco-German relations.[1] Wilton agreed to serve, and France's and Germany's positive responses to Drummond's feelers on Wilton's appointment helped solve what might have become a strained situation between Paris and Berlin.[2]

Though tensions were rising Drummond's forecast to the Secretary-General of the Belgian Foreign Ministry was that a war with Germany was not likely to occur for the next ten years.[3] Within fourteen months, however, he would drastically reduce this figure based on his experience in the disarmament negotiations which had commenced. Initially in early 1931 Drummond was attracted by the notion that disarmament might be implemented by budgetary limitations which in the world's depressed economic state would have the added advantage of great popular support. He thought that direct armaments limitation would prove impracticable because of the demands which would be pressed by every state, acting on the advice of their military and naval staffs. If this proved to be the case, Germany might agree to accept a very low budgetary figure. Drummond believed that a system limiting German armaments by a budgetary device would be of far greater advantage to France than the Versailles Treaty's clauses. Indeed, it might be arranged for this budgetary limitation to take precedence over any prior international agreements on the subject of disarmament. What had to be avoided was any specific reference to a revision of the peace treaties or of Article 19 of the Covenant. From the calculations of budgetary experts Drummond understood that 'budgetary limitation was really a practical and feasible proposition' and that adequate safeguards could be devised against any budgetary frauds. Progress in budgetary limitation, he believed, would be stimulated further if the United States changed her attitude on this matter. He was firm, however, that it either had to be direct limitation or budgetary limitation.

---

[1] Drummond to Wilton, 4 Oct. 1930, ibid.
[2] D[rummond] to Wilton, 25 Nov. 1930, ibid.
[3] *DDB, 1920–1940*, ii. 631. See also, E[ric] D[rummond], Record of Interview, 20 Nov. 1930, FO/371/14938.

Simultaneous but different forms of limitation would be somewhat dangerous. Likewise Drummond did not believe that Germany would agree to the inclusion of the Versailles Treaty's military clauses in any disarmament convention. He felt that she would not accept this inclusion as a voluntary obligation under the League's aegis unless it was accompanied by large armaments reduction by France and other states.[1]

Drummond conveyed these thoughts to Cecil who accepted them for under his leadership the League's Preparatory Commission on disarmaments in its draft convention added the principle 'of limitation of the annual budget for the armed services'. Germany, however, opposed this principle since her armaments expenditure had not been limited by the peace treaties. Thus she had concentrated on quality to make up for the the quantity denied her under the Versailles settlement. The Americans also opposed the principle but did not object to its inclusion in the draft convention. With Germany and the United States opposed the budget limitation principle died a quick death.

By the time the disarmament conference convened on 2 February 1932 little had been achieved. Disagreement over naval questions had occurred between the French, the Germans, and the Italians. France had declared to the League that she had reduced her armaments to a dangerously low point and would not undertake further reductions unless she received new security guarantees, for example, the establishment of an international military force under the League's control.[2] Discussing the situation that was developing with Hymans, Drummond thought that Germany during the conference would assume a moderate position. If a general and real control was organized on all the armaments of all the states Germany would view it as an application of the parity principle which would actually satisfy

---

[1] Drummond (Geneva) to Cecil, 24 Feb. 1931 and E[ric] D[rummond], Record of Interview, 26 Feb. 1931, Add. MS. 51112, Robert Cecil Papers, BL. See also, [Walter A. Riddell], Interview with the Secretary-General, 23 Jan. 1932, Walter A. Riddell Papers, YUT; Riddell to Bennett, 23 Jan. 1932, MG 26, K, Vol. 432, Richard Bennett Papers, and Riddell to Skelton, 23 Jan. 1932, MG 25, D1, Vol. 103, Oscar Skelton Papers, PAC.

[2] Walters, pp. 440–4. See also D[rummond] to Aghnides, 17 June 1931, Add. MS. 51112, Robert Cecil Papers, BL.

her. He also appeared to think that it was necessary that the disarmament conference end with an understanding which could very well prolong the truce. He noted to Hymans that Germany was appropriating considerable sums for rearming. When asked by Hymans his opinion on the possibilities of a war Drummond responded that one might erupt in five years time. What then, Hymans asked? In keeping with his notion that the League was nothing more than a reconstituted but improved concert of powers system Drummond retorted: 'have a great conference'.[1]

By July the disarmament conference had bogged down, primarily because there was no consensus among the great powers. France tied any further arms limitation to greater security guarantees, especially from Great Britain and the United States, and both countries were unwilling to give these guarantees. Germany in turn claimed *gleichberechtigung*—parity or equality of armaments.[2]

Drummond believed that a theory propounded by Count Albert Apponyi, Hungary's League representative, offered a reasonable way out of the impasse that had developed. According to Apponyi, Drummond wrote to the Foreign Secretary, Sir John Simon, the reduction and limitation of armaments should be based for all states on Article 8 of the Covenant. By doing so there was obtained 'legal equality', though Article 8 carefully avoided 'any mention of actual equality of armaments'. Under this arrangement 'it would be theoretically possible for the French' to maintain their existing armaments intact, provided they could present a reasonable case based on national security, geographic location, and special circumstances, all provided for in paragraph 2 of Article 8, while the 'German armaments remained at their present level'. Under such an arrangement the Germans would be given the *gleichberechtigung* they claimed while the French would be allowed a considerable *de facto* armaments superiority over the Germans. To such a proposed arrangement there were many obstacles, especially ones created by the Russians, but Drummond thought that Apponyi's proposed solution could harmonize the French and German positions. When Apponyi first proposed this possibility he believed that

[1] *DDB, 1920–1940*, iii. 33.
[2] Walters, pp. 502–12.

though the Germans would raise objections, in the end it would go far toward satisfying their demands.[1]

Nothing really developed from this suggestion. The disarmament negotiations continued into 1933. Concessions that the ex-Allied states were unwilling to give Germany in 1932 were now proffered. They were too late. On 30 January the Nazis came to power in Berlin. To the Nazis, disarmament was out of the question.

It was at this point that the Danzig question again presented itself. Ominously in mid-June 1932, during an official visit to the Free City by a British naval force, the Poles dispatched the destroyer *Wicher* to pay respects to the British flotilla, neglecting, however, to notify the Danzigers beforehand as was required by the World Court's advisory opinion given the previous year and adopted by the Council.[2] Since a German naval force was expected to visit Danzig on 24 June it was feared that a repetition of the Polish action on that date might lead to very serious difficulties. Naturally, Drummond wished to avoid any special Council meeting on this question in view of strained Polish–German relations. His suggestion was that Simon, as the Rapporteur, 'might speak strongly' to the Polish Foreign Minister, August Zaleski, about the responsibility which he would incur, if, in defiance of the World Court's opinion endorsed by the Council, he allowed Polish warships to enter the Free City without previously informing the Danzigers.

Acting on Drummond's suggestion Simon pressed Zaleski. When Zaleski called on Drummond to discuss what had occurred he found him less than friendly to the Polish position. Faced by an unfriendly Drummond and threatened by Simon with a special Council meeting, an action which Paris also supported, Zaleski gave in to the pressure.[3] Several months later, with some behind-the-scenes help from Drummond, a Polish–Danzig

---

[1] Drummond to [Simon], 31 July 1932, John Simon Papers.

[2] Kimmich, p. 119; John Brown Mason, *The Danzig Dilemma* (Stanford: Stanford University Press, 1946), pp. 224–5.

[3] Edward Hallett Carr, Memorandum, 15 June 1932, E[ric] D[rummond], Note by the Secretary-General, 16 June 1932, E[ric] D[rummond], Record of Interview, 18 June 1932, E[ric] D[rummond], Record of Interview, 20 June 1932, Administrative Commissions Danzig 1928–32: 2B/37463/688, LNA; Kimmich, pp. 119–20.

protocol was signed governing the entrance and stay of Polish warships in the Free City's port area.[1]

The incident should have been a forewarning that Poland would not hesitate to use force to maintain her position in the Free City. The Nazi acquisition of power in January 1933, their destruction of internal opposition, and their blatant anti-*status quo* orientation, was answered by Warsaw on 6 March when a Polish force, unauthorized by the Danzigers, was landed ostensibly to reinforce the guards at the Westerplatte munitions depot. Whether this act was part of some larger Polish scheme to wage preventive war against Germany or to commence some sort of action to force her to execute the peace treaties is not exactly clear. What is clear, however, is that this descent was a flagrant breach of all existing agreements governing Danzig. It was justified by the Poles on the grounds that revolutionary forces in Danzig jeopardized the depot's security. The Danzigers immediately requested through the High Commissioner, Helmer Rosting, a former Danish Secretariat official, that the troops be quickly withdrawn. The Poles politely refused to do so and Rosting referred the issue to the Council which was in session.[2]

With tensions running high in Germany, Danzig, and Poland, and the matter construed in Geneva as a challenge to the League's prestige, Drummond adopted a strong position. He pointed out to the Polish representative, Count Edward Raczynski, 'that any action in the present inflammable situation which was likely to increase ill-feeling between Poland and Germany ought to be avoided'. Drummond noted that he did not know the facts and had not spoken to Rosting. Nevertheless, he felt bound to draw Raczynski's attention to the situation and asked that Warsaw do everything possible to see that it reverted to normal. Drummond observed that if it was true that the security of the Westerplatte depot was threatened, it was unfortunate that Poland had not first consulted and attempted to obtain Rosting's consent for the action she had taken. He trusted that once the excitement over the recent German elections subsided—an allusion to the Nazis' electoral success—the men

---

[1] D[rummond] to [Zaleski], 4 July 1932, E[ric] D[rummond], Record of Interview, 11 July 1932, Administrative Commissions Danzig 1928–32: 2B/35667/688, LNA; Mason, p. 255.
[2] Kimmich, pp. 131–2.

landed at the Westerplatte would be withdrawn as quickly as possible.[1]

Several days later the German representative, August Keller, on instructions from Berlin, discussed the question with Drummond who recognized 'the gravity of the situation'.[2] Drummond then broached the matter with René Massigli of the French Foreign Ministry who informed Paris of the Secretary-General's complete preoccupation with the Westerplatte business. Drummond desired that Poland reconsider her move and spontaneously withdraw her troops. In the hope that France might pressure her Polish ally Drummond explained pointedly that his problem was how to get this advice understood in Warsaw. Massigli, unfortunately, did not respond, preferring not to understand the obvious appeal for French intervention in Warsaw which was certainly in Drummond's observation.[3]

Drummond then had another talk about the matter, this time with Ernst Ziehm, the President of Danzig's Senate. Ziehm's protest about Poland's action naturally found Drummond in agreement. He would do everything possible, he assured Ziehm, to have the Polish troops withdrawn. At the same time Drummond noted the Polish fear of Nazi influence in Danzig and emphasized that there must be no disturbances in the Free City.[4]

Drummond's assurances to Ziehm were not idle words. His attitude and influence are reflected in Keller's report to Berlin that the position assumed by the British delegation corresponded approximately with Drummond's views.[5] Nor was there any French or Italian support for Poland. Faced by hostility on all sides Warsaw's position was untenable. The question, however, was not aired publicly before the Council. Undoubtedly, in order not to humiliate and embarrass the Poles—something which Drummond wished to avoid[6]—the negotiations leading to a compromise solution were handled in the Secretariat.[7] The Poles departed from Danzig in mid-March and the situation in the Free City quickly reverted to normal.

---

[1] E[ric] D[rummond], Record of Interview, 6 Mar. 1933, FO/371/17226.

[2] *DGFP 1918–1945*, C, i. 124.   [3] *DDF 1932–1939*, I, ii. 755.

[4] Ernst Ziehm, *Aus Meiner politischen Arbeit in Danzig 1914–1939* (Marburg/Lahn: Bahr, 1960), pp. 167–9; Kimmich, p. 132.

[5] *DGFP 1918–1945*, C, i. 138.

[6] Ziehm, p. 168.   [7] Kimmich, p. 133.

In the remaining months of Drummond's tenure no further difficulties developed in German–Polish relations. His last involvement in German affairs was in trying to select and appoint a High Commissioner for Danzig.[1] Polish objections to possible candidates delayed the replacement of Rosting until October 1933 when the Irish representative, Sean Lester, was appointed High Commissioner. This same month Germany departed from the League. By this point Drummond was no longer Secretary-General but the British Ambassador in Rome. He could only have mused at the turn of events.

Drummond had spent almost seven years attempting to expedite Germany's admission into the League. His actions during this period remind one of Second World War convoys in which fast ships like Drummond were forced to move at the speed of the slowest ship, in this case France. Drummond's ability to influence and affect German events was largely limited by the very nature of the political struggle. The political stakes were of so high an order that Drummond even in the best of situations could do no more than attempt to act as a buffer between the parties and whenever possible offer solutions and advice on how particular questions might be handled. His dependence for a time upon French, not to say British support, and the deep-seated suspicions in Paris about any Secretariat moves that could be construed as pro-German required him to move with the caution of a footpad. Would a more active intervention on his part have helped to bridge the gap between the victorious and defeated powers? Not likely. Germany during this period was basically an anti-*status-quo* state regardless of the government in power. No Secretary-General could really bridge the gap that was an outgrowth of Germany's defeat and the Versailles settlement. Perhaps with time, and a continuing balance of power, the League might have been able to produce a situation which could have led to an acceptable accommodation of Germany's foreign policy desires. But this was not to be. Germany remained a League member for only seven years,

---

[1] Drummond (Geneva) to Cadogan, 9 Jan. 1933, H.M. Consul (Geneva) from Cadogan to the Foreign Office, No. 4, 18 Jan. 1933, Drummond (Geneva) to Cadogan and the two enclosed records of conversation, 23 Jan. 1933, Drummond (Geneva) to Eden, 11 May 1933, Eden to Drummond, 22 May 1933, Drummond (Geneva) to Eden, 23 May 1933, FO/371/17227.

withdrawing from the organization about three and a half months after Drummond's own departure. As the lyrics of the Horst Wessel Lied echoed through the cities of the Third Reich, Drummond's prediction to Hymans of a war with Germany in five years' time did not appear to be either pessimistic or wide of the mark. The Munich settlement was a mere five years away following Germany's withdrawal from Geneva.

V

DRUMMOND AND LATIN AMERICA

The League and Latin America

Drummond's relationship with Latin America was complicated by a number of factors none of which were of his own making. Foremost was Latin American resentment over the Monroe Doctrine's inclusion in Article 21 of the Covenant.[1] Another was the interest shown in possible employment of the Pan-American Union or some other body as a political counterweight or substitute for the League in Latin American affairs. This interest seemingly contradicted one of the motives that animated some Latin American states in joining the League: the belief that the organization might balance American power and influence in the southern hemisphere. A further complication was the United States' negative attitude toward League involvement in Latin America. This in turn was compounded by the organization's physical remoteness from Latin America and the public disinterest shown toward the League in many Latin American countries. There was also the vexing problem of the power struggle among the Latin American states themselves, especially the ABC powers.[2]

As to the Pan-American Union, Drummond feared that any scheme proposed by it which did not leave the League free to intervene in Latin American questions 'must in the end diminish largely the authority of the World League'. Accordingly, the only possible arrangement that he could envisage was for the League to delegate to the Pan-American Union 'certain of its powers as regards American disputes', but he thought the League could not and should not 'relinquish its position as the final court

---

[1] Frank P. Walters, *A History of the League of Nations* (London: Oxford University Press, 1960), p. 56.

[2] Stephen P. Duggan, 'Latin America, the League, and the United States', *Foreign Affairs*, XII, No. 2 (January 1934), pp. 281–93; Warren H. Kelchner, *Latin American Relations with the League of Nations* (Philadelphia, 1930), *passim*; Walters, p. 524.

of appeal and supreme authority in all matters relating to international peace'.[1]

The question was then raised in a slightly different form in 1920 by Agustín Edwards, the Chilean Minister in London, who argued that up to a certain point the League had to recognize the 'principle of continental political autonomy'. This entailed allowing the American states to regulate through a kind of sub-council their political affairs. This procedure, Edwards maintained, would be a means of resolving American objections to the League.[2] Although he sympathized greatly with Edwards's views, Drummond did not think that he had sufficiently realized the importance of the contrary arguments. The main thesis underlying the League, Drummond maintained, was that a dispute which might conceivably lead to war was a matter of concern to the entire world and not merely to one particular continent. Therefore, the whole world's influence should be brought to bear in order to settle such a dispute before war actually erupted.

If this underlying thesis was admitted, Edwards's main contention seemed to disappear. The predominant position that President Wilson enjoyed in Paris was due to the general knowledge that the United States could play the role of the impartial and disinterested third party in all European matters. For this reason, Drummond thought it would be a disaster if the Council did not contain members who held similar disinterested views regarding European questions. Indeed, if Edwards's views were adopted he feared that Washington would refuse to join the League or would agree to serve only on the proposed American sub-council. This would cause a political division of the world into continents which was exactly the reverse of the League ideal. Drummond agreed, however, that if possible some steps were desirable to meet Edwards's point that Latin American

[1] E[ric] D[rummond], Notes on the Pan American Union Scheme, 14 May 1919, General 1919: 40/1011/1011, LNA. See also, Arthur W. Rovine, *The First Fifty Years. The Secretary-General in World Politics 1920–1970* (Leyden: Sijthoff, 1970), p. 64; Terry L. Deibel, *Le Secrétariat de la Société des Nations et l'internationalisme américain, 1919–1924* (Genève: Dotation Carnegie, 1972), p. 93.
[2] Conversation between Edwards, Chilean Minister and Pierre Comert, 16 July 1920, Political 1920: 11/5549/5549, LNA. See also, Deibel, p. 92.

disputes should be resolved by American states themselves. Drummond thought this might be handled by extending the Monroe Doctrine's application. His suggestion was that in a purely American dispute the Council should designate its American members, as well as three representatives of other American states, to act as a Council sub-committee and invest it with powers similar to those held by the Council.[1] Though objections to such a plan might be raised, it seemed to him that it would make easier Washington's decision to become a League member. Moreover, the plan was justified to a certain extent by the fact that the Monroe Doctrine was specifically mentioned in Article 21 of the Covenant.[2]

The question was again raised in 1922 when Uruguay's Foreign Minister, Juan Buero, proposed the establishment of a League of Nations for the Americas in which all disputes between American states would be settled by arbitration. Under Buero's proposal membership in the Geneva League would in no way be incompatible with membership in the American League of Nations.[3] Though Drummond was troubled by this proposal he doubted it would develop further at the Pan-American Conference scheduled to convene in March 1923 in Santiago, Chile. Both Chile and Brazil, he pointed out, were warm League supporters and would, he thought, 'use their influence to prevent any action detrimental to the League' from being taken at the conference.[4] He was right. As the conference was about to convene Edwards announced that Buero's proposal would not be a topic for discussion[5]—an attitude also assumed by the United States during the course of the conference.[6]

---

[1] [Eric Drummond], Memorandum, 20 July 1920, Political 1920: 11/5549/5549, LNA. See also, Rovine, pp. 64–5.

[2] Minutes of a Directors' Meeting, 21 July 1920, General 1920: 40/5697/854, LNA.

[3] *New York Times*, 16 July 1922, p. 15, and 23 July 1922, p. 14. See also, *PRFRUS, 1923*, i. 293–4.

[4] Drummond (Geneva) to Fosdick, 10 Aug. 1922, File 9027, Raymond B. Fosdick Papers, PU.

[5] *New York Times*, 24 Mar. 1923, p. 3.

[6] Samuel Guy Inman, 'Pan-American Conferences and Their Results', *The Southwestern Political and Social Science Quarterly*, IV, No. 4 (March 1924), p. 354; Duggan, 'Latin America, the League, and the United States', pp. 290–1.

Of course, Drummond's attitude toward this question was also partially dictated by the fear that by devolving power and authority to regional organizations, whether they be Far Eastern or Latin American, the League would be 'reduced to a purely European machine'. If this occurred the first step toward the ultimate dissolution of the organization would have been effected. He could not see how in that event the League would be able to maintain Latin American and Asian states, nor any of the Dominions as members of the organization. The League's financial contributions would be so reduced that the greater part of the Secretariat's humanitarian and technical activities would have to be scrapped. This would be a serious blow, not merely from the League's point of view but also from that of the causes which the League had undertaken to support.[1]

Though no devolution along the lines desired by the Latin Americans occurred, Drummond was willing within certain limits to make special arrangements or devise special programmes in order to smooth the League's relationships with the Latin American states. Accordingly, in the spring of 1921 he proposed that four or five Latin Americans be taken into the Secretariat and that they be formed into an Advisory Committee on Latin American Affairs. Drummond thought the proposal might be reasonably advanced to the Assembly which decided the organization's expenses. Objections, however, were raised by members of the Secretariat who argued that it would be an error for them to begin treating Latin America 'in any way [either] collectively or as a unit'. Though they opposed the establishment of such an advisory committee they believed that it would be possible to place four or five Latin Americans within the Secretariat's different sections. Faced by this opposition Drummond thought it might be sufficient to state to the Assembly that these Latin Americans in the Secretariat 'would be consulted individually or collectively when South American questions arose'.[2]

It was this decision which led to the establishment within the Secretariat of the Bureau for Liaison with Latin America presided over by a Panamanian, Cristibal Rodriguez. Originally

---

[1] Drummond (Geneva) to Sweetser, 6 Dec. 1921, Box 31, Arthur Sweetser Papers, LC. See also, Deibel, p. 94.
[2] Minutes of a Directors' Meeting, 28 May 1921, LNA.

dependent upon this bureau were the League's Latin American correspondents who were regarded as its external collaborators and not League officials. They neither enjoyed the privileges of League officials nor were they fully subject to the Secretariat's staff regulations; they were to be found in El Salvador, Bolivia, Dominican Republic, Paraguay, Colombia, and, in 1930, in Chile.[1]

In the Secretariat's important first division, however, Latin American representation was meagre. This reflected the low political priority and influence assigned to Latin America. It is true that the argument can be made that these states contributed only a small part of the League's budget and some of them were often in arrears and thus were not entitled to many Secretariat posts. Yet no finer way to build bridges with Latin America could have been devised than through greater Secretariat representation for the states of the southern hemisphere. Though these states comprised one-third of the League's membership they had no officials in the Secretariat's first division in 1920, only four by 1930 and the high point of six was not reached until 1938. Because of their small number and the unimportance of their functions Latin American officers 'carried little weight' in the Secretariat.[2] Nor was any attempt made during Drummond's tenure to establish contacts or to collaborate closely with the Pan-American Union. Granted, some Latin American members of the Secretariat did attend Pan-American Conferences, but they did so without formal accreditation and thus were in a sense only semi-private observers.[3]

Brazil's withdrawal from the League in 1926 led to renewed attempts to strengthen the organization's arrangements with Latin America. The difficulty was that Drummond and the Secretariat's top officials agreed that it was not 'in the general

[1] Egon F. Ranshofen-Wertheimer, *The International Secretariat: A Great Experiment in International Administration* (Washington, D. C.: Carnegie Endowment for International Peace, 1945), pp. 187–8; Duggan, 'Latin America, the League, and the United States', p. 290; Kelchner, pp. 142–3, 147–62.

[2] Ranshofen-Wertheimer, pp. 356–61.

[3] *Proceedings of the Exploratory Conference on the Experience of the League of Nations Secretariat, held in New York City on August 30, 1942, under the auspicies of the Carnegie Endowment for International Peace* (Washington, D.C.: Carnegie Endowment for International Peace (roneographed), 1942), p. 64; Ranshofen-Wertheimer, pp. 186–7.

interests of the League that any special treatment should be accorded to the Latin American states as a whole'. They also thought such a policy contrary to the desires of the Latin American representatives at Geneva. They decided, however, that the Secretariat's functional sections (Economic and Finance, Health, Transit and Social, and so on) should give more attention to ascertaining if there were Latin American questions which could be studied with a view to some sort of action by the pertinent section. Of course, the Secretariat could not act unless requested to do so by a Latin American state.

Simultaneously, the Bureau for Liaison with Latin America would be abolished, but the valuable services rendered by Rodriguez would continue by attaching him to the section handling protocol questions. In substitution, there would be monthly meetings of the Secretariat's Latin American members in what was later called the Committee on Latin American Questions. Presided over by Drummond, the meetings would discuss any problems considered to affect Latin America as a whole, as well as the views of the Secretariat's sections which had dealt with any problem especially affecting a particular Latin American state. They hoped that these meetings would be used by the Secretariat's Latin American members to convey suggestions about subjects that could most usefully be treated by the Secretariat's various sections. Lastly, it was agreed that it would be useful from time to time to have meetings of the League's different bodies in Latin America provided it was not too expensive and a sufficient number of League members found it possible to make so long a journey. Of course, the initiative for such meetings would have to emanate either from a Latin American state or from a Latin American member of the particular League body.[1]

Thus, though the Bureau for Liaison with Latin America was abolished, its work continued albeit along a broader front and in a more decentralized manner. This liaison procedure, Drummond pointed out, would be 'executed by means of personal contacts and of unofficial, personal and confidential correspondence'. Since the liaison work was more likely to be effective when directed by Latin American nationals it was to these very

[1] Minutes of a Directors' Meeting, 31 Aug. 1926, LNA.

individuals in the Secretariat that the work was delegated. Rodriguez was to act as the liaison man with the Secretariat's various sections as well as the contact man with Latin American ministers, ex-delegates, and so on.[1] By mid-1927 this new approach commenced in earnest when, for the first time, Secretariat personnel dealing with health matters were dispatched to Latin America on a technical mission.[2]

Though contacts between the League and the Latin American states increased, they were often negated by the indifference and lack of interest in the organization to be found in most of Latin America. In many states of the southern hemisphere 'the League was not a living thing but a far-away organization'.[3] Drummond was not unaware of this fact though he clung to the hope that the Latin American states would sooner or later realize the organization's value and 'become immediately the strongest partisans of the League'[4] like the Latin American delegations at Geneva.[5]

The difficulty, however, in effecting a closer association was the Monroe Doctrine's inclusion in the Covenant. It was a burden that Drummond had to bear. He emphasized, however, that the doctrine's inclusion in Article 21 could not warrant a refusal to a legitimate request for help from a League member, whether it was or was not a Latin American state. At the same time he insisted that it 'would be a mistake for the Secretariat to give any official advise as to the exact scope and meaning of that Article'. If a country wished to raise a question about the interpretation of any Covenant article, it clearly had an opportunity to do so at the Assembly's yearly meeting. In the interim, until an exact interpretation was given and accepted by the Assembly, a League member had the right to interpret an article in a manner

[1] E[ric] D[rummond], Note by the Secretary-General, 27 Oct. 1926, General 1926: 40/56227/56227, LNA. See also, Rovine, p. 67.

[2] Drummond (Geneva) to Murray, 12 Jan. 1927, Gilbert Murray Papers, BLOU; Duggan, 'Latin America, the League, and the United States', p. 290; Kelchner, pp. 175–8.

[3] Ranshofen-Wertheimer, pp. 189–90.

[4] Drummond (Geneva) to Murray, 12 Jan. 1927, Gilbert Murray Papers, BLOU.

[5] Drummond (Geneva) to Bullard, 19 Mar. 1928, Arthur Bullard Papers, PU.

that it believed proper, provided of course that such an interpretation was not opposed to the article's obvious sense.[1]

Reservations by the United States in 1926 in accepting the Statute of the World Court mirrored the practical difficulties that the Monroe Doctrine produced. Under the Senate's fifth reservation, prior consent was necessary before the World Court could handle a request for an advisory opinion on any question in which the United States could 'claim to have an interest'. Drummond pointed out that correctly or incorrectly many Latin American states believed that this reservation reaffirmed in the widest possible terms the Monroe Doctrine, and that it 'would give international sanction to that doctrine being interpreted in any manner that suited the administration of the United States at the moment'. This feeling had been so aroused that the acceptance of this reservation by the League's membership 'would prove that the League did not care a jot whether the Latin American states stayed inside it'. These states feared that in a situation in which two of them desired the Council to have the World Court give an advisory opinion on a matter that affected them, Washington would certainly intervene claiming that the Monroe Doctrine was being violated. Drummond thought that the United States was not likely to do so if the country was actually a member of the World Court. Nevertheless, if the country was from Latin America, it would not feel happy, as the American press often seemed to lose completely its self-control whenever the Monroe Doctrine was mentioned. Of course, Drummond agreed that American entry into the League was much more important than the loss of several Latin American states, but had to point out that the Latin Americans were already League members while the Americans were not. Every time a Latin American state departed from the League it strengthened the argument of the League's opponents that the organization was a European affair and they had better avoid getting involved with it.[2]

The question was raised again several years later in the

---

[1] D[rummond] to Nogueira, 5 Feb. 1924, Admissions to the League 1923: 28/31501/3076, LNA. See also, Rovine, p. 65.

[2] Drummond (Geneva) to Gilchrist, 26 Aug. 1926, Huntington Gilchrist Papers, LC.

Committee on Latin American Questions. Since the Secretariat's involvement in the question would have been politically unwise, Drummond's comments reflected his desire to avoid the issue. He wondered whether any useful purpose would be served in discussing the Monroe Doctrine from any point of view other than its precise legal significance in the Covenant. Different views had been expressed about it at different times and by different countries, and the doctrine's interpretation tended to vary according to circumstances. From the League's point of view, according to Drummond, its meaning obviously had to be the one it possessed at the moment the Covenant was signed, and League members could only be bound by the interpretation given to the doctrine at that time. He was firm in his belief that it was not the Secretariat's task to adopt any official opinion as to whether the doctrine was or was not to be regarded as a regional understanding. Indeed, legal experts themselves disagreed on the question.[1]

Privately, Drummond was even more frank. The United States, he wrote to an American associate, did not want the League, and the Latin Americans would naturally hesitate before invoking the League in any dispute in which Washington might have a direct interest. Drummond did not believe that this would be the case in a dispute only between Latin American states. But the Latin Americans were frightened—he was convinced wrongly—that Washington might in such a dispute 'invoke and perhaps enforce the Monroe Doctrine, as prohibiting any proposal to an international body' like the League.[2]

The Monroe Doctrine was a cross that the League and Drummond had to bear and it complicated their relationship with the Latin American states. When pressed by the Latin Americans the Council, like Drummond, avoided any definition of the Monroe Doctrine and restricted itself in a statement to Costa Rica in 1928 that mention of the doctrine in Article 21 neither extended its scope nor enhanced its validity and asserted

[1] Minute of the 11th Meeting of the Committee on Latin American Questions, 10 Feb. 1928, General and Miscellaneous 1928–32: 50/882/882, LNA.

[2] Drummond (Geneva) to Bullard, 23 Apr. 1928, Arthur Bullard Papers, PU.

in clear language that the Covenant conferred upon League members equal rights and equal obligations.[1]

The Wayward States: Mexico and Argentina

The exclusion or absence from the League of certain Latin American states increased Drummond's difficulties in dealing with the southern hemisphere. Keeping in mind his firmly held belief that an international organization to be successful had to 'be based on the principle of universality'[2] it was only natural that he would devote a large part of his energies in attempting to have these states become fully-fledged members of the organization.

One of the most important states excluded at the organization's inception was Mexico. This was largely due to American influence because of Mexico's nationalization of American oil and land interests.[3] In July 1922, on the grounds that the Mexicans were contemplating possible admission to the League, Drummond attempted to ascertain the Foreign Office's attitude.[4] Since Mexico was not recognized by Great Britain he pointed out that admission to the League did not necessitate a state's *de jure* recognition by other League members and cited several precedents. Although Drummond welcomed Mexico's 'spontaneous application', he doubted the wisdom of giving the Mexicans 'any definite encouragement' to make an application, otherwise troubles might develop with the Americans.[5]

The Foreign Office's attitude, however, was not encouraging. Balfour's opinion was that Great Britain could hardly favour Mexico's admission to the League since she was in default of her financial obligations and it was for this reason that London refused to recognize her government. When Mexico fulfilled her obligations Great Britain would be willing both to recognize her and to welcome her as a League member.[6]

Drummond was unhappy with London's stance and hoped

[1] Kelchner, pp. 132–3; Walters, pp. 391–2.
[2] See Chapter II, p. 27, fn. 2.
[3] Duggan, 'Latin America, the League, and the United States', p. 286; Walters, pp. 37–8, 462.
[4] Drummond to Tufton, 18 July 1922, FO/371/7232.
[5] Drummond to Tufton, 21 July 1922, ibid.
[6] Sperling to Tufton, 27 July 1922, ibid.

that it might modify its attitude. The League's somewhat difficult position in Latin America, he argued, would make Mexico's admission to the organization very valuable. It might cause Argentina to return to the League since her president was favourably disposed toward it but needed a pretext for reversing the country's previous policy. The Mexicans, however, would not apply for admission unless they were assured of a unanimous vote in favour of their application. They had already made sure that they would be supported by the other Latin American states as well as by France and Italy, and except for the British vote unanimity could be had. Accordingly, he hoped that at the Assembly's upcoming session at the minimum the Foreign Office would 'promise benevolent neutrality'. He asked whether it would not be a great mistake if Great Britain appeared as the only opponent to Mexico's admission. While Drummond understood why Mexico's desire to enter the League could not be supported, he wondered whether Mexico's recent agreement regarding her foreign debts did not now remove one of the Foreign Office's principal objections. For these reasons he earnestly hoped that London would assume a more considerate attitude in the question of Mexico's admission.[1]

Drummond's arguments appear to have made some impression. The Foreign Office noted that nothing had occurred to modify its previous attitude since Mexico's agreement covering her foreign debts was in some respects unsatisfactory to British bond holders. However, if other League members proved to be unanimously in favour of Mexico's admission, London would be reluctant to appear as the only obstacle and Great Britain 'could at any rate promise benevolent neutrality as desired' by Drummond.[2]

For reasons that are obscure Mexico's bid to join the League was not made during the Assembly's autumn session. Indeed, it was not until the following year, 1923, that any moves were undertaken and then by Drummond himself. Since he did 'not think it would be possible or wise for the British Government to take any initiative' in this matter even if it was willing to do so, Drummond proposed to work through some Latin American

[1] Drummond to Tufton and the enclosed memorandum, 17 Aug. 1922, ibid.
[2] Seymour to Tufton, 24 Aug. 1922, ibid.

state or Spain.[1] His final selection fell on Brazil and Chile who then made overtures to Mexico to join the League. To this move, Lord Curzon was informed, 'Mexico had offered a shocking response'[2]—though publicly Mexico explained that she had declined the invitation since she was not diplomatically recognized by Great Britain.[3]

This failure caused Drummond to think that for the moment it would be unwise for the Secretariat to take any further steps regarding Mexico's admission and that it 'would be better to let events gradually prove to Mexico the advantages which would accrue' to her if she became a League member. A little time might have to elapse before Mexican statesmen realized the fact, but he thought that this realization would ultimately occur. The recent overture, he argued, had been inopportune since the strains in Mexican–American relations had made the Mexicans somewhat intransigent regarding any international matter which they considered might in the slightest way affect Mexico's national dignity and self-esteem.[4]

For the next five years Drummond bided his time and no more was heard of the matter. During these years the fervour of the Mexican revolution subsided, Mexican–American relations slowly returned to normal, and Brazil departed from the League. In the summer of 1928 the question was again raised this time by Alberto Pani, the Mexican Minister in Paris, who explained that for prestige reasons it was impossible for his government to apply for League membership without an invitation being addressed to it. The representative of El Salvador, J. Gustavo Guerrero, explained to him that it might be possible for the Assembly to issue such an invitation provided Mexico gave an encouraging response since the League did not want to run the risk of tendering an invitation which would be refused or rebuffed.[5]

---

[1] Drummond to Cecil, 13 Aug. 1923, Add. MS. 51110, Robert Cecil Papers, BL.

[2] Tilley (Rio de Janeiro) to Curzon, 26 Sept. 1923, FO/371/9441.

[3] *New York Times*, 15 Sept. 1923, p. 15.

[4] E[ric] D[rummond], Note by the Secretary-General, 4 Oct. 1923, and D[rummond] to Nogueira, 5 Feb. 1924, Admissions to the League 1923: 28/31501/3076, LNA.

[5] E[ric] D[rummond], Record of Conversation, 27 Aug. 1928, General and Miscellaneous 1928–32: 50/6832/6832, LNA.

The situation was slowly changing and Mexico's increased interest in the League was reflected the following year, 1929, when she accredited an observer to the organization.[1] Changes in the Mexican Foreign Ministry in early 1930 were also encouraging and were mirrored in a discussion between Drummond and Antonio Castro Leal, the Mexican observer in Geneva, on the possible expansion of Mexico's role in different League organs, especially the International Labour Organisation. The fact that Mexico felt insulted by being excluded from the list of original League members caused Drummond to remark that it might be possible for him to address a letter to Leal on this question to be communicated to his government and possibly published. His letter would point out that this feeling was based on a misunderstanding since the League could not be held responsible for an action that had been taken before it was founded, and that Drummond was convinced that all the Council's members were moved by the friendliest feelings toward Mexico. Drummond was even willing to submit such a letter to the Council for its approval.

As to a unanimous Assembly invitation to Mexico to join the League, Drummond noted that it was most unlikely that any League member would disagree with the Council on this matter. He foresaw, however, great difficulty in securing such an invitation and besides, it could not be attempted unless the states concerned were all assured that the Mexican reply would be favourable. There was the added disadvantage that this procedure would delay matters to such an extent that it would be most difficult for Mexico to be admitted at the forthcoming Assembly session.[2] As he promised Drummond wrote his letter. He emphasized that no legal, political, or even moral responsibility of any sort could rest on the League for actions taken previously by others. Drummond was convinced that all League members were animated in regard to Mexico with the friendliest feelings as had been shown by various Assembly declarations.[3]

However, despite Drummond's efforts there were no further developments. Again, as in 1922, Mexico made no move to join

[1] Duggan, 'Latin America, the League, and the United States', pp. 286–7.
[2] Eric Drummond, Record of Interview, 1 May 1930, FO/371/14988.
[3] D[rummond] to Leal, 26 May 1930, General and Miscellaneous 1928–32: 50/6832/6832, LNA.

the League. A full year elapsed before Drummond on 13 June 1931 broached the question with Cadogan. Comments in the Mexican press, especially an article in a semi-official government newspaper stating that Mexico might adopt a friendlier attitude toward the League provided something was done to right the Paris insult of 1919, attracted Drummond's attention. His proposal, following a conversation with the new observer, Salvador Martinez de Alva, was that a *démarche* might be made on the subject by the British Minister in Mexico, a suggestion he had offered to Cadogan previously. If a promising reply was received Drummond thought it might be arranged for the Assembly to declare on the motion of the Irish Free State or Germany, countries which were not original members, that it regretted that Mexico was not originally invited to become a League member and that it would always be pleased to welcome Mexico as a member of the organization. This would not be a direct invitation which Drummond thought would be impossible unless there were assurances that Mexico was ready to accept immediately. The Mexican observer told him that if some such Assembly declaration was made and then followed up by separate diplomatic moves there would be a favourable response. He passed this information along, Drummond explained, because if Mexico were admitted it would greatly improve the League's position in Latin America. The Foreign Office, however, was not receptive to Drummond's suggestion. 'No. Our attitude has already been decided', minuted the Permanent Under-Secretary, Robert Vansittart.[1]

Before Vansittart's rejection was received, however, Martinez de Alva suggested an alternative to Drummond's proposal that involved sending telegrams directly to Mexico by various foreign ministers inviting her to join the League in view of the Assembly's resolution. His attempt to raise the ante was too much for Drummond who responded that this would be far from easy since a diplomatic overture was one thing, but invitations by foreign ministers was another.[2]

If Martinez de Alva's proposal annoyed him Vansittart's

[1] Drummond (Geneva) to Cadogan, 13 June 1931 and the attached minute by R[obert] V[ansittart], FO/371/15733.

[2] Drummond (Geneva) to Cadogan, 16 June 1931, and the enclosed Record of Interview, ibid.

decision disappointed him. He knew, he informed Vansittart, that London's relations with Mexico were not very good and that various difficulties existed. Drummond thought that this situation might in part be traced to the strongly held Mexican feeling that Great Britain was largely responsible for their exclusion as original League members. Every Mexican he met emphasized this point though they did admit that the main responsibility rested with President Wilson and the Americans.

Vansittart might think he was 'over-emphasizing' Mexico's importance, he observed, but this was not so. In Latin America as a whole Mexico enjoyed an 'extraordinary position'. Drummond supposed that this was due to the fact that she was looked upon as the champion of the southern hemisphere's independence as against the American danger which loomed very large in most Latin American states. Drummond felt convinced that if Mexico joined the League, the organization's position in Argentina would be greatly enhanced and, in a short time, with Mexico, Argentina, and Chile all attending Geneva meetings, Brazil could not long remain separated from the League. Vansittart was still unreceptive. Drummond, he minuted, showed himself an expert at understatement when he wrote that London's relations with Mexico were not very good. It was curious to Vansittart that 'we should be expected to run after half-savage crooks. We are "glad to meet them", but I really feel too old for this form of sprinting'.[1]

In late August as the Assembly session drew nearer, Martinez de Alva again called on Drummond to secure a British initiative regarding an invitation to Mexico to join the League. Drummond thought that while no British initiative would be possible—he gave no hint of Vansittart's attitude—it might be possible to arrange to have the Assembly pass a resolution presented by certain states including Great Britain. Of course, he insisted he could not assume any responsibility in stating that an Assembly invitation would be issued and he could not be quoted in this sense. If things looked promising, Drummond thought an Assembly resolution could be arranged, but assurances that Mexico would accept the invitation if it was offered were also

---

[1] Drummond (Geneva) to Vansittart, 18 June 1931 and the attached minute R[obert] V[ansittart], 19 June [1931], ibid.

necessary. He really believed it would be in British interests, Drummond informed Cadogan, to give the Mexicans satisfaction on this point. He thought that Mexico's attitude which had been somewhat unfriendly would, from what Martinez de Alva had said, certainly change.[1]

When pressed for assurance by Martinez de Alva that the plan they had discussed would go through, Drummond replied that he could give no such assurances beyond stating that he would do everything possible to bring the question to a successful conclusion. The difficulty, he maintained, was Mexico's request that London play a prominent role in the proceedings while the chances of the alternative proposal, namely, a unanimous Assembly resolution presented by certain powers including Great Britain, would be overwhelming. Mexican insistence on a British role made it impossible for him to go beyond what had already been said. When Martinez de Alva divulged that Mexico would publicly declare that she was in no way hostile to the League, Drummond noted that such a declaration would be helpful.

Since Drummond had not wavered in his insistence that the simplest procedure was a resolution proposed by the Council's permanent members plus Spain, Martinez de Alva finally agreed to it and formally assured Drummond that when offered, Mexico would accept the invitation to join the League.

Martinez de Alva then raised the possibility of a reservation to the Monroe Doctrine which he pointed out had never been recognized by his country. Drummond's response that this was not really possible led them to devise a formula whereby Mexico's declaration accepting admission to the League took note of the Council's statement on the doctrine to Costa Rica in 1928. This information was then conveyed to Cadogan as well as to Cecil who would be the British representative at the Council's and Assembly's September meetings. Cecil was someone who would be favourably inclined toward assisting Drummond to get Mexico into the League, and London's reaction to this conversation showed the need for such assistance. 'Drummond

---

[1] Drummond (Geneva) to Cadogan, 27 Aug. 1931 and E[ric] D[rummond], Record of Interview, 24 Aug. 1931, ibid.

has been unnecessarily sympathetic', minuted Alexander Leeper of the Foreign Office.[1]

In early September as promised the Mexican President publicly explained that Mexico had a friendlier attitude toward the League than was previously the case.[2] As agreed with Drummond, the permanent Council members led by Great Britain and including Spain then submitted a resolution to the Assembly which pointed out that Mexico was not included in the League's original members and proposed that this unjust omission be repaired by inviting her to accede to the Covenant. Strongly supported by Cecil, Briand, and Curtius, as well as by others, the draft resolution was then passed unanimously by the Assembly.[3] Less than a year later, in July 1932, a somewhat similar procedure fostered by Drummond was again used to admit Turkey to the League, a country which he had contacted and tried to interest in the League as early as 1922.[4]

Cadogan was less than pleased with the whole performance. He thought that Drummond had been 'hypnotized' by Martinez de Alva 'with the deplorable result' that the Assembly meeting 'in a time of almost unprecedented crisis, could do no better for the best part of a day than make speeches imploring Mexico to enter our counsels'.[5] Cadogan's annoyance was understandable in view of the poor nature of Anglo–Mexican relations during this period. For Drummond, however, whose responsibilities were more catholic, Mexico's and subsequently Turkey's admission by invitation were attempts to improve the League's general position especially in Latin America and the Near East.

---

[1] Drummond (Geneva) to Cadogan, 29 Aug. 1931, E[ric] Drummond, Record of Conversation between Sir E. Drummond and M. de Alva, 29 Aug. 1931, and the attached minute by A[lexander] W. A. Leeper, ibid.

[2] *New York Times*, 5 Sept. 1931, p. 1.

[3] League of Nations, *Official Journal*, Special Supplement, No. 93, pp. 34–7.

[4] Drummond (Geneva) to Tyrrell, 29 Nov. 1922 and the enclosed Record of Conversation between Sir Eric Drummond and Veli Bey at Geneva, 29 Nov. 1922, FO/371/7967; Drummond (Geneva) to Cadogan, 9 Dec. 1929, FO/371/13828; Drummond (Geneva) to Cadogan, 14 Apr. 1932, E[ric] D[rummond], Record of Interview, 14 Apr. 1932, E[ric] D[rummond], Note by the Secretary-General, 16 Apr. 1932, Drummond (Geneva) to Clerk, 10 May 1932, D[rummond] to Clerk, 7 June 1932, FO/371/16473; League of Nations, *Official Journal*, Special Supplement, No. 102, pp. 9–10, 17–23.

[5] Cadogan (Geneva) to Vansittart, 9 Sept. 1931, FO/371/15733.

During these years of increasing world tension and corresponding pressure on the League, Drummond, and for that matter others, believed that increasing the League's membership would be one way to strengthen the organization. One can question, however, whether the method of invitation achieved this purpose for the intrinsic strength of any organization like the League is not its numerical membership but its political importance in world politics and the use made of it by the organization's member states. If the League's political importance during this period had been in the ascent, both the Mexicans and the Turks would have assumed a far different attitude and Drummond would have had to play the role of the seduced rather than the seducer.

Cadogan's annoyance must have increased when Mexico's acceptance arrived in Geneva. Rather than the formula discussed with Drummond the message declared that Mexico had never taken cognizance of the regional understanding—the Monroe Doctrine—cited in Article 21 of the Covenant.[1] In Geneva it was understood, *The Times* of London reported, that this reference in Mexico's reply to the Monroe Doctrine was 'not opportune'.[2] On this part of the arrangement there had been a hitch, but not one of Drummond's making. Indeed, difficulties developed within a year after Mexico's admission. In late September 1932 plans were announced to withdraw from the League because the money expended for the organization could, in view of the world financial crisis, be better employed for education and other public works in Mexico.[3] Understandably, Drummond was troubled by this news and discussed the matter with the American Minister in Bern, Hugh R. Wilson. It appeared to Drummond that Mexico's action was really the result of personal feuds within the Mexican Government. In Drummond's opinion while it was always regrettable when a state withdrew from the League, especially after having just been admitted, it would be most unfortunate to have anything like this occur on the eve of the debate on the Lytton Commission's Manchurian Report. He thought that Washington might also feel this way but obviously hoped, Wilson noted, that it might find it possible to put in a

---

[1] *The Times* (London), 11 Sept. 1931, p. 11, and 14 Sept. 1931, p. 11; *New York Times*, 10 Sept. 1931, p. 1.

[2] *The Times* (London), 12 Sept. 1931, p. 10.

[3] *New York Times*, 28 Sept. 1932, p. 7.

word in the proper Mexican quarters. Wilson thought the fact that Drummond had brought his question to his attention, despite his obvious reluctance to do so, was evidence of the importance that he attached to it from the 'point of view of League prestige and the urgency' with which he regarded it.[1]

That Mexico's intended action was no ploy was verified some weeks later when she closed her Geneva office. Though it was explained that this was an administrative action and the activities of the office would be executed by the Mexican diplomatic mission in Paris it was an ominous move. This was followed in early December with an official letter to Drummond informing him that Mexico was withdrawing from the League. In late May 1933, a reversal occurred and Mexico renounced her withdrawal from the League. It was explained that this about-face was due to President Roosevelt's programme of peace through disarmament and non-aggression pacts announced some days before.[2] It must be noted, however, that about two weeks before this reversal Pani, now the Finance Minister and opposed to Mexico's continuance in the League, visited Washington and held a series of talks on economic issues with President Roosevelt and the State Department's experts.[3] It is possible to conjecture that during this visit someone put in the word with Pani that Drummond had suggested.

The second most important Latin American state absent from Geneva was Argentina. The situation with Argentina, however, was somewhat different from that with Mexico and accordingly had to be handled in a different manner. Whereas Mexico had never been an original League member and joined only when formally invited to do so, Argentina had through her executive accepted the Covenant but had done so without legislative approval as required by the constitution. Nevertheless the executive's adherence to the Covenant made it legally binding on Argentina according to the norms of international law. Technically, therefore, Argentina was a League member which was mirrored in the fact that when her delegation appeared for

---

[1] Wilson (Geneva) to the Department of State, 28 Sept. 1932, File 500.C001/742, RG 59, NA.

[2] *New York Times*, 17 Nov. 1932, p. 5, 15 Dec. 1932, p. 6, 16 Dec. 1932, p. 17, 28 May, Part IV, 1933, p. 3; *The Times* (London), 16 Dec. 1932, p. 13.

[3] *PRFRUS, 1933*, i. 506, 516–17, 548–51.

the Assembly's first session no question was raised as to its proper standing.[1] The difficulty that led to the schism between the League and Argentina was a series of Covenant amendments proposed by her Foreign Minister, Honorio Pueyrredon, during this first Assembly session. When the Assembly set these proposed amendments aside for future consideration Pueyrredon and his delegation announced in a fit of pique that their mission had ended and departed from Geneva.[2] Argentina was not to return until Drummond's tenure as Secretary-General had ended.

Initially, Argentina's continual absence from the League despite her technical membership raised certain administrative problems which had important political implications. One such problem was Argentina's contribution to the League budget and the arrears in payments that had developed. What Drummond wanted to avoid of course was the creation of 'unnecessary difficulties' to her return to the League; difficulties political and within Argentina herself or of a nature necessitating that she reapply for membership.

One could assume, he noted, that Argentina was a member dating from her adhesion to the Covenant. Naturally this implied that she was liable for all her unpaid budget contributions. The second approach was to hold that Argentina's membership had been in abeyance pending the legislature's ratification of the Covenant. The advantage here was that it liquidated the arrears and the position started afresh from the date on which Argentina resumed her membership. Personally, Drummond was partial to the former approach which clearly implied that the League did not consider Argentina's arrears should form any impediment to her return. Accordingly he thought it advisable that a note be drawn up which Edwards could take with him to Argentina to help him during negotiations aimed at returning Buenos Aires to Geneva. The note might outline his two approaches and leave it to Argentina to decide which she preferred to adopt. In

[1] Kelchner, pp. 46–9, 91–2. On the question of the norms of international law see William W. Bishop, Jr., *International Law: Cases and Materials* (2nd edn.; Boston: Little, Brown, 1962), p. 107 and fn.

[2] Kelchner, pp. 93–8; Walters, p. 124; Duggan, 'Latin America, the League, and the United States', pp. 285–6.

Drummond's mind, however, the important thing was to get Argentina to return to the League.[1]

Obviously the scheme adopted was the first one, for the legislature was requested to appropriate the funds to pay Argentina's quota to the budget. This was consented to in June 1924 and Argentina then paid her contributions including her arrears for the budgets of 1922 and 1923 even though in these budgets quotas had not been assigned for Argentina. In 1924, 1925, and 1926 the question of Argentina's relationship with the League was considered by the legislature but no decision was arrived at.[2] In mid-December 1926 Drummond informed Cadogan that the Chilean representative, Enrique Villegas, had suggested to him that it might prove very helpful if the British Minister in Buenos Aires said something to the Foreign Minister or to the President about Britain's desire to see again Argentina's delegation at Geneva. According to Villegas the question would probably be raised in the legislature during the coming spring and some outside impulse would be most helpful.[3]

Nothing however appears to have developed from Drummond's probe and in May of the following year, 1927, he again returned to the problem. He informed Cadogan that the British Minister in Buenos Aires had proposed that Drummond himself or one of the under secretaries-general should come to Argentina. Drummond feared that such a proposal at the present time was out of the question since there was no invitation from the government and in such a case an invitation was essential. Moreover, it would be very difficult to visit only Argentina among the Latin American republics. If he visited one country he would have to visit all of them. In addition, Drummond did not see how he could possibly depart from Geneva. The workload was getting heavier and he had three new under secretaries-general. There was also the danger that if he left for several months friction might possibly erupt between the Secretariat's French and Italian members.

Personally Drummond feared that a purely political visit

---

[1] E[ric] D[rummond], An untitled memorandum, 6 Oct. 1922, Finances and Accounts 1922: 31/23975x/23975, LNA.

[2] Kelchner, p. 101.

[3] Drummond (Geneva) to Cadogan, 10 Dec. 1926, FO/371/11901.

might appear as if the League desired to apply pressure on Argentina in what was an internal matter, or as interference in domestic politics, a danger that might be lessened if the government extended an invitation to visit the country. The forthcoming visit, he noted, by Secretariat personnel dealing with health matters might prove very useful, however, and everything would be done to get the mission's activities played up in the Argentine newspapers.

The other suggestion the British minister had made and one that Drummond did not dismiss was that a cabinet minister or an important national of one of the Great Powers should visit Buenos Aires. Then there was the added suggestion of a joint *démarche* by the Great Powers, though he feared that this would involve too many diplomatic exchanges to be practical. It would not be too difficult to secure provided London were willing to take the initiative in this matter, and thought the possibilities of a joint *démarche* might be discussed at the forthcoming Council meeting by the concerned representatives. Drummond was sure that he could secure French, Italian, and German support for such a joint move through the under secretaries-general.[1] In fact, he pointed out that the visit of the Secretariat personnel to Argentina might be a very opportune moment for such a move provided the *démarche* could be made either shortly before or perhaps directly after their arrival.[2] London's reaction was negative. Austen Chamberlain, Cadogan informed Drummond, was of the opinion that neither the League's authority nor its dignity would be served by a joint *démarche* of the Great Powers unless it was definitely ascertained beforehand that any such step would be agreeable to Buenos Aires, and would lead to a quick and acceptable response. Chamberlain also dismissed the possibility of sending a cabinet member to Argentina.[3]

Rebuffed by Chamberlain and with no added proposals Drummond for the next three years allowed things to continue more or less as before. Argentina paid her budget quota for the years 1924 through 1929 and in 1928 her minister in Bern was

[1] Drummond (Geneva) to Cadogan, 3 May 1927, FO/371/12685. Drummond had made some of these points a year before. See the minute by Cavendish-Bentinck, 26 July 1926, FO/371/11901.

[2] Drummond (Geneva) to Cadogan, 11 May 1927, FO/371/12685.

[3] Cadogan to Drummond, 25 May 1927, ibid.

also appointed permanent observer at Geneva.[1] It was not until October 1930 that Drummond again moved to have Argentina return to the League. This time the Foreign Secretary was Arthur Henderson, like Chamberlain a good friend, but far more sympathetic to the League and Drummond's advice. Unlike Chamberlain, and in line with Drummond's suggestion, Henderson instructed the British Ambassador in Buenos Aires to impress upon the Foreign Ministry the importance which Great Britain and undoubtedly other League members attached to the resumption by Argentina of her collaboration with Geneva. The present government could do nothing, it was explained to the British ambassador, since Argentina's active participation depended on the legislature's acceptance and ratification of the Versailles Treaty. It was hoped that Argentina would inevitably return to Geneva and if Drummond's visit to Latin America materialized he might do much to influence the country's public opinion in the League's favour.[2]

The only thing necessary, Drummond insisted, was that Argentina who on strong legal grounds had always been regarded as being a League member, should resume sending an Assembly delegation and pay her budget contribution. The question of legislative acceptance and ratification, he correctly pointed out to Cadogan, was purely a matter of internal politics.[3]

In late December Drummond received the opportunity to press personally the case for Argentina's return to the League when he arrived in Buenos Aires after having attended Uruguay's centenary celebrations. This time-consuming and tiresome trip by ship, train, and car to the various Latin American states, can be contrasted with the speed and convenience that is offered by jet travel and modern communications to the United Nations' Secretary-General. To accentuate the unofficial and private nature of his visit the Foreign Minister asked that when Drummond called on him he be accompanied by the British ambassador. At this meeting as well as subsequently with the Acting President, where again he was accompanied by the ambassador, Argentina's relationship with the League was discussed. During his four day stay in Buenos Aires Drummond

[1] Kelchner, p. 102.
[2] Cadogan to Drummond, 24 Oct. 1930, FO/371/14193.
[3] Drummond to Cadogan, 30 Oct. 1930, FO/371/14956.

met many of the leading political personalities of the country and kept the problem to the fore by inquiring when a delegation would attend the next Assembly session. The friendliness shown to him caused Drummond to feel that if the legislature had been in session during his visit the Versailles Treaty would have been ratified.[1]

By August 1931 the euphoria had worn off and Drummond had to admit to Cadogan that for the moment there did not appear much more that could be done regarding Argentina, though he admitted being reasonably optimistic as to an ultimate success.[2] In April 1932 ultimate success appeared to be on the horizon. The new Foreign Minister, Carlos Saavedra Lamas, it was reported, was very anxious to have Argentina return to the League 'as quickly as possible and without difficulty'. The question of Argentina's arrears presented problems, however, but Drummond agreed to a formula under which Argentina would pay her 1932 budget contribution and the delegation upon its arrival in Geneva could discuss the question of arrears with the Assembly's pertinent sub-committee. Drummond observed that though Argentina's budget contribution was a very important financial question her presence as a League member 'possessed much greater significance'. Therefore he did not think that there would be much difficulty in coming to some sort of satisfactory settlement of the whole financial question.[3] Though Drummond confirmed with Argentina's Minister in Bern the arrangements made, no delegation appeared at the Assembly's autumn session.[4]

To make sure that a delegation from Argentina would be present at the Assembly's 1933 session Drummond in February contacted the British Foreign Secretary, Sir John Simon, and asked whether in his London conversations with Argentina's Vice-President the question of her League membership had been broached. Drummond pointed out that though Argentina's

---

[1] E[ric] D[rummond], Note by the Secretary-General on his Visit to Buenos Aires, 28–31 Dec. 1930, General and Miscellaneous 1928–32: 50/25677/722, LNA.

[2] Drummond (Geneva) to Cadogan, 17 Aug. 1931, FO/371/15720.

[3] E[ric] D[rummond], Record of Interview, 18 Apr. 1932, Financial Administration 1928–32: 17/38905/661, LNA.

[4] D[rummond] to Ruïz-Guinazú, 20 Sept. 1932, ibid.

policy was to resume her membership and this had been approved by the legislature's lower house, in the upper house action had been postponed when the legislative session ended. There was no reason to believe that Argentina had changed her policy but in view of her strong proclivity to delay final action in such matters, Drummond was anxious that advantage be taken of every possibility to confirm Argentina's good intentions. Without doubt Argentina's readiness to act would be greatly increased if she felt that her League membership was a matter of interest to London. Drummond understood that the strictly official part of the Vice-President's mission had now ended, but that he was remaining to carry on some commercial negotiations. He therefore hoped that it was not too late—assuming the point had not already occurred to Simon—for Simon to speak to him on this matter. If this was not possible, did Simon think he could suggest it to Walter Runciman, the President of the Board of Trade, who Drummond supposed would be seeing the Vice-President in regard to commercial questions?[1]

Simon was not receptive. He had not discussed the matter with the Vice-President, he informed Drummond, and doubted the advisability from London's point of view of even broaching the subject with him. Personally, Simon did not think that Latin America would be affected by anything which London might say on the matter. He rather felt that if Argentina considered that it was in her interests to co-operate with the League she would do so without outside prompting. Moreover, now that conversations with the Vice-President on commercial questions had commenced Simon did not believe that it was desirable to raise any matter which did not strictly pertain to the matter being discussed.[2]

Within four months after this exchange Drummond had departed from Geneva. In late September Argentina resumed her League association,[3] and her absence from Geneva largely due to internal politics and constitutional complications had been reversed. Though it is difficult to gauge what effect Drummond's actions had in bringing Argentina back to the League it can be

[1] Drummond (Geneva) to Simon, 18 Feb. 1933, FO/371/17391.
[2] Simon to Drummond, 27 Feb. 1933, ibid.
[3] League of Nations, *Official Journal*, Special Supplement, No. 115, p. 36.

safely said his endeavours gave hope to those in Argentina who wanted to return to Geneva and assured successive governments in Buenos Aires that at least within the Secretariat everything possible would be done to make her return as smooth and advantageous as possible. One can question, however, whether in the short run or even in the long run Drummond's constant pleading was not somewhat demeaning to the League and, perhaps, even unwise. Argentina was no Germany, and the type of supplication that Drummond made in Berlin, considering the prize to be won, was not worth the same effort in Buenos Aires. At least in Germany there were some political elements who saw the advantage to their country of a League membership, something that was not as true in Argentina. Simon was perhaps right. When it suited Argentina's interest to co-operate with the League she would return to Geneva without any prompting. What Drummond perhaps failed to see was that Argentina's absence from Geneva was more than merely an internal constitutional and political question, but was like Costa Rica's withdrawal and Peru's, Guatemala's, and Honduras' lack of interest, a reflection of the League's basic political unattractiveness to a country as geographically remote and regionally powerful as Argentina; a country which saw no use for the League within the international politics of the southern hemisphere where its immediate interests lay, especially its competition with Chile and Brazil. Indeed, Argentina's absence from Geneva caused Drummond to devote most of his energies to Brazil which was the most powerful and the most important of all the Latin American states. It is these labours that we will now examine.

The Brazilian Problem

As we have seen in the struggle for Germany's admission to the League, Drummond did not support Brazil's bid for a permanent Council seat. Drummond's stance was that in a reorganized Council one non-permanent seat should on a rotational basis be reserved for the ABC powers; the allocation of another two seats to be decided by the Latin American states themselves.[1]

Though the Brazilian reaction was to withdraw from the

[1] Chapter IV, pp. 186, 188.

Council and resign from the League Drummond continued to be optimistic that Brazil would or could be returned to the League and in the years that followed used every occasion that presented itself to bring this about. He initially presumed that the whole issue depended on Brazil's president, and hoped that when the incumbent departed a policy reversal might set in, especially if Brazil was re-elected to the Council—a risky step he admitted, particularly if Brazil refused. As between Spain and Brazil, however, Drummond was more worried over the latter's defection because, as he explained to Cecil, Latin American states had 'so little direct contact with all interests affected by the League'.[1]

When Brazil's formal notice of withdrawal from the League arrived Drummond made no moves to contact Rio de Janeiro since he had been advised that any *démarches* would be useless and would only encourage the government's intransigence. However, he considered Brazil's action dangerous since other Latin American states hinted that they too might follow Brazil's example. Moreover, responsible Americans, he feared, were aiding this movement. The suggestion that he go to Latin America and mend fences he dismissed on the grounds that it meant a prolonged absence since he would have to visit every state in the southern hemisphere. This could not be done at the very moment when Germany entered the League. In addition, the Latin American states, he asserted, were very touchy and quarrelled among themselves, but they were united in placing the blame and responsibility for these quarrels on the League's shoulders.[2]

The immediate impact of Brazil's withdrawal was that Drummond proposed that the three non-permanent seats allotted for Latin America by the Committee on the Composition of the Council should be reduced to two. Brazil and Argentina, he pointed out, were not candidates for these seats. Bolivia, Peru, and Honduras were perpetual League absentees. Costa Rica had withdrawn from the League. That left only ten Latin American

---

[1] Drummond (Geneva) to Cecil, 11 June 1926, Add. MS. 51111, Robert Cecil Papers, BL.

[2] Drummond (Geneva) to Cecil, 14 June 1926, ibid. Six weeks later Drummond repeated some of the objections about his visiting Latin America. See the minute by Cavendish-Bentinck, 26 July 1926, FO/371/11901.

states that were eligible. Of these ten states Haiti and Santo Domingo (Dominican Republic) could hardly become Council members, and therefore only eight states were left which were really eligible. To attempt to divide three seats among these eight states appeared to Drummond politically unacceptable. He suggested that the committee announce that while in principle it favoured that three non-permanent seats should be reserved for Latin America such a view was of course based on the presumption that all Latin American states presently League members were available for election. Until that occurred two non-permanent seats would appear to be a fair proportion for the Latin American states. If this was done, Drummond observed, there would be a reserve seat for Latin America which might be used in any future negotiations either with Brazil or with Argentina whenever the latter formally resumed her relationship with the League.[1]

Faced by Cuban and Venezuelan objections,[2] however, Drummond reversed his position. He accepted Cecil's original scheme of three non-permanent seats for Latin America, though he thought it desirable, if Spain refused Council membership if elected to a non-permanent seat, to reduce the non-permanent seats from nine to eight.[3]

This suggestion, as we have seen, was not followed and as June gave way to July Drummond remained somewhat optimistic about keeping both Brazil and Spain, but especially Spain, in the world organization.[4] On 2 July he pursued the Brazilian possibility in an interview with the president elect of the Brazilian state of Minas Gerais. Drummond noted that Raul Fernandes, who had served as Brazil's League representative, and who had been offered the Directorship of the Secretariat's Legal Section did not want to accept this prominent post if Brazil was no longer a League member. Drummond appreciated Fernandes's sensitivity on this matter, but at the same time it

[1] Drummond (Geneva) to Cecil, 15 June 1926, Add. MS. 51111, Robert Cecil Papers, BL.

[2] Drummond (Geneva) to Cecil, 16 June 1926 and E[ric] D[rummond], Record of Conversations with Dr. de Agüero y Bethancourt and M. Cesar Zumeta, 16 June 1926, ibid.

[3] Drummond (Geneva) to Cecil, 24 June 1926, ibid.

[4] Chapter IV, pp. 189–90.

made the Secretariat's situation difficult. Drummond did not know what arrangements could be made during the forthcoming Assembly session. It might well be that it would be prepared to re-elect Brazil to one of the non-permanent seats, but before it did this the Assembly would have to have some assurances that Brazil would accept.

Drummond explained that it was impossible for him to give any assurances that Brazil would be re-elected, though he felt sure that there would be French and Italian support for such a move. Regarding Great Britain who was important because of the votes of the Dominions, Drummond believed that support was possible if by giving this support the present difficulties were solved.[1]

In conveying the record of this interview to Tyrrell, the Permanent Under-Secretary, Drummond believed that much could be accomplished through his interviewee. He thought it would be very useful if he could transmit to him orally a message as to the attitude London would assume, provided it knew that Brazil would accept the Assembly's offer of a non-permanent Council seat. The Foreign Office's reaction was unfriendly. The Secretariat, minuted Ivone Kirkpatrick of the Western Department, naturally was very anxious that Brazil and Spain should not exit from the League. In trying to prevent this, however, it was exceeding its functions. Furthermore, it was 'very doubtful whether action by the Secretariat will do any good; it may even do harm'. The notion of pressuring Brazil through the Secretariat or through Brazilian nationals was unattractive. Kirkpatrick noted that everything had been done through the normal channels to influence her. It had been decided that there was nothing to do but to allow events to run their course. He thought it 'would be undignified and fruitless to change our mind now' and to dispatch further messages. No one disagreed with this minute. It was capped by Chamberlain who wrote: 'I am shy of negotiations carried on through people who speak only in an "individual" capacity'.[2]

Despite the Foreign Office's negative attitude Drummond

---

[1] [Eric Drummond], Record of Interview with Carlos Ribeiro de Andrada, 2 July 1926, FO/371/11896.
[2] Drummond (Paris) to Tyrrell, 2 July 1926 and the attached minutes, ibid.

appears to have pursued the idea of some sort of Assembly declaration about Brazil.[1] Without London's support, however, it was doomed. Therefore he did not tackle the question again until late March 1927. A suggestion by Barbosa Carneiro with whom Drummond had maintained contact,[2] that private conversations between Brazil's Foreign Minister and the diplomatic representatives of the Great Powers 'would have a good effect' prompted Drummond to contact Cadogan. Great Britain's position in Rio de Janeiro, according to Barbosa Carneiro, was stronger than France's and a British move would perhaps prove successful. The difficulty Drummond noted to Cadogan was to find the right moment which would allow Brazil to return to the League without any loss of face. Cecil's reaction was that if the subject turned up the ambassador might observe to the Foreign Minister that London was surprised that Brazil which had always supported peaceful settlement should withdraw from the League and might even add that it was British policy to strengthen the League.[3]

Drummond returned to the question in early June when a report from Rio de Janeiro as well as a conversation with Barbosa Carneiro gave him the impression that a joint *démarche* of the Great Powers plus Belgium to the Foreign Minister might inevitably lead to Brazil's return to Geneva.[4] Inquiries by the ambassador in Rio de Janeiro on instructions from the Foreign Office and his reply that the report was erroneous confirmed Chamberlain's 'determination not to move in the matter', Drummond was informed, 'and his conviction that Brazil will not be won by the League or the Powers running after her'.[5]

The decision in January 1928 to have the Council appeal to Spain to continue as a League member caused Drummond to

[1] Drummond (Geneva) to Cadogan, 19 Aug. 1926 and Barbosa Carneiro to Drummond, 18 Aug. 1926, FO/371/11897.

[2] [Eric Drummond], Record of Interview, 10 Dec. 1926, FO/371/11899.

[3] Drummond (Geneva) to Cadogan, 30 Mar. 1927, E[ric] D[rummond], Record of Interview, 30 Mar. 1927, and the attached minute by R[obert] C[ecil], FO/371/11965.

[4] Drummond (Geneva) to Cadogan, 3 June 1927, Drummond (Geneva) to Cadogan, 4 June 1927, and [Eric Drummond], Record of Conversation, 4 June 1927, ibid.

[5] An unsigned copy of a letter to Drummond, 20 July 1927, ibid.

request that Brazil also be included in the appeal. He did not see
how it was possible, he informed Chamberlain, for the Council
to avoid it. Certainly the Council's Latin American members
would insist on Brazil's inclusion. Drummond argued that
Brazil's exclusion from the appeal would strengthen those Latin
American elements who were hostile to the League and who
repeatedly declared that it was a solely European instrument. A
favourable reply by Spain to the Council's appeal might cause
Brazil to follow suit in view of the optimistic accounts of political
changes in Brazil received by Thomas. Personally Drummond
thought it more likely that Brazil would be influenced by events
in Argentina rather than what Spain did. In the meantime he
had prepared a statement which the Council might adopt at its
March meeting. It had been difficult to draft and no one had seen
it, not even in the Secretariat.[1] Actually it appeared to
Drummond that if March was ripe for a Council appeal it might
be effective not only in Spain but also in Brazil.[2] Chamberlain
was not convinced. He thought Drummond had 'always been
and still is far too sanguine. The wish is father to the thought'.
Drummond had reported this type of information several times
previously. 'His informants have always been wrong. Our
information has always been proved right'. On 14 February
while in London Drummond called on Chamberlain and
discussed the situation with him. 'I threw a little cold water this
morning', Chamberlain minuted in the pertinent file.[3]

Following this talk with Chamberlain, Drummond had an
interview with Barbosa Carneiro and, as he had promised,
conveyed to Chamberlain a copy of the conversation. Though he
feared it did not appear to lead beyond the point already
reached, it did show that the Council could hardly refrain from
appealing to Brazil when it appealed to Spain. This was Barbosa
Carneiro's 'usual talk and quite futile', Chamberlain minuted.
'He only misleads Sir Eric as to the real position'. Several weeks
later Chamberlain was more blunt about Barbosa Carneiro: 'I

[1] Drummond (Geneva) to Chamberlain, 30 Jan. 1928, AC55/131, Austen
Chamberlain Papers, UB.
[2] Drummond (Geneva) to Selby, 7 Feb. 1928, Austen Chamberlain Papers,
FO/800/262.
[3] Minutes by A[usten] C[hamberlain], 10 Feb. and 14 Feb. 1928, ibid.

continue to distrust the information which reaches Sir Eric thro'
this channel'.[1]

Chamberlain's caustic minutes were well-founded and Drum-
mond himself was not unaware of the difficulties involved. When
a former Brazilian representative suggested that the Great
Powers would lose nothing by renouncing their permanent
Council seats for ten-year mandates, Drummond noted to
Cadogan that if the thought was that Brazil would not return to
Geneva until this condition was fulfilled then the wait would
have to be indefinite.[2] Of course the reports like the one from his
Italian Under Secretary-General Paulucci caused Drummond to
believe that if a simultaneous appeal was made to Brazil and
Spain, Brazil would decide to continue in the League. Chamber-
lain's secretary, however, thought Paulucci's report was overly
optimistic. Chamberlain agreed that 'this optimism is a mere will
of the wisp'.[3]

Drummond's persistence paid off, however, and Chamberlain
finally agreed to include Brazil in the Council's appeal to Spain.
Before the Council took this action Drummond thought it would
be desirable if Brazil was made aware of its intentions and
suggested that the British Ambassador in Rio de Janeiro might
convey this information. His idea was not to ask Brazil's consent
to the Council's action, but to inform her with the explanation
that in view of the matter's great importance the Council would
not feel justified if it took no action. He did not know whether it
would be wise to suggest that if Brazil did not wish to reply to the
Council's appeal the Brazilians should consider the possibility of
extending the *status quo* for another two years. But Drummond's
proposal did not appeal to Chamberlain and he rejected it.
Chamberlain expected that the 'Council will get a snub for its
pains'. Accordingly he saw 'no good reason why the British
Ambassador ... should get snubbed too!'[4]

---

[1] Drummond to Selby, 15 Feb. 1928, [Eric Drummond], Record of
Conversation, 15 Feb. 1928, and minutes by A[usten] C[hamberlain], 16 Feb.
and 1 Mar. [1928], ibid.

[2] Drummond to Cadogan, 16 Feb. 1928 and Mello Franco to Drummond, 25
Jan. 1928, FO/371/12743.

[3] Drummond (Geneva) to Selby, 20 Feb. 1928, Paulucci's report and the
minutes by Walford Selby and A[usten] C[hamberlain], 23 Feb. [1928], ibid.

[4] Drummond (Geneva) to Selby, 23 Feb. 1928 and the attached minute by

As arranged the Council at its March meeting invited Brazil and Spain to continue as League members.[1] The gist of Brazil's rejection of the appeal, however, raised certain fundamental political and constitutional questions. In essence although the Brazilians reaffirmed their decision to withdraw from the League they desired to continue as members of the International Labour Organisation, the World Court, and the League's technical organizations.[2] This desire could have come as no surprise to Drummond for in October 1927 he had raised the possibility of this kind of collaboration with the Brazilian chargé d'affaires in Bern.

Drummond's dilemma was 'whether it was politically desirable that a State could choose the organization to which it desired to belong and refuse its contribution to the organization in which it was not particularly interested'. This type of collaboration, he realized, might create a dangerous precedent and might result in a fall in League contributions and inevitably lead to states which might wish to belong only to certain technical organizations. At the same time he saw the possible advantages. A state might withdraw from the League but remain closely associated with it. After a period of time it might find it unsatisfactory not to be represented in the Assembly and the Council. Since he was unsure of the 'legal and political aspects of the matter' he asked the Legal Section to study the whole question.[3]

By the time Brazil rejected the Council's appeal, however, and proposed this very collaboration Drummond had second thoughts about the matter. He took the legal position that at the expiration of Brazil's two years notice of withdrawal under Article 1 of the Covenant, she automatically ceased to be a member of any League organization. Since Drummond and Thomas disagreed as to whether this also applied to the International Labour Organisation, Drummond was inclined to ask the World Court for an advisory opinion. Regarding the League's technical

A[usten] C[hamberlain], 25 Feb. [1928], Austen Chamberlain Papers, FO/800/262.

[1] League of Nations, *Official Journal*, IX (1928), pp. 405–7, 584–5.

[2] Drummond (Geneva) to Cadogan, 20 Apr. 1928, FO/371/12743.

[3] E[ric] D[rummond], Record of Interview, 3 Oct. 1927, Minutes of a Directors' Meeting, 5 Oct. 1927, LNA; Minutes of a Directors' Meeting, 5 Oct. 1927, LNA.

organizations the only one which specifically provided for non-members of the League was the transit organization. This constitutional clause was framed for the purpose of including those states which had never been League members. Therefore the question was open when one dealt with states which withdrew from the League, but sought election to this organization. In other technical organizations it might be held that there was provision by which states not fully entitled to League membership could become members of these organizations, but this, Drummond claimed, could in no way apply to Brazil. Respecting the World Court there was obviously no participation by states in it, except as members of the Assembly. Brazil would not be eligible to vote at the Assembly's next election for the court's judges unless the court's statute was changed.

Though Drummond believed all this was correct constitutionally the political question that developed was whether it was or was not desirable that Brazil should be allowed to continue as a member of the labour organization and of the League's technical organizations without being a full League member. Brazil's Foreign Minister suggested that these League contacts might ultimately lead to his country's returning to the League, and Drummond had been told that Brazil's next president was likely to be a warm League supporter. Yet against this one had to balance the distinct and real danger that other Latin American states might follow Brazil's example since what appealed to them was the League's technical organizations and not its political functions. If these states could retain their membership in the former while freeing themselves of the latter responsibilities they would be only too pleased to do so. Drummond's own inclination was to adopt the approach that Brazil must realize that she ceased all forms of international co-operation by resigning her League membership, even though this might create difficulties and a vexing dispute with the International Labour Organisation. He was particularly interested in knowing, he asked Cadogan, the Foreign Office's thoughts on this question. Of course, he believed that it was far easier to be accommodating to Brazil, but he honestly feared the dangers that lay in a precedent and his Latin American contacts stressed this very much. He thought it useful that the British delegation which would come to the conference of the International Labour Organisation should be aware of the constitutional situation regarding Brazil's withdrawal from the League and its effects on the labour organization. It was very likely, he noted, that Thomas would try to get the conference to move some resolution to the effect that Brazil should continue as a member of the organization even if she withdrew from the League. Personally, Drummond doubted whether the conference had any valid powers to pass such a resolution.[1] Drummond's attempt to drum up support against Brazil's membership in the labour organization proved abortive. When Brazil's position was raised at the meeting of the labour conference on 28 May, the chairman observed that the conference 'was not competent to settle the legal question raised by the special situation of Brazil'.[2]

Though Drummond was unsatisfied at the way the constitutional question had been avoided and personally believed that Brazil legally was not a member of the labour organization he appears to have said nothing publicly. Brazil continued as a member of Thomas's organization, the World Court, and participated in the League's various technical organizations; she paid contributions to all of them.[3]

Drummond did not return to the question until February 1930. Private information reached him that Julio Prestes, who would become Brazil's president in November, intended during May to visit London, Paris, and Rome. If this trip materialized it would prove a fine opportunity, he informed Cadogan, to discuss with Prestes Brazil's position toward the League. He felt

[1] Drummond (Geneva) to Cadogan, 20 Apr. 1928, FO/371/12743. See also, E[ric] D[rummond], Note by the Secretary-General, 20 Apr. 1928, General and Miscellaneous 1928–32: 50/4061/2537, LNA.

[2] Draft Minutes of the Second Sitting of the Governing Body of the International Labour Office, 28 May 1928, General and Miscellaneous, 1928–32: 50/4061/2537, LNA.

[3] E[ric] D[rummond], Record of Interview, 19 Oct. 1928, ibid.; [Eric Drummond], Note by the Secretary-General, 20 Apr. 1929, FO/371/13469; E[ric] D[rummond], Note by the Secretary-General, 14 Aug. 1929, Administrative Commissions Danzig 1928–32: 2B/12404/12404, LNA; E[ric] D[rummond], Record of Conversation, 3 Sept. 1929, E[ric] D[rummond], Note by the Secretary-General, 6 Sept. 1929, E[ric] D[rummond], Record of Conversation, 17 Sept. 1929, General and Miscellaneous 1928–32: 50/4061/2537, LNA; E[ric] D[rummond], Note to a memorandum by M. Buero, 25 Oct. 1929, Administrative Commissions Danzig 1928–32: 2B/12404/12404, LNA; Walters, pp. 196, 389–90, 788.

sure that it would be very useful if during Prestes's London visit he could be made aware of the importance which Great Britain attached to Brazil's return to Geneva. Drummond held that the advantages that would accrue to Brazil by returning to the League would be considerable, keeping in mind that since her departure from Geneva she had played only a secondary role in world affairs. He expected that the French would certainly do what they could along the lines he had indicated. Perhaps Cadogan, he observed, at the proper moment would bring the matter to the attention of those who could implement his suggestion.[1]

He raised the issue with Cadogan again in late March.[2] In mid-May Drummond arranged to have an interview with Prestes. It was agreed that it would be wiser if this interview occurred after Prestes had been in Europe a little because if Drummond attempted to see him too soon after his arrival, it would appear like too direct an approach on the League's behalf and might have an effect contrary to that desired. When pressed to give Prestes assurances that a high position in the Secretariat would be reserved for a Brazilian, Drummond responded that he regretted that he did not think he could do this. However, it could be explained to Prestes that if Brazil returned to the League such a possibility was in no way ruled out and as proof of this he could remind him of the offer that had previously been made to Fernandes. Drummond pointed out that as a League member Brazil would have a finer chance of electing a Brazilian to the World Court since the elections took place in Geneva and tended to work in favour of nationals from countries who were League members.[3]

When Drummond did see Prestes in July he explained that he had never been able to understand why Brazilian public opinion thought that the League's decision to give only Germany a permanent Council seat was harmful to its own country's prestige. Only Germany, he noted, had been assured of everyone's support. This included the Latin American states who also objected to any one of their own receiving a permanent seat. This feeling had worked against Brazil, but her position was no

[1] Drummond (Geneva) to Cadogan, 26 Feb. 1930, FO/371/14206.
[2] Drummond to Cadogan, 24 Mar. 1930, ibid.
[3] Eric Drummond, Record of Interview, 17 May 1930, ibid.

worse than Spain's. In fact, it was more advantageous than Spain's since Madrid's hopes had been raised by a promise that it would be given a permanent seat. Spain had, however, returned to the League while unfortunately Brazil remained outside. Drummond argued that Brazil's prior statements that she was not working for herself in seeking a permanent seat but for Latin America had now come to fruition. There was now a definite but informal arrangement that Latin America would always have three of the Council's non-permanent seats, and Drummond wondered whether this great achievement had been fully understood by Brazil's public opinion. Though Prestes did not want to promise anything that might commit him for the future he did formally assure Drummond that when he became president 'he would examine the whole situation with the greatest care'. No reasonable man, Drummond responded, could ask for more. The interview had gone 'better than I expected', he informed Cadogan.[1]

What Prestes would have done will never be known. Before he could assume office a *coup d'état* was staged by Getúlio Vargas, and Prestes along with the incumbent president were exiled to Europe. By this point Drummond was preparing for his Latin American trip and Brazilian events were obviously a setback. In order to make his trip as successful as possible Drummond asked the Foreign Office whether it thought that the Prince of Wales, who would also be in Latin America at about the same time, could be induced to say some words at each Latin American capital that he visited in support of Drummond's mission or in praise of the League. Drummond felt sure that if the Prince acted as he had suggested the result would be very beneficial. If he refrained from saying anything it would be thought that Great Britain was not really interested in the League or in the success of Drummond's mission.[2]

Because of the completely informal nature of the Prince's visit the Foreign Office instead offered to arrange that if the Prince and Drummond's itineraries crossed to give full publicity to the warm reception which the Prince would doubtlessly wish to give Drummond. The Foreign Office hoped that its proposal would

[1] Drummond to Cadogan, 4 July 1930 and the enclosed interview with Prestes, 4 July 1930, ibid.
[2] Drummond to Selby, 14 Nov. 1930, FO/371/14186.

help to achieve the purpose that Drummond had in mind.[1] The Foreign Office's proposal was far short of what Drummond had envisaged and although he did not realize it at the time it was a blessing in disguise. As he subsequently admitted to Cadogan, it was on the whole probably a wise decision for during his trip there were too many people who appeared to think that there was some sort of connection between his journey and that of the Prince of Wales.[2]

In view of Vargas's *coup d'état* Drummond upon his arrival in Rio de Janeiro was careful about discussing the possibility of Brazil's return to the League. However, in an interview with Vargas he pointed out that the world economic crisis showed the 'inter-dependence of all nations, and therefore the value of the League at least as a clearing-house'. His general impression after his visit was that there was nothing to be done in Brazil, at least for the moment. When things had settled down and a 'favourable opportunity arose it ought not to be impossible' to devise a method for Brazil's return to the League.[3]

Drummond's six weeks' Latin American tour in which he showed the League flag, so to speak,[4] surpassed his expectations.[5] Interestingly, he used his presence in Latin America to plead for greater British support for the League in that region since Drummond did not believe that London would likely lose any prestige or material benefits by rendering such support. Likewise he alerted Henderson to the fact that in the whole area there was the general feeling that a European war was in the offing. This resulted in a lack of confidence in any collaboration with Europe whether commercial or otherwise, and although he had had some success in dissipating this feeling, fortnightly syndicated newspaper articles by Lloyd George, he noted, had a considerable and very negative impact.[6]

[1] Selby to Drummond, 14 Nov. 1930, ibid.

[2] Drummond (Geneva) to Cadogan, 21 Feb. 1931, FO/371/15052.

[3] E[ric] D[rummond], Note by the Secretary-General on his visit to Rio de Janeiro, 19–20 Dec. 1930 and E[ric] D[rummond], Note by the Secretary-General on his visit to Santos and São Paulo, 21 Dec. 1930, General and Miscellaneous 1928–32: 50/25677/722, LNA.

[4] All the pertinent memorandums can be found in General and Miscellaneous 1928–32: 50/25677/722, LNA, and in FO/371/15052.

[5] Drummond (Geneva) to Cecil, 2 Mar. 1931, Add. MS. 51112, Robert Cecil Papers, BL.

[6] Drummond to Henderson, 7 Jan. 1931, FO/371/15720.

To dispel the feeling that a war was imminent Drummond during his visit to Cuba left a letter for the Prince of Wales with the British chargé d'affaires. He drew the Prince's attention to the matter, as he thought that he might desire during his Latin American tour perhaps to correct this misconception as to Europe's stability.[1] Regarding Lloyd George's articles, Drummond attempted to handle that problem through Kerr. Aside from being pessimistic and giving the impression that a war was impending these articles also disturbed Drummond for they were 'continuously attacking the League indirectly'. Why this was so Drummond did not know. As one of its founders Lloyd George, he noted, should be very proud of it. These articles did not make for League popularity in Latin America. The end result was to make Latin America turn increasingly to the United States rather than to Europe and the League. He told Kerr all this, Drummond admitted, 'because you may think it possible to pass it on [to Lloyd George] in some discreet form'.[2] What Kerr did, if anything, is unclear, but spurred by Drummond's messages the Foreign Office attempted by a circular dispatch to all British missions in Latin America to cover the points he had raised.[3]

Drummond's other observations about American influence in the area were not amenable to immediate Foreign Office action. Though he thought American policy in Latin America was somewhat obscure, consciously or unconsciously it appeared to be directed toward disparaging Europe, Great Britain, and the League. Washington did this in order to turn Latin America toward Pan-Americanism as well as to turn its economic and financial relations toward the United States rather than elsewhere. On the other hand, this American attempt to monopolize Latin America was largely, if not entirely, offset by Latin America's instinctive fear that it will be absorbed by the United States. Of course this was helpful regarding its relationship with the League. The strongest anti-American feeling was to be found in Argentina and it also existed in other countries. It seemed that some of these countries were caught in a struggle which they themselves disliked, but had not perhaps the energy

---

[1] Morris (Havana) to Henderson, 4 Feb. 1931, ibid.
[2] Drummond to Kerr, 7 Jan. 1931, File GD40/17/247, Lothian Papers, SRO.
[3] Drummond (Geneva) to Cadogan, 17 Aug. 1931, FO/371/15720.

to escape from. Nor did Drummond know they would be able to escape even if they possessed such energy.[1]

Actually, the Latin Americans had a greater instinct for survival than Drummond gave them credit for. Thanks to Drummond's endeavours, the exigencies of world politics, and the shifting balance of forces in the southern hemisphere, within a year after his departure from Geneva almost every Latin American state was an active League member with the exceptions of Costa Rica and Brazil who never rejoined the organization. To Rio de Janeiro acceptance of the League had been a kind of high risk adventure in which successes in Europe would be used to enhance Brazil's own position in Latin America where her immediate interests lay. It undoubtedly thought that Argentina's absence from the League could be used, in conjunction with the general rearrangements that would have to be made when Germany entered the League, to secure a permanent Council seat. A legal and symbolic recognition of great power status, the acquisition of a permanent Council seat would have given Brazil a position among the Latin American states second to none. But the gamble failed and the loss of face and prestige by the acceptance of any lesser seating arrangement in the Council necessitated withdrawal from the organization. As in the case of Argentina it can be questioned whether attempts to entice Brazil back to Geneva were wise—whether the flame was worth the candle. On the other hand, to have made no attempt might also have been unwise, if even the remotest possibility existed that Brazil might return. As in the case of Argentina Drummond perhaps failed to see that the will to use the organization, and the political advantages that would accrue by doing so, would in the last analysis decide whether Brazil would or would not return to Geneva. As in the late 1930s when there was an exodus of Latin American states from Geneva, Brazil's departure was largely due to events and conditions external to the League setting. To a certain extent Brazil's attitude was also shaped by the League's inability to control effectively inter-state conflicts in Latin America itself. This was largely due to America's non-membership and the simultaneous need to have her political co-operation in the area plus the political competition among the Latin American states themselves, especially the ABC powers.

[1] Drummond (Geneva) to Cadogan, 21 Feb. 1931, FO/371/15052.

Latin American Disputes

Preceding the League's establishment inter-state relations in Latin America had been little different from those of Europe. Balancing alliances, marked by border disputes and armed conflict were not unfamiliar in the political landscape of the southern hemisphere. The Tacna–Arica dispute, emanating from the War of the Pacific (1879–84), which pitted Chile against Bolivia and Peru was potentially one of the most complicated and vexing problems that the League might be asked to tackle.

The Chileans feared in June 1920 that an appeal to the League over this dispute might be made either by Bolivia or Peru or by both states acting together. Santiago maintained that questions relating to prior treaties dealing with this territorial dispute did not fall within the League's competence. Indeed, Chile's Edwards argued that it was the League's very existence which led to the dispute not being solved since it raised Peruvian hopes of League intervention. Could Drummond think, Edwards asked, of a way by which the League could declare to Chile, Bolivia, and Peru that this particular dispute lay outside its competence? Drummond feared that the League could not adopt such an attitude. He assured Edwards that the League would greatly prefer to see disputes settled by direct negotiations between the parties themselves than by having them brought before the League for a decision. Drummond also thought it impracticable to have the League declare that it would not take notice of any Latin American dispute unless the approbation of the Pan-American Union was first secured. It would create a new precedent, he argued, since in the past Latin American states had submitted disputes to European arbitration, for example to the Kings of Great Britain and Spain, without any reference to the Pan-American Union. Drummond asked Edwards to consider whether it would not be possible for his country to bring the Tacna–Arica dispute before the Council. It could state that the dispute had existed for a long time and that it would be very willing, provided the Council agreed, 'to accept the mediation of three arbitrators appointed by the League to study the question on the spot'. Would not this be a grand gesture on Chile's part, he observed, and take the wind out of Peru's sails since she could hardly reject such mediation?

Though Edwards did not commit himself he explained that Chile intended to claim that the peace treaty of 1883 was a regional arrangement meant to maintain the peace and therefore fell outside the Council's purview under Article 21 of the Covenant. Naturally he could not comment on it officially, Drummond observed, but personally he doubted very much whether this Chilean argument was valid.[1]

No moves were made until the Assembly's first session. In separate notes to Drummond both Bolivia and Peru requested that the dispute be placed on the Assembly's agenda and that under Articles 15 and 19 the League revise the prior treaties dealing with this question. Pressure from other delegations and American absence from the League caused the Bolivians and the Peruvians to withdraw their requests. Resubmitted by Bolivia at the Assembly's 1921 session the relevancy of Article 19 involved in the request was examined by a jurists' committee. They concluded that the Bolivian request was not in order since the Assembly could not on its own modify any treaty. The modification of treaties, the committee correctly pointed out, was solely within the competence of the organization's member states.[2] Thus the Tacna–Arica dispute was not examined by the League. It was finally solved some years later outside the League system,[3] but the Assembly's rejection of the request soured both countries toward the organization. Until the dispute was settled Bolivia and Peru absented themselves from League meetings and activities and fell further and further behind in their budget contributions.[4] The very nature of the dispute, however, and the inflexible position assumed by the parties gave Drummond little room for manœuvre.

Drummond assumed a more active role in February 1921 when Costa Rican forces seized and occupied a disputed area on the border with Panama. According to contemporary press reports Drummond instructed the Council's 'political advisers',

[1] E[ric] D[rummond], Record of Interview, 9 June 1920, Political 1920: 11/4773/12, LNA.

[2] Kelchner, pp. 75–82, 103–4, 113.

[3] William Jefferson Dennis, *Tacna and Arica; An Account of the Chile–Peru Boundary Dispute and the Arbitrations by the United States* (New Haven: Yale University Press, 1931), pp. 194–289.

[4] Kelchner, pp. 104–6, 114.

which one must assume meant the Secretariat's Political Section, to investigate this dispute with a view to the League's intervention. Though Drummond based this action on newspaper reports, neither Costa Rica, Panama, nor any other League member brought the matter to the Council's attention.[1] Technically, by his instructions to the Political Section to investigate the dispute Drummond had not officially submitted the question to the Council which under Article 11 of the Covenant could only be done by a League member. This fine point was missed by Senator William Borah of Idaho, one of the mainstays in the Senate's opposition to the Versailles Treaty and the Covenant. Borah strenuously objected to Drummond's action, claiming that it confirmed the opposition that had been raised against the League and violated the Monroe Doctrine.[2] It was a fine point that has also been missed by subsequent chroniclers of this event.[3] In view of the raw nerve that had been irritated in Washington, discretion was necessary and at the Council's meeting of 1 March Drummond explained that he had prepared a telegram to be sent to both governments since it appeared from press reports that the dispute had now been satisfactorily settled and that therefore it was unnecessary for the Council to intervene. The Council agreed and the telegram was sent. Several days later, however, the Council reversed itself when it observed that 'certain reports' had been brought to its attention showing that tension still existed between the two governments. It felt obligated to bring these reports to their attention since both states were League members who had solemnly accepted the Covenant's principles and obligations. The Council's request was for factual information. When informed by Panama that she had accepted an American offer of good offices the Council expressed its pleasure and divorced itself from the dispute despite subsequent Panamanian objections that Washington's attempts to settle the question were unacceptable to her.[4]

It is obvious from these events that although Drummond had

---

[1] *New York Times*, 1 Mar. 1921, p. 3; Kelchner, p. 120.

[2] *New York Times*, 1 Mar. 1921, p. 3; Rovine, p. 65.

[3] Walters, p. 137; Rovine, p. 65.

[4] League of Nations, Council, *Minutes of the Twelfth Session of the Council of the League of Nations Held in Paris, February 21–March 4, 1921*, pp. 27, 42, 199–201; League of Nations, *Official Journal*, II (1921), pp. 214–19.

not officially submitted the question to the Council since this was not allowed under the Covenant, he had behind the scenes brought the question to its attention. Seven years later in December 1928 he was less circumspect in his actions when fighting broke out between Bolivian and Paraguayan forces in the Chaco Boreal, the first skirmish of what later was to develop into one of Latin America's bitterest wars.

As the Council was about to convene in Lugano, press reports describing what had occurred appeared. Bolivia had broken off diplomatic relations with Paraguay and there was a strong possibility of open hostilities.[1] In this situation Drummond, one of his chief collaborators recorded, 'took upon himself the responsibility of laying the question before the Council'. Obviously this kind of action took place only behind the scenes since, as we have seen, this could be done only by a League member. Drummond, however, felt 'certain that most members, at least, of the Council would agree that it ought not to disregard what looked like a real threat to peace'. By this point Drummond had been in power for over nine years and his influence, experience, and expertise were beginning to carry some weight in the League's antechambers. Fortuitously, the Council's President was Briand and their long and close collaboration helped smooth and expedite Drummond's action.[2] In order to avoid the pitfall posed by the Monroe Doctrine the Council anodynely reminded both sides of their obligations as League members, warned against military action that might aggravate the problem, and requested Briand to follow events and convene a special Council session if further fighting erupted.[3]

Drummond pointed out to the Bolivian Minister in Bern, Alberto Cortadellas, that though both governments were willing to continue the mediation or arbitration procedure instituted by Argentina to ascertain where the real frontier was in the Chaco, Bolivia had declared that she could not continue this procedure until she had received reparations for the injuries she had suffered stemming from the recent frontier incident. He felt that the two matters could be separated and that they should discuss

---

[1] Kelchner, p. 180.   [2] Walters, pp. 393–4.
[3] League of Nations, *Official Journal*, X (1929), pp. 21, 40–1, 56, 71–3, 253–6, 264–6; *PRFRUS, 1928*, i. 686.

only the matter of reparations. He reminded Cortadellas that under Article 13 of the Covenant there was provision for reparations for exactly such incidents. Bolivia could very well ask for arbitration over this matter and be awarded such damages as proved to be owed it. Drummond felt bound to observe that above all the Council desired that the problem should be peacefully settled. It had no special desire to be the instrument that arranged the settlement. If there were other preferred means, he noted, for example Argentina's arbitration, the Council would be just as happy. Drummond thought it well to make this point since Cortadellas in his comments appeared to imply that it was the League's desire to settle the matter itself. Cortadellas remarked that the matter was more likely to be solved now than before.[1]

He was right. Briand and Drummond working closely together assisted in having both Bolivia and Paraguay accept the good offices of the Pan-American Arbitration Conference.[2] Drummond later admitted that at one point he was most anxious about the dispute. After spending a day at Geneva on his return from the Council's Lugano meeting he had gone to Paris to be at Briand's disposal during the crisis. Drummond feared that the question was likely to run through Christmas and that he would have to remain in Paris. Unexpectedly matters turned out well and he thought that the League's action had been both 'effective and justified'. He observed that interestingly the Council had acted without receiving any appeal from either Bolivia or Paraguay or from any League member. If its action had been criticized he thought it would have relied and rightly so on Article 4 paragraph 4 of the Covenant—which allowed the Council to deal with any matter within the League's sphere of action or affecting world peace. In addition, the obligations that both Bolivia and Paraguay acknowledged were those found in the Covenant and this gave the Council a most effective weapon

---

[1] E[ric] D[rummond], Record of Interview, 17 Dec. 1928, Political General 1928–32: 1A/8946/2042, LNA.

[2] E[ric] D[rummond], Results of a Conversation with M. Briand, 18 Dec. 1928, E[ric] D[rummond], Record of Interview, 19 Dec. 1928, Political General 1928–32: 1A/8946/2042, LNA; League of Nations, *Official Journal*, X (1929), pp. 266–9; *PRFRUS, 1928*, i. 698–700; Margaret La Foy, *The Chaco Dispute and the League of Nations* (Bryn Mawr, 1941), pp. 22–3.

which it utilized to the utmost.[1] Drummond disengenuously noted that the question had been treated by the Council as it would have treated a European one, if allowance was made for the geographical disparities.[2]

In early January 1929 the Pan-American Arbitration Conference arranged for the suspension of hostilities and appointed a commission of inquiry and conciliation, also called the neutral commission. Though the neutral commission arranged a settlement of the December 1928 border incident its efforts to solve the Chaco dispute by proposing arbitration were unsuccessful. In early October 1929 the five governments whose representatives composed the neutral commission warned that unless the fundamental question was settled there would be a reoccurrence of the December 1928 border incident. Their warning went unheeded.[3] 'We are following the matter as closely as possible', Drummond noted on 14 January 1930, 'but I do not think it would be possible or desirable in present conditions to take any action vis-à-vis either Bolivia or Paraguay'. He felt sure that the League was in a position to be informed if the situation deteriorated or if there was danger of open conflict.[4] Indeed, two days after writing this note Drummond was informed by the Paraguayan Minister in Paris that fighting had again erupted in the Chaco. Drummond limited himself to forwarding these messages to the Council's president who was assured by both sides that they would continue to seek a solution by peaceful means. By May the diplomatic contacts which had been ruptured in December 1928 were re-established, but the fundamental question remained unsolved.[5]

For the next two years the intermittent but unsuccessful negotiations continued. In June 1932 serious fighting erupted once again which the neutral commission attempted to control. Since Bolivia had never accepted the Kellogg–Briand Pact the only obligation against war common to both sides was the Covenant. With the neutral commission involved in the question and the Council also competent to intervene, a jurisdictional

---

[1] Drummond (Geneva) to Bullard, 9 Jan. 1929, Arthur Bullard Papers, PU.
[2] Drummond (Geneva) to Bullard, 28 Jan. 1929, ibid.
[3] *PRFRUS, 1930*, i. 818–933.
[4] A note by Eric Drummond, 14 Jan. 1930, FO/371/14182.
[5] La Foy, pp. 28–30.

clash between the two bodies was possible. To avoid this, the procedure suggested by Drummond, and the one that was accepted by both the Council and the neutral commission, was that the Council should point out to Bolivia and Paraguay their Covenant obligations and strongly urge both of them to entrust the question to the neutral commission. In turn Drummond desired to be kept informed of what the neutral commission was doing and what progress it was achieving. He especially wanted this information during the Assembly session. Drummond thought he could 'keep the matter entirely within the bounds of co-operation with the work of the Commission of Neutrals'.[1]

By November this co-operation was being strained by the neutral commission's delays in keeping the Council informed. Argentina spoke of presenting a plan for League action. Drummond observed that naturally if Argentina presented a plan under the Covenant the League would be obliged to consider it but he hoped the plan would not be presented in view of the neutral commissioners' efforts which seemed to be going well. By mid-November because of the continued fighting there was a growing feeling in the Council that something should be done. If this feeling could not be contained Drummond hoped to propose that the Council inform Bolivia and Paraguay that it was happy to note that in line with Article 12 direct negotiations were taking place under the neutral commission's auspicies; that the Council regretted that severe fighting continued and that it called on both parties to cease hostilities; that the Council insisted that both sides accept the neutral commission's proposal of dispatching a military commission to examine the facts and arrange that there be no resumption of fighting; and lastly, that the Council consider that a refusal by either side constituted a denial of its Covenant obligations. Drummond thought that this Council communication would have a beneficial effect, aid the efforts of the neutral commission, and run no risk of upsetting actions taken by Washington and the neutral commission. As previously, Drummond's suggestion was duly channelled into

---

[1] *PRFRUS, 1932,* v. 220–30, 234–6, 241; League of Nations, *Official Journal,* XIII (1932), pp. 1720–1, 1923–5, 1944–6; Walters, p. 529.

the Council's bosom and with slight modifications accepted by it on 25 November.[1]

In early 1933 Drummond was again enmeshed in the Chaco question. In late January he pointed out to the American Minister in Bern, Wilson, that the continued fighting had upset the Council. It felt that it had to act and hoped that Washington would support it in the same way the Council had supported the efforts of the neutral commission. The Council proposed that in view of the present deadlock that it send a commission of inquiry to Bolivia and Paraguay, and if necessary and practicable to the Chaco itself. The commission would attempt to propose a substantive solution to the dispute. It would be instructed to act in consultation, as far as this was possible, with those states which had also been involved in attempting to find a solution to this question. Its first duty would be to arrange an immediate cease-fire. This three-man commission, according to Drummond, would be composed of an American, an Argentine, and someone from a small European power. He explained to Wilson that there was no desire to remove the matter from the hands of the neutral commission. It was only because of the present deadlock that this step had been felt desirable in view of the League's obligations. Both of them knew that there was a certain rivalry between Argentina and the United States regarding this dispute. La Paz wanted a settlement arrived at in Washington while Asunción favoured one reached in Buenos Aires. It seemed to Drummond virtually impossible to secure a solution to the conflict unless both of these positions were abandoned. The Council's proposal seemed to allow for a way out. The United States and Argentina would both be on the commission and the commission need not operate out of Buenos Aires.

In view of Drummond's ability to disguise his own thoughts and proposals as those of others, especially in the Chaco dispute,

---

[1] *PRFRUS, 1932*, v. 242–4; League of Nations, *Official Journal*, XIII (1932), pp. 1951–2. According to Argentina's Foreign Minister, Saavedra Lamas, Drummond had asked him if the League should intervene in the Chaco dispute and he had replied in the affirmative. *DDF 1932–1939*, I, i. 601. Since Saavedra Lamas is described as a 'devious and audacious diplomat' it would be safe to say that his comment was really a trial balloon which he credited to Drummond. See Bryce Wood, *The United States and Latin American Wars 1932–1942* (New York: Columbia University Press, 1966), pp. 31–2 and *passim*.

it would be safe to assume that this proposal was one that he had nurtured himself. Regardless, Washington was unfriendly to the proposal and its rejection by Bolivia and Paraguay sealed its fate.[1] Drummond's last venture in the Chaco dispute was in May following Paraguay's formal declaration of war against Bolivia. At this point it was resolved to dispatch a League commission to the Chaco for the purpose of bringing about an effective armistice and, if possible, of negotiating an agreement under which the dispute would be submitted to arbitration. In handing this draft proposal to Wilson several days before it was considered and adopted by the Council, Drummond anticipated that both parties would not immediately accept its recommendations. He explained that the Council felt that it had no alternative but to act in the question. The conflict's duration, the failure of all efforts to effect a settlement, Paraguay's declaration of war, and finally the appeals of both governments to the Council at different periods had created a situation where the Council had to act according to the Covenant's obligations. Drummond sincerely hoped, he noted to Wilson, that the manner in which the Council would act was agreeable to Washington and if it was, that it might be possible for the neutral commission to advise Bolivia that it regarded the Council's procedure as a reasonable solution to the question and hoped that both sides would accept it. The neutral commission agreed, but despite the Council's action the Chaco dispute dragged on long after Drummond departed from the League.[2]

During this same period Drummond was involved in another Latin American conflict when Peruvian forces in September 1932 occupied the Colombian district of Leticia which Peru had ceded to Columbia in 1922. Peruvian resistance to any Colombian reoccupation of the area plus the failure of Brazilian mediation,[3] prompted Drummond in mid-January 1933 to dispatch messages reminding both states of their obligations as League members.[4]

[1] E[ric] D[rummond], Record of Interview, 27 Jan. 1933, and E[ric] D[rummond], Record of Interview, 30 Jan. 1933, FO/371/16519; *PRFRUS, 1933*, iv. 262–7.

[2] *PRFRUS, 1933*, iv. 323, 325–7, 330–1.

[3] Walters, pp. 536–7.

[4] E[ric] D[rummond], Note by the Secretary-General, 13 Jan. 1933, Political 1933–40: 1/751/531, LNA.

When Drummond explained his intended action, the Irish representative, Sean Lester, agreed that the messages should be immediately dispatched in the name of his fellow countryman, the Council's President, Eamon De Valera, and should be circulated and published. When the Council met De Valera would explain what he had done and ask his colleagues to support his action. Lester likewise agreed that Drummond should convey a private message to the Great Powers and to Spain, asking either on his own behalf, or if necessary he could say after consultation with De Valera, for their diplomatic support of De Valera's action.[1] Actually when the messages were sent to Colombia and Peru they were signed by Lester himself.[2]

Peru then appealed to the League to have Colombia suspend all military measures. Drummond's attitude was that this appeal as well as Colombia's appeal to Washington under the Kellogg–Briand Pact 'were so alike in spirit as to exert a coordinated influence'. To mobilize world public opinion and bring pressure to bear from as many states as possible on Colombia and Peru Drummond thought it would be most useful if the Department of State's communication to Peru on 25 January examining the whole situation could be formally conveyed to him—it was—with permission to circulate it. Following these comments to the American Consul, both the Bolivian and Peruvian representatives called on Drummond to discuss possible methods for solving the dispute. Drummond noted that a Brazilian proposal offered a possible solution to the question; a proposal that Peru surrender Leticia to Brazilian army units which would occupy it for ten days after which Leticia would be returned by these same army units to the Colombian authorities. When the Peruvian representatives explained that it was the ten-day time period that posed difficulties, the idea developed that the Brazilian occupation might be prolonged for a month or six weeks. Drummond made it clear to both men that this suggestion was a purely personal one on his part, and that in offering it he in no way committed the League or any member of the organization.

Reflecting their faith in Drummond, two days later these same representatives again called on him. On his own responsibility

[1] E[ric] D[rummond], Record of Interview, 14 Jan. 1933, ibid.
[2] League of Nations, *Official Journal*, XIV (1933), pp. 527–8; *PRFRUS, 1933*, iv. 405, 421.

the Colombian submitted to Drummond certain proposals which in his opinion might form the basis for a settlement of the dispute. Drummond suggested and both representatives agreed that in view of proposals that had been tendered to Lima, including those of the United States, it was advisable to abstain from further action in Geneva. This would allow the governments which had intervened in the dispute 'sufficient time to develop their action particularly as it was felt that any new suggestions emanating from Geneva now might create confusion and result in a misunderstanding'.

In the weeks that followed Drummond's contacts as well as his collaboration were close with the Department of State through the American Minister in Bern. Frustrated, however, at her inability to reoccupy Leticia, Colombia in late February requested that the dispute be dealt with under Article 15. Drummond hoped that the Council would not be content merely with the adoption of a report under paragraph four of Article 15. The Leticia issue, he observed, was clear-cut and all states agreed that Peru was the aggressor state. He doubted the advisability of breaking diplomatic relations with Peru since he recognized the danger and even the disaster that this might involve for foreign interests. He believed, however, he informed Wilson, that an arms embargo perhaps followed by other forms of embargo could be applied against Peru. Several days after expressing these opinions Drummond had a number of talks with the Peruvian representative. From these talks it was Drummond's impression that Peru was unsure of what course she should pursue and was especially apprehensive at the possibility of sanctions.

This led Drummond to express the opinion to Wilson that it would be most useful if he could have some indication of how Washington would view the possibility of an arms embargo against Peru. No arms embargo was imposed. Instead the Council recommended that Peru withdraw her troops from Leticia and only after this had been done should negotiations commence on the various grievances raised by Peru against Colombia. Though Colombia accepted the Council's recommendation Peru rejected it. The situation deteriorated. Peruvian warships were sent through the Panama Canal with orders to go up the Amazon River and join the Peruvian forces near Leticia. The Council asked member states of the League to refrain from giving this naval force any assistance. Despite this request the Peruvian ships were re-supplied at Curaçao, Trinidad, and Haiti. The Council's endeavour was of course undercut by these actions of the Dutch, British, and Haitian authorities. This was too much for Drummond who declared that giving facilities to the Peruvian warships played into Lima's hands. The best possible support for the Council's settlement proposals, he observed, was to withhold these facilities and delay the arrival of the Peruvian ships at Leticia. The assassination of the Peruvian dictator, Sanchez Cerro, soon led to further negotiations and an agreement for settling the dispute. Leticia was surrendered by Peruvian forces to a League commission which administered the area with Colombian troops. A year later, following negotiations between the two sides under a Brazilian chairman, the commission relinquished Leticia to Colombia.[1]

For Drummond, the League, and the world at large, the peaceful settlement of the Leticia dispute was a very small ray of light in a world community where increasingly by 1933 a small number of powerful states were committed to an anti-*status quo* policy, a policy which in turn led to feelings of insecurity among a greater number of smaller and less powerful states. The United States' lack of involvement in the League and her general withdrawal from world affairs was especially crippling to the League in Latin America where Washington's influence was considerable and its co-operation and support indispensable if the League was to succeed in controlling the level of inter-state violence in the southern hemisphere. This explains Drummond's constant preoccupation with Washington's attitude reflected in his continuing contacts with the American Minister in Bern. European affairs also contributed to the League's and Drummond's often weak or aborted moves in Latin America. The European balance of power and the avoidance of armed conflict in Europe understandably dominated the League's and Drummond's actions during these years to the detriment of Latin America, a situation compounded by Latin America's geographical remoteness and its minimal political impact on Europe in a global political system which was far less interdependent than it is today. In turn Latin America's limited economic development

---

[1] *PRFRUS, 1933,* iv. 423–8, 430–1, 433–4, 438, 457, 459, 460–1, 482, 490–3, 495–6, 527–8, 530–2; Walters, pp. 537–40.

and its very geographic remoteness and political isolation from European events made it difficult to coerce individual Latin American states either by the League or by other outside powers, including the United States, especially when they dealt with the ABC powers.

In a sense Latin America's position was not unique for even states within Europe were immune to Drummond's and the League's endeavours. Italy was one such state. Indeed, it was one of the most important of the anti-*status quo* countries during Drummond's tenure and it is his relations with Italy both before and after Mussolini's acquisition of power that we will now examine.

VI

ITALY AND THE *STATUS QUO*

From Versailles to Corfu

Long after his retirement Drummond observed that by the end of his first year he had largely succeeded in gaining the complete confidence of every League member and in inspiring the belief that he was an international officer ready to serve and help in their international difficulties as far as was compatible with the Covenant's principles.

This confidence was initially earned when he strongly took issue with British proposals to reduce the League's budget. Many of the Assembly's representatives were astonished and, Drummond thought, pleased by his action. They seemed to have expected that he would submit without objection to the British proposals and when Drummond resisted they concluded that he was truly impartial. There were, however, variations of confidence in Drummond. On this sliding scale confidence in him 'was far less in the case of Italy than in the countries of the Little Entente and Scandinavia'. Drummond thought the smaller the state the greater trust it placed in the Secretary-General.[1]

Italian suspicion of Drummond was not something personal but based on concrete political considerations. Whether right or wrong, as a member of the victorious Allied coalition Italy was convinced that she had not been sufficiently compensated in the Paris peace treaties for the role she had played and the contribution that she had made to the war effort. Thus she was the one ally which also happened to be anti-*status quo* oriented. In particular Italy's inability to secure what she desired especially along the Adriatic's Istrian–Dalmatian littoral encouraged the thought that a British Secretary-General might be unresponsive to Rome as was his government. Drummond's position therefore was far more complicated in dealing with Italy than in dealing

---

[1] Handwritten comments by Sir Eric Drummond (Lord Perth) 31 Jan. 1951, which were prepared and sent in response to questions posed by Stephen M. Schwebel. These notes were kindly made available to the author by Mr. Schwebel.

with Germany. Basically his task was to moderate Italy's claims especially in areas where Rome felt it had legitimate rights: the Balkans, East Africa, Albania, and so on. The rise of the Fascist state under Benito Mussolini only aggravated this relationship, for the Duce's regime was willing to use force on the international scene to achieve its goals as well as coercive diplomatic methods, including, for example, support of dissident elements within a neighbouring country against which Italy had demands, as in the case of Yugoslavia. At the same time in his attempts to moderate or accommodate Italy's drives Drummond had to make sure that his attempts never aggravated Rome to such a point that it would withdraw from the League or that it would complain about him in London or Paris. At the minimum in order to be successful any action that he took with Rome necessitated the consent and preferably the active support of London and Paris.

Working against Drummond of course was his prior service as a British diplomat and especially his close collaboration as Secretary-General with successive London governments and their instruments of foreign policy: the Foreign Office and the various political personages who represented Whitehall during League meetings. Therefore in dealing with Italy Drummond, as in the case of Germany, had to move warily. What Italy demanded always had to be juxtaposed against what the League could allow. The problem was complicated by the fact that Italy was not only a Great Power or the greatest of the small powers as one wit put it, but a Great Power which—unlike Germany— was a member of the victorious Allied coalition.

Even before the League was officially established Drummond became involved in the Adriatic question and its possible implications for the organization. This was triggered by the proposal in December 1919 that Fiume (Rijeka) be established as a buffer state between Italy and Yugoslavia. Fiume would be controlled by the League which would also determine its future. Likewise the historic Italian city of Zara (Zadar) on the Dalmatian coast would be independent under the League, but within Yugoslavia's customs system. Finally Italy would be given a League mandate over Albania.[1]

---

[1] *Correspondence Relating to the Adriatic Question.* Miscellaneous No. 2 (1920), Cmd. 586 (London: H.M. Stationery Office, 1920), pp. 3–9.

On the whole Drummond was favourably disposed toward the proposal. His principal point, however, was that the League should not be considered as a personality since all it really represented were the members of which it was composed. The League through its members, he admitted, could extend protection to a particular country. However, a discussion of sovereignty conflicted with the very idea of the League and was 'open to the accusation of the creation of supernational government'. Personally, Drummond thought it would be most undesirable for the League to guarantee territory placed under the sovereignty of a national state. For example, Italy proposed that certain territories should be assigned to her and to Yugoslavia. These territories would be guaranteed by the League. Drummond was strongly opposed to the acceptance of this Italian proposal. There was already, he pointed out, a guarantee against external aggression for such territories under Article 10 of the Covenant. To go beyond this seemed to imply a guarantee of permanent peaceful possession and against internal movements, something Drummond thought the League ought to avoid.[1]

Though a compromise was worked out in January 1920 the Adriatic question was not resolved. Writing to Kerr in February Drummond noted that whatever solution was adopted one thing was perfectly clear, namely, that Gabriele D'Annunzio, the poet and modern-day *condottiere* who had led a group of Italian adventurers to occupy Fiume, would have to be turned out of the city. If the 1915 Treaty of London was applied, Drummond claimed that the responsibility of turning D'Annunzio out would fall squarely on Italy's shoulders, but if either the December or January proposals were adopted, which in different terms gave Fiume to the League, then in theory the responsibility would fall specifically on the League. If this was correct it seemed to Drummond that the League 'would be placed in an impossible position'. He hoped that Lloyd George might make it very clear that whatever course of action was adopted it was the Italians who had to turn D'Annunzio out and that this had to be done within a given time. If this was not done they would 'be up

---

[1] Drummond to Kerr, 10 Dec. 1919, D[rummond] to Nicolson, 10 Dec. 1919, File GD40/17/56, Lothian Papers, SRO; Minutes of a Directors' Meeting, 10 Dec. 1919, General 1919: 40/2391/854, LNA.

against all the old difficulties'.[1] In the end Drummond thought that Fiume would come to the League in the same way as did Danzig. If this proved true, he hoped that many of Danzig's precedents would be followed and none of its mistakes repeated. The important point, however, was that the League should not be saddled with Fiume until the city had 'settled down and [was] in a position to govern itself'.[2]

Another Danzig in the Adriatic was not to be. After direct negotiations Italy and Yugoslavia agreed in November 1920 under the Treaty of Rapallo to constitute Fiume and a small surrounding area into a free state. D'Annunzio was forced out of the city, but a local Fascist *coup d'état* in March 1922 led to Fiume's occupation by Italian troops. Seven months later Mussolini's Fascist government came to power. There was little that Belgrade could do given Yugoslavia's weak position and faced by a *de facto* Italian occupation of the city plus a seemingly resurgent Italy under the Duce. In January 1924 under the Treaty of Rome, Fiume was formally annexed by Italy[3] and the question was removed as a potential burden for both the League and Drummond.

Another matter which attracted Drummond's attention prior to Mussolini's assumption of power was the question of Austria's financial reconstruction. Her deteriorating financial situation would have inevitably led to greater political instability in what was already a dangerously unstable area. Accordingly, the Allied powers asked the League in March 1921 to set up a plan for Austria's financial reconstruction. The question was then taken up by the League's Financial Committee,[4] but as Drummond pointed out to his Foreign Office friend, Gerald Spicer, the Allied promise to release their liens on Austria and to convince other states to do the same had not been fulfilled. It seemed to Drummond that this was obviously a task for the Allies to tackle

---

[1] Drummond to Kerr, 10 Feb. 1920, File GD40/17/56, Lothian Papers, SRO.

[2] Drummond (Paris) to Kerr, 11 Mar. 1920, ibid.

[3] Ivo J. Lederer, *Yugoslavia at the Paris Peace Conference* (New Haven: Yale University Press, 1963), pp. 276–308; Maxwell H. H. Macartney and Paul Cremona, *Italy's Foreign and Colonial Policy 1914–1937* (London: Oxford University Press, 1938), pp. 85–95.

[4] Nicole Pietri, *La Reconstruction financière de l'Autriche, 1921–1926* (Genève: Dotation Carnegie, 1970), pp. 25–37; Frank P. Walters, *A History of the League of Nations* (London: Oxford University Press, 1960), p. 206.

and not for the League. Further action by the Financial Committee depended on releasing the liens. Drummond therefore wanted Spicer to bring the matter to the Foreign Office's attention, asking them to consult the Treasury as to the best way of proceeding in this matter. Drummond thought that probably it would be through joint Allied instructions to the Reparations Commission.[1]

Other difficulties, however, soon developed with the Italians. In early June the Financial Committee drew up a scheme that was accepted by both the British and French Governments. One of the scheme's main features, Drummond explained to Balfour, was that a control commission be established in Vienna and that it be dependent on the Financial Committee. The Italians were opposed. They desired that the control commission should be dependent on the three principal Allied powers. Drummond held that Italy's stance was contrary to previous British and French declarations. The desire had been not to exercise any control over Austria's finances. To do so would make it appear that the Allies were to some extent responsible for these finances. Moreover, it was felt that it was important to make Austria feel that her independence was being impaired as little as possible. The two conditions, he insisted, were fulfilled by having the control commission under the Financial Committee.

Drummond therefore hoped that London would urge Rome very strongly to accept the Financial Committee's proposals. If these proposals were not accepted, and should the Financial Committee's scheme fail to materialize, 'the League would obviously be placed in a somewhat difficult position should Austria apply to the Council for permission to join Germany'[2]— an allusion to the possibility of Austria's economic collapse and to the procedure allowing for *Anschluss* with Germany under Article 88 of the Treaty of St. Germain. Drummond's suggestion was soon submerged by the course of events. Though most countries agreed to suspend their liens the United States would not. The Financial Committee's scheme could not be implemented. Austria's economic situation teetered on the edge of the abyss. The Council's solution was to establish a special committee

---

[1] D[rummond] to [Spicer], 12 May 1921, Economic and Financial 1921: 10/12825/11730, LNA.

[2] Drummond to Balfour, 8 June 1921, George Curzon Papers, FO/800/152.

to deal with the situation. The committee was composed of French, Italian, Czech, and Austrian representatives with Balfour presiding as chairman. Political questions were handled by the committee, while the financial, economic, and legal work was entrusted by the committee to the League's and the Secretariat's technical organizations.[1]

Drummond's attitude could not have gone unnoticed in Rome which considered Austria along with Albania, Bulgaria, and Hungary as falling within Italy's sphere of influence. To offset what Rome might have construed as Drummond's anti-Italian orientation, Daniele Varè, an Italian member of the Secretariat's Political Section, attempted to persuade Drummond to visit Rome. If they got used to seeing him in Rome, he argued with Drummond in November 1921, 'they will begin to consider him as a collaborator and not as an opponent'. Varè repeated this argument with Monnet. He appears to have made his point, for Drummond wisely decided to go to Rome,[2] and some days later in early December he arrived to confer with the Italian authorities.[3] As we shall see in the years to come, he took Varè's advice to heart. However, perhaps because of Italy's worsening internal situation at the time, Drummond made no move to visit Rome during 1922. Instead, in October 1922 on the eve of Mussolini's take-over, Drummond journeyed to Belgrade rather than Rome.[4] This visit might have been prompted by what the Yugoslav Minister in Bern described as 'a distinct antipathy to the League [found] throughout all classes in his country' who felt that it was largely an English controlled organization where Drummond in particular exercised 'great power' and English Secretariat officials outnumbered those of other nationalities.[5]

Drummond's first indirect contact with Mussolini appears to have occurred in November 1922 when he conveyed to Tyrrell information requested by the Italian representative at the Lausanne Conference, no doubt to answer Mussolini's query, as

[1] Pietri, pp. 43–200; Walters, pp. 206–10.
[2] Daniele Varè, *Laughing Diplomat* (London: John Murray, 1938), p. 205.
[3] *New York Times*, 4 Dec. 1921, p. 1; *The Times* (London), 6 Dec. 1921, p. 9.
[4] Varè, pp. 211–12; Dodge (Belgrade) to the Secretary of State, No. 1662, 4 Nov. 1922, File 500.C113/11, RG 59, NA.
[5] Joseph C. Grew, *Turbulent Era*, ed. Walter Johnson (Boston: Houghton Mifflin, 1952), p. 449.

to what force the League possessed.[1] Indirect contact continued
during early 1923 over the question of Italian representation in
the upper reaches of the Secretariat.[2] Though this problem had
developed from the Secretariat's inception it became more acute
following the establishment of Mussolini's government.

Direct contact with Mussolini really commenced in July 1923
when the Ethiopian heir and regent Ras Tafari (Haile Selassie)
contacted Drummond and requested Ethiopia's admission to the
League. Since the Assembly dealt with admissions Drummond
inscribed the request on its agenda. Interestingly, the Italian
Minister in Addis Ababa, Gino Macchioro Vivalba, opposed the
Ethiopian move. He argued that Ethiopia's admission would not
be in Italy's interest. Though he did not say so, it was obvious
that Ethiopia's precarious independence would be strengthened
and further protected by the Covenant's stipulations. Macchioro
Vivalba noted, however, that the existence of slavery in Ethiopia
could be used in order to reject her request for admission. Because
it was impolitic for Italy to oppose openly the Ethiopian request
he suggested that the best solution would be if Rome could
arrange to have other less interested powers propose a postponement of the question in the hope that Ethiopia would consent to
anti-slavery measures.

Clearly Mussolini was annoyed by Drummond's response to
the Ethiopian request. He desired to know, he informed Bernardo
Attolico, the Italian Under Secretary-General, his judgement of
Drummond's conduct and if Drummond was able to respond to
Ethiopia's request on his own initiative. Mussolini also wanted
information about Drummond's 'personal disposition' in this
question and Attolico's opinion on the possibility of having the
Ethiopian request postponed by powers less interested than
Italy—Macchioro Vivalba's solution. Since Ethiopia's request
for admission appears to have been sponsored by France[3]
Drummond very wisely was unwilling to get himself involved in
any struggle between Paris and Rome. He personally intended,
he wrote to Cecil, to divorce himself from this question and let

[1] D[rummond] to [Tyrrell], 27 Nov. 1922, Drummond Folder, LNA.

[2] James Barros, *Betrayal from Within: Joseph Avenol, Secretary-General of the League
of Nations, 1933–1940* (New Haven: Yale University Press, 1969), pp. 9–10 fn.
See also *DDI*, 7, ii. 79.

[3] *DDI*, 7, ii. 107–9, 114, 119–21, 124, 257.

those states for and against Ethiopia's admission fight it out between themselves.[1] Mussolini's resistance soon melted, however, when he realized that in this question strong British support was not forthcoming and that Ethiopia's admission merely required a two-thirds Assembly vote.[2] In September Ethiopia was unanimously accepted as a League member only after agreeing that slavery was not an internal problem but one in which the League could intervene and that she would make special efforts to suppress it within the country.[3]

The period that led to the compromise over Ethiopia's admission also saw the League face the most serious crisis since its establishment. It stemmed from the Italian naval bombardment and occupation of the island of Corfu. This coercive act was prompted by the assassination on Greek soil by persons unknown of the Italian members of an international commission appointed by the Ambassadors' Conference to delimit the Greek–Albanian border. Concurrently France, because she needed Italy's support in the Ruhr occupation, loyally supported Italy throughout the crisis. In a sense, therefore, Drummond's position during the Corfu crisis was quite similar to his position in the Ethiopian question. There was, however, one important qualitative difference and this was that in the Corfu crisis, unlike the Ethiopian question, the stakes were much higher and the question of Italy versus the League and all that this implied was obvious to everyone. Correspondingly, Drummond as in the Ethiopian question was unobtrusive. This is not to say, however, that he was completely inactive. On the contrary, from the very beginning of the crisis, as we shall see, he was involved in trying to discover a political formula which would be acceptable to all and which would lead to a quick settlement of the incident. His subsequent actions were an attempt to salvage from the Corfu crisis as much as possible for the League, a task that he pursued in his own quiet way.

The Greeks inadvertently complicated the question by submitting it to both the Ambassadors' Conference and the

---

[1] Drummond to Cecil, 13 Aug. 1923, Add. MS. 51110, Robert Cecil Papers, BL.

[2] *DDI*, 7, ii. 119–24, 131–2, 256.

[3] League of Nations, *Official Journal*, Special Supplement, No. 13, pp. 124–5; Walters, p. 258.

League. The League was therefore faced with the difficult task of trying to mesh the Council's actions with those of the Ambassadors' Conference. Toward this end, meetings outside the Council on 6 September from which the Greeks and Italians were excluded developed proposals, largely inspired by Cecil, for a settlement of the dispute.[1] In conveying to Cecil copies of the draft proposals which Drummond had the Secretariat translate and type—an action he asked not be publicized—he pointed out that Antonio Salandra, Italy's representative, should be either shown the draft proposals beforehand or the general lines which the Council proposed to adopt should be discussed with him. He hoped that Cecil would be completely sure of French support before he finally decided to present the draft proposals, since Drummond thought it possible that Salandra would raise the procedural argument that the League had no competence in this question. Much, however, depended upon the actual wording used in the draft proposals and it was for this reason that Drummond advocated that Quiñones de León discuss them with Salandra, making him understand that the Council was determined to press them if this indeed was the case.[2]

At the Council meeting late that afternoon Quiñones de León formally presented the draft proposals. They were a clever compromise between the demands Italy had presented to Athens and the recommendations made previously by the Greek representative. Objections by Salandra as well as the delaying tactics of the French representative caused Cecil to move that the *procès-verbal* of the meeting be conveyed to the Ambassadors' Conference, a neat way of getting the Council's draft proposals before them without engaging in a battle with either Salandra or the French representative.[3]

In the days that followed, Drummond and the Council watched the tortuous negotiations in the Ambassadors' Conference which finally led to a compromise formula to handle the question. These negotiations were hastened by Mussolini's threats to leave the League if the Council attempted to intervene in the

[1] James Barros, *The Corfu Incident of 1923: Mussolini and the League of Nations* (Princeton: Princeton University Press, 1965), pp. 157–8.

[2] Drummond (Geneva) to Cecil, 6 Sept. 1923, Add. MS. 51110, Robert Cecil Papers, BL.

[3] Barros, *The Corfu Incident of 1923*, pp. 158–69.

question, as well as the fear that Rome contemplated remaining in permanent occupation of Corfu unless some sort of settlement was hammered out. Drummond was dismayed by what had occurred. To avoid the Council's intervention in the question, Rome had argued that Italy's action at Corfu was not an act of war or threat of war, that the issue concerned national honour and dignity and hence was outside the Council's purview, and that the question really fell within the sphere of the Ambassadors' Conference since the murdered Italians had been acting as its agents. The events stemming from the Corfu crisis, Drummond wrote on 14 September, had 'done much to weaken both the moral authority of the Council and the general confidence that the precise obligations of the Covenant will be universally accepted and carried out'. A powerful League member had 'refused to carry out its treaty obligations under the Covenant, and has succeeded in doing so with impunity, some might even say, with an increase of prestige'. The Covenant's fundamental principles had been brought into question and until they were universally re-established the uncertainty produced would quickly undermine the League's power. Drummond thought that some of the problems raised during the Corfu crisis—the Italian objections to the Council's competence were obviously uppermost in his mind—could be handled as abstract questions and given to the World Court for an advisory opinion.[1]

As usual, Drummond made no move himself but had the issue introduced by Viscount Ishii. With the support of Cecil and Branting and despite Salandra's delaying tactics, the Council finally agreed to submit five questions for an advisory opinion, not to the World Court as desired by Drummond, but to a special commission of jurists. The first three questions that the jurists' commission was asked to deal with involved the Council's right and duty to act when one party to a dispute claimed that the procedure of Article 15 for some reason did not apply. The fourth question dealt with whether coercive measures not intended as acts of war were consistent with the Covenant's obligations. The last question related to state responsibility for crimes committed on its territory.[2] The next question that

---

[1] Ibid., pp. 254, 317–20.
[2] Ibid., p. 253 fn.; Walters, pp. 252–3.

Drummond tackled was the presidency of the jurists' commission. Since he obviously wanted the commission to succeed and London had been Rome's adversary during the crisis, a British president would have raised Italian objections. Therefore, Drummond pointed out to Cecil that though the British nominee, the ex-Chancellor, Lord Buckmaster, was obviously the most important member it would be a mistake to have him preside over the commission. He observed that Japan's Mineitciro Adatci was also a member and it seemed to Drummond that he would be a very suitable president. If Lord Buckmaster, Drummond explained, proposed Adatci as the commission's president there would be no further difficulties. His other point was that no Latin American jurists had been included on the commission.[1] Drummond made his point.[2] Not only was Adatci chosen as president, but a Uruguayan and a Brazilian were also appointed, furnishing the commission with Latin American representation.

Drummond's labours, however, were only partially successful. Though the replies of the jurists' commission in March 1924 were unanimous on all questions posed and thus clearly vindicated the Covenant and really denied most of the arguments raised by Italy, the commission's reply to the fourth question— coercive measures not intended as acts of war—was ambiguous.[3] It was a reply that left League members, and one can safely assume Drummond, dissatisfied since many member states held that all coercive acts were forbidden by the Covenant at least until the League's provisions for peaceful settlement had been utilized.[4]

The possibility of debating the jurists' reply to the fourth question was voided by Salandra's behind-the-scenes argument to Drummond, conveyed through Attolico, that the Council immediately, unanimously, and without discussion approve *en bloc* the jurists' replies. Salandra warned that should any Council member raise a question he would reserve his freedom regarding question four and other questions posed to the jurists. His own view, Drummond explained to the Foreign Office in February

---

[1] Drummond (Geneva) to Cecil, 13 Oct. 1923, Add. MS. 51110, Robert Cecil Papers, BL.
[2] [Cecil] to Drummond, 23 Oct. 1923, ibid.
[3] League of Nations, *Official Journal*, V (1924), pp. 523–4.
[4] Walters, p. 253.

1924, was that 'it would be the happiest conclusion' if the Council members would agree to Salandra's demands, express their appreciation of the jurists' work, and transmit their replies to the Assembly for its information. He pointed out to Attolico that naturally no arrangement could be made that Council members would not give reasoned statements for accepting the jurists' replies, and he hoped that Salandra would be prepared to do likewise, provided the jurists' replies were accepted. However, Drummond did 'agree with Salandra that the less discussion the better, as otherwise all sorts of awkward questions may crop up'.[1] Since by this time it was in everyone's interest to avoid further difficulties with Mussolini, the Council at its March meeting acted in the manner Drummond had suggested[2] and thus removed from its agenda the legal questions raised by Mussolini's action at Corfu.

Drummond could also not have been pleased with the crisis' denouement—the decision of the Ambassadors' Conference in late September that Greece pay Italy a sum of 50 million lire for the alleged wrongs that she had committed according to a report filed by the commission of inquiry established by the Ambassadors' Conference. Justice had to surrender to realism and it still rankled Drummond almost twenty-four years later. The sum paid by Greece was doubtlessly excessive, he wrote, but the Ambassadors' Conference's acceptance of the figure Mussolini claimed was, he feared, 'due to the theory so prevalent today— that the preservation of unity between the Great Powers was essential, even at the cost of injustice'.[3]

If Drummond looked askance at Mussolini's coercive actions against Greece, he was no less perturbed over a year later by Britain's coercive actions against Egypt following the assassination by Egyptian nationalists of Sir Lee Stack, the Governor of the Anglo-Egyptian Sudan and grand Sirdar of the Egyptian army. In this matter Drummond had to tread carefully, and considering his nationality, perhaps even more carefully, than in the Corfu crisis. A false step would have quickly destroyed any

[1] Drummond to [Noel-] Baker, 14 Feb. 1924, Add. MS. 51106, Robert Cecil Papers, BL.

[2] League of Nations, *Official Journal*, V (1924), pp. 525–7.

[3] [The Earl of] Perth, 'The Corfu Incident', *The Spectator*, 14 Feb. 1947, p. 206.

influence or trust that he had previously inspired in Whitehall. His approach therefore was indirect and cautious.

Though he thought that the circumstances and the legal situation were different in Stack's assassination from that of the Italian members of the international commission, nevertheless Britain's actions in Egypt, he noted, were compared to Mussolini's at Corfu. Since Drummond had not seen from the British side any adequate explanation of what had occurred he believed that an authoritative statement of this kind was badly needed. Indeed, because it was desirable for Britain's 'own good name to give some explanation, and if possible to do it through the League' he asked Cecil to persuade Chamberlain to send him a statement to be forwarded to the League members explaining the British action in Egypt, and advancing reasons why the question was not one for the League. If this was done he thought it would have a great impact.

Drummond pointed out that prior to the League's establishment such a declaration would have been circulated in a dispatch to all the powers. Such a move would, he thought, have great advantages in this particular case and certainly help in regards to the League if London's explanations were given through him, and therefore to the League members in general. It was very clear of course, he believed, that Great Britain was in no way obligated to make any statement to the League. There were, however, times when voluntary statements of this nature were of the greatest value.[1]

Since Chamberlain made no statement to the League Drummond's pleas fell on deaf ears. His supplications to Chamberlain, however, were not unusual, for he had also made them to Mussolini a year earlier following the Corfu crisis. Yet his Rome talks were far more serious and important since the Duce, unlike Chamberlain, had threatened to leave the League. After the Corfu crisis ended, in October 1923, Drummond informed Cecil that he was going to Rome—doubtlessly moved by Varè's previous advice. He hoped to 'beard the lion' with no unsatisfactory results though he did not relish putting his head between the bars of the cage. In his discussions with the Italians

[1] Drummond (Geneva) to Cecil, 26 Nov. 1924, Drummond (Geneva) to Cecil, 27 Nov. 1924, Drummond (Geneva) to Cecil, 3 Dec. 1924, Add. MS. 51110, Robert Cecil Papers, BL.

Drummond insisted that if he came to Rome he would try to have an audience with Pope Pius XI. He would attempt, though he did not think he would succeed, to get a Vatican pronouncement in favour of the League. If he could not do this Drummond hoped at the minimum to secure from the Vatican some encouragement for the League which he thought would be useful.[1]

Drummond had his first Rome interview on the morning of 5 November with Salvatore Contarini, the Foreign Ministry's all-powerful Secretary-General. Their two-hour conversation was an attempt by Contarini to prime Drummond for his interview with Mussolini later that day. Special emphasis was laid on Italy's lack of adequate Secretariat representation, to which Drummond replied that he had done much to remedy the situation and pointed to the administrative and other problems involved. Drummond did agree that on the question of the League's various High Commissionerships Rome had a legitimate grievance, but unfortunately this matter was almost completely out of his hands. He suggested that before one of these posts fell vacant Rome should propose a candidate and prepare the way beforehand by diplomatic negotiations. Of course if Italy really manifested, he noted, an interest in the League this would make Italian appointments easier. Drummond argued that a League policy was really in Italy's interest, for example, in the question of Tangier, and observed that there were certain Italian elements that perhaps desired territorial expansion, and they obviously could not view the League in a sympathetic light. Judging from Contarini's comments to Drummond's not overly disguised remarks, it had been a frank and on the whole a successful interview.[2]

In the afternoon Drummond was closeted with Salandra. The substance of the discussion dealt with the report of the jurists' commission and the Italian desire to avoid its discussion before the Council when Branting was its president. Drummond warned that this was a delicate matter and would have to be arranged beforehand. He then pointed out that if the jurists failed to agree it was likely that either the British or Swedish representative

[1] Drummond (Geneva) to Cecil, 15 Oct. 1925, ibid.
[2] [Eric Drummond], Record of Interview, 6 Nov. 1923, ibid.

would propose to the Council an immediate reference of the
whole matter to the World Court for an advisory opinion.
Drummond's comments were something of a disguised threat for
Rome desired to avoid any reference to the World Court.
Salandra's response showed this when he stated his belief that it
would be possible for the jurists' commission to reach an
agreement without any reference to the court. It was Drummond's
impression that Salandra was anxious to arrive at a settlement
and to get the entire question out of the way. To this purpose, he
thought Salandra was ready to use his personal influence to the
utmost.[1]

Since the jurists' report was unanimous on all questions and
diplomatically ambiguous on the important fourth question, we
can assume that Salandra used his influence in Rome to avoid
complications. In turn when the report was considered by the
Council, Uruguay's Alberto Guani, sat as President,[2] and
Salandra's apprehensions about Branting being the presiding
officer, what Drummond called this 'delicate matter', was
'arranged beforehand'.

Drummond's most important interview of course took place
that evening with Mussolini. The Duce made it clear to
Drummond that 'Italy had no parti pris' regarding the League
and was not opposed to the League's idea. Indeed, he thought the
organization could serve a very useful purpose. However, he
complained about Italian representation in the Secretariat which
caused Drummond to repeat more or less what he had told
Contarini that morning, and reiterated that the discussion of
Italian appointments often raised the argument that Italy was
indifferent or even unfriendly to the League and that this
indifference diminished the chances that the Italian candidate
would be selected. If, on the other hand, Italy were considered
favourably disposed toward the League and working in its
interests, the appointment of Italians would be far easier.

Surely, Mussolini observed, neither Britain nor France would
refuse to recognize Rome's claims regarding the League, and
thus add to their problems with Italy. Drummond felt that as
regards Britain Mussolini's 'just demands' would be considered

---

[1] [Eric Drummond], Record of Interview, 6 Nov. 1923, ibid.
[2] League of Nations, *Official Journal*, V (1924), pp. 501, 523.

sympathetically. As to France he was uncertain. Drummond promised, however, to explain the Italian position in London and to do what he could to ensure that Italy was equal in the League with other powers. Drummond's impression was that if Italy's prestige regarding her position in the League could be met Mussolini would become a warm supporter of the organization. He noted that Mussolini had explicitly stated a number of times his desire to collaborate closely with Great Britain, while simultaneously keeping on friendly terms with France. He held that in Mussolini's view Italian and British foreign policy were moving on converging lines and the Duce intended to do all he could to remove difficulties which at the moment existed between both countries.[1] Though Drummond had not noted it, Mussolini probably realized that the Corfu crisis had badly strained his relations with London. Therefore, a more conciliatory tack toward the League especially through Drummond, an excellent conduit to the Foreign Office, would be a convenient way to re-establish the correct if not increasingly warm relations that he had developed with Britain prior to the Corfu crisis.

He honestly believed, Drummond wrote to Cecil, that his Rome visit had proved useful. He felt that the small and just price to be paid was to treat Italy in the League on an equal footing with France and Great Britain, particularly regarding Secretariat appointments. Regarding his audience with Pope Pius XI the Foreign Ministry had warned that he had to be most careful. For if it were thought that he was negotiating with the Vatican in any way, a great deal of good which his visit could generate would be cancelled.[2]

During his first Vatican visit, probably in 1921, Drummond had 'urged the possibility of a special encyclical', but had been told that all previous encyclicals had urged international peace and co-operation, and it was not possible to do more in supporting the League as long as it was opposed in certain countries.[3] The

[1] [Eric Drummond], Record of Interview, 6 Nov. 1923, Add. MS. 51110, Robert Cecil Papers, BL. For a sanitized version of this interview see E[ric] D[rummond], Interview of the Secretary-General with the President of the Council of Italy, 7 Nov. 1923, in Minutes of a Directors' Meeting, 15 Nov. 1923, LNA.

[2] Drummond (Rome) to Cecil, 7 Nov. 1923, and Drummond (Geneva) to Cecil, 12 Nov. 1923, Add. MS. 51110, Robert Cecil Papers, BL.

[3] Drummond (Geneva) to Cecil, 1 May 1923, ibid.

Vatican's natural reticence in this matter and perhaps the Foreign Ministry's admonition to Drummond might explain the Pope's desire during Drummond's short visit to avoid any conceivable reference to the discussions dealing with liaison between the Holy See and the League.[1]

Drummond then called on Cardinal Pietro Gasparri, the Vatican's Secretary of State. Cardinal Gasparri surveyed the European scene and pointed out that the 'Vatican had unrivalled knowledge of what was happening in the different countries'. He asked how Drummond found relations between Italy and the League. The Cardinal was astonished when Drummond replied that he hoped his visit had helped to improve these relations and that he had had a very satisfactory discussion with Mussolini.[2]

But Drummond was not satisfied by his talks in the Vatican. He felt that his audience with the Pope had been much less fruitful than his interview with Mussolini. In fact he doubted whether much could be done with the Vatican for some time to come. A great deal depended on Italy's relations with the League since Rome was on very good terms with the Vatican and the Holy See would wish to avoid anything in the international sphere which might upset this relationship.[3]

Mussolini likewise found his interview with Drummond 'very gratifying'.[4] Initially following Drummond's meeting with Mussolini, there were some violent attacks against the League in the Italian press. The word, however, was soon passed along for immediately after Drummond gave a press conference describing in guarded terms his talk with the Duce the tone of the Italian press changed.[5] In the Foreign Office there were some who were not as pleased as Drummond, or Mussolini for that matter, over what had transpired. It was regrettable, Harold Nicolson minuted, that 'Drummond should have purchased the support of M. Mussolini for the principles of the League (which he could never comprehend) at the price of posts for the Italians on the

---

[1] [Eric Drummond], Record of Interview, 7 Nov. 1923, ibid.

[2] [Eric Drummond], Record of Interview, 7 Nov. 1923, ibid.

[3] Drummond (Geneva) to Cecil, 12 Nov. 1923, ibid.

[4] *DDI*, 7, ii. 314.

[5] Drummond (Geneva) to Cecil, 12 Nov. 1923, Add. MS. 51110, Robert Cecil Papers, BL; Graham (Rome) to Curzon, No. 982, 9 Nov. 1923, FO/371/8900.

League Secretariat (which ought to be a perfectly independent executive body)'. It was an understandable criticism from a Wilsonian idealist like Nicolson who had served for a short while in the Secretariat. A more hardheaded criticism was made by Miles Lampson. He thought that Drummond had let Mussolini off very lightly throughout their interview. This, however, was Drummond's affair. Presumably, his main object had been to prevent Italy's defection from the League. Personally, Lampson had always been 'more than doubtful whether, when it came to the punch, Italy would in fact "defect"'.[1] Crowe was openly sceptical of Mussolini's new League orientation and especially his desire for increased Italian representation in the Secretariat.[2] He was not far off the mark. Mussolini soon reiterated his dissatisfaction with Italy's League position. The idea was widely held in Italy, Mussolini told the Italian Senate on 16 November, that the League represented a kind of insurance for those states which were satiated, but Italy did not come under this category.[3]

The Balkans and East Africa

Italy's unsatiated desires manifested in Albania, Bulgaria, and Hungary, her actions in Corfu, and her strained relations with Yugoslavia, prompted Drummond in 1924 to pay particular attention to Balkan affairs.[4] The Prime Minister, MacDonald, appreciated the information that Drummond conveyed to him. Indeed, he hoped that Drummond would continue to write very freely to his secretary in order that MacDonald be kept informed of Drummond's 'own views, and informed as to the direction in which other minds are working'.[5]

In line with this request Drummond informed MacDonald in

[1] Minutes by Harold Nicolson and Miles Lampson, 15 Nov. 1923, ibid.

[2] *DDI*, 7, ii. 319.

[3] Graham (Rome) to MacDonald, No. 675, 31 July 1924, FO/371/10575. See Benito Mussolini, *Opera Omnia*, eds. Edoardo and Duilio Susmel (Firenze: La Fenice, 1956), XX, pp. 98–111.

[4] Drummond (Geneva) to Waterhouse, 13 Feb. 1924, W[aterhouse] to MacDonald, 16 Feb. 1924, Drummond (Geneva) to Waterhouse, 4 Mar. 1924, Drummond (Geneva) to Waterhouse, 5 Mar. 1924, File 1/201 (1924), MacDonald Papers, PRO.

[5] [Waterhouse] to Drummond, 19 Feb. 1924, ibid.

early March of 'intimate conversations' that Attolico had had with Mussolini. Italy, according to Drummond, appeared somewhat irritated with Great Britain, complaining of a number of incidents that she claimed showed that the present London government was not inspired by any friendly feelings toward Rome. When asked whether he thought these incidents were unconnected or whether they represented a deliberate British policy, Mussolini had taken the former view. Mussolini did add, however, that he was finding it somewhat difficult to restrain the Italian press although, personally, he was anxious that nothing should occur to disrupt Italian–British relations. Drummond thought it right to pass this news on because MacDonald knew that the Italians were at the moment sensitive on the question of prestige, and particularly in having their position as a Great Power recognized. Inasmuch as this was largely a question of form and not of substance, Drummond believed it might not be overly difficult to give Rome some satisfaction.[1]

Drummond's information was no surprise for MacDonald was not unaware of Mussolini's irritation. His decision, therefore, was to recognize realities and settle with Mussolini those questions which could be settled amicably. Accordingly, he offered to Mussolini to settle concurrently the question of Jubaland and the Dodecanese Islands without the settlement of one issue dependent on the other. MacDonald's conciliatory move was an attempt to normalize Italian–British relations and though it meant the loser in any such arrangement would be Greece, Mussolini delayed a month before he reacted to MacDonald's proposed formula.

Mussolini's reserve was understandable since MacDonald's government was Britain's first Labour government—albeit a minority government—containing elements, unlike the previous Baldwin government, which for ideological reasons were ill-disposed toward Italy's Fascist regime. Certainly, the difficulties encountered in the autumn of 1924 in having the Council hold its December session in Rome rather than Geneva and, especially, the uncertain attitude manifested by the British representative, Lord Parmoor, can probably be traced in part to this ideological

[1] Drummond (Geneva) to Waterhouse, 4 Mar. 1924, ibid. See also, *DDI*, 7, ii. 417, 422, 423, 426, 427, 430, 432, 433–7, 440, 448–9, 454, and ibid., iii. 2–5, 12–13, 16–17.

hostility. Drummond supported the proposal and convinced Parmoor to accept it,[1] no doubt thinking that a Council session in Rome would assist in smoothing the League's relations with Italy. Unfortunately, the acceptance of Italy's invitation only weeks after the discovery of the body of the murdered Socialist leader, Giacomo Matteotti, played into Mussolini's hands. A December Council session in Rome gave the regime's soiled reputation and declining prestige a badly needed boost in the aftermath of the Matteotti murder.[2]

During the Council's meetings in Rome, Drummond had the opportunity to survey the European scene with Beneš and then with Contarini. In view of the fact that Czechoslovakia along with Yugoslavia and Rumania were members of the Little Entente and Beneš would be privy to Belgrade's thoughts, Drummond took this opportunity to discuss the Italian–Yugoslav negotiations over Albania. He was 'troubled' by these conversations since it was reported that both governments were plotting a revolution against the Albanian Prime Minister, Orthodox Bishop Fan Noli. This appeared to Drummond a somewhat dangerous approach for Belgrade to adopt. Postwar arrangements among the Great Powers gave Italy under certain conditions the right to intervene in Albania. Surely it was not in Yugoslavia's interests, he noted to Beneš, to promote the possibility of such Italian intervention. Was it possible, Drummond asked, that Rome and Belgrade were arranging Albania's partition? If this was the case, the situation from the League's point of view could be very serious. Drummond 'did not think that the League could possibly admit and survive the partition' of a member state by other member states.

Beneš predicted that a revolution would erupt against Noli in the spring—unknown to either of them it had already commenced—but assured Drummond that Yugoslavia had no designs on Albania and would not agree to her partition. Belgrade wanted an independent Albania between Italy and Yugoslavia. Drummond noted that if this was the case and if incidents did occur, they probably would be settled through the League. Beneš explained that regarding Balkan questions he left

---

[1] *DDI*, 7, iii. 76–7, 102–4, 290, 304, 306–7, 318–19.
[2] Alan Cassels, *Mussolini's Early Diplomacy* (Princeton: Princeton University Press, 1970), pp. 234–5, 251.

things to Yugoslavia, only arranging to be kept informed so that he could remonstrate if Belgrade's proposed moves might lead to international disturbances.

Drummond then inquired about Greek–Yugoslav relations. Beneš explained that Belgrade's real objective was to secure greater railway facilities between Yugoslavia and the Greek port of Salonika and the free use of the latter in case of war. He added that Drummond doubtlessly knew that for the past five years Italy had been trying to influence Yugoslavia's expansion toward Salonika. Beneš, however, was not apprehensive on this score since he felt that Belgrade was not at the moment strong enough to embark on such a dangerous course.[1]

The significant aspect of this conversation was not merely the information that Beneš divulged to Drummond, but that he spoke so openly to him about such sensitive subjects. This was partly inspired by the trust and confidence that Drummond generated because of his discretion and tact, but also because Beneš could safely assume that in conveying the information to London, which Drummond did, it would be received with greater credence since Beneš's own reputation for veracity in the Foreign Office, especially with Chamberlain, was far from high.

The next day, 15 December, Drummond continued his surveillance of the Albanian scene. In a long conversation Contarini assured him that Italy had absolutely no desire to intervene in Albania but warned that difficulties might develop if revolutions in Albania persisted. According to Contarini, Albania had nothing to fear from either Belgrade or Rome if only she set her own house in order. Drummond's impression was that Contarini's general attitude toward the League continued to be very friendly, although he was inclined to regard the organization as still too weak to undertake important tasks.[2]

On Christmas Day Ahmed Zogu's forces entered Tirana. Once more the pendulum had swung. During this period of Albanian turbulence, Mussolini remained inactive. The Matteotti affair and its aftermath caused the Duce to concentrate on internal affairs and consolidate his position, producing a corresponding

---

[1] Two memorandums by E[ric] D[rummond], Record of Interview, 14 Dec. 1924, AC51/29, Austen Chamberlain Papers, UB.
[2] [Eric Drummond], Record of Interview, 15 Dec. 1924, ibid.

inactivity in foreign affairs which persisted into the spring of 1925. With Mussolini inactive, Drummond's contacts with Rome virtually ceased. By mid-1926, described by Mussolini as Fascism's Napoleonic year, an aggressive foreign policy recommenced[1] which again found Drummond apprehensive.

In early May Drummond conveyed his concern to Cecil. Giuseppe Bruccoleri, of the Secretariat's Press and Information Section, who had returned from Rome had reported that 'unhappily, the mot d'ordre among the newspaper and Fascist circles there is that the League must be hampered in every way possible'. On the other hand, from what Drummond had gathered, Italy's League representative, Vittorio Scialoja, who was coming to a Geneva meeting later in May, was not prepared 'to carry out instructions in this sense'. Bruccoleri also informed Drummond that he believed that it would be of the greatest value if Chamberlain could explain frankly to the Italian ambassador that difficulties against the League would not be viewed by London with any sympathy and indeed might adversely affect the friendship between both countries.[2]

In late June, Drummond registered a further complaint with Cecil about Rome's actions. By this point both of them were deeply involved in the whole question of Germany's admission to the League and her acquisition of a permanent Council seat as well as the difficulties that this had raised with Brazil and Spain. Quiñones de León seemed to think, he informed Cecil, that the Spanish Foreign Minister was 'in close touch with the Fascists'. In fact Italian and Spanish members of the Secretariat appeared to think that much of the opposition to Germany's admission to the League was 'being stirred up from Rome'. When the Spanish Ambassador to the Vatican went to Rome he had favoured a compromise over Spain's request for a permanent seat. When he returned to Geneva 'he was very stiff'. Everyone knew, Drummond observed, how much the Brazilians and the Italians had fraternized during the special March Assembly called to consider Germany's admission. There were also, as Cecil doubtless had seen, 'distinct signs in the Italian press, of a campaign against the entry of Germany to the Council in

---

[1] Cassels, pp. 230–55, 390.

[2] [Cecil] to Tyrrell, 6 May 1926, Add. MS. 51098 and 51111, Robert Cecil Papers, BL.

September, and the final putting into force of the Locarno Treaties'. Drummond did not believe that Rome would dare take public responsibility for such action, but it was 'looking for tools'. Cecil might have likewise noticed some ominous pieces in the Polish press, and these too, Drummond understood, had come from pro-Fascist elements.[1]

Chamberlain's reluctance to raise the question of Mussolini's machinations against the League at this time can probably be traced to his desire to maintain and improve his personal friendship with the Duce whom he had met for the first time during the Council's December 1924 meetings in Rome. This personal association helped to contribute by December 1925 to a settlement of Ethiopian issues which had been raised by Italy in November 1919. Through an exchange of notes between Mussolini and the British Ambassador, Sir Ronald Graham, it was agreed that in the event that Great Britain with Italy's support obtained Ethiopia's consent to build a barrage on Lake Tsana, the source of the Blue Nile and Egypt's prosperity, Britain would recognize Italy's exclusive economic influence in western Ethiopia and in the area crossed by an Eritrean–Somalian railway to be constructed west of Addis Ababa.

The texts of the Mussolini–Graham exchange were not made known to the Ethiopians until June 1926. Addis Ababa protested about the agreement not only to the British and the Italians but also to the League. This was soon followed by British and Italian assurances to Drummond that they never had any intentions of pressuring Ethiopia. These assurances, however, were unsatisfactory to the Ethiopians. They felt that the Mussolini–Graham exchange was incompatible with Article 10 of the Covenant and maintained that under Article 20—treaty obligations inconsistent with the Covenant were not binding—they had no right to conclude such an agreement. Since Great Britain and Italy intended to register with the Secretariat the Mussolini–Graham agreement as required under Article 18 of the Covenant, Ethiopia felt 'entitled and bound to request' that Drummond publish a note by Addis Ababa together with the Mussolini–Graham correspondence in order that the public might become acquainted with its views and the reassurances given by London

---

[1] Drummond (Geneva) to Cecil, 24 June 1926, Add. MS. 51111, Robert Cecil Papers, BL.

and Rome to its protests. Thus everyone would know, as London and Rome had recognized, that Addis Ababa had 'full and complete freedom' to decide further requests and to judge what was in Ethiopia's interests.[1]

When presented with this unusual request by Ethiopia, Drummond thought that there would be no difficulty in giving the letter full publicity by conveying it to the press as well as to the League's membership. On the matter of registration under Article 18 this was a problem that raised some difficulty as Drummond 'did not know whether it was possible to register a uni-lateral declaration'. He promised to look up and follow the precedents. The Ethiopians could 'rest convinced' that their letter would have as far as the League was concerned the 'same validity' as the Mussolini–Graham agreement.[2]

From the tenor of Drummond's remarks it was clear that he was not pleased with what had occurred. His subsequent actions confirmed it. When the Mussolini–Graham exchange was published in the League of Nations *Treaty Series*, as required under Article 18, the somewhat unusual procedure was followed of having a footnote inserted drawing the reader's attention to the fact that a letter relating to this agreement had been addressed to Drummond by the Ethiopian Government. The Ethiopians had requested that their letter be published but since the letter was not 'in fact susceptible of being registered and published in this Series under the applicable rules', it had been published in the League's *Official Journal* and the exact citation was then given.[3]

If Chamberlain was reticent to take steps that might annoy Mussolini, so was Drummond though for slightly different reasons. In August 1926 a series of *komitaji* raids against Yugoslavian and Rumanian border posts caused Athens, Belgrade, and Bucharest to issue a collective note of protest which impressed on Sofia the necessity to suppress immediately and for all time *komitaji* activities in Bulgaria.[4] A recent trip to

[1] League of Nations, *Official Journal*, VII (1926), pp. 1517–27; *DDI*, 7, iv. 289; Walters, pp. 396–8.
[2] E[ric] D[rummond], Record of Interview, 4 Oct. 1926, Political 1926: 11/54518/52770, LNA.
[3] League of Nations, *Treaty Series*, L (1926), pp. 282–93 and fn.
[4] *The Times* (London), 11 Aug. 1926, p. 11, and 12 Aug. 1926, p. 9.

Greece in April[1] may have further sensitized Drummond to the tensions and the political climate of the Balkans, that microcosm of European politics. Also somewhat similar events in October 1925 had quickly led to a Greek invasion of Bulgaria. With Germany's admission to the League virtually assured, and keeping in mind Italy's interests in Bulgaria, any Balkan adventure which led to the League's involvement and to a possible clash between the powers at this time was to be avoided and this is the line that Drummond followed. He declared to the Bulgarian Minister in Bern that it might not be expedient for his country, for various reasons of a practical nature, to make an appeal to the League in connection with the collective note of protest handed to Sofia. Drummond's suggestion was that provided the Great Powers could agree, their military attachés at Sofia and Belgrade could proceed to make inquiries if new disorders erupted at the Bulgarian frontier. They would have this right to undertake local inquiries from the Great Powers and this in turn would exclude every interference by the League.

What Drummond was proposing therefore was direct negotiations between the parties—an approach that the minister admitted was favoured by his government which would not appeal to the League except in the case of an actual invasion.[2] The Great Powers appear to have seen eye to eye with Drummond on this problem for in Sofia their diplomatic missions advised a direct settlement of the question, an avoidance of any appeal to the League, and a conciliatory and non-contentious Bulgarian reply to the collective note of protest. Whether Drummond influenced the Great Powers or vice versa or whether Drummond and the Great Powers simultaneously but independently came to the same notion of how to handle the matter is unclear. What is clear is that Sofia followed the advice tendered, and the acceptance of its conciliatory note by Athens, Belgrade, and Bucharest[3] brought the incident to a close only days after Germany's formal admission to the League.

---

[1] Eric Drummond, Record of Interview, 13 Apr. 1926 and Drummond (Geneva) to Selby, 19 Apr. 1926, FO/371/11356.

[2] *DDI*, 7, iv. 305.

[3] *The Times* (London), 21 Aug. 1926, p. 8, 23 Aug. 1926, p. 9, 28 Aug. 1926, p. 9, 1 Sept. 1926, p. 11, and 13 Sept. 1926, p. 10.

The Appointment of Paulucci de Calboli Barone

It was only after Germany was admitted to the League and a number of colonial issues were settled with Italy that Chamberlain in January 1927 undertook to approach Mussolini about the organization. He used for the occasion an address dealing with the League that he had delivered at the University of Glasgow. He was sending this address to Mussolini, Chamberlain explained to Graham, the British Ambassador, in order to 'maintain the personal relationship which happily existed between' them. Moreover, he wanted the Duce to see the League as he saw it and because Chamberlain thought that Italian foreign policy was being injured 'by the constant attacks upon the League in certain Fascist journals'. These anti-League attacks fed the notion that Italy was aggressive and that Mussolini disliked the League because it was an obstacle to aggression. Chamberlain believed that Mussolini's policy was sane and for the present a peaceful one. He regretted these constant suspicions. He did not suppose that his Glasgow address would produce great results but if it caused Mussolini to think a little about the League it would not be a bad thing either from London's point of view or from Mussolini's. The Duce's reply was on the surface seemingly sympathetic[1] and, as we shall soon see, gave the false impression that it had mellowed the Italian dictator's attitude toward the organization.

In actual fact it had not. Indeed, Mussolini at this point was busy purging from the Italian diplomatic service those elements which had endeavoured to moderate Fascist attempts to engage in an adventurist foreign policy. Those purged included the ambassadors in Berlin, London, and Paris, as well as Contarini whose dismissal soon left the Foreign Ministry without a helmsman. At the same time, it was also decided to unload on the League Mussolini's *chef de cabinet*, an important post held by Marchese Giacomo Paulucci de Calboli Barone, an aristocrat who had previously served as secretary to several former foreign ministers.[2] Paulucci had 'ably supported' Contarini in his attempts to restrain the Duce and had 'constantly urged the

[1] *DBFP, 1919–1939*, IA, ii. 709–10 and fn.
[2] Cassels, pp. 7, 165, 284–7, 388.

counsels of prudence and moderation'.[1] To open up the League slot Under Secretary-General Attolico was appointed Ambassador to Brazil which Drummond felt was a blow to the Secretariat. Therefore Drummond decided to go to Rome to discuss the question of Attolico's successor. He hoped, he informed Cecil, that in his Rome discussions he would 'be able to get someone who, while being a solid Fascist, equally believes in the League'— a seeming contradiction in terms.[2]

Before Drummond even contacted Cecil, however, Paulucci called on Graham to inform him confidentially that he had been proposed as Attolico's successor. Mussolini suggested his appointment, Paulucci noted, to emphasize the 'interest and importance he attached to the League'. In fact, London might consider the Duce's 'actions as the first fruits' of the recent private letter which he had received from Chamberlain. Paulucci went on to explain that personally he had always done as much as he could for the League and hoped that if his appointment was approved he would be able to strengthen what had to be regarded as Italy's weak link in foreign policy.

Whitehall hoped that Paulucci's appointment would be approved, and thought that Drummond would agree that his appointment was a promising one, which would contribute to strengthening Italy's attachment to the League and the principles for which it stood.[3] Whitehall's comments, however, reached Geneva after Drummond had departed for Rome. It was in a sense a superfluous communication for Drummond was too wise and experienced to ignore the writing on the wall: Mussolini was offering Paulucci as Attolico's successor, like it or not.

[1] H. Stuart Hughes, 'The Early Diplomacy of Italian Fascism: 1922–1932', in Gordon A. Craig and Felix Gilbert (eds.), *The Diplomats 1919–1939* (Princeton: Princeton University Press, 1953), p. 217. The information that Mussolini had to remove Paulucci because he found him 'absolument ridicule, grotesque, pas intelligent' appears to be a planted Italian tale. 'The Reminiscences of Thanassis Aghnides' (typewritten manuscript), Oral History Collection, CUNY. For Secretariat reaction to Paulucci's appointment see also 'The Reminiscences of Branko Lukac' (typewritten manuscript), Oral History Collection, CUNY.

[2] Drummond (Geneva) to Cecil, 20 Jan. 1926 [*sic*], Add. MS. 51111, Robert Cecil Papers, BL.

[3] Selby to Drummond, 21 Jan. 1927, Austen Chamberlain Papers, FO/800/260.

Accordingly when he arrived in Rome and initially discussed the matter with Dino Grandi, the Foreign Ministry's Under-Secretary, an early Fascist, and a member of the party's Grand Council, Drummond expressed his pleasure with Paulucci's nomination.[1] That evening, 26 January, Drummond also discussed the subject with Mussolini. He repeated what he had said to Grandi and divulged that in the interim he had spoken to Paulucci. Drummond was completely convinced, he told Mussolini, that he could not get a better collaborator in the Secretariat's work. He hoped, therefore, that he could formally offer Paulucci the Under Secretary-Generalship. Mussolini agreed that it was of 'considerable constitutional importance that the initiative' for the appointment should formally come from Drummond. When Drummond asked whether he could draw up the communiqué stating that he had asked for Paulucci's services and that Mussolini had consented though he regretted losing him, the Duce agreed, asking only that he examine the communiqué before it was released.

They then discussed Chamberlain's recent letter and his address at the University of Glasgow. Mussolini noted that in his letter to Chamberlain he had explained that the League had to 'remain a federation of states and not become a super-state'. Drummond remarked that if the League attempted to become a super-state it would very likely disappear. He also observed that if it were possible for Mussolini to come to Geneva he would realize how groundless his fears were about the undue influence of the small states. In fact, it was the Great Powers which dominated the Geneva situation. If these powers agreed, the small states never raised objections. Drummond, however, thought that it was wise for the small states to be present and an opportunity afforded them to express their views and even criticize. This way they might feel they were participants in general world policy. Mussolini retorted that if this was the case he completely agreed. He thought by having them in the organization it gave small states a safety valve should their interests be threatened and that a kind of control might be exercised over them so that disputes should not erupt among

---

[1] [Eric Drummond], Record of Interview, 26 Jan. 1927, FO/371/12683.

them which might drag in the Great Powers.[1] If the interview had gone well it was largely due to the fact that Mussolini had achieved what he wanted: Paulucci out of Rome and in Geneva.

Drummond noted to Chamberlain that his letter, as well as his University of Glasgow address, 'had evidently made a great impression on [Mussolini] favourable to the League'. He thought that perhaps the 'first fruits' of this positive impression was the Duce's suggestion that Paulucci should succeed Attolico as Under Secretary-General. From the Secretariat's point of view this was fine since Paulucci was considered by everyone as a friend of the League, very loyal and trustworthy, and had Mussolini's complete confidence. He hoped, therefore, that events in Italy might now take a favourable turn regarding League affairs.[2]

Drummond was 'greatly pleased with the friendly spirit' shown by Mussolini and Grandi, he informed Graham. It was also Drummond's impression that the atmosphere regarding the League 'had undergone a considerable change for the better' since his previous visit to Rome in December 1924. An indication of the new atmosphere was that press attacks against the League during his stay in Rome caused Grandi to admonish the erring editor. He pointed out to him that such articles did not represent the government's view and were especially out of place and discourteous at the very moment when the Secretary-General was visiting Rome.

Before departing from Rome Drummond issued a press communiqué expressing his satisfaction over the friendly and hospitable reception accorded him. He noted with pleasure that the League's importance as an organ of international life was increasingly recognized in Italy, and thought that the hostility to the organization, which was marked in certain circles, and not merely in Italy, was based on misconceptions. It was believed that the League wished to intervene in internal affairs. This was absolutely untrue. Any attempt to become a super-state would be the League's own death warrant. Nor was it true that patriotism and discipline were incompatible with the League's principles.[3]

In the Foreign Office the Head of the League of Nations

---

[1] E[ric] D[rummond], Record of Interview, 26 Jan. 1927, Austen Chamberlain Papers, FO/800/260.

[2] Drummond (Rome) to Chamberlain, 27 Jan. 1927, ibid.

[3] Graham (Rome) to Chamberlain, No. 70, 28 Jan. 1927, FO/371/12683.

Department, Ronald Campbell, minuted that perhaps he was being too scrupulous but it struck him as somewhat improper that Drummond should issue a communiqué touching on the League attitude of the country he was visiting. Chamberlain did not agree. He saw 'no objection to so tactful a statement—except the precedent'.[1]

Drummond explained to London that in selecting Paulucci 'reasons of principle' dictated that he show that the initiative for the appointment rested with him. He pointed out that the first candidates offered by Germany had not been up to scratch and he had negotiated with Berlin on this matter for some time before securing Dufour-Feronce. There was also a practical consideration in Paulucci's case. If it was thought in certain countries that Mussolini had imposed his *chef de cabinet* on the Secretariat, Paulucci's own position would have been intolerable. On the other hand, if Drummond took the initiative this type of objection could not be raised. Drummond was pleased with Paulucci and glad that he was coming to Geneva. The added advantage was that it would be unnecessary for Paulucci 'to prove himself a super-keen Italian!'[2] Though the points that Drummond made were well taken, in actual fact the appointment had been forced upon him not merely by Mussolini but also by the British Government—something which he was neither willing to admit nor come to grips with.

At the same time London was not shy about soliciting information unconnected with Paulucci's appointment. Had Mussolini, London queried, referred to Italy's relations with Yugoslavia and Albania. He exercised great discretion about the problem, Drummond replied. He mentioned the matter only in connection with the Secretariat's registration of the November 1926 Tirana treaty as required under Article 18 of the Covenant. As to the treaty Drummond failed to see how either Paris or Belgrade who were displeased with it could request its interpretation when it was registered with the Secretariat. He believed that the only way they could get an interpretation was to raise the subject before the Council, but he sincerely hoped that they

---

[1] Minutes by R[onald H.] Campbell, and A[usten] C[hamberlain], 2 Feb. [1927], ibid.

[2] Drummond (Geneva) to Selby, 31 Jan. 1927, Austen Chamberlain Papers, FO/800/260.

would not do this.[1] Drummond's caution was justified. The Albanian problem was a political tinderbox.

The Duce in World Politics

Nothing had really changed, although on the surface everything was going well and it appeared to Drummond that Italy might assume a new tack toward the League. Because of his British nationality, distrust of Drummond in Rome persisted.[2] By the spring of 1927, it must have been obvious to Drummond himself that nothing indeed had changed in view of Italy's attitude toward Yugoslavia and the sphere of influence that she was developing in Albania. The Yugoslav desire to change the Treaty of Tirana from a bilateral to a tripartite arrangement was rejected by Mussolini and tensions between Belgrade and Rome increased.[3]

In March Drummond was approached by Kosta Fotić, the Yugoslav representative, following an announcement by Mussolini that military preparations by Belgrade along the frontier with Albania foreshadowed an attack against that country.[4] Fotić desired to know the procedure that his goverment could follow in case it decided to bring the question of its relations with Albania before the League. Drummond replied that the only provision in the Covenant that he thought could be invoked in this situation was Article 11 paragraph two. On the other hand, he hoped that the situation might be handled by direct negotiations between the two governments. This comment was probably triggered by Drummond's knowledge, based on prior soundings, that there was no interest in having any League investigation along the Yugoslav–Albanian frontier. In turn it explains why he envisaged an investigation along the frontier only by the military attachés of the Great Powers in Belgrade.

This particular aspect of the question did not develop further and soon faded from the international scene. In the Secretariat, however, the tensions of the Italian–Albanian–Yugoslavian

[1] Selby to Drummond, 28 Jan. 1927 and Drummond (Geneva) to Selby, 31 Jan. 1927, FO/371/12064.
[2] *DDI*, 7, v. 15–16 and fn.
[3] Cassels, pp. 332–7; Macartney and Cremona, p. 109.
[4] *DDI*, 7, v. 89–90; Macartney and Cremona, pp. 107–8.

triangle continued to be felt. Arriving in Geneva in March to assume his duties, Paulucci was informed that Avenol would leave immediately for Sofia to deal with the question of the League's loan and would also visit Belgrade. Paulucci quickly made Drummond aware that he found Avenol's trip to Belgrade inopportune at the present time. Regardless of why Avenol went to Belgrade, the impression would be that the highest French Secretariat official had gone in order to collect 'laments and protests'. A Frenchman like Avenol was especially unsuitable following Briand's recent pro-Yugoslav declarations. He feared hostile reactions, especially in Italy, as much against the League as against France. Drummond responded that the reports from Belgrade showed that it feared Albania's occupation by Italy and an eventual attack against Yugoslavia consented to by Britain. These reports had decided him to intervene indirectly and informally in order to pacify the situation. The dispatch of a British Secretariat official was out of the question. Drummond hoped that a Frenchman welcomed in Belgrade without suspicion would be able to do useful work. Paulucci disagreed. He thought it better to leave the matter to the Great Powers. Avenol's hurried departure for Belgrade, he claimed, would allow the interpretation that Paris managed to get the League to place itself at Belgrade's disposal. The end result of this conversation was that Paulucci obtained a postponement of Avenol's trip. He also suggested that during any Belgrade trip Avenol be accompanied by an Italian Secretariat official.

Mussolini approved of Paulucci's action. He desired the cancellation of Avenol's trip but if this was impossible it would be acceptable if he departed within fifteen days provided he bypassed Belgrade. What was of particular interest to the Duce was Drummond's behaviour. The Secretary-General's resolve to 'intervene indirectly and in an informal manner' to pacify the situation on the basis of the fantastic fear that Italy would occupy Albania constituted in Mussolini's opinion an 'excessive initiative' since an action of this sort could not concern the 'mere person' of the League's Secretary-General. Therefore, Paulucci was instructed, in disregard of his status as an international civil servant, to see whether Drummond might be induced to consider if his initiative might not exceed 'the limits of his competence' and therefore 'raise regrettable impressions and discussions'.

Acting on Mussolini's orders Paulucci explained to Drummond Italy's point of view in the Albanian–Yugoslav question and again raised the possibility of cancelling Avenol's Belgrade trip. He questioned if Drummond's initiative did not exceed his competence and whether it was worth taking upon himself grave responsibility in a question which had not yet been entrusted to the Council and thus 'raise regrettable repercussions'. Drummond attempted to explain that Avenol's trip was the usual courtesy visit employed by the Secretary-General and the Under Secretaries-General with the governments of various League members. Avenol, he maintained, would in no way be involved in dragging the League into a question which had not been entrusted to it for solution.

Prudently Paulucci put his thoughts into a letter to Drummond and supplemented them with oral arguments that he did not want to put into writing. Drummond's reply was conciliatory and Paulucci recommended that Mussolini accept the bargain struck. He pointed out to the Duce that his desire to have an Italian Secretariat official accompany Avenol was so that this official could observe Avenol's actions and then report to him upon his return—an extraordinary statement if the Secretariat was supposed to be a non-political international civil service. Regarding the argument in Drummond's letter relating to Albania's integrity as a League member based on Article 10 of the Covenant, Paulucci proposed that he convey to him in writing a 'precise reservation' on this point.

Mussolini approved of all of Paulucci's actions. The gist of the arrangement devised appears to have been that Avenol would go to Sofia but not Belgrade before May except if circumstances counselled a further postponement. In his trip Avenol would be accompanied by an Italian Secretariat official who Mussolini thought should be Marcello Roddolo of the Political Section.[1] In late April Avenol arrived in Sofia.[2]

Drummond, however, was 'somewhat alarmed at the continuance of this wretched ... business', he informed Tyrrell, the Foreign Office's Permanent Under-Secretary. From his conversations with Paulucci, he feared that Italy would never consent to discuss with Yugoslavia the Treaty of Tirana and its

[1] *DDI*, 7, v. 100, 111, 120–1, 138–9 and fn.
[2] *The Times* (London), 29 Apr. 1927, p. 13 and 3 May 1927, p. 15.

implications. Nor unfortunately would Italy agree to furnish explanations regarding the Tirana treaty to the League. What could be done? Drummond noted that the Ambassadors' Conference in November 1921 concluded a definite arrangement whereby Italy had practically pledged herself that if Albania's frontiers were threatened, she would only dispatch troops into Albania after coming before the Council. This arrangement is followed five years later by the Treaty of Tirana which is considered by some critics and especially by Yugoslavia as giving Italy the right to send troops into Albania without first coming before the Council.

Drummond thought that there was a clear distinction between the two commitments. The arrangement with the Ambassadors' Conference concerned Albania's frontiers and independence. The Treaty of Tirana maintained the political *status quo*. But was it not fair to say, Drummond queried, that if troops could not be dispatched in the arrangement made with the Ambassadors' Conference without first bringing the matter before the Council, troops could not be dispatched in the second case unless similar action was also taken? The point was that the powers represented on the Ambassadors' Conference had the right to clear up the matter. Of the four powers on the Ambassadors' Conference Great Britain appeared to be the only one that could, without causing offence, approach Italy on this question. Was it possible, Drummond asked Tyrrell, for London to request officially from Rome assurances that the Tirana treaty neither altered nor restricted the arrangement made with the Ambassadors' Conference? Naturally, this would have to be done confidentially, but if the official reply could be made public either by a Parliamentary question or in some other way, the 'whole sting of the present situation' would, he thought, vanish. He disclosed that he felt compelled to make this suggestion for when he mentioned the idea to Paulucci, he did not appear hostile to it.[1]

The Foreign Office was not receptive. On the advice of Orme Sargent, Head of the Central Department, Tyrrell pointed out to Drummond that two interpretations could be given to the 1921 arrangement. Mussolini interpreted it as being an unconditional recognition by the Ambassadors' Conference of Italy's special right to intervene in Albania as provided for in the

[1] Drummond (Geneva) to Tyrrell, 23 Apr. 1927, FO/371/12216.

Tirana treaty. In fact, as Mussolini interpreted the 1921 arrangement, the Tirana treaty merely elaborated Italy's right which the Ambassadors' Conference had already granted in 1921. Thus Mussolini would deny that the 1921 arrangement imposed any kind of obligation upon Italy or in any manner restricted her liberty of action. This was not to say that the League's legal advisers could not make an excellent case interpreting the arrangement in the opposite sense. However, in view of Rome's attitude, Drummond would understand London's reticence to commit itself at this stage to one interpretation over another. Furthermore, Great Britain had no special claim in interpreting the 1921 arrangement, and she did not wish the onus of doing so if it could be avoided.

Then Tyrrell's warning was delivered. Though no concern of his, he was 'inclined to think that the League Secretariat General would do well to exercise a similar circumspection'. Whatever Paulucci may say Mussolini would strongly resent Drummond's 'proposed interpretation and treat it as an attempt to defraud him of his just rights'. If Mussolini thought that Geneva would approach the question along these lines it would not help in reconciling him to League procedure. It was Tyrrell's opinion that if the Council was asked to deal with the question it would be 'well advised to treat it, not as a juridical problem, but on broad practical and unlegal lines'. He apologized for this policy attitude which also caused the rejection of Drummond's second suggestion. Chamberlain felt that in the 'interest of general and particular peace' he had gone as far as a British Minister ought to go. He did not support the idea that because Great Britain alone among the Great Powers had preserved really good relations with Italy, London was 'therefore to demand explanations at Rome for other people's benefit, give continual and usually unpalatable advice and even exert pressure' where no British interest was involved.[1]

Drummond got the message but also rose to the occasion. He fully understood the Foreign Office's 'anxiety not to commit itself to any opinion', he replied to Tyrrell. Personally, from the text of the Ambassadors' Conference's 1921 arrangement, he could not find any support for the theory that Tyrrell implied in

[1] Minute by O[rme] Sargent, 26 Apr. [1927] and Tyrrell to Drummond, 5 May 1927, ibid.

his letter was Mussolini's, namely, that Italy had a right under this arrangement to take action in Albania without first going to the Council. Tyrrell likewise had no need to worry about the Secretariat's exercising circumspection. It had absolutely no intentions of interfering or of tendering proposals. It was not the League's business if the Ambassadors' Conference made arrangements which were considered capable of two diverse interpretations. Drummond trusted, on the other hand, that Tyrrell's letter did not mean that he objected to his writing to him occasionally, in order to ascertain whether the information which came to Geneva from so many varied sources might be of some use.[1] Tyrrell's rejoinder assured him that his communications were appreciated. Nor had he feared that the Secretariat would act without circumspection. However, Tyrrell felt that it would be as useful for Drummond 'to know our point of view as for us to learn yours'.[2] It was a stand-off.

Lacking British support Drummond was in no position to give assurances when he discussed the whole matter with Fotić. Since there were several interpretations possible of the relationship between the 1921 arrangement and the Treaty of Tirana Drummond thought that the wiser policy would be to 'leave the whole question somewhat obscure'. Thus if it was raised in the future the signatories to the 1921 arrangement would be in a position to appeal to Italy 'on the ground of goodwill rather than on a legal point'.

Fotić then strongly pressed Drummond as to whether he believed that the Tirana treaty and the recent Italian–Albanian declaration—that the treaty concerned no other state and would not be reopened—were in fact consistent with the Covenant. Drummond replied that personally he could see no legal inconsistency. It seemed to him that the only way to approach this whole matter was on the basis of prior Italian–Yugoslav treaty commitments providing for friendly and neighbourly relations between the two states.[3]

Devoid of support and negotiating from a position of weakness, any sort of understanding with the Italians eluded the Yugoslavs whose own relations with Albania steadily deteriorated leading

[1] Drummond (Geneva) to Tyrrell, 9 May 1927, FO/371/12217.
[2] T[yrrell] to Drummond, 16 May 1927, ibid.
[3] [Eric Drummond], Record of Interview, 17 May 1927, ibid.

in the summer of 1927 to a diplomatic rupture. In November Yugoslavia signed a treaty of friendship, alliance, and arbitration with France which had been initialled in March 1926. Briand maintained that it was not directed against Italy, and the French press insisted that it was in step with both the Covenant and the Locarno principles. Rome's answer soon followed on 22 November, when it concluded a second Treaty of Tirana with Albania which formed a defensive alliance between the two states. The situation had gone from bad to worse.[1]

In discussing the new situation with Drummond, Paulucci complained about the attitude in British political circles and the Foreign Office over the latest developments. Drummond hastened to assure Paulucci that a few days previously when he was in London he had ascertained that Chamberlain equally disapproved of the two recent treaties. Paulucci observed, perhaps with some annoyance, that in holding the same opinion about both these treaties Chamberlain 'probably did not exactly understand the profound difference both in the spirit [and] in the purpose of these two international acts'.[2]

Things for the moment did not develop further. Instead, difficulties involving Italy unfolded in another direction. On New Year's Day 1928, Austrian customs officers at Szent-Gotthard on the frontier with Hungary discovered that a consignment labelled machine parts really contained machine-gun parts. Though the consignment had come from Verona its final destination could not be ascertained from the bills of lading. As one of the vanquished states, Hungary was committed to an anti-*status quo* policy which was hindered by the fact that under the Treaty of Trianon her armaments were restricted. Naturally, the news of what had been discovered at Szent-Gotthard caused an immediate reaction among the states of the Little Entente. Since Hungary was Italy's quasi-ally in eastern Europe, their understanding based on a common anti-*status quo* orientation, it was obvious that these machine-gun parts were meant for Hungary. It was probably only one of many undetected consignments dispatched to Hungary after prior consultation and agreement with the Italian authorities.[3]

[1] Macartney and Cremona, pp. 109–12.
[2] *DDI*, 7, v. 597–8.
[3] Walters, pp. 400–1.

Though this was only conjecture at the time and firm evidence
was lacking to prove it, the publication of the Italian Foreign
Ministry's archives after the Second World War shows that this
indeed was the case. Like it or not Italy had to support Hungary
in this question and Mussolini informed Paulucci that Rome
viewed the matter as a 'simple smuggling affair'.[1] The other
permanent Council members were of course not interested in
raising questions that might prove embarrassing to their Locarno
partner. So between enforcing one aspect of the Paris peace
settlement and not jeopardizing the recently ratified Locarno
Pacts they chose the latter course over the former. Along with
this the small states were also afraid that any independent action
on their part would incur Rome's diplomatic enmity.[2] In this
kind of setting there was not much that Drummond could
accomplish.

In fact, initially when the Little Entente approached him over
the question, Drummond did not want to convene the Council
and asked them to put their protests in writing.[3] When they did
so,[4] Drummond observed to Cadogan that the Szent-Gotthard
question was more a matter for investigation by customs officials
rather than military experts. This approach dovetailed with
Mussolini's claim that it was a smuggling matter. How much
Drummond was influenced by the Duce's claim which might
have been communicated by Paulucci is difficult to say.
Drummond's proposal, however, would lead at least to some sort
of investigation. Something was better than nothing. General
opinion in Geneva appeared to be that the Permanent Advisory
Commission on Military, Naval, and Air Questions would have
to convene since the Council would want its opinion. Personally,
Drummond thought it would be far better if the Council would
request the Transit Committee to establish a small group of
experts to investigate the Szent-Gotthard question, including the
place of origin of the machine-gun parts and their destination.
This group would then report directly to the Council and to the
Transit Committee. The latter body might then furnish its

---

[1] *DDI*, 7, vi. 17, 70, 72–3, 99, 126–7, 291.
[2] Walters, p. 402.
[3] Elek Karsai, *Számjeltávirat Valamennyi Magyar Királyi Követségnek* (Budapest:
Táncsics Könyvkiadó, 1969), p. 368.
[4] League of Nations, *Official Journal*, IX (1928), pp. 545–8.

observations and recommendations for the purpose of solving certain customs problems relating to international frontier railway stations like Szent-Gotthard.[1]

Drummond's case for some sort of investigation was strengthened along two fronts. Though he knew it would be of limited value, Beneš desired such an investigation from the 'psychological point of view' and to 'prevent future infractions' of the Treaty of Trianon.[2] Though Beneš's desires, and those of the Little Entente for which he was often the spokeman, could not be entirely disregarded, of far greater importance was the French reaction. Drummond pointed out to the Foreign Office that although the Szent-Gotthard question was of little intrinsic importance, it was being considered in France both by Briand's friends as well as by his enemies to be something of a test case. Those Frenchmen who were opposed to both Briand and the League would be pleased if no League action was taken in this matter, and it was because Briand's friends felt 'this so strongly that they [were] very earnest in insisting that the League must make an inquiry'. Avenol believed that Briand would be very willing to limit sharply the scope of any League inquiry. What was of particular interest to Drummond was that the enemies of the League and of international conciliation desired that nothing be done in the Szent-Gotthard question in order to 'frustrate Briand's policy of relying on and supporting the League'.[3]

Before the Little Entente requested that the Szent-Gotthard question be placed on the Council's agenda Hungary announced in the press that in vew of the irregularities associated with the consignment, the machine-gun parts would be broken up and the metal sold for scrap.[4] Drummond at first ignored the warnings of the Little Entente over this move.[5] On 23 February, almost six weeks after the Hungarian announcement had been made and after the question was inscribed on the Council's agenda, this intended action was checked by a message from the Council's Acting President, the Chinese representative, Tcheng

---

[1] Drummond (Geneva) to Cadogan, 1 Feb. 1928, FO/371/12935.

[2] Drummond to Selby, 6 Feb. 1928, Drummond Folder, LNA.

[3] Drummond (Geneva) to Selby, 4 Feb. 1928, Austen Chamberlain Papers, FO/800/262.

[4] Walters, p. 401.

[5] Karsai, p. 368.

Loh.[1] By the time Loh's message arrived the plan had been partially executed making any subsequent inquiry more difficult than would have otherwise been the case.[2] This move prompted the Hungarian representative, General Gabor Tánczos, to call on Drummond to discuss Loh's action. Since Loh was inexperienced[3] it is possible that he was persuaded to send this message either by the Little Entente, or by Drummond who might have had second thoughts about the disappearance of the machine-gun parts which would have complicated any future investigation.

The Hungarians might have suspected this, which accounts for Tánczos's visit. Drummond, however, refused to be drawn into any discussion about Loh's message. He claimed that he had not been consulted about its contents, and it was impossible for him to say anything since his relationship with Loh would be involved. He did admit that Loh's action raised a constitutional question which had to be separated from the Szent-Gotthard incident itself. Drummond pointed out that Loh's message did not suggest that he had authority to require that the break up of the machine-gun parts cease. The message merely suggested that certain conservation measures be followed.

Drummond did not think that Budapest's policy had been wise. It seemed to him that the Council was likely to be somewhat annoyed that Hungary, after having been informed that the Szent-Gotthard question was going to be considered, then took steps to destroy the material about which the complaint had been made. When Tánczos correctly pointed out that Budapest had announced this action as early as 5 January Drummond retorted that if this had been Budapest's intention surely it would have been more proper to have informed the Council through him rather than to assume that it would take official notice of government statements appearing in the press. Nor did Drummond accept Tánczos's explanation that the sale of the scrap metal was necessary to defray the expenses of the freight trains which had carried the consignment and were still in Hungary. Drummond repeated that the whole matter was one of

---

[1] League of Nations, *Official Journal*, IX (1928), pp. 548–9; Walters, p. 401.
[2] Walters, p. 401.
[3] Drummond (Geneva) to Cadogan, 25 Oct. 1927, FO/371/12686.

impressions rather than of facts and he was willing to admit that legally Hungary was within her rights in taking the action she had taken.[1]

Several days after this interview Drummond informed Paul de Hevesey, Tánczos's associate, that an investigation by a small committee limited to the frontier railway station at Szent-Gotthard was 'unavoidable'. Drummond appeared friendly and wanted to settle the whole question quietly. He observed to Hevesey that naturally the origin of the machine-gun parts could not in any case be investigated.[2] Italy was now off the hook but Drummond had achieved at least half of what he wanted. Though Hevesey should have been pleased at how things had developed he was on the contrary annoyed at the decision, and his comments caused Drummond, as Cadogan noted to the Foreign Office, to reply 'quite properly to all these truculent observations'.[3] On 7 March the Council decided to establish a three-man committee composed of the Dutch, Finnish, and Chilean representatives to study—not to investigate—the Szent-Gotthard question and present a report. The committee was also empowered to seek the assistance of experts chosen from the League's membership. Finally, in June the matter was brought to a close when the Council issued a public statement of the facts as ascertained by the committee, a general warning of the inherent dangers of an illicit traffic in arms, and a mild censure of the Hungarian authorities for their uncooperative attitude.[4] It was a 'very anodyne' report, Drummond observed to Chamberlain,[5] but it was also in line with Beneš's desires and Briand's needs. Considering the constraints under which Drummond had worked it was as good an ending as one could expect.

The Council's action allowing Italy, not to mention Hungary, to escape censure must have been particularly galling to Yugoslavia which was at odds with both states. As 1928 gave way to 1929 the tensions between Italy and Yugoslavia already exacerbated by the French–Yugoslav Treaty of November 1927

[1] Eric Drummond, Record of Interview, 24 Feb. 1928, FO/371/12935.

[2] Karsai, p. 379.

[3] A note by A[lexander] Cadogan, 2 Mar. 1928, FO/371/12935.

[4] League of Nations, *Official Journal*, IX (1928), pp. 387–97, 905–18.

[5] Drummond (Geneva) to Chamberlain, 14 May 1928, AC55/139, Austen Chamberlain Papers, UB.

and the second Treaty of Tirana were further heightened by a series of events in Albania, Italy, and Yugoslavia. During May, June, and August a series of anti-Italian riots and demonstrations swept a number of Yugoslavian cities in protest against ratification of the Nettuno Conventions of 1925 which guaranteed the rights of Italian residents in Dalmatia. In Italy there were counter-demonstrations. These Yugoslav riots may have been fed by the fear of Italy's growing sphere of influence in Austria, Bulgaria, and Hungary and the well-founded suspicion that she was supporting and financing *komitaji* intrigues in Macedonia and separatism in Croatia. Mussolini's revisionist speech in the Italian Senate on 5 June 1928, therefore, merely confirmed officially what the Yugoslavians had already come to accept as established Italian policy. This was followed in September by the proclamation and election of Ahmed Zogu as King Zog I of Albania—an action unacceptable to Yugoslavia. That same month Rome signed a treaty of friendship with Athens which gave Belgrade cause to wonder about its southern neighbour. With the New Year Italy refused to renew the Rome treaty of friendship and cordial collaboration signed in 1924.[1]

Tensions continued during 1929. In mid-October the execution of a Slav student of Italian nationality who had been convicted at Pola with firing on Fascists on their way to vote produced anti-Italian riots and demonstrations in Belgrade and other Yugoslavian cities. Italy protested these acts and though Yugoslavia promised to punish the offenders, she objected to interference in her internal affairs.[2] Italian–Yugoslavian relations had hit a new low and, fearful of an attack, Yugoslavia began taking military precautions. Inasmuch as Drummond was scheduled to make an official visit to Belgrade, he 'took the opportunity of first going to Italy to see Mussolini and discuss the matter with him'.[3]

[1] *DDI*, 7, vi., vii. *passim*; Macartney and Cremona, pp. 113–14, 196–7; Hughes, 'The Early Diplomacy of Italian Fascism: 1922–1932', p. 223. *New York Times*, 26 May 1928, p. 6, 27 May 1928, p. 18, 29 May 1928, p. 5, 31 May 1928, p. 1, 1 June 1928, p. 27, 15 June 1928, p. 27, 16 Aug. 1928, p. 5, 18 Aug. 1928, p. 5 and 19 Aug. 1928, p. 26.

[2] *New York Times*, 17 Oct. 1929, p. 26, 18 Oct. 1929, p. 18, 19 Oct. 1929, p. 4, 22 Oct. 1929, p. 10, 23 Oct. 1929, p. 23.

[3] Stephen M. Schwebel, *The Secretary-General of the United Nations* (Cambridge: Harvard University Press, 1952), p. 8.

Since his last visit to Italy, suspicions against Drummond had increased thanks to Paulucci who had reported that his chief supported the notion of regional security pacts on the Locarno pattern, especially an association of Austria and Hungary with the countries of the Little Entente. Such a notion was unacceptable in Rome which feared that any Danubian Confederation or Mediterranean Locarno would be a threat to Italy's security or contrary to her interests. This was followed by later observations that he detected in Drummond a Yugoslavophilia and that Drummond had attempted to pressure the Italian President of the Mandate's Commission following Zionist complaints about his partiality.[1] These comments as well as Rome's traditional suspicion of Drummond based on his nationality did not make his task easier.

In his first interview which appears to have been with Grandi, who had recently been appointed Foreign Minister, greater collaboration between Italy and the League dominated the conversation.[2] Grandi's comments clearly reflected his conviction that 'international conciliation had now become the accepted goal of Italian policy'—the end result of what appeared to be a successful Italian foreign policy capped in February 1929 by the Lateran Treaty which finally normalized Italy's relations with the Vatican.[3]

Drummond did not see Mussolini until the afternoon of the following day, 30 October. Initially, the conversation dealt with Italian representation in the Secretariat. Drummond then turned the conversation to his real purpose for coming to talk to Mussolini: Italian–Yugoslavian relations. He noted that during his last visit Mussolini had remarked that even if he desired to make war—which he did not—it would be impossible to do so without endangering his government's present policy. Mussolini retorted that this was still his stance. He could not envisage war, except if Yugoslavia attacked Albania, in which case war would inevitably follow. Drummond observed that if Yugoslavia did attack Albania she would have to contend not only with Italy but probably with all the League's members. Mussolini appeared

---

[1] *DDI*, 7, vi. 110–11, 278–9 and viii. 50, 188, 193, 221. See also, *DBFP, 1919–1939*, IA, iv. 272–4.

[2] [Eric Drummond], Dino Grandi, 29 Oct. 1929, FO/371/13694.

[3] Hughes, 'The Early Diplomacy of Italian Fascism: 1922–1932', pp. 230–1.

surprised by this statement. Drummond then inquired whether there were any indications of difficulties in Albania. There were none, Mussolini replied. Everything appeared quiet. Of course, a time may come when internal difficulties in Yugoslavia might cause her to engage in an adventurous foreign policy so as to promote national unity.[1]

That same day Drummond also discussed with Grandi the Italian nationals in the Secretariat. Too often he thought that these officials 'were considered as part of the Italian diplomatic machine and entrusted by the Government with duties which really lay outside their scope'. It was this type of suspicion which had led to considerable 'concealed criticism' of the Secretariat's Italian officials during the past two Assemblies. Drummond had attempted to defend them but moves by Rome would certainly assist him and he believed would be to Italy's benefit. For example, Rome sometimes sent official communications directly to Paulucci rather than address them to the Secretary-General. Drummond thought the precedent was unfavourable as there were people looking for reasons to criticize. Grandi maintained that this action was due to the Foreign Ministry's disorganization. Paulucci and the other Italians in the Secretariat, he disingenuously claimed, did not exist as far as the Italian Government was concerned. He really understood the need to observe completely the forms which had been established for organizations like the Secretariat.

It was not until that evening that Drummond was able to broach to Grandi the question of Italy's relations with Yugoslavia. Grandi noted that Yugoslav–Albanian relations were the danger point and reminded Drummond that Italy under the second Treaty of Tirana had an alliance with Albania and would be duty bound to execute its terms. To these comments Drummond observed that if Yugoslavia committed aggression the question would come to the League and he was convinced that Italy would not be the only state protecting Albania.[2]

Drummond also had an interview with Cardinal Gasparri,

---

[1] [Eric Drummond], Signor Mussolini, 30 Oct. 1929, FO/371/13694.

[2] [Eric Drummond], Signor Grandi, 30 Oct. 1929, ibid. By the spring of 1931 Paulucci's antics behind the scenes had annoyed Drummond to the point that he desired Paulucci's removal from the Secretariat. *DDI*, 7, ix. 356 fn.

but with the Lateran Treaty in mind Drummond's main interest
centred around the question of the treaty's registration with the
Secretariat as stipulated in Article 18 of the Covenant.[1] When
the Lateran Treaty was signed in February Drummond had
been keen on having it registered with the Secretariat. At the
same time he felt that the Vatican should avoid League
membership because it would be contrary to its interests and
lessen its prestige. He hoped that the Holy See would express
publicly its approval of the League's activities in maintaining
peace. To press these points with the Vatican Drummond
mentioned to Paulucci in January his intentions of visiting the
Pope. Mussolini, however, opposed any such visit. Paulucci was
informed by the Duce that the Italian Government wanted
neither a visit by Drummond to Rome nor did it want the
Lateran Treaty to be registered with the Secretariat. Drummond's initiatives along these lines would provoke both the
discontent and probably the opposition of the Italian Government.[2] Since Drummond did not proceed to Rome until October
because of the rising tensions between Belgrade and Rome,
though it had been reported in mid-February that he would go,[3]
we can safely assume that he heeded Mussolini's warnings.

When Drummond mentioned Cardinal Gasparri's reference
to the possible registration of the Lateran Treaty with the
Secretariat, Grandi expressed his surprise. He thought that the
registration of the treaty with the Secretariat 'would be viewed
with dislike in Italy as a whole'.[4] Drummond got the point, and
when he continued his discussions with Cardinal Gasparri he
was less enthusiastic about the treaty's registration than he had
been previously. 'Could a State which was constituted by a
special treaty', he queried the Cardinal, 'ask for the registration
of that special treaty?' Drummond's general impression after this
interview was that the Vatican desired the treaty's registration.
It felt, however, that any attempt to register the treaty would

[1] [Eric Drummond], Cardinal Gasparri, 30 Oct. 1929, FO/371/13694.

[2] *DDI*, 7, vii. 278–9 and fn., 281–2, 286. On the question of the Vatican's
relations with the League, Drummond was much more cautious than either
Lords Parmoor or Cecil. See Drummond (Geneva) to Lampson, 17 June 1924,
FO/371/9935, and Drummond (Geneva) to Cadogan, 7 Mar. 1927,
FO/371/12685.

[3] *New York Times*, 17 Feb. 1929, p. 4.

[4] E[ric] D[rummond], Signor Grandi, 30 Oct. 1929, FO/371/13686.

raise the opposition of the Italian Government and in that situation the Vatican wanted to know whether if it persisted in the face of such opposition the treaty would be registered. Though Drummond was embarrassed by the whole situation, in the end Mussolini had his way for the Vatican had second thoughts and the Lateran Treaty was never registered with the Secretariat.[1]

Drummond's trip to Rome on the whole appears to have been a successful one and that was the attitude held in the Foreign Office. Drummond, John Balfour minuted, had 'put in a useful word of warning against the danger of Italy embroiling herself with Yugoslavia over Albania'.[2] Cecil also agreed that the visit had been worth while and scribbled that Drummond had 'shewed his usual tact'.[3]

Proceeding to Belgrade Drummond spoke with the Foreign Minister, Voijslav Marinković, on the morning of 4 November and conveyed to him what Mussolini and Grandi had both said on the subject of Italian–Yugoslav relations. He quoted Mussolini's statement regarding the impossibility of Italy making war unless Albania was attacked by Yugoslavia. Drummond noted that personally he was not alarmed at the situation since the Italian press had made outbursts at various times against Great Britain as well as France. Clearly, Yugoslavia's friendship with France contributed to the feeling against her in Italy. But he was convinced that nothing was being prepared in Rome's government circles against Yugoslavia. He suggested that if anything occurred on the Albanian frontier which might be inflated into an incident and possibly give rise to Italian action, Belgrade should immediately appeal to the League explaining what had occurred and requesting a commission of inquiry. Drummond believed that this would greatly strengthen Belgrade's hands in such a situation. Lastly, Drummond observed that Grandi especially emphasized Italy's anxiety to maintain Albania as a buffer state.[4]

[1] [Eric Drummond], The Pope and Cardinal Gasparri, 31 Oct. 1929, ibid., and *DDI*, 7, viii. 215–16, 452.

[2] Minute by J[ohn] Balfour, 6 Nov. [1929], FO/371/13709.

[3] Minute by R[obert] C[ecil], 16 Nov. [1929], FO/371/14126.

[4] [Eric Drummond], Record of Conversation, 4 Nov. 1929, FO/371/13709; *DDI*, 7, viii. 160, 178–9.

Following this interview Drummond was received by King Alexander and repeated to him much of what he had said to Marinković. The King commented that he was unafraid of Italy's embarking on a war against his country. What he really feared was a possible Italian *coup* similar to the occupation of Corfu in 1923. Drummond tried to explain to the King the real facts regarding the Corfu incident and maintained that if the League had not existed in 1923 Italy would still be occupying that Greek island. Anyway, Drummond did not believe that an incident similar to Corfu could occur at the present time. The League was far stronger and he did not think that any state could commence an aggressive act without incurring for itself the gravest risk.

King Alexander replied that he was pleased to hear this, because if Italy occupied one of Yugoslavia's Adriatic islands the national reaction would be such that he would be forced to act on Italy's frontier. Even if this occurred, however, he would at the same time appeal to Geneva.[1]

Drummond thought that his combined visits to Rome and Belgrade had 'been distinctly useful'.[2] Years later he cited this episode as an example of his political effectiveness behind the scenes.[3] There is no doubt that conveying assurances to Belgrade that nothing was being plotted in Rome helped allay Yugoslav fears. His own arrival in Rome, however, in no way contributed to a pacific Italian foreign policy orientation. This pacific orientation had been established weeks before and had been capped by Grandi's appointment as Foreign Minister.

With Rome quiescent Drummond's Italian contacts virtually ceased. Briand's proposal in May 1930 for a European union caused Drummond to doubt that it would ever be generally accepted. The security aspects of Briand's proposal, he noted to Cecil, which were part and parcel of the plan were unacceptable to Great Britain. If London disapproved so would Switzerland, the Scandinavian states, and The Netherlands who might also feel that the organization of Briand's proposed European union might be harmful to the League. Certainly Italy would do what she could to 'wreck the scheme', not only because the initiative

---

[1] E[ric] D[rummond], Record of Conversation, 4 Nov. 1929, FO/371/13709.
[2] Drummond to Cadogan, 9 Nov. 1929, ibid.
[3] Schwebel, pp. 7–8.

was French but because Italy would view it as a French attempt to 'secure European leadership in perpetuity'. Likewise opposed would be Germany and Hungary. Drummond felt, however, that Briand's scheme contained valuable elements and if it was rejected outright and nothing substituted, the 'general cause of international progress would undergo a real setback'.[1] As Drummond foresaw, objections to Briand's scheme were raised by Italy as well as by other states and it was not accepted. The first tremors of the great depression had already hit Europe and economic nationalism and insecurity were the order of the day, not political and economic union as mirrored in Briand's proposals.[2]

When Drummond next arrived in Rome in mid-April 1931 the picture was fast changing. The question of a French–Italian naval understanding was still unresolved. Ominously Mussolini was again espousing a strongly revisionist line after having for several years exclusively concentrated on internal affairs.[3] Though Drummond's discussions with Mussolini and Grandi dealt with the forthcoming Disarmament Conference Italy's hostility to France and her Czech protégé, Beneš, did not go undisguised.[4]

The removal of Grandi as Foreign Minister in July of the following year and his appointment as ambassador to London portended more difficult times ahead. They were not long in coming. In early January 1933 an arms shipment from Italy was discovered in Austria on its way to Hungary: it was Szent-Gotthard all over again. London was opposed to having the question considered by the Council. Maintaining friendly relations with Mussolini continued to be Great Britain's policy while France with a new ambassador in Rome did not want to jeopardize any conversations leading to a *détente* and a possible understanding with the Duce. Naturally neither the Italians nor the Hungarians were interested in an open Council debate which would have embarrassed both of them. Italy's views were made known to both London and Paris through Grandi and her

[1] Drummond (Geneva) to Cecil, 26 May 1930, Add. MS. 51112, Robert Cecil Papers, BL.
[2] Walters, pp. 430–4.
[3] Hughes, 'The Early Diplomacy of Italian Fascism: 1922–1932', pp. 231–2.
[4] [Eric Drummond], Record of Conversation, 18 Apr. 1931, FO/371/15704.

League representative, Baron Pompeo Aloisi. Drummond himself, it appears, thought that unlike the Szent-Gotthard incident the best way to handle the question was through normal diplomatic channels even though the Treaty of Trianon had been violated. In the end, thanks to London and Paris, the question was settled by Austria's returning the arms to Italy and Italy accepting them—a tacit admission by Rome that it had violated the Treaty of Trianon.[1]

Of course all of this occurred after Drummond had publicly expressed his desire to depart as Secretary-General and Avenol had been selected to succeed him. In retrospect one could argue that Drummond during his tenure as Secretary-General had treated Mussolini with great deference. This did not mean, however, that he was unaware of the dangers that emanated from Rome. A more active policy on Drummond's part would probably have been of limited value. Who would have supported him? Certainly not London which under Chamberlain and his successors regardless of party affiliation went to great lengths to cultivate Mussolini. French support in certain given situations might have been forthcoming but without British backing would have only led to a stalemate. Drummond, once he had committed himself against Italy, would have no longer been *persona grata* and whatever small influence that he had in Rome would have been quickly undermined. To talk of support that Drummond might have built up among the small nations would be to deal with illusions. In the inter-war period it was only the actions of the Great Powers that really counted and Mussolini's ability to play a 'seesaw diplomatic game with skill worthy of a better cause'[2] locked Drummond into a system and into a situation where his possibilities for action were extremely limited. The same was also true, as we shall see, in the Manchurian crisis.

[1] *DDF 1932–1939*, I, ii. 434–41, 460, 470, 486, 496–9, 534–5, 540–2, 544–5, 555, 559–60, 572–3, 601–3, 626–7, 691–3; Baron Pompeo Aloisi, *Journal (25 Juillet 1932–14 Juin 1936)*, trans. Maurice Vaussard (Paris: Plon, 1957), pp. 47–8, 49, 52, 53, 54–5, 56, 62, 64, 67, 70.

[2] Walters, p. 432.

VII

THE MANCHURIAN CRISIS

The League in China

Initially five states from what is labelled the Afro-Asian world accepted the Covenant. By the outbreak of the Second World War eleven states from this group were League members. Wartime events did not appreciably increase this figure, for the United Nations Charter was ratified in 1945 by only twelve Afro–Asian states.[1] This situation is easy to understand: until the mid-1950s African and Asian territories were largely controlled by European powers. Of the League's Afro–Asian states the most important were China and Japan. The latter was especially important because she was considered one of the world's great powers mirrored in the fact that she was a permanent Council member.

Throughout the early 1920s the League's and Drummond's attentions were understandably focused on European affairs. China only slowly began to attract the League's attention as the civil strife between the various factions and elements within the country led to political upheaval as well as economic and social dislocation. Within the Secretariat the Polish Director of the Health Section, Ludwik Rajchman, saw the possibilities of assisting China through the League. Following a Far Eastern trip in 1925–6 Rajchman prophetically described to Drummond the probable trend of events in China and the many ways in which her League membership could be used, both to assist her economic and social development and to place her international position on a firm and normal basis. Rajchman perceived that China's continuing turmoil was a danger to peace and was convinced that if the nationalist Kuomintang received western support, it would be able to establish a platform on which a new governmental authority might base itself. As a League member China had the right to ask for such help without loss of prestige.

[1] Leland M. Goodrich, Edvard Hambro, Anne P. Simons, *Charter of the United Nations: Commentary and Documents* (3rd rev. edn.; New York: Columbia University Press, 1969), pp. 650, 663–4.

League meetings dealing with the political aspects of the China problem would place China on an equal footing with other states and surround her with countries that enjoyed no special privileges within her territory—a far different arrangement from diplomatic conferences in Peking. The League's social and economic organizations could offer China expert advisers and technical assistance, at moderate cost, and devoid of the danger that China's interest would be second to those of another state.[1]

Drummond found Rajchman's report of 'extreme interest both from the technical and from the political point of view'. Drummond had no objection to Rajchman's suggestion that there should be a special study for the settlement of Far Eastern disputes. In his view, however, the Covenant afforded a 'sufficient basis to cover any special case' which might arise and had the 'advantage of elasticity so that it can be shaped to particular circumstances'.[2]

As disorders in China increased and incidents involving foreigners expecially British nationals multiplied, Drummond conveyed to Cecil in early 1927 the Secretariat's thoughts on how the situation in China might be handled. If Cecil's reaction was favourable the possibility of acquiring British support to implement Rajchman's recommendations would have greatly improved. It was not to be. In early February Cecil persuaded Chamberlain to address a statement to the League explaining British policy toward China and especially the dispatch of troops to protect Shanghai's International Settlement. The statement did not see how the League might assist in solving British–Chinese tensions but promised to invoke its good offices if the opportunity arose.[3] Cecil believed that the Secretariat's plan lacked 'commonsense'. You could not negotiate with the Kuomintang in Canton, he pointed out to Drummond, which controlled about a third of China and was seeking to overthrow the established order, as China's only government. Such a move would be a 'gross insult' to the government in Peking which

[1] Frank P. Walters, *A History of the League of Nations* (London: Oxford University Press, 1960), pp. 328–31.

[2] E[ric] D[rummond], A note by the Secretary-General, 25 Feb. 1926, General 1926: 40/49378/49378, LNA.

[3] League of Nations, *Official Journal*, VIII (1927), pp. 292–3; Walters, p. 330.

might inevitably disappear but was for the moment in control of most of the country.[1]

Though rebuffed by Cecil, Drummond kept the Secretariat informed about Far Eastern affairs by holding whenever necessary meetings on questions dealing with the Pacific area. The Japanese Under Secretary-General, Yotaro Sugimura, presided over these meetings. Included were nationals of Pacific countries and some of the Latin American states though the group's composition varied depending on the nature of the problem to be considered.[2] During the latter part of 1927 Drummond's difficulties with the Chinese centred almost exclusively on the professional competence of Peking's League representatives.[3]

By February 1928 Drummond's difficulties with the Chinese had again moved back to a more sensitive political plane. Late that month Drummond warned Cadogan that an attempt would be made to have the Red Cross address a message to the Council, drawing attention to the famine in China. He understood that this move was part of a larger plan to have the League take up the Chinese question. The idea was that on receipt of the Red Cross' communication a commission would be dispatched to China to examine the famine's effects. The commission while reporting on the famine would equally refer to its cause, namely, China's civil war. It would indicate that until this condition had been remedied there would be no hope of any appreciable amelioration in the situation. It was then thought that on receipt of the commission's report the League might find some way of intervening in China's affairs.[4]

This information had been conveyed to Drummond by Hsia Chi-feng, a Chinese member of the Press and Information Section. Drummond was obviously not interested in having the League become directly embroiled in China's civil strife. He

[1] [Cecil] to [Drummond], 24 Feb. 1927, Add. MS. 51111, Robert Cecil Papers, BL.
[2] E[ric] D[rummond], Note by the Secretary-General, 6 Apr. 1927, General 1927: 40/58623/47610, LNA.
[3] Drummond (Geneva) to Cadogan, 25 Oct. 1927, E[ric] D[rummond], Record of Interview, 17 Nov. 1927, E[ric] Drummond, Record of Conversation, 2 Dec. 1927, Eric Drummond, Record of Interview, 3 Dec. 1927, FO/371/12686.
[4] Cadogan to Mounsey, 23 Feb. 1928, FO/371/13223.

thought, he informed Hsia Chi-feng, that any possible League appeal on the question of China's famine was somewhat difficult and was complicated by the fact that there was also a similar appeal by Albania. Though Drummond felt that the League could not refuse to communicate the Chinese appeal to all its members, it would state that any response to the appeal should be addressed to one of the two international Red Cross societies which would be invited to make arrangements for the joint administration of the funds provided. Drummond was apprehensive over whether such an action was likely to harm the League in China and emphasized that by this action the 'matter would be treated solely as a humanitarian question, and have no political bearing'.[1]

It is difficult to say whether the Peking government contemplated any such move. What can be said is that no such appeal was made to the League. At the time Hsia Chi-feng contacted Drummond the Kuomintang controlled sixteen of China's twenty-two provinces. By early June Peking fell to the Kuomintang's troops. When the Assembly convened in autumn 1928 China was represented for the first time by a Kuomintang delegation. Since China had been elected as a non-permanent Council member in 1926 and because of the new procedure adopted following Germany's admission to the League, China could retain her seat only if she received a two-thirds Assembly vote. Though a majority vote was cast in China's favour it fell short of the two-thirds vote needed. China's loss of her non-permanent seat was resented in Nanking where the erroneous view was held that the Assembly was not well disposed toward the Kuomintang as it had been toward the prior discredited government in Peking. This view added to China's budgetary arrears made it appear as though China, like Brazil, might depart from the League. At this point Drummond attempted to head off any such move by implementing Rajchman's scheme. He proposed to Nanking that he send Avenol on an official visit in order to establish closer relations between China and the organization, and to explain the League's activities and its organization to the leaders of Nanking's government. It was

[1] Drummond to Hsia Chi-feng, 23 Feb. 1928, ibid. See also, Hsia Chi-feng, *China and the League and My Experiences in the Secretariat* (Shanghai: The Commercial Press Ltd., 1928), pp. 129–34.

clearly understood, though it was not openly stated, that the real purpose of Avenol's trip would be to discuss the various ways in which China could utilize the League's expert committees in its huge reconstruction task.[1]

This move into the Far East required immediate fence mending and certainly one of the most important entities to be contacted was the State Department. As so often in his dealings with the Americans, Drummond's approach was indirect and through a third party. His conduit was the American, Arthur Bullard, of the Press and Information Section, who was returning to the United States. Inasmuch as Bullard was going to Washington Drummond asked him if he could take the opportunity of explaining unofficially to the State Department the reasons for Avenol's mission. He did not think that the State Department 'would in any way believe that such a mission could be antagonistic to American interest or policy'. This was the last thing that would occur to him, and so much was to the contrary, Drummond observed, that he would ask Avenol before he departed to contact and keep in touch with the American Minister in China so that Avenol might, if it was practicable, have the benefit of the minster's 'views and experience'. Because 'misrepresentation on such a subject might be dangerous' Drummond was grateful if Bullard would undertake to contact the State Department and explain his actions.[2] Several days later Drummond must have realized that there would be some delay before Bullard arrived in Washington. Accordingly he contacted the American Minister in Bern and explained what had occurred as well as the purpose of Avenol's mission.[3]

In discussing Avenol's forthcoming visit with Wang King-ky, China's representative, Drummond reiterated that the mission's purpose was 'to promote closer relations between the Chinese Government and the organs of the League', as well as the 'establishment of direct contact between the Secretariat and the Chinese Government'.[4] When Wang King-ky subsequently

---

[1] Walters, pp. 331–2.

[2] Drummond (Geneva) to Bullard, 6 Oct. 1928, File 500.C112/426, RG 59, NA.

[3] Wilson (Bern) to the Department of State, No. 95, 8 Oct. 1928, File 500.C112/424, RG 59, NA.

[4] D[rummond] to Wang King-ky 18 Oct. 1928, Minutes of a Directors' Meeting, 18 Oct. 1928, LNA.

noted reports concerning the League's possible usefulness to his country in the matter of its 'financial reconstruction' as well as ideas circulating in the Secretariat as to possible ways of assisting it through the League's technical organizations, Drummond replied that of course if Nanking's authorities wished such information Avenol would be prepared to give it. Naturally the initiative could only originate with the Chinese Government and neither he nor Avenol possessed 'authority to arrange Technical missions of, or studies by the League in China'.[1]

Avenol's trip proved successful and from 1929 onwards there was a steady stream of League experts and Secretariat officials headed for China. Led by Rajchman they established very close relations with Nanking's authorities. In time China liquidated her budgetary arrears and these sums of money Drummond convinced the Assembly should be utilized to promote the League's activities in China.[2]

As the Kuomintang expanded and consolidated its hold it came into conflict with a number of powers having special rights in China, especially Japan and Soviet Russia. A clash with Japanese troops at Tsinan-Fu in May 1928, which caused Japan to issue a statement to Drummond explaining what had occurred, was not settled until March 1929.[3] Much more serious were a number of armed clashes between Kuomintang and Russian troops from July through November 1929. Though this conflict was never tackled by the League and was settled by direct negotiations between the Chinese and the Russians, Drummond was prompted by Secretariat memorandums dealing with the affair to make some interesting comments on what had transpired.

Since Soviet Russia was not a League member the thrust of Drummond's observation was that each case that developed

---

[1] E[ric] D[rummond], Record of Interview, 29 Oct. 1928, Minutes of a Directors' Meeting, 29 Oct. 1928, LNA.

[2] Walters, pp. 332–3. It should be pointed out that aside from China the League also carried out non-political activities in India. V. Shiva Ram and Brij Mohan Sharma, *India and the League of Nations* (Lucknow: Upper India Publishing House, 1932), pp. 135–60; Jehangir C. Coyajee, *India and the League of Nations* (Waltair: Thompson, 1932), pp. 148–239; Dina N. Verma, *India and the League of Nations* (Patna: Bharati Bhawan, 1968), pp. 147–238.

[3] League of Nations, *Official Journal*, IX (1928), pp. 792–5; Masatoshi Matsushita, *Japan in the League of Nations* (New York: Columbia University Press, 1929), pp. 159–60.

ought to be treated solely on its merits. Accordingly he did not think that the Secretariat should in any way blame itself for the League's inactivity during the recent Chinese–Russian fighting. It had to be borne in mind that neither China nor Soviet Russia desired the League's intervention at any time. From the inception of the fighting the strong possibilities were that it would be peacefully settled. Indeed, it was known that China had considered a League appeal but that because of internal Chinese politics an appeal was a very delicate matter. If the Secretariat 'had come to the conclusion that League intervention was desirable', Drummond was confident that it *'could probably have provoked it'*. On the other hand, as it was believed that League intervention could not have been useful, but would only have increased the friction, 'surely it would have been unwise to attempt it'. He admitted frankly that if he was again faced with the question he would not change in any way the policy the Secretariat had adopted.

He noted that an ingenious proposal had been put forward that the Council might discuss these questions without taking any action and this very discussion would have a salutary effect on public opinion. The problem, he pointed out, was that to talk and do nothing opened one to criticism, and it had to be remembered that in this particular conflict China and also Russia would have had to be invited to attend any discussions. Russia would have refused. China might have attended, but would not have found herself in a difficult position if the Council did not formally face her with the question. It should not be thought, Drummond observed, that he ruled out the possibility in all cases of such Council discussion, but he was 'convinced that in the particular case in question it would not have served any useful purpose'.[1]

Some days before Drummond wrote these comments he observed to Hymans that in Belgium's possible election to the Council China was a very important consideration which, to his mind, 'outweighed everything in the present circumstances'. Rajchman who had recently returned from China reported that

---

[1] Italics added. E[ric] D[rummond], Note by the Secretary-General, 27 Feb. 1930, Political General 1928–32: 1A/19175/13390, LNA. See also, Russell M. Cooper, *American Consultation in World Affairs* (New York: Macmillan, 1934), pp. 97–8.

she was being pulled in three different directions. These were American, Soviet Russian, and European. The American direction previously strong had since diminished. This left Soviet Russia and Europe. To the Chinese the League represented Europe. It was possible that the direction in which China might move would be decided by the end of the year. If this was so, the question of a non-permanent Council seat for China might become a matter of the greatest importance. Naturally it depended on whether the civil war in China ceased and also whether Nanking paid at least a sizeable portion of its budgetary contributions. The major difficulty was that to become a non-permanent Council member China needed a two-thirds Assembly vote. Drummond thought, however, that all these points were of minor import, in comparison with the great matter which was at stake.[1]

Drummond returned to the matter on 30 April when he was visited by General Tsiang Tso-ping, China's Minister in Berlin. Pressed by the General, Drummond declared that if China desired to be considered for a non-permanent Council seat he would do what he could to assist but pointed out that it was a question which, both in theory and in fact, was largely beyond his competence. The greatest obstacle that had to be overcome, he observed, was that China needed a two-thirds Assembly vote in order to become a non-permanent member. The difficulty was that some states as a matter of principle opposed countries being immediately re-elected to the Council. If they opposed China on this issue it would be solely on this ground and in no way directed against China *per se*. He noted that Belgium despite the support she had received from her wartime allies had failed to obtain this two-thirds vote. This showed how strong feelings were on the matter. The problem was aggravated by other considerations. First, from press reports it appeared that political difficulties persisted in China and that the country was still not completely stabilized. Second, that China had unfortunately, for reasons Drummond understood, been unable to pay her budgetary contributions. Drummond recommended that China work for a non-permanent seat the following year at which point a two-thirds vote would not be required. There was an additional

[1] [Eric Drummond], Record of Conversation, 21 Feb. 1930, Add. MS. 51112, Robert Cecil Papers, BL.

factor, Drummond insisted, that had to be taken into consideration and that was that China's election to the Council at this time would give the Far Eastern states three seats on it. This representation was excessive if one took into consideration the number of Far Eastern states who were League members. He thought this argument could be used against China by any country which also was a candidate for a Council seat.

General Tsiang Tso-ping replied that China's size, population, and her place in world affairs really justified giving her a permanent Council seat and it was only because it appeared virtually impracticable at the moment to acquire such a seat that Nanking had decided to press for a non-permanent seat. Drummond retorted that he used many of the General's own arguments in discussing this matter with others, but he felt bound to insist on the difficulties which he foresaw. He stressed these difficulties not because he wished to dissuade China from offering her candidature this year. He did so because he was very apprehensive that if the attempt failed the reasons for this failure should be understood in China and that it should not be thought that China's rejection constituted a serious rebuff or be laid at the Secretariat's door. Drummond thought that it would be wise that as soon as the decision had been definitely made to press China's candidature, to inform other governments of this fact and request their support. He could do no more than give advice if he were consulted. Any initiative in this matter had to be taken by the Chinese themselves.[1]

In the months that followed there was renewed fighting between the Kuomintang and a northern anti-government coalition. Drummond's attitude was to avoid League involvement in this struggle since the Kuomintang believed it would win. Furthermore, the Kuomintang would bitterly resent the League's involvement as an attempt to prevent its final victory and its complete unification of the country. The situation would only change if a deadlock developed and Nanking felt it could not win. The furthest that Drummond was willing to go was for Henderson, the British Foreign Secretary, to sound out, if he thought it right, the Chinese representative as to the situation in his country and the possible assistance that might be given

[1] Eric Drummond, Record of Interview, 30 Apr. 1930, File 65K, Box 265355, Department of External Affairs, PACRMB.

provided he understood that Henderson had no desire to intervene in any way in the Kuomintang's struggle with the anti-government coalition.[1]

By August it was obvious to Drummond that China could not be elected to the Council. The difficulty that he saw was to convince Nanking that this was the case, and that its prestige would be enhanced if it consented to have its representative elected as the Assembly's President.[2] Drummond's endeavours along this path proved fruitless for the Chinese persisted in proposing their candidature for a non-permanent Council seat— and were rejected.[3] The following year, September 1931, as Drummond had foreseen, the pendulum swung the other way and China was unanimously elected by the Assembly to a non-permanent seat.[4] By this point Chinese affairs, peripheral during the League's first decade, had now moved to the centre of the Geneva stage.

The Manchurian Occupation

On the night of 18–19 September there was an explosion on the south Manchurian Railway line a few miles north of Mukden. Arranged by staff officers of Japan's Kwantung Army, the explosion was an excuse to occupy Mukden and other Manchurian cities.[5] The Tokyo authorities were caught unawares and their attempts to solve the question with Nanking by direct negotiations were frustrated by the spreading hostilities. The Chinese, unable to resist the Kwantung army's onslaught, chose to appeal to the Council under Article 16 of the Covenant.

[1] Drummond (Geneva) to Cecil, 17 June 1930 and Cecil (Geneva) to Henderson, 18 July 1930, FO/371/14723.

[2] Drummond (Geneva) to Cecil, 25 Aug. 1930, Add. MS. 51112, Robert Cecil Papers, BL; [Walter A. Riddell], Interview with Sir Eric Drummond, 29 Aug. 1930, Walter A. Riddell Papers, YUT.

[3] League of Nations, *Official Journal*, Special Supplement No. 84, p. 127.

[4] Walters, p. 470.

[5] See Takehiro Yoshihashi, *Conspiracy at Mukden. The Rise of the Japanese Military* (New Haven: Yale University Press, 1963), pp. 185–9; Sadako N. Ogata, *Defiance in Manchuria: The Making of Japanese Foreign Policy, 1931–1932* (Berkeley: University of California Press, 1964), pp. 70–1; Chin Tung Liang, *The Sinister Face of the Mukden Incident* (New York: St. John's University Press, 1969), pp. 45–54, 71–6; Westel W. Willoughby, *The Sino-Japanese Controversy and the League of Nations* (Baltimore: The Johns Hopkins Press, 1935), pp. 29–46.

The initial problems that Drummond faced were a lack of impartial information about what had occurred, and the attitude of the United States since Manchurian events ran counter to long-held American goals, namely, maintenance of the Kellogg–Briand Pact and the integrity of China. His first move, therefore, was to press Secretary of State Henry L. Stimson for information, as well as his opinion as to whether the Kellogg–Briand Pact was involved in the matter and the basis for his views. Since Stimson represented that portion of the Republican Party which was friendly to the League, Drummond undoubtedly hoped that he would be willing to co-operate with the organization. Stimson likewise admitted that he lacked sufficient information though he held that the Japanese military had initiated an aggressive action over a wide area only after prior preparation and that the military and Tokyo were at odds both as to what happened and as to Japan's intentions. It was therefore advisable that Japanese nationalist feelings not be aroused in support of the military and against the Tokyo authorities; that Washington was closely following events and their relationship to treaty obligations, especially the Kellogg–Briand Pact and the Washington Nine Power Treaty of 1922, which bound the signatories, including Japan, to respect China's territorial integrity.

The Council's first move on 22 September was to appeal to both sides to abstain from further action which might endanger the situation as well as to promulgate in consultation with both sides means to enable them to proceed to the *status quo ante*. In addition, a Council committee was established composed of its Spanish president, all the permanent members plus China—the so-called Committee of Five. This committee contemplated sending to Manchuria a commission of inquiry which would investigate, if necessary, merely with Nanking's authorization since China alone was sovereign in Manchuria. In view of the lack of impartial information as well as the uncertainty of American co-operation the committee considered premature the possibility of joint action. In conveying this information to Stimson, Drummond desired that Stimson give his opinion as quickly as possible as to whether Washington, if invited, could consider participating in the steps contemplated by the committee. The Council, Minister Wilson informed Stimson, was greatly impressed with the urgency and the seriousness of the situation.

Never had Wilson seen a League situation as tense or one in which America's co-operation was so earnestly desired.

Drummond thought there were two steps that Washington might adopt. The first was that an American representative be invited to sit on the Council—subsequently done but with qualifications. Drummond regarded this as the boldest and perhaps the most effective step possible because of the effect it would have on Japan's public opinion. The second was the appointment of a regular Council committee of France, Germany, Great Britain, Italy, and Spain along with an American representative. Of these two possibilities, the first, Drummond pointed out, required Council approval. In his opinion a suggestion that America participate in the Council would be quickly accepted, except perhaps by Japan. There was a League precedent for the second step in the appointment of an American to the Council's special Liberian Committee. While Drummond thought Stimson might find the appointment of an American to the proposed Council committee easier, he felt that the first step, American representation on the Council, would of course be more effective. Should he adopt the first step, Wilson noted to Stimson, Europe would be thankful and relieved, especially France, but he naturally realized that the decision as to the feasibility of such a move would depend on the mood of American public opinion. As to possible Japanese resistance to American participation, its mere suggestion in the Council's deliberations might help strengthen the hand of Japan's foreign minister against the military.

Though Stimson sympathized with the League's efforts he rejected any American participation on the Council's proposed commission of inquiry. Nor was he willing to have a representative sit either on the Council or on its special committee. Indeed, unlike Wilson he thought that the establishment of the commission of inquiry would make it more difficult for Tokyo to impose its will on the military. He likewise believed that for the moment direct negotiations between the parties was the best procedure for solving the crisis.

Stimson's rejection of the Council's and Drummond's overtures caused Cecil to suggest the establishment of a different type of commission, one that would merely ascertain the facts. Cecil's suggestion was an obvious attempt to have the Council's actions dovetail with Stimson's desires. Drummond explained to Wilson, however, that the reports from Manchuria were so contradictory regarding the number of Japanese troops and their location that the Council felt it essential to ascertain the actual facts. The commission, he assured him, would be given the narrowest terms of reference. Again as in the previous days Drummond asked if Stimson would agree to an American appointment to the commission if the Japanese accepted this proposal and he offered to base his invitation on either the Nine Power Treaty or the Kellogg–Briand Pact or on America's general world interest.

But Stimson was not moved. He pressed for a settlement through direct negotiations and did not expect the Japanese would accept this form of inquiry which if imposed on them, would play into the hands of the military. He preferred a commission appointed by both sides. Appointing an American to Cecil's proposed commission, he argued, would be used by the League to threaten Japan and this he felt would not produce the results anticipated; and it would also destroy Washington's usefulness as a mediator should the League's efforts fail.

Naturally, with Stimson pressing for bilateral negotiations, the Japanese would not agree to any commission of inquiry. They declared that there was no military occupation of Manchuria; that they had no territorial designs; that they had withdrawn most of their troops back to the South Manchurian Railway zone; that they intended to withdraw as quickly as possible the remainder of their troops as soon as Japanese lives and property were no longer in danger; that they hoped to enter into direct negotiations with the Chinese; and that the Council could help by refraining from intervening in the question. Tokyo's assurances were accepted by the Council on 30 September. In addition, on the suggestion of the Japanese representative, it was agreed that Council members might convey to Drummond for the Council any information which they might receive from Manchuria which would be of importance to the Council's work.

The Council's decision was really an acceptance of Stimson's desire that the Chinese and the Japanese settle the issue and avoid League intervention in the question. Drummond's attitude was that Japan's willingness to allow League members to transmit to him any information that they obtained from

Manchuria had resulted from the Council's continuous pressure. It was about as far as the Japanese could be brought to accepting any form of impartial information from Manchuria.

Drummond's information caused him to divulge to Wilson that the Chinese had threatened to conclude an alliance with the Russians if the League failed to achieve results in this question. On the other hand, the Japanese had also been talking to the Russians and anticipated no difficulty. Drummond admitted that the Chinese and the Russians were discussing an alliance though this might have nothing to do with intervening in Manchuria. For the moment, in his opinion, any Chinese and Russian discussions had been headed off by what he felt was the favourable turn which the Manchurian affair was taking. He was anxious to avoid being placed in a position where he was continually exposed to Chinese protests and threats. The Chinese should now do their share during the period that lay immediately ahead and he desired that Washington make a suggestion to them in this sense. Wilson noted to Stimson that it was a delicate matter for him to make such a suggestion without having the Chinese draw the implication that there was a lack of confidence in Drummond or that the Chinese case was being minimized. Drummond, however, was assured by Stimson that he supported the Council's actions and that he was pressuring both sides to abide by its decision. Moreover, Stimson was ready to comply with Drummond's suggestion that Washington forward to him any pertinent information which it might be able to make available.[1]

Instinctively Drummond also pressed Cadogan for any information that the Foreign Office might be able to furnish regarding Manchuria, a request that he also made to all the Council's permanent members.[2] He also suggested to Cadogan that perhaps the diplomatic missions of the Great Powers in Peking could jointly arrange to acquire trustworthy information as to what was occurring in Manchuria. He feared that not only

---

[1] *PRFRUS, 1931*, iii. 22, 26, 36–7, 39–40, 43–52, 57, 60–1, 66, 72–3, 82, 88–89, 93, 96–9, 110, 116–17; League of Nations, *Official Journal*, XII (1931), pp. 2307–8. See also, Henry L. Stimson, *The Far Eastern Crisis* (New York: Council on Foreign Relations, 1936), pp. 46–52; Hugh R. Wilson, *Diplomat Between Wars* (New York: Longmans, Green, 1941), pp. 260–2.

[2] Drummond (Geneva) to Cadogan, 1 Oct. 1931, FO/371/15490.

would the League's authority be endangered by failure in Manchuria but so would the success of the Disarmament Conference set to convene in February. Furthermore, if the Council met on 14 October, the presence of the foreign ministers of the states represented on the Council would be of the highest importance.[1] Unfortunately, Drummond's pleas for information led nowhere. It appears that aside from some information furnished by London and a few reports furnished by Paris and Berlin he received no real information from any Council member on the latest developments in the disputed zone.[2]

Such information might have been of some value for the situation in Manchuria steadily deteriorated. The actions of the Kwantung Army belied Tokyo's assurances in Geneva. Each passing day made it obvious that a military occupation was in progress. This lack of information is reflected in Drummond's discussion on 6 October with Prentiss Gilbert, the American Consul in Geneva. Events had now brought them into close contact and despite the social and personal tension between them[3] in the coming days they would work well and very closely together. Drummond's only information was from Rajchman in Nanking. In respect to Soviet Russia's attitude Drummond believed that they were more or less playing a double game, 'on the one hand telling the Chinese that they are their closest friends with perhaps insinuations of support and on the other hand telling the Japanese that they will stand completely aside in the dispute'. He admitted, however, that he had no firsthand knowledge of Russia's diplomatic or military posture. Naturally Drummond welcomed Stimson's news that American military attachés were in the area and that diplomatic officers would soon be dispatched there. Drummond emphasized that all interested states should as far as possible obtain and mutually exchange information and noted the actions that he had taken along this

[1] *DBFP, 1919–1939*, 2, viii. 712.
[2] Christopher Thorne, *The Limits of Foreign Policy: The West, the League and the Far Eastern Crisis of 1931–1933* (London: Hamilton Hamish, 1972), p. 144 fn. See also, Walters, p. 474.
[3] Drew Pearson and Constantine Brown, *The American Diplomatic Game* (New York: Doubleday, 1935), pp. 310–11. See also, Drummond (Geneva) to Cadogan, 2 Nov. 1931, FO/371/15496.

line.[1] Unfortunately, even Rajchman's information was of limited value. It was Gilbert's impression, based on Drummond's manner in discussing this information as well as Gilbert's knowledge of Rajchman's very pro-Chinese orientation, that Rajchman's views might be considered as inspired by the Chinese.[2]

Drummond's anxieties during this period centred on the Chinese. He pointed out to Gilbert the difficulties they posed. The Council in its discussion of what had occurred had insisted on using the term, the 'withdrawal of [Japanese] troops within the [South Manchurian] railway zone'. The Chinese, however, had used and tried to have the Council adopt the phrase 'the reestablishment of the *status quo ante*'. Drummond observed that the Chinese representative, Alfred Sze, had urged him personally that the term '*status quo ante*' be used. Drummond had countered by suggesting the use of the term, 'in accordance with prior treaty stipulations'. Drummond's suggested expression caused Sze to withdraw his proposal since China held that she did not recognize the validity of these prior treaties under which Japan was entitled to more troops in the railway zone and to the occupation of more territory than was possible in the use of the term, '*status quo ante*'.

Like Gilbert, Drummond believed that the League's intervention was a Chinese diplomatic victory and that it was their intention to involve the Council as much as possible in all aspects of the Manchurian situation. Personally, he thought that if the Japanese successfully withdrew within the railway zone the League would then attempt to adjust other outstanding problems between China and Japan through direct negotiations between the two parties. China's attitude might make this difficult but he thought that this was the desirable procedure otherwise the Chinese would bring every minor question to the League or appeal to it at every hitch. Should China persist in trying to keep the Manchurian situation on the international level, Drummond could not foresee the outcome. Drummond agreed with Gilbert that an extremely difficult situation would develop if Japan proved recalcitrant in executing the Council's programme. In

[1] Gilbert (Geneva) to the Department of State, No. 158, 7 Oct. 1931, File 793.94/2015, RG 59, NA.
[2] Gilbert (Geneva) to the Department of State, No. 159, 7 Oct. 1931, ibid.

view of the world situation—the *Kreditanstalt* in Vienna had failed in mid-May, President Hoover had proposed a moratorium on inter-governmental debts in June, and Great Britain had abandoned the gold standard 21 September—Drummond concurred that pressure on Japan through the use of 'economic sanctions would be entirely out of the question'. If worse came to worst he envisaged the withdrawal from Tokyo of the diplomatic representatives of the important states. This move, he believed, would be a type of pressure which would be very difficult for Japan to resist. If one keeps in mind that in this early period Drummond could not envisage the use of the League's coercive measures because of the world situation and the attitude of the Great Powers, and especially the attitude of the United States, then many of his subsequent actions become understandable.

Drummond perceived the relationship of the political and economic aspect of the Manchurian problem to the world situation, Gilbert reported to Washington, and especially to the disarmanent problem. He strongly held that nothing should be omitted and nothing left unsaid which might contribute to a speedy settlement of the question. In this connection he pointed out the 'restraining effect upon the Japanese and the good effect in quieting world anxiety' if Stimson or Drummond himself 'were able to make known the fact that the United States and the League entertain similar views on certain of the more vital aspects involved'.[1] The farthest, however, Stimson was willing to go was to have Gilbert assure Drummond that he supported the Council's action and was pressuring both sides to abide by its decision.[2]

Though Drummond thought it might be desirable to postpone convening the Council until 21 October so that additional information could be received, he acknowledged that a postponement might inflame Chinese public opinion. To calm this opinion he suggested to the Japanese that on their own initiative they should invite individual powers to send representatives to the area to inform their governments on what was occurring. Drummond pointed out that such an action would be in line with their Council statement and the Council's decision.

[1] *PRFRUS, 1931*, iii. 128–32.
[2] Gilbert (Geneva) to the Department of State, No. 162, 7 Oct. 1931, File 793.94/2013, RG 59, NA; *PRFRUS, 1931*, iii. 136.

Chinese action which might complicate the situation was a continuing matter of concern. When approached by Sze who was especially apprehensive about reported Japanese naval movements near Shanghai, Drummond emphasized that everything depended on China's ability to exercise self-restraint. He discounted the reported naval movements and his information, he optimistically noted, led him to believe that the Japanese withdrawal in Manchuria was slowly proceeding. If China continued her restraint Drummond was sure that Japanese troop withdrawal into the railway zone would be assured, though it was not likely to be completed by the time of the Council's mid-October meeting. Drummond thought that the withdrawal would occur in weeks or even days, and on Sze's suggestion agreed to warn the Japanese strongly not to land marines at Shanghai as this might lead to hostilities. On his part Sze would attempt to calm the Chinese and concurred with Drummond that the Council's mid-October meeting might have to be delayed a week. To make sure that the Chinese would take no action Drummond informed Rajchman in Nanking that to obtain Japan's complete execution of the Council's resolution depended on China's ability to control anti-Japanese movements and exercise moderation. He realized the great difficulties that were involved but he begged Rajchman to urge the Chinese authorities to do everything possible along these lines. Even if a Japanese withdrawal by the time the Council was set to convene was doubtful, progress would certainly have been made toward a full withdrawal of troops. It was necessary, Drummond cautioned, to assist the Tokyo authorities in their struggle with the military.[1]

Drummond was alarmed at the turn events had taken during the previous few days. He feared that the anti-Japanese tide sweeping Chinese public opinion and the rumoured action being mounted by the Japanese for the purpose of protecting their nationals in China—the reported naval movements at Shanghai—might lead to war. He hoped that others would also advise restraint on the Chinese and in line with this showed Gilbert a memorandum of his conversation with Sze. Drummond correctly observed that the Kwantung Army's action had been long planned and was initiated in the belief that the opportunity was

---

[1] *DBFP, 1919–1939*, 2, viii. 717–18, 721–3, 731–3. See also, Ogata, p. 86.

favourable in view of the preoccupation of the interested powers in other questions. The Japanese were now alarmed, he believed, at the international reaction which had been manifested and they were doing what they could to settle the question.[1]

Again Drummond raised with Cadogan the matter of receiving impartial information from Manchuria, arguing that its mere conveyance to the Council would help calm Chinese public opinion—which at the present moment should be feared most. According to Sze, Nanking was having a difficult time controlling the communists who were stirring up a violent nationalist agitation in order to bring down the government. It was obvious, Drummond observed, that the communists would be delighted to see a Chinese–Japanese war since they thought that they would acquire advantages in both countries from such a conflict. To restrain Japan he urged his Japanese Under Secretary-General, Sugimura, to press Tokyo to do everything possible to prevent the landing of marines at Shanghai. He also correctly pointed out to him that it was difficult to restrain the Chinese and urge them to moderation if simultaneously Japanese troops in Manchuria were occupying territory and expanding their area of occupation. Sugimura agreed, and promised to contact Tokyo which was done several days later.[2]

This same day 7 October, unknown to Drummond, Japanese planes bombed Chinchow where a considerable portion of the civil and military authority of Manchuria's Liaoning (Fengtien) Province had gathered. Any postponement, as Drummond desired, of the Council's scheduled mid-October meeting was now out of the question. He concurred with Sze that this Japanese action was deliberate and provocative. Drummond hesitated between the necessity to placate Chinese public opinion by an immediate summons to the Council to convene, and objections to calling the Council when the only information available was from conflicting Chinese and Japanese sources without impartial information serving to stabilize the Council's action. Drummond proposed that the Council's president immediately dispatch identical notes to both sides reminding them of their agreement not to aggravate the situation. In light of recent developments

---

[1] Gilbert (Geneva) to the Department of State, No. 163, 8 Oct. 1931, File 793.94/2014, RG 59, NA.
[2] *DBFP, 1919–1939*, 2, viii. 728–30; Ogata, pp. 86–7.

this move was really aimed at the Japanese. It was hoped, however, that the publicity would assist in calming Chinese public opinion which was looking for an immediate move by the League. Because of these developments which Drummond considered alarming, the Council would meet on 12 October. Drummond hoped that Stimson would have information for him to present to the Council. He felt the tide might turn if he had impartial information to present to the Council when it convened.

Stimson thought that although a negotiated settlement was preferable, the situation now developing raised the question whether it had become necessary to remind both sides formally of their obligations under the Kellogg–Briand Pact. He welcomed Drummond's views regarding how attention might quickly and effectively be called to the Pact's obligations in the event that such action became necessary. If this question was raised during the Council's upcoming meeting, Gilbert was authorized, if he was invited, to contribute to the discussions on this point.[1]

Drummond, however, 'was afraid of invoking the Pact', Gilbert informed Stimson, fearing that 'it might bring up other issues which would make settlement of the Manchurian problem more difficult'. In Drummond's opinion any formal invocation of the Kellogg–Briand Pact had 'certain practical disadvantages'. First, it would create a question of dual jurisdiction and competence which would allow either China or Japan to chose one instrumentality and deny the other thereby making negotiations much more difficult. Based on prior experience the League had reasons to fear this and Drummond cited the Corfu Incident of 1923. He maintained that it would allow China or Japan to remove the present discussions to a different plane, namely, whether the Kellogg–Briand Pact had actually been violated and in this way have the engagements given to the Council assume a secondary role. Any of the parties seeking to delay matters would certainly utilize this procedure.

Assuming, however, that the only breach of the Kellogg–Briand Pact was a resort to war, then such a resort to war at the present state of the Manchurian dispute was a violation of Article 12 of the Covenant, with everything that such a violation entailed under Article 16. Obviously, American policy would be extremely important in such a serious issue. On the other hand,

[1] *PRFRUS, 1931*, iii. 144–6, 154.

Drummond suggested that if Stimson saw fit he might communicate to the Chinese and Japanese that he had great doubts whether the Kellogg–Briand Pact 'was not in imminent danger of violation'; that he did not intend at the moment to invoke the Pact since the League was seized with the question and had assurances from both sides, which if loyally executed would prevent any danger of the Pact's violation; that while he fully supported the League's action, neverthless he felt obligated to remind both states of their obligations under the Pact; and that a violation of the Pact by resort to war might be considered by League members as implying a violation of the Covenant. Since these were his 'personal views', Drummond asked that Stimson keep them confidential.[1]

Drummond then attempted to explain his role as Secretary-General and its relation to this matter. He pointed out to Stimson that his position was in no way analogous to a foreign minister's. In actual fact he was only an agency for the transmission of information in the relationship between the League and various governments. To exchange information only with him was in no way an exchange of information with either the Council or its members. Regarding the valuable information that Stimson had made available, he remained handicapped in using it in any practical way as he was restrained by the injunction not to reveal its source. Should he transmit the information to anyone, the first question that would be raised would be the information's source. Depending on his reply the information either would not be given its due weight or its source would be surmised. In the latter case he might be placed in the position of appearing to breach Stimson's and Gilbert's confidences.

Drummond envisaged three ways of utilizing the factual information on Manchuria received from neutral sources. In order of their effectiveness they were: to circulate the information among the Council members and make it public; to transmit it confidentially to the Council members; and to make the information known for confidential use by the Committee of Five. Drummond trusted that Stimson would understand the

[1] Ibid., 164–5; Gilbert (Geneva) to the Department of State, No. 179, 11 Oct. 1931, File 793.94/2058, RG 59, NA. See also, Armin Rappaport, *Henry L. Stimson and Japan, 1931–33* (Chicago: University of Chicago Press, 1963), p. 32; Thorne, p. 154.

spirit in which his position in this question was being made
known to him, and he solicited Stimson's assistance in whatever
way he felt able to give it.

Stimson was not moved. To disclose the reports of the
American diplomatic observers in Manchuria, he insisted, would
make their task more difficult, put them in peril, and compromise
their subsequent service in the Far East. Disclosing sources to the
Council 'would tend to encourage controversy'. When Gilbert
explained Stimson's position Drummond agreed that it was
unwise to identify the sources of the information transmitted to
him. As to the Kellogg–Briand Pact Stimson was aware that
independent action by Washington might embarrass the League's
work, but he saw no danger of any embarrassment to the League
if the Pact's invocation were left, as he suggested, specifically to
the Council. Drummond's suggestion that Washington alone
should call Japan's and China's attention to the Pact was to
misunderstand the entire purpose of invoking it, namely, to bring
as many of the signatories of the Pact into action, and by doing
so mobilize what was essentially the 'world's public opinion
against a breach of the peace in Manchuria'. Though Stimson
was aware of the danger of dual jurisdiction he did not see how
invoking the Pact, under the Council's auspices, could possibly
involve such a danger. Indeed, this danger might arise if
Washington on its own were to send China and Japan a note
under the Pact. Drummond saw Stimson's point and admitted
that he had been wrong in his approach and explained that the
Committee of Five, like Stimson, saw no conflict whatsoever and
no reason why action could not be simultaneously attempted
through both the League and the Pact.[1]

On 13 October, the Council convened and heard the Chinese
and Japanese explanation of what had occurred.[2] The next day
Drummond was visited by Setsuzo Sawada, Japan's substitute
representative. It was obvious from Sawada's comments that
American participation in the Council's proceedings was
uppermost in his mind. Initially he dwelt on Japan's desire for
direct negotiations with China. Drummond commented that any
attempt along these lines would prove difficult, and recommended
that the points on which Japan desired to negotiate might better

[1] *PRFRUS, 1931*, iii. 155–6, 159, 167–8, 178, 181.
[2] League of Nations, *Official Journal*, XII (1931), pp. 2309–21.

be embodied in a Council resolution. Surely it would be better to obtain a Council resolution embodying these points which was also accepted by China, he noted, rather than to insist on direct negotiations in order to secure them.

Sawada's fear of an adverse Japanese reaction to American participation in the Council's proceedings which would be considered as directed against Japan's interest and little short of a threat, caused Drummond to remark that any such notion would be quite erroneous. Washington, he maintained, had stated that it wished to base its move on the Council's prior action and support it in every way possible. Moreover, the Americans were one of the joint authors of the Kellogg–Briand Pact whose second article referred to the settlement of disputes by peaceful means. It was far better, Drummond argued, that in a situation where there was a common basis for discussion that all opinions be co-ordinated rather than that the League and the United States, working toward a common end, should attempt different means. Drummond observed that it was really a matter of getting the right formula. He was sure that a formula could be devised which would avoid the impression that Japan was being pressured.

Since the American would only be sitting in the Council in an advisory capacity Drummond felt sure that it was within the Council's competence to extend an invitation for that purpose. The Council, he noted, was free to do what it thought proper in order to maintain the peace. Things would be completely different, of course, if an invitation was issued to a non-member state of the League to sit on the Council with the same power as that of a Council member. In fact, if the invitation to the American was a procedural question it could be decided by a majority vote of the Council. Surely no Council member would wish to oppose such an invitation. As to having the question examined by a committee of jurists, Drummond foresaw some difficulty with this approach since he doubted whether many of the delegations had their legal advisers with them, but he promised to try to have the point examined at least individually.[1]

The following day, despite Japanese objections, the Council accepted Briand's proposal that the United States be invited to

---

[1] Eric Drummond, Record of Interview, 14 Oct. 1931, FO/371/15494.

participate in the Council's proceedings. The invitation was accepted and on the afternoon of 16 October, Gilbert took his seat at the Council table. In the days that followed, the Council, led by Briand and basing its action on Japan's prior assurances, pressed the Japanese to agree to their promised withdrawal within a given time period and to state precisely the conditions that governed this withdrawal. In these discussions Drummond played an active role and although the Japanese were willing in general to repeat their previous promises and assurances, they refused to be specifically tied down to any public statement. Briand then attempted to force the issue on 24 October when he proposed a Council resolution essentially recapitulating the Council's resolution of 30 September but with the important proviso that a Japanese withdrawal begin immediately and be completed within three weeks—that is by the Council's scheduled meeting on 16 November—and that once the withdrawal was completed China and Japan should commence direct negotiations for the settlement of the questions outstanding between them. Since this resolution was obviously unacceptable to the Japanese they formally vetoed it.[1]

This veto, however, went uncontested for everyone still hoped that Japan might be dissuaded from her Manchurian adventure. Moreover, they were not convinced that open hostilities against Japan were necessarily in China's interests.[2] The anticipated Japanese veto did not visibly shake Drummond. But he was understandably disturbed by Stimson's unexpected decision to withdraw Gilbert from the Council's proceedings and to have him reassume his role as an observer and auditor once discussions of the Kellogg-Briand Pact had been concluded and action reinstituted under the Covenant.[3] Resilient, Drummond quickly recovered, for on 26 October we again find him trying to devise a compromise formula with Naotake Sato, Japan's other substitute representative. Drummond proposed that in line with a message from the Chinese representative that his country would scrupulously fulfil her treaty obligations, Tokyo might be

---

[1] League of Nations, *Official Journal*, XII (1931), pp. 2322–62; *PRFRUS, 1931*, iii. 272–3, 299–301; *DBFP, 1919–1939*, 2, viii. 818–20; E[ric] D[rummond], Record of Interview, 26 Oct. 1931, FO/371/15495.

[2] Walters, pp. 477–8.

[3] *PRFRUS, 1931*, iii. 267; Thorne, p. 155; Stimson, pp. 52–69.

able to contend that its action had been intended to secure this very admission from China. Since this Chinese admission had now been secured and Japan's stance vindicated, Tokyo was ready to commence the withdrawal of its troops in Manchuria on the condition that the Council obtain from the Chinese an undertaking that the direct negotiations referred to in the Council's rejected resolution would begin on the same day that the troops' evacuation in Manchuria was completed. Drummond pointed out that in fact the Spanish representative had suggested this during the Council's deliberations, but it seemed to have escaped the attention of the Japanese. He believed that the case could be presented to Tokyo in such a way as to make it appear as a Japanese victory. A great deal, he maintained, could be made out of the Chinese engagement to respect treaties. Sato appeared impressed by his proposal and Drummond was sure that upon his return to Japan he would do his best to have it accepted as a possible solution to the present crisis.[1]

This was wishful thinking and Drummond's comments several weeks later showed it. Like ink on a blotter the area of Japanese occupation and control in Manchuria began to spread. In Tokyo the authorities found themselves less and less capable of controlling the military. Drummond appeared apprehensive that new Japanese demands were being raised, and he speculated regarding possible American action in connection with the Council's rejected resolution of 24 October. He believed that the Japanese position was hardening, Gilbert reported to Washington, and that Japan's next move would be the establishment 'in Manchuria of a puppet government'—a prophetic comment. When Drummond queried if conversations were going on between Washington and London as well as Paris regarding possible action, Gilbert replied that he knew nothing. It was Gilbert's impression that Briand along with Drummond continued handling the Council's negotiations and that Drummond would play an important part.[2]

Several days later Drummond was alarmed by information from an unidentified but reliable source that Washington had abandoned the Council's stance that it would not recommend

---

[1] E[ric] D[rummond], Record of Interview, 26 Oct. 1931, FO/371/15495.
[2] *PRFRUS, 1931*, iii. 341–2.

direct negotiations between the parties while Japanese troops
were in possession of Manchurian territory beyond that specified
in treaty arrangements.[1] Accordingly, Drummond correctly
pointed out to the Chinese that since the Council's 24 October
draft resolution was vetoed by the Japanese it was not binding
and that only the Council's 30 September resolution was valid.
Consequently, as in the past, he recommended that China
exercise great caution and take all steps necessary to avoid a
clash with Japanese forces. When Gilbert explained that
Washington was uninformed of what the League wished it to do,
Drummond repeated what he had told the Chinese. Although
Drummond thought the Council's rejected resolution of 24
October was not legally binding, he thought it did possess 'a
moral force' denoting what the states represented on the Council
considered to be both 'right and fair under the circumstances'.

However, Briand's note of 29 October to the Japanese, he
pointed out, stressed the fifth point in the Council's rejected
resolution of 24 October, namely, the immediate appointment of
representatives by both sides to make arrangements for the
Japanese evacuation of occupied territory and its reoccupation
by the Chinese authorities. If this procedure was followed
satisfactorily then Drummond thought that everything else was
of secondary importance. He suggested that Washington impress
on the Japanese the immediate implementation of this procedure.
Indeed, the Chinese had approached the Japanese on this
question but Tokyo had not yet responded. If the negotiations on
the Japanese evacuation could commence, then in effect, he
argued, the Japanese position would have been turned and both
Washington's and the League's wish that the evacuation should
commence as soon as the Chinese authorities and troops could
give security would have been achieved. Drummond recommended that any American action in Tokyo should not be made
public as the government might resent public pressure, but
simultaneously it would be useful if Washington made a public
announcement that it generally agreed with the principles
spelled out in the Council's rejected resolution of 24 October.
Such a statement would not commit the United States to the
three-week time period for Manchuria's evacuation which

---

[1] *DBFP, 1919–1939*, 2, viii. 862–3.

Drummond believed the State Department considered an obstacle in the negotiations.

He hoped, Drummond informed Cadogan, that what he had said to Gilbert was in line with the Foreign Office's endeavours. The important thing, in Drummond's mind, was to induce the Japanese to enter into direct negotiations with the Chinese on the evacuation and security questions, in which case even if the Japanese evacuation was not far advanced by 16 November when the Council would reconvene, the situation would certainly be much improved. He had also impressed on Gilbert that his presence at the Council would be important even if he was only an observer. Drummond noted that he had looked into Article 15 of the Covenant—what could be the first step in the implementation of sanctions under Article 16. He did not believe that utilization of this article would be as serious a matter as some people feared. Would not the first step under this article, he queried, be that he should ask the Council that a commission of inquiry be established and sent to Manchuria to make a full investigation of what had occurred as stipulated in the first paragraph of Article 15? The commission's report would have to follow within six months after the submission of the question under this article but this could easily be done and it might assist in clearing up the whole Manchurian question. This was a thought for the future for if the Japanese evacuation could commence everyone could pause for developments in the next phase of the question.[1]

However, the seizure by Japanese forces of Manchuria's salt revenue made any future evacuation less likely and caused Sze to observe to Drummond that this act was a clear interference with Chinese administration and contrary to prior Japanese pledges. Drummond expressed his alarm and promised to transmit Sze's protest note to the Council. He observed that he could not advise whether an earlier Council meeting was or was not desirable. The Council and its president would decide the question after reading the Chinese note. Then Sze commented that he was also considering the application of Article 15 and asked for Drummond's advice. Since everyone, it appears, desired for the moment to avoid the use of that article Drummond

[1] Ibid., 865–6, 868–70; *PRFRUS, 1931*, iii. 350, 352–3.

replied that this was a difficult question and he did not feel he was in a position to offer advice. He agreed with Sze that Article 15 allowed a commission of inquiry, but noted that if such a body was established it was unlikely that the Council would act until its report had been received. Drummond also explained to Sze that if a commission was established according to Article 12, its report did not necessarily have to be available for three to four months. He likewise reminded him that under Article 11 the Council acting unanimously was able to take any measures which it thought wise and effectual in safeguarding the peace.[1]

During these early November days Drummond supported the attempts of Japanese Under Secretary-General Sugimura to solve the crisis. Sugimura's formula was that two independent but concurrent negotiations commence between the Chinese and Japanese. The first would concentrate on Japanese evacuation of Manchurian territory and its reoccupation by Chinese authorities. The second would be direct negotiations on all other points previously raised, especially by the Japanese, even before the evacuation was completed. This formula seemed to Drummond really to give the Japanese what they desired, for they could claim they had received satisfaction from the Chinese regarding direct negotiations. The hitch in the proposed formula was that it required a certain amount of Japanese goodwill and the information that he received from Sugimura was not optimistic.[2]

Drummond complimented Sugimura's spirit and endeavours which showed that 'he was in every sense of the word, an international official'. This was especially true since he was working under the most trying conditions and had aroused against himself the extremist elements in his own country. Though Drummond thought the Manchurian question serious, there was a 'glimmer of hope' and 'reason to believe' that a way would be found to avoid a break between Geneva and Tokyo. In fact, no rupture with the League, he observed, was desired by the responsible authorities who made Japanese policy and it was this condition which permitted the thought that a satisfactory method for settling the question would be found. Of course the method used by the Japanese in Manchuria could not be sanctioned by

---

[1] E[ric] D[rummond], Record of Interview, 3 Nov. 1931, FO/371/15496. See also, *PRFRUS, 1931*, iii. 357–61.
[2] *DBFP, 1919–1939*, 2, viii. 875–6.

the League. If this Japanese action was to be repeated in other parts of the world the League's utility as an organization created to maintain the peace 'would be greatly diminished if not destroyed'. The hope was to find a method of settlement which would not humiliate either party.[1]

The Secretariat at this time was apprehensive at the way things were developing and Avenol was no exception. Although Drummond agreed with him that there were 'certain special circumstances' which differentiated the Manchurian question from an ordinary European clash, he nevertheless felt that the question had to be viewed in a more general way, namely, whether the occupation of territory could be accepted as a means to enforce claims long contested by the other party. If such an admission was made, it was Drummond's view that belief in the League as an organ of security against such procedures would be seriously shaken, if not completely given up, at least when a Great Power was involved, and it was this which made the question of such importance for the future.

At the same time Drummond was convinced that American co-operation was helpful, especially since other states appeared afraid to move unless American support was assured. He denied that Washington had stated that it would refuse to impose sanctions. In fact it could not be assumed that if certain measures were envisaged it would not want to participate. Whether this covered economic santions, he did not know. If the situation, however, was unchanged when the Council reconvened on 16 November then the Council would have to decide whether it was prepared to exercise any pressure to execute Article 11. A 1927 report on this article, approved by the Council, had stated that if any parties to a dispute disregarded the Council's advice or recommendations the Council would consider the measures to be taken; it could manifest its formal disapproval; it might recommend to League members to withdraw their diplomatic representatives from the state in question; or it might also recommend measures of a more serious nature. Whether the Council would even be prepared to consider these steps Drummond could not say, but a great deal would depend on the attitude of the Great Powers and he was sure that it would have to be faced since the Japanese aims were now very clear: to

[1] Minutes of a Directors' Meeting, 4 Nov. 1931, LNA.

obtain Chinese recognition of certain Manchurian treaties which China up to the present had contested and to remove Manchuria from any direct dependence on Nanking.

If the League failed in this matter, Drummond maintained, not only were the value of the Covenant's peace-keeping clauses destroyed—its technical non-political work could of course continue—but the success of the Disarmament Conference would be seriously endangered since if the Covenant and other international conventions afforded no security, each country could rightly argue that it had to depend on its own armed strength.

This was why, rightly or wrongly, he considered the Manchurian question of paramount importance from the League's point of view and for the general principles for which it stood. It might be that the Great Powers were not yet ready to assume the engagements they had undertaken in such a case, but if this was so, it was far better that the world be aware of it than that nations should be asked to trust to what would then be proved to be a failure.[1]

Establishing the Lytton Commission

Drummond's faith in the Americans appeared vindicated for Stimson conveyed to Tokyo a message which attempted to clarify that Washington's and Geneva's objectives in the Manchurian question were similar, namely, to prevent war and to bring about a peaceful settlement. He therefore endorsed the Council's prior actions. As to the 24 October resolution which was aborted by the Japanese veto, Stimson invoked its spirit but deliberately refrained from mentioning the three-weeks time limit that it had stipulated for the Japanese evacuation of Manchurian territory.

Drummond was very satisfied with Stimson's note which he felt dovetailed with the present negotiations and would thus be of great assistance. He informed Gilbert of the difficulties being experienced by Briand in Paris where there were elements, especially in the Quai d'Orsay, which were clearly pro-Japanese

---

[1] D[rummond] to Avenol, 6 Nov. 1931, Avenol Folder, LNA. For an extract from this letter see Arthur W. Rovine, *The First Fifty Years. The Secretary-General in World Politics 1920–1970* (Leyden: Sijthoff, 1970), p. 83 and Thorne, pp. 183–4.

in their orientation. Correspondingly, French policy in this question largely depended on Briand's leadership. Stimson took the hint and the American chargé d'affaires in Paris was quickly instructed to convey informally to Briand Stimson's message to Tokyo.[1]

On 6 November, Sze again raised the question of invoking Article 15 of the Covenant and asked for Drummond's advice. Since everyone, it appeared, continued to wish to avoid the use of that article at least for the moment, Drummond replied, as he had before, that this was a difficult query. All things considered he doubted whether it would be wise to invoke the article. Probably an inquiry under Article 15 would take months. Would not the invocation of this article, he asked, and the establishment of a commission of inquiry allow Japan to state that she would continue her Manchurian occupation until the report of the commission had been received? Drummond therefore thought that it was probably in China's own interest to avoid for the present the use of Article 15 but to see how matters developed in the Council. Sze responded that he had come to the same conclusion.[2]

However, a Japanese reply to Briand's note of 29 October narrowed the options and made the invocation of Article 15 almost inevitable. Drummond regarded the reply as outside the scope of the Council's resolution of 30 September since it posited the argument that considering the state of tension in Manchuria no security would be afforded to foreign and especially Japanese residents if the area were evacuated by Japanese forces. In Drummond's view, regardless of Tokyo's contentions its actions had violated the spirit as well as the letter of the obligations it had assumed in the resolution of 30 September. It had also violated Article 10 of the Covenant, Article 2 of the Kellogg–Briand Pact as well as Article 1 of the Nine Power Treaty. Drummond believed that unless the situation altered the Council when it reconvened on 16 November would probably be faced with a most serious situation.

Accordingly, he felt it essential that the Council and the United States co-ordinate and agree on policy questions that

[1] *PRFRUS, 1931*, iii. 387–9, 404–5. See also, Drummond (Geneva) to Cadogan, and the enclosed Record of Interview, 6 Nov. 1931, FO/371/15497.
[2] E[ric] D[rummond], Record of Interview, 6 Nov. 1931, FO/371/15497.

might arise. He correctly pointed out that co-ordination between the United States and the Council would be useful because he was sure that its members would wish to act in unison with Washington in so serious a matter. Since Tokyo's public opinion appeared somewhat ignorant of the feeling in other countries aroused by Japan's Manchurian adventure he wondered whether Washington would not consider publishing the text, or at the least, the substance of Stimson's recent note to Tokyo.

To Cadogan, Drummond noted that Japan's reply seemed to show that at the moment she was 'absolutely unyielding'; likewise the reply was 'entirely unsatisfactory'. He believed that Briand shared his opinion. Sugimura was dejected and did not see what more he could possibly do. His formula which had been adopted by the Japanese representative as his own seemed to have been rejected by Tokyo. 'In short', Drummond observed to Cadogan, 'it is a vile situation'.[1]

Since America's continual co-operation was of the greatest importance Drummond pressed Gilbert on the matter and expressed his hope that there would be no change of the American representative attending the next Council meeting scheduled to be held in Paris on 16 November. He argued that solidarity in the Manchurian question in opposition to the use of armed force in any form would carry to the forthcoming Disarmament Conference so that the conference would open under auspicious circumstances enhancing its likelihood of success. Alteration of American representation, Drummond maintained, might be used by the Japanese press to both stiffen public opinion and to support Japan's present stance, giving the extremists a shot in the arm which might substantively affect the negotiations. In fact, any change in American representation would lead to press speculation which perhaps might be unfortunate and damaging. Moreover, Drummond pointed out that previous problems over American representation in the Council had produced for Briand the greatest difficulties. The main reason that the Council acquiesced in an invitation was the feeling that it would be responsive to Washington's desire. Hence Council members would misunderstand an American with-drawal which doubtlessly would hurt their sensibilities. The

---

[1] *DBFP, 1919–1939*, 2, viii. 877–9; *PRFRUS, 1931*, iii. 397–9.

position of an American auditor attending Council sessions in Paris would be clearly understood. Drummond did not see how the attendance of an auditor could prejudice America's general position.

Stimson desired to continue his co-operation with the League but fearful of America's isolationist elements who had complained about Gilbert's instructions, he wanted any co-operation to be less open than before. Therefore, Stimson instructed the American Ambassador in London and ex-Vice President, General Charles G. Dawes, to proceed to Paris and to partake in the coming negotiations but not to attend any of the Council's meetings. In fact, he informed Dawes, 'we want them to come to you'.[1] Considering the sensitive task assigned, Dawes's selection was unfortunate, for Dawes was dogmatic, ill-mannered, and even more important, anti-League and pro-Japanese.[2]

On the same day that Stimson made his arrangements with Dawes, Drummond responded to Avenol who had complained of the Council's handling of the question and had observed that though the League's principles were unchanging its procedures were flexible.[3] Drummond noted that everywhere it was the extreme nationalist newspapers, the military, plus armaments manufacturers, that complained the most about any added pressure being applied against Japan—an allusion especially to the French press, and to French munitions manufacturers. These very elements, he noted, were also opposed to the success of the Disarmament Conference.

To this degree the Manchurian and disarmament questions were connected and likewise connected because Europe's general public did not distinguish between the Far East question and one which might develop in Europe. This theory was justified for if it was admitted that a state had the right to occupy the territory

---

[1] *PRFRUS, 1931*, iii. 397–401, 407.

[2] Charles G. Dawes, *Journal as Ambassador to Great Britain* (New York: Macmillan, 1939), pp. 424–5; Robert H. Ferrell, *Frank B. Kellogg. Henry L. Stimson. The American Secretaries of State and Their Diplomacy*, ed. Samuel Flagg Bemis (New York: Cooper Square Publishers, Inc., 1963), xi. 229–32; Sara R. Smith, *The Manchurian Crisis 1931–1932* (New York: Columbia University Press, 1948), pp. 160–4; Walters, p. 479; Thorne, pp. 172, 185, 198 fn.; Pearson and Brown, pp. 319–22.

[3] A[venol] to Drummond, 7 Nov. 1931, Avenol Folder, LNA. See also, Thorne, p. 183.

of a country violating its treaty obligations and not evacuate from that territory until it had obtained satisfaction, then obviously such an admission had to alarm a large number of European powers. The principle underlying such an action was inadmissible. If this was so the question arose as to what could be done in the Manchurian question.

Investigating the circumstances surrounding the Manchurian problem Drummond thought was right, and it would be to Japan's advantage that the League should do this, since it would prove the legitimacy of Japan's grievances against China. To undertake the investigation the Council would have to have a Chinese appeal under Article 15. This would allow the Council to establish a committee of inquiry as stipulated under that article. Though the Chinese government had been persuaded by Briand and others not to invoke this article, the Chinese government simultaneously did not wish to invoke it—although Drummond knew that Sze had been instructed to do so—because China did not wish the entire Manchurian problem impartially examined.

On the question of Japan's actions in Manchuria, it was claimed, and perhaps rightly, that China had ceaselessly violated her treaty commitments there. Yet Japan did not claim that her present Manchurian action was taken under these treaties. The only thing that Japan clearly maintained was that she had acted in defence of these Manchurian treaty rights. Accordingly, it would be wise to obtain from Tokyo a clear statement as to the treaties she was referring to. It then might be possible to see whether China accepted the validity of these treaties and, if she stated that she did not, Drummond could not see any reason why the Council should not ask the World Court for an advisory opinion on the validity of the contested treaties. As far as he could gather, based on a superficial examination of the problem, the Japanese contention on the validity of most of these treaties was probably well-founded and the World Court's advisory opinion would be in Japan's favour. His fear was that Japan might be unwilling to take the risk of submitting the issue to the World Court. But it appeared to Drummond that this was a step that should be taken.

Drummond was sure that when Japan agreed to the Council's 30 September resolution that the evacuation of her troops in

Manchuria depended on effective assurances for the safety of Japanese lives and property, she had not had in mind that this safety depended on China's execution of the Manchurian treaties that Tokyo now referred to. This claim was an after-thought: Tokyo now talked not only of the safety of Japanese lives and property but also of a return to normal conditions in Manchuria. He had proof that this was so for the Japanese had in September been ready to make a statement that troop withdrawals within the railway zone did not depend on direct negotiations between China and Japan on issues not directly connected with the troop evacuation. Indeed, the Japanese delegation had been authorized to make such a declaration at the Council, but unfortunately because of Chinese blundering this step was abandoned.

Japanese intentions had now changed and there was no indication that Tokyo was prepared to scale down its present demands. Personally, Drummond was inclined to believe that the Council members would be most unwilling in view of the general situation to take any action under Article 11—which dealt with war or the threat of war. He also feared that such a stance would also be taken by the United States. Unless such action was universal, he felt that it would be less than useless. Certainly no power or group of powers would be prepared to take action unless they were certain that they would be universally supported.

Drummond did not see if action continued under Article 11 how a commission of inquiry could be established to investigate the entire Manchurian problem, unless the Japanese would agree. This brought one back to Article 15. Here the obstacle was the general unwillingness to invoke the article and this was not an easy dilemma to solve.[1]

During this period Drummond became apprehensive over press reports that Tokyo appeared preoccupied by the Secretariat's attitude and its absolute impartiality. He appealed to his colleagues to exercise the greatest caution in their conversations, especially outside the Secretariat. Often their declarations, he observed, were considered as expressing the authorized opinion not only of the Secretary-General but also of the Council's

---

[1] D[rummond] to Avenol, 10 Nov. 1931, Avenol Folder, LNA. See also, Rovine, pp. 83–4 and Thorne, pp. 183–4.

members. It was for this reason that the greatest prudence was necessary.[1]

His comments did not mean, however, that the Secretariat within its own domain should remain inactive. Henri Vigier, a French member of the Political Section, proposed to Drummond that if a deadlock developed during the coming Council meeting then Briand should invoke Article 7 of the Nine Power Treaty which stipulated that when a situation arose involving, in the opinion of one of the signatories, the application of the treaty's agreements, there would be a complete and frank communication between the contracting states. Briand, Vigier argued, by invoking Article 7, would allow the Council to continue operating under Article 11 of the Covenant, permitting it perhaps to find within the framework of the 1922 treaty and in conjunction with Washington, a solution which would facilitate the execution of the Council's resolution of 30 September. The principal advantage was that this procedure would avoid—at least for the moment—any invocation of Article 15. An added advantage was that it would put to an end the Japanese campaign which maintained that the question was now between the various states and not one for the League.

Vigier's scheme was a 'brilliant idea', Drummond informed Cadogan, and worth being considered in the Foreign Office because it would to some extent take the responsibility for the Manchurian question off the League's shoulders if at the next Council meeting there was a deadlock. If Cadogan thought that something might be done along these lines, perhaps the best procedure would be to contact Briand since Vigier's scheme might require some consultation with Washington. Desirous of keeping his hand on the pulse, Drummond hoped that if there was a conference or commission of the signatories of the Nine Power Treaty, he would be 'allowed to attend, for liaison purposes, adopting in this case the American precedent, of a silent observer'.[2]

Drummond then broached Vigier's scheme to Under Secretary-General Sugimura who liked it since he was obviously very keen in avoiding, if possible, any strong measures being taken

---

[1] Minutes of a Directors' Meeting, 11 Nov. 1931, LNA.

[2] Drummond to Cadogan, 11 Nov. 1931 and the enclosed copy of Vigier's proposal, FO/371/15498. See also, Thorne, p. 184.

against Tokyo, especially the invocation of Article 15. As to Vigier's observation that the Japanese might raise some difficulty by contending that Article 7 of the 1922 treaty really only referred to a diplomatic exchange of notes and not to the convening of any conference or committee, Drummond did not believe that such a position could long be maintained since it would be quite proper to ask the concerned powers to meet in conference and in that case he could not envisage any possible Japanese refusal. The more he thought of Vigier's scheme, the more he liked it.[1]

Avenol's suggestion was that conversations under the Council's aegis should commence in order to bring about direct negotiations between China and Japan. Held in secret session these discussions would be free and the American representative might use his influence. Likewise, questions could be posed, he argued, to the Japanese representative without fearing the effects on Japan's public opinion that public sessions would have.[2] Drummond's response was that no practical progress in settling the question developed from such secret Council meetings because the Japanese representative would not reply to the explicit questions posed. Moreover, he was alarmed by the suggestion that the Council's conversations should be directed toward obtaining direct Chinese–Japanese negotiations. China had stated, and Drummond thought rightly, that she would not engage in direct negotiations on any points not connected with the question of security, as long as they had to face the pressure of a Manchurian military occupation. On this issue he did not think that the League could pressure China to give way, for if it did, a dangerous precedent would be created for the future. In fact, he could envisage military elements in certain states applying similar reasoning and thinking joyously of the results. He therefore did not feel that the League could possibly make such a recommendation at least as things stood now.

Lastly, Drummond was not sure that China was unable to maintain order in the territories which would be effected by the withdrawal of Japanese troops. The Chinese were prepared to dispatch a large contingent of first-class troops and these forces would be as capable as was the small Japanese force of

[1] Drummond (Geneva) to Cadogan, 12 Nov. 1931, FO/371/15499.
[2] A[venol] to [Drummond], 12 Nov. 1931, Avenol Folder, LNA.

maintaining order, provided the Japanese gave them the opportunity to do so. The only thing to do now was await the Council's meeting, though he admitted that he was not at all optimistic over its prospects.[1]

Avenol observed that Drummond had misunderstood him. Since Japan had not respected the resolution of 30 September it belonged to the Council to discover why and to find out whether direct negotiations were possible and, if not, what were the obstacles. Drummond agreed that a cross-examination of the Japanese representative was most desirable, but the difficulty was to induce a capable Council member to undertake the assignment. In addition, he feared that the American represent-ative would not attend a secret Council meeting.[2]

His exchanges with Avenol had led nowhere and Drummond's pessimism must have increased even more when Cadogan warned him that the initial Foreign Office reaction to Vigier's scheme was unsympathetic. The Foreign Office objections were that the Nine Power Treaty was merely a renunciatory act and that Article 7 contained no machinery for dealing with infractions of the treaty. Moreover, if the League by this device transferred the question to another body it would lose more prestige beyond its simple failure to settle the question. There was also the danger of dual authority which Drummond had foreseen when Stimson proposed invoking the Kellogg–Briand Pact. By invoking the Nine Power Treaty, might not the Japanese play one authority off against another, Cadogan asked, and perhaps escape between both of them?[3]

Drummond responded that perhaps he had not sufficiently emphasized that Vigier's scheme could only be utilized as a last resort and did not envisage its use at the present time. If not Vigier's scheme then what? The only thing that remained was the Council's resolution of 30 September. Drummond argued that the two-part resolution, the first part dealing with Japanese troop evacuation, the second with security of Japanese lives and property in Manchuria, were mutually interdependent. His

[1] D[rummond] to Avenol, 13 Nov. 1931, ibid. See also, Thorne, p. 183.

[2] A[venol] to Drummond and D[rummond] to Avenol, 14 Nov. 1931, Avenol Folder, LNA.

[3] Cadogan to Drummond, 14 Nov. 1931, FO/371/15500. See also, Vansittart to Simon, 16 Nov. 1931, FO/371/15498, and *DBFP, 1919–1939*, 2, viii. 913 fn.

point, therefore, was that the Council should recommend to both sides that direct negotiations, 'separate but parallel, or else merged', should immediately begin on the issues of evacuation and security. To do this Japan had to declare what she meant by security. Also she would have to define her intentions on the matter of the Manchurian treaties, and, if treaty interpretation was included, how was it to be reconciled with the question of security? This was an important point since Washington's attitude up to the present had been that it could not recognize territorial occupation as a method for securing the interpretation or the recognition of the validity of treaties that were contested. Tokyo might also be asked what treaties it was referring to and if it responded, Sze could be asked if China accepted these treaties. If Sze's reply was negative the Council could then declare that since there was a disagreement about the interpretation or the validity of these treaties it would be willing to ask the World Court for an advisory opinion. Drummond was certain that Japan would refuse. The Council might then ask Japan whether she would agree to negotiations commencing immediately on the issues of evacuation and security, with a solemn promise by Sze before the Council that the day the troop evacuation was completed direct negotiations on the question of the treaties would begin. This suggestion had already been made to Japan and until now she had not agreed to it, but it had never been made public and he could not help feeling that Tokyo would be in a very difficult position if this was done.

If all these moves failed then Drummond felt that the Council could only state that it would continue its work under Article 11 and that it expected the resolution of 30 September to be executed. Moreover, it could express its formal disapproval under Article 11 of Japan's refusal to accept proposals which appeared to the Council to be both 'fair and equitable' and which had gone far to satisfy her desires, and would be glad to be informed by Tokyo of the steps it took to execute the engagements it had accepted under the resolution of 30 September.

Drummond admitted that this approach was of course 'rather weak', but he thought it was the best that could be achieved. He felt it would be far worse if the Council endeavoured to force China to accept direct negotiations on all points raised by Japan, especially the one dealing with treaties, as long as Manchuria was occupied. It would create a very dangerous precedent and, anyway, he did not think China would agree to it.

Apparently the Japanese would be willing to institute direct negotiations for troop evacuation with the local Manchurian authorities, but for the League it meant recognizing that these authorities were independent of China's central government. In the end Drummond thought that Japan would 'have to come to terms' with China's central government because the boycott of her goods was beginning seriously to affect her. If Geneva assisted Tokyo on this point, Tokyo had to be prepared to give Geneva something in return and for the moment it showed no signs of doing this. Perhaps Cadogan, he ended, might think it worth while to pass this preliminary explanation of his present views to the Foreign Secretary, Sir John Simon, who Drummond hoped would be able to see him before long.[1] Drummond then called on Dawes and gave him this missive which he disguised as a personal and confidential memorandum by deleting Cadogan's name. He claimed that the Council's general feeling, subject to changed conditions, was that in any recommendation the suggestion be included to consider the question along the lines spelled out in the memorandum.[2]

Whatever slim hopes Drummond might have harboured, despite his agreement with Gilbert that economic sanctions were out of the question, that London would be willing, either alone or more likely in conjunction with others, to take forceful measures were dashed when Simon informed him that Great Britain was 'not willing to take any sanctions whatever against Japan'. Simon's admission was at least frank and open and, as Drummond later wrote to him, naturally under 'these circumstances ... there [was] a very severe limitation on what [was] possible as regards League action'.[3] Unfortunately, Stimson was not as frank, nor for that matter were the French, Germans, and Italians, all of whom likewise wanted for various reasons to avoid coercive measures under the Covenant.

In Washington, President Hoover, who like Stimson was friendly to the League, opposed the application of sanctions

---

[1] *DBFP, 1919–1939*, 2, iii. 913–15.

[2] Shaw from Dawes (Paris) to the Department of State, No. 748, 16 Nov. 1931, File 500.C112/723, RG 59, NA; *PRFRUS, 1931*, iii. 455–8.

[3] *DBFP, 1919–1939*, 2, viii. 885 fn., 951.

which he felt would lead to war.[1] This explains Stimson's cautious policy and his attempts to limit American actions whether with the League, China, or Japan to one of diplomatic pressure and the use of public opinion. The French view was that China was to Japan what Germany was to France. They saw Japanese actions in Manchuria which involved China's treaty commitments as analogous to French actions in the Ruhr which involved Germany's Versailles commitments. Japan's actions in Manchuria might therefore be an added precedent for French actions in Germany tomorrow. This attitude was reflected in the French press, by the Quai d'Orsay, as well as by business and financial interests. Moreover, it was conceivable that if China disintegrated, France could repeat in Yunnan what Japan did in Manchuria and thus protect further her Indo-Chinese colony.[2] Naturally, Germany looked askance at Article 16 and Berlin 'strongly deprecated' China's intended Council request for the application of Articles 15 and 16 of the Covenant. Italy was no different. Indeed, Drummond informed Cadogan that he had learned confidentially that with Grandi absent people in Rome were encouraging the Japanese, informing them that they disagreed with the Council's aborted resolution of 24 October, despite the fact that Italy had formally supported it. Drummond observed that Rome might have in mind its attitude at the time of the Corfu Incident of 1923, and desired to be consistent. At the same time, he could not 'help being somewhat suspicious', and thinking that the people in Rome 'have equally in their thoughts the possibility of an occupation of Albania'.[3]

The Council, and, one might add, Japan, faced a dilemma. The Council could either confess an inability to control the situation or invoke Article 15 of the Covenant. The former possibility was out of the question while the latter possibility might inevitably lead to the invocation of Article 16.[4] For Japan, therefore, the invocation of Article 15 posed a real threat.

[1] Herbert Hoover, *Memoirs* (New York: Macmillan, 1952), ii. 365–72; Henry L. Stimson and McGeorge Bundy, *On Active Service in Peace and War* (New York: Harper, 1948), pp. 232–4.

[2] Rappaport, pp. 20–1; Thorne, pp. 146–7; *DBFP, 1919–1939*, 2, viii. 681, 714–15, 746, 771–2, 916; *PRFRUS, 1931*, iii. 165, 388.

[3] *DBFP, 1919–1939*, 2, viii. 885, 916.

[4] Walters, p. 479.

Though probably unaware of the desire to avoid imposing sanctions against it, Tokyo decided in line with recommendations from its diplomatic missions in western Europe and, most important, the Kwantung Army's high command, to propose that a League commission of inquiry proceed to Manchuria to examine the whole question of Sino-Japanese relations and especially the relations of both countries to Manchuria.[1] This proposal, however, was tied to a request for direct Chinese–Japanese negotiations on troop withdrawal, security for Japanese lives and property, as well as the question of the Manchurian treaties. The latter request Drummond pointed out to Sugimura was an obstacle in the proposal and offered some suggestions for skirting the issue. They both agreed, however, that in any discussion of the Japanese proposal public meetings should be avoided.

Drummond's alternative proposal was based on whether Japan would be willing to ask only for the commission of inquiry, leaving the other questions aside; the situation regarding Manchuria's occupation would for the moment be left as it was. Drummond argued that any commission of inquiry would take close to a year to complete its mission. It would allow the League an opportunity to inquire into the whole situation as though it was operating under Article 15, but the advantage would be that the commission would be appointed and the whole procedure executed under Article 11. He thought the commission of inquiry and the other points in the Japanese proposal could be separated and recommended that Simon contact Tokyo on this possibility. If the Japanese were willing to make this amended proposal the Chinese might be persuaded to accept it. Dawes, he observed, could speak to them. Should these conversations prove productive Simon might see Briand shortly before the Council meeting and inform him of what had transpired and then report these developments to the Council. Drummond then pressed at a private meeting of the Council at which the Chinese and Japanese were absent that an attempt be made to ascertain their views on the question of the Manchurian treaties. He proposed that both delegations be questioned separately in order to explain privately to the Council their views on these treaties. This

[1] Ogata, pp. 115–16.

suggestion was accepted, but it led to no solution and the deadlock continued.[1]

Drummond's alternative plan, however, to establish a commission of inquiry which was divorced from other Japanese requests was accepted by Tokyo, and the Council agreed that such a commission be established under Article 11 of the Covenant. The next step that remained was to draw up a mutually acceptable draft resolution.[2] It was not an easy task. Tokyo's aim was to keep Japanese military supervision outside any commission's competence and thus avoid the army's indignation. It demanded exclusion from the draft resolution of any clauses referring to troop withdrawal within a fixed time period. In addition, the resolution was to state that nothing precluded Japanese forces from taking military measures to protect the lives and property of Japanese subjects against bandits and other lawless Manchurian elements.[3]

There then ensued for several weeks a tortuous bargaining process in which Drummond played a very active role[4]—complicated by a thwarted Japanese advance toward Chinchow and Tientsin. But there was dissatisfaction: from Avenol, who had been excluded from these negotiations, perhaps because of a suspected pro-Japanese orientation and a lack of political acumen;[5] and from Cecil who thought that, 'in spite of Eric and Co.', the negotiations could have been considerably shortened if there had been firm insistence on public meetings of the Council.[6]

Finally on 10 December the Council unanimously established a five-man commission of inquiry to study and report on all circumstances affecting international relations which threatened to disturb peace and good understanding between China and Japan. The commission, however, could not control the military situation in Manchuria or initiate negotiations between the two

[1] *DBFP, 1919–1939*, 2, viii. 923–9, 934 and fn., 962–3.
[2] League of Nations, *Official Journal*, XII (1931), pp. 2364–71.
[3] Ogata, p. 116.
[4] Eric Drummond, Record of Interview, 26 Nov. 1931 and the attached preliminary draft resolution, FO/371/15502; *PRFRUS, 1931*, iii. 529, 535–9, 551–2, 561, 649–53; *DBFP, 1919–1939*, 2, viii. 947–9, 951–2, 956–8, 971, 973–974, 980–1 and fnn., 983–4, 991–3, 1003–4; Dawes, p. 427; Walters, p. 480.
[5] A[venol] to D[rummond], 26 Nov. 1931, Avenol Folder, LNA. See also, Thorne, p. 184.
[6] *DBFP, 1919–1939*, 2, viii. 1000.

parties or offer recommendations for settling the dispute. The Japanese representative in his Council comments promised troop withdrawal as quickly as possible, but declared that Tokyo was not precluded by the establishment of the commission from acting to protect Japanese lives and property against bandits and other lawless Manchurian elements.[1]

Drummond held that the Council had done as well as could be expected in a 'very delicate situation'. Both parties had in a sense achieved something from what they had demanded. Though China had not obtained an immediate troop withdrawal, she had brought the dispute to the international plane and saw a commission dispatched to the area. As to Japan, though she could not compel China to enter into direct negotiations and to consider the dispute as concerning only themselves, she had secured that no fixed time limit would be set for a troop withdrawal and that the commission's mandate would be broad.[2]

Briand assigned Drummond the task of arranging the commission's membership. It was to be composed of British, French, German, and Italian commissioners, as well as an American provided Washington acquiesced to his appointment. An additional commissioner from a smaller state might also be added if this was necessary, and although the Council had specified five commissioners no objection to this increase was envisaged. Drummond's impression was that Washington would be disposed to having an American serve on the commission. He and Briand had Walker D. Hines in mind, the former Director General of Railroads. Since Manchurian railway problems were involved his expertise would make him a valuable member of the commission. It was hoped, Drummond explained to Gilbert, that the commission would proceed to Manchuria by mid-January and its task completed after nine months.[3]

Simon's initial desire was to have Lord Macmillan, a Lord of Appeal in Ordinary, appointed to the commission. If he was unavailable Drummond hoped that 'either [a] first class jurist will be selected or better still Sir A[usten] Chamberlain if he would serve'. In the end Lord Lytton, the former Governor of

---

[1] League of Nations, *Official Journal*, XII (1931), pp. 2371–83; Walters, pp. 480–1.

[2] Minutes of a Directors' Meeting, 16 Dec. 1931, LNA.

[3] *PRFRUS, 1931*, iii. 682–3.

Bengal, was approached and on the second request consented to serve on the commission and was subsequently elected its chairman. America's choice was General Frank R. McCoy; France's General Henri Claudel; Germany's Dr. Heinrich Schnee, the former Governor of German East Africa; and Italy's Count Luigi Aldrovandi Marescotti, its former ambassador in Berlin.[1]

Like Cecil, Drummond thought that the Manchurian crisis had dealt the League a 'severe blow'. He entirely disagreed, however, with Cecil's suggestion that this was due to the secrecy of the Paris negotiations. The real reasons were the complexity of the Far East's peculiar conditions and the seeming inability of the Great Powers even with American assistance to apply what the public thought were the Covenant's obligations. Naturally this made the League's position difficult, but would publicity, he queried, have improved things? Since he had more to do with the negotiations than anyone else Drummond believed that if public negotiations had been attempted no agreement on a resolution would have been secured. The choice was between complete failure and a public confession of this and agreement on a resolution ultimately accepted by the Council. Personally, Drummond thought the latter was the right course. He knew that the press had largely ignored the resolution and the importance of the Lytton Commission to the Far East's future, but he trusted that in the end the results would show the Council's wisdom. Public negotiations, he argued, would have propelled Japanese public opinion, already inflamed by the military, to reject the compromise resolution. In this situation world public opinion would have had no impact in Japan. While publicity was the League's strongest weapon where European and American states were concerned, it might well have a reverse effect in the Far East. By understanding or studying the Council's resolution the press would have seen that it contained for China a number of advantages. Though he was willing to assume responsibility for the secret negotiations, Drummond was not prepared to assume 'it as regards the limits within which the Great Powers and chiefly Great Britain forced us to work'. This is what really damaged the Geneva organization. He could 'no

[1] *DBFP, 1919–1939*, 2, ix. 51, 61, 75–6 and fnn.; *PRFRUS, 1931*, iii. 688 and fn.; Walters, p. 482.

longer confidently affirm to foreigners that a British Government will always scrupulously carry out all its engagements under the Covenant at whatever cost'.

Of course there were other factors that worked against the League. There was a very unfair feeling that the League was pro-French, while in Paris, of course, it was held that it was pro-British. There was the isolationism which expressed itself in tariffs and anti-foreign feeling. All these factors would now come into play in the Disarmament Conference. It was useless now to apportion blame. They had to do their best to pull through under very difficult circumstances.[1]

Similar but more guarded comments were made by Drummond to the Canadian Advisory Officer on the League in Geneva. He argued that if Articles 10 and 16 had been invoked Japan would have immediately occupied China and defied the world community, such was the present Japanese attitude. He hoped that the Lytton Commission would find China and Japan 'more amenable to the influence of world public opinion' and that a reasonable solution might finally be devised.[2] Certainly by his actions behind the scenes Drummond had done as much as anyone to find or devise some solution to the problem that had developed. By maintaining the confidence of both sides he had been able to play an active and constructive role in establishing the Lytton Commission. If most of his suggestions and proposals to solve the question were not acceptable this was due less to their originality or intrinsic merit than to his inability to bridge the gap between the League's envisaged role and what support states were willing to give it and especially, the widening gap of hostility and distrust between China and Japan.

Non-Recognition of Manchukuo

While Drummond busied himself with the Lytton Commission the Kwantung Army occupied Chinchow in early January and

---

[1] *DBFP, 1919–1939*, 2, ix. 22, 26–7 and fn., 56–7, 61.

[2] [Walter A. Riddell], Interview with the Secretary-General, 23 Jan. 1932, and Riddell Diary, 23 Jan. 1932, Walter A. Riddell Papers, YUT; Riddell to Bennett, 23 Jan. 1932, MG 26, K, Volume 432, Richard Bennett Papers; and Riddell to Skelton, 23 Jan. 1932, MG 25, D1, Volume 103, Oscar Skelton Papers, PAC.

Harbin in early February. Even more serious was the clash between Japanese and Chinese forces at Shanghai on the night of 28 January. On the afternoon of 26 January as the Shanghai situation deteriorated, the permanent Council members as well as Drummond received separately and privately the Chinese and Japanese representatives to express clearly and unequivocally the Council's alarm regarding the situation and to feel them out over other aspects of the dispute. When the Japanese representative explained that Tokyo was getting accustomed to protests, Drummond observed 'with some heat' that it surely had to take into consideration 'the expressions of general world opinion'. The Chinese representative's observation that he had been instructed to invoke Articles 15 and 16, but had refrained from doing so, hoping he would receive satisfaction under the present procedure, caused Drummond to comment that he understood that China would be satisfied by the Council's endorsing Stimson's note of 7 January to China and Japan—the forerunner of the Stimson Doctrine. In this note Stimson informed both sides that the United States would not recognize any Chinese–Japanese agreement impairing American treaty rights in China, including those relating to China's sovereignty, independence, or territorial and administrative integrity, or to the Open Door policy, or to any arrangement arrived at contrary to the Kellogg–Briand Pact. The Chinese representative did not think that such Council action would be sufficient.

Drummond was pessimistic that either Japan or the Council could be persuaded to take the proper action. On 29 January China invoked Articles 10 and 15 of the Covenant. Under the latter article Drummond was charged with the immediate task of arranging for a full investigation of the dispute. He proposed that since the Lytton Commission would take three weeks to arrive in Shanghai that in the interim the states whose nationals were on the commission should be invited by the Council to form a temporary commission until the Lytton Commission arrived in Shanghai. This temporary commission, composed of their diplomatic or consular officials on the spot, would report on the facts and the causes of the Shanghai fighting. Stimson replied that since the temporary commission would be acting under Article 15 Washington could not appoint its Consul-General in Shanghai as a commission member. However, he would be instructed to co-operate with the commission's members in studying and reporting upon the facts and causes of the fighting. Drummond had managed to get more or less what he wanted—continued American support and co-operation with the League's processes.[1]

At the same time Drummond was 'greatly disturbed' at London's suggestion that the British Government was inclined to send essentially a negative response to an American proposal for a common front in the Shanghai affair. Drummond favoured a policy of very great patience. He was willing to admit that perhaps it might have been preferable if Washington had waited longer before making any serious moves, but he strongly emphasized that if London returned a discouraging answer to Washington now it would certainly 'cause great resentment in America with all its possible consequences'. Moreover, a negative response to the American proposal would encourage Tokyo in the belief that it will not meet any effective opposition whatever it does in Shanghai. It was highly probable that as a result of the latter situation Great Britain would have to intervene in the immediate future more so than before and would then find herself unsupported by Washington. Drummond had made his point: 'I entirely agree with this view', Simon minuted.[2]

During these days Drummond again raised the possibilities of using the Nine Power Treaty and attempted, without recommending any course, to ascertain British, French, and Italian views on the matter. Though the treaty provided specific means for American collaboration they simultaneously feared that Japan might take advantage of the dual jurisdiction created to obfuscate the question and perhaps escape from some of her obligations. They especially did not wish to lose the advantage now afforded under Article 15—an investigation conducted, if necessary, even without Japan's assent. The consensus was that invoking the treaty now was undesirable.

Drummond was aware that China was considering its invocation. If China did so Drummond felt that the procedure followed became a matter of importance. Although the treaty's implementation did not necessarily involve the convening of a

---

[1] *PRFRUS, 1932*, iii. 72, 76, 94, 123–4, 129–31, 156–7.
[2] *DBFP, 1919–1939*, 2, ix. 221 and fn.

conference, Drummond believed that to 'accomplish any tangible results a conference would be essential'. If no conference was convened, he argued, Tokyo might merely state its willingness to engage in full and frank communication with the other signatories—as required by the 1922 treaty—and the situation would remain static. Gilbert believed that Drummond was advising the Chinese representative that if his country invoked the Nine Power Treaty she should simultaneously suggest that the presence of the various powers' representatives in Geneva afforded an occasion for a meeting. This would not only serve the purpose of a quick and convenient place to meet but also assist in co-ordinating the efforts of those states who were signatories to the treaty and those states who were League members. However, Gilbert believed that Drummond's general line with the Chinese representative was to dissuade China from invoking the 1922 treaty at least for the moment.[1]

China's invocation of Articles 10 and especially 15 caused Sugimura to propose a compromise under which the Chinese would withdraw their appeal to Article 15 provided the Lytton Commission's members were utilized as the neutral observers to oversee Chinese–Japanese negotiations to solve all outstanding differences between them in Shanghai in the spirit of the Kellogg–Briand Pact and the Council's resolution of 10 December. Though Drummond did not know whether this plan would work, he encouraged Sugimura to make the attempt with the Japanese delegation. This same day, 3 February, Drummond was visited by Naotuke Sato, and Tsuneo Matsudaira, the Ambassador in London. The thrust of the Japanese comments were that though Article 15 would be acceptable if it was limited to events in Shanghai, it would not be acceptable if applied to Manchuria. Drummond replied that the Japanese unfortunately misunderstood. It was not within their competence either to refuse or accept Article 15. China requested that the whole dispute be submitted to the Council under Article 15. The Council had no choice but to consider it under that article. Japan had no power to limit the question China submitted under Article 15. Drummond held the view that the Council was already seized of the dispute under Article 15 by China's very

[1] *PRFRUS, 1932*, iii. 177–8.

submission of the matter. It would require, he noted, the Council's assent to remove consideration of the dispute under Article 15. Drummond likewise dismissed the Japanese contention that the Council could not deal with the dispute simultaneously under Articles 11 and 15. These articles, he maintained, ran concurrently. If in considering the dispute under Article 11 a danger of war arose, the Council was quite competent to deal with the war danger under Article 15. Indeed, it had a duty to do so. The first two paragraphs of Article 15 required automatic action. It was only when the two parties made their statements and brought them to the Council's knowledge that the Council could decide whether the dispute was of a type contemplated under Article 15—one likely to lead to a rupture. If Tokyo had strong legal doubts, he would recommend to the Council that the World Court be urgently requested for an advisory opinion on the points at issue. The procedure under the first two paragraphs of Article 15 would of course continue. He warned Sato that he was convinced that his interpretation of Article 15 was legally correct and that the World Court would rule against the Japanese thesis. The situation therefore should be carefully considered by Tokyo from that point of view.

In addition, Drummond thought that Article 10 was not in question. Sato's contention that the vote of both parties had to be counted appeared to him to lack common sense. If a state violated the territorial or political integrity of another state its Council representative would never admit it. Therefore it would be intolerable if the vote of the aggressor state was permitted to stop Council action to protect the attacked state's integrity.

Drummond observed that Japanese criticism should be directed against China, not the Council. He noted reports that Tokyo was considering withdrawing from the League owing to the pressure of public opinion. No one would regret this more than himself. Yet he would prefer that this occur to abandoning the principles laid down in Article 15. To agree to Tokyo's contention would simply destroy the Covenant's effective value. He hoped that Sato and Matsudaira would forgive him for having expressed his views so frankly, but he thought that it was far wiser to explain things as he saw them. This conversation obviously had its impact, for Sugimura was unable to persuade the Japanese delegation to accept a compromise scheme. They contended that it 'would be impossible to persuade [the] Chinese to withdraw their submission of the case under article 15'.[1]

Within the narrow options that remained to him and undoubtedly in the hope that greater pressure both diplomatic and from world public opinion might be generated against Tokyo, Drummond contemplated convening the Assembly. He thought that this would be an easy step since the Disarmament Conference was now in session. Drummond recognized that there was a risk that this might 'turn into a public condemnation of Japan', but he thought that this danger might be skirted by careful preparation. He likewise considered whether a Council appeal to Japan might not be advisable. The appeal would point out that Japan's power was far greater than China's and call on it 'in the interests of peace, justice and chivalry' not to use this power. Drummond appeared to think that such an appeal might favourably affect the Japanese elections set for 20 February.

He also toyed with the possibility of economic sanctions, but not, according to Minister Wilson, as if he was contemplating such action. Drummond correctly pointed out that there was a legal problem involved, for under the Covenant economic sanctions were provided for only in the case where war had erupted and not as a measure for preventing war. Even if this legal difficulty could be avoided there remained the serious question whether Japan would not react to economic sanctions either by a declaration of war against all the states involved in applying the sanctions or by blockading the Chinese coast which in turn led to a serious risk of war.

Drummond's thoughts were soon followed by Chinese action. Exercising their right under paragraph nine of Article 15 the Chinese quickly referred their appeal to the Assembly. What role Drummond played in this action is difficult to document. His thoughts, however, raise the strong suspicion that it was Drummond himself who recommended this procedure to the Chinese. Drummond explained that China's purpose in appealing to the Assembly appeared to be to reserve her right to do so which otherwise would have lapsed. He pointed out that the Chinese did not suggest a specific date for convening the Assembly, in fact they did not want to set either a date or have

[1] *DBFP, 1919–1939*, 2, ix. 413–17; *PRFRUS, 1932*, iii. 202–5, 206.

an immediate meeting.[1] When pressed by Simon to have the Chinese dissuaded from proceeding with their demand convoking the Assembly, Drummond responded that he doubted this could be done. Having discovered that the Council would do little to help her China probably wished to mobilize Assembly sympathy for her cause and record publicly its disapproval of Japan's action. This support China might expect to garner, he observed, from among the Assembly's 'more irresponsible members'.[2]

Since Stimson perceived no objection to a 'special and strong' Council appeal to Japan, Drummond officially proposed that such an appeal be made, though Wilson noted that the draft appeal was 'more vigorous in tone than this appellation would indicate'. On 16 February, to Simon's annoyance, the Council appealed to Japan, which subsequently rejected the appeal. Three days later the Council on Drummond's suggestion also acquiesced to China's invocation of Article 15 and her request that the question be considered by the Assembly which was asked by the Council to convene on 3 March.[3]

The question that was now raised was whether the United States should not be formally invited to associate herself openly with the League and to act in conjunction with the organization. Drummond demurred. He did not believe that the time for such action had arrived. He thought the entire situation was changing with the convening of the Assembly. Also consideration had to be given to inviting not only the United States but other countries attending the Disarmament Conference which were not League members—a clear allusion to Soviet Russia. The situation, he noted, could change radically in ten days' time. In the interim great caution had to be exercised in connection with any new steps.

Naturally, Soviet Russia's presence at the Disarmament Conference made it difficult to extend an invitation to the Americans without one also being extended to the Russians. The problem was whether Moscow would want to co-operate with Geneva in finding a solution to the Manchurian problem or

[1] *PRFRUS, 1932*, iii. 285–6, 298, 308.

[2] *DBFP, 1919–1939*, 2, ix. 488.

[3] *PRFRUS, 1932*, iii. 305, 323, 346; Walters, p. 487; *DBFP, 1919–1939*, 2, ix. 491–4, 500–2, 520–1; League of Nations, *Official Journal*, XIII (1932), pp. 371–2.

whether it would fish in troubled waters by urging the Assembly to censure Japan, thereby inflaming the situation even more. Accordingly, Drummond for the moment doubted the wisdom of issuing an Assembly invitation to non-member states because of these reasons. Simultaneously, he wanted Washington's views conveyed to him in writing as to the problems that might be under discussion. Unless these views were written, he argued, they were of limited use and would not receive either the circulation or the weight they otherwise merited. Such a move, Drummond added, would go far in preventing the Assembly from taking steps which might be distasteful to Washington, and in repeating the autumn episode in which the Council insisted for a time limit on Japanese troop withdrawal in Manchuria.

Stimson also wanted to avoid an Assembly invitation. He saw only danger and no advantage in discussions between Washington and Geneva, since the League had not yet come to any decision or report even for so simple a situation as the one in Shanghai. Therefore the League was in no position to ask Washington about the eventual application of sanctions as it had to render a judgement before it could discuss punishment. Moreover, economic sanctions were not the only sanctions under the Covenant.

Drummond was no doubt pleased by Stimson's attitude and admitted that he himself was dubious whether the Assembly could legally invite a non-member state to its deliberations. On the question of sanctions his comments were far from radical. He observed that there had been much loose talk about sanctions, mostly by states which had nothing to lose. Drummond thought that it was most important to avoid giving the Japanese any pretext to declare war on the League or any member state. At the same time everything possible had to be done short of giving the Japanese excuses for such extreme action. In Drummond's opinion, 'at the present moment the Japanese state of mind might be ready to go to war with even Great Britain' should the League impose economic sanctions against Japan under the Covenant. Because of this he felt that any proposal to impose sanctions would not be supported by members of the League. The danger, however, was that the Assembly might attempt to pass judgement on Japan claiming that she had violated the Covenant which would appear to entail the application of Article 16. Drummond agreed with Stimson that it would be a mistake 'to punish a prisoner before sentence was passed'. The better procedure was to avoid coming to any decision till all the facts were at the Assembly's disposal, since the Covenant provided that the judgement itself involved immediate punishment. As to the Assembly Drummond believed that it would 'probably adopt a resolution whereby all states undertook not to recognize solutions reached in this matter which were contrary to existing treaties'. Thereafter the Assembly would establish a committee for executive action followed by a report to the Assembly.[1]

Drummond's own version of this interview with Wilson which he sent to Simon makes interesting reading. As the editors of the British diplomatic documents point out, Drummond's account tallies closely with what Wilson reported, except that where Wilson reported it was Drummond's opinion that the Japanese state of mind might be ready to go to war with Great Britain if sanctions were applied, Drummond recorded that he thought that even if 'America and Great Britain together were prepared to take economic sanctions, Japan in her present state of mind might be ready to go to war with both of them'. Because Simon was opposed to coercive measures against Japan the inclusion of the Americans in Drummond's statement could only have pleased Simon and lulled him into the false impression that Drummond shared and supported his Far Eastern policy. We of course know that on his own initiative Drummond had nourished the idea of a Council appeal to Japan and that he had probably advised the Chinese to transfer their appeal under Article 15 to the Assembly. The suspicion that Drummond was trying to direct Simon's attention away from his own activities is strengthened by the fact that the last paragraph in Wilson's report saying that Drummond envisaged an Assembly resolution not to recognize solutions contrary to existing agreements was not covered in Drummond's own version of this interview which he sent to Simon.[2]

Such a resolution would of course have contributed to the League's co-operation with the United States, which throughout the crisis Drummond attempted to foster, by dovetailing it with

[1] *PRFRUS, 1932*, iii. 430–1, 452–3, 456–7.
[2] E[ric] D[rummond], Record of Conversation, 27 Feb. 1932, FO/371/16160. *DBFP, 1919–1939*, 2, ix. 640 fn.; Walters, p. 487.

Stimson's letter to Senator Borah. This letter was a warning to Japan and a suggestion to the Assembly that 'by adopting the principle of non-recognition of any new situation brought about by means contrary to the Kellogg–Briand Pact, it should build up a formal barrier against military conquests such as might impress not only Japan but also any other prospective aggressor'.[1] As we have seen, the earliest manifestation of this policy, to be labelled the Stimson Doctrine, had been displayed in Stimson's note of 7 January to both China and Japan, and Drummond himself soon after the note had been issued had shown interest in having it endorsed by the Council.

Drummond was unintentionally assisted in this task by the Kwantung Army which arranged on 1 March the proclamation of Manchuria's separation from China and her establishment as the independent State of Manchukuo. This action which was taken on the day following the Lytton Commission's arrival in Tokyo faced the commission with a *fait accompli* and acted as a catalyst in propelling Simon and the Assembly to adopt Stimson's suggestion. Drummond's objective was to make the Assembly's resolution more palatable to the Japanese by making 'the statement of principles in the form of a declaration instead of a resolution'. Along these lines he drafted a text which he sent to Simon and, at the same time, warned him of a possible attempt to introduce new principles of international law into any Assembly resolution. In particular he thought the Latin Americans might attempt to secure a statement that intervention by one state in the affairs of another state could not be justified. Since various resolutions might be proposed Drummond wondered whether Simon 'thought it wise or possible to submit a draft resolution in the sense of the text I gave you'.

Since Drummond's draft resolution cannot be traced it is difficult to say whether it was the draft resolution proposed by Simon which was used as the basis for the discussion of principles and, with very slight amendment, adopted by the Assembly on 11 March—the Japanese and the Chinese abstaining, the former because the resolution dealt with both Manchuria and Shanghai, the latter because they were without instructions. Under Spanish pressure, wording was added to the resolution that it was contrary to the Covenant's spirit that settlement of the

[1] Walters, p. 488.

Manchurian dispute should be attempted by military pressure by either party. Simon himself considered the resolution 'satisfactory' and it was acceptable to the League's 'extremist circles' because it strongly reaffirmed the Covenant's principles and the Kellogg–Briand Pact and proclaimed that it was incumbent upon League members 'not to recognize any situation, treaty or agreement which may be brought about by any means contrary' to the Covenant or the Kellogg–Briand Pact. However, the resolution did 'not directly declare a violation of the Covenant or condemn Japan' and emphasized the League's mediatory procedure under paragraph three of Article 15.[1]

Under the resolution there was created a Committee of Nineteen to arrange an armistice at Shanghai and bring about a settlement of the Manchurian question. The committee was composed of the Assembly's president, six states elected by the Assembly, and the Council's twelve members minus China and Japan. Initially, the British Minister and his colleagues in China wanted to know whether the Committee of Nineteen would authorize the Lytton Commission to delay their Shanghai departure in order to assist when appropriate in the negotiations relating to a Shanghai cease-fire and the withdrawal of Japanese forces. Drummond pointed out that the commission was responsible only to the Council, and although the Council had decided it should have a free hand as to plans, he presumed that the Council could issue instructions or at the minimum make recommendations to the commission. Discussion in the Committee of Nineteen, he divulged, showed that it very much wanted the commission to proceed to Manchuria as quickly as possible. Naturally, if both China and Japan, he noted, asked for the commission's good offices at Shanghai the situation would be different. On the other hand, he understood that the Chinese were anxious that the commission depart for Manchuria as soon as possible. Personally, Drummond considered the commission, which had been informed by the Committee of Nineteen that it needed an early report on the general situation in Manchuria, should be given the greatest freedom to decide questions of this nature on their own responsibility. Simon, however, was keen on keeping the commission in Shanghai so that it could take part in

[1] *DBFP, 1919–1939*, 2, x. 52, 95, 103–4, 107, 124–5, 138 and fnn. For the Assembly's 11 March resolution see Willoughby, pp. 299–301.

the negotiations. By doing so, of course, the investigation of the key question, Manchuria, would have been further delayed, a step that would have assisted the Japanese. In the end, more effective than Drummond's objections were Washington's that the commission's delay in tackling the Manchurian problem would be playing into Tokyo's hands. Though the commission remained in Shanghai until 26 March it does not appear to have played any role in contributing to a settlement of the Shanghai question.[1]

In fact it was not until 5 May that the Committee of Nineteen was able to arrange an armistice in Shanghai. In the complex discussions over details which finally led to the withdrawal of the Japanese forces, Drummond contributed in no small way to the inevitable settlement by his comments and the advice he tendered to the Chinese and Japanese representatives in Geneva.[2] During this period he approached Cadogan to ascertain the British response to Tokyo's request for advice regarding the attitude it should assume toward the Assembly's 11 March resolution.[3] More substantive was the information Drummond conveyed to Cadogan on 19 April from Robert Haas, the Director of the Communications and Transit Section, who was acting as Secretary to the Lytton Commission, that the commission was encountering constant difficulties with the Japanese over its forthcoming trip to Manchuria. It was so important, Drummond pointed out to Cadogan, that the commission be able to execute its task that he suggested that London make representations to Tokyo on this issue. It was certain, he added, that a proper word from the Japanese capital would remove all these difficulties. Though initially Drummond also thought of complaining to René Massigli of the French delegation and to Wilson, he thought it better not to suggest anything to Wilson but merely to send him a copy of Haas's message, since the Lytton Commission was a League body and although Washington approved of the commission it had not formally participated in establishing it.[4]

[1] *DBFP, 1919–1939*, 2, x. 151, 153, 154, 163; *PRFRUS, 1932*, iii. pp. 598–9, 600–1.

[2] *DBFP, 1919–1939*, 2, x. 290–7.

[3] Drummond (Geneva) to Cadogan, 9 Apr. 1932, FO/371/16164.

[4] Haas (Shanghai) to the Secretary-General, 19 Apr. 1932 and two letters Drummond (Geneva) to Cadogan, 19 Apr. 1932, FO/371/16165. See also, *DBFP, 1919–1939*, 2, x. 336 fn.

The following day Drummond informed Moscow that Lytton felt that information or evidence from Russian officials in Manchuria would be of help, and inquired whether this could be furnished by the Russian authorities, but Moscow's reply was in the negative.[1] More favourable was Simon's reaction who, in line with Drummond's advice, instructed the British Ambassador in Tokyo to make representations to the authorities over the difficulties being encountered by the Lytton Commission.[2]

Unfortunately, Drummond's actions were not appreciated by everyone. Nor was there any real understanding of the difficulties under which he was working if one kept in mind the similar attitude in London, Paris, and Washington, namely, the avoidance of coercive measures against Japan in the Manchurian question. Drummond's use of the Secretary-General's office to maintain and continue American co-operation between Washington and Geneva, to have the Council appeal to Japan, and all his other activities were unknown to outsiders. Thus it is understandable if criticisms were voiced even by friends, though these criticisms were factually incorrect. Noel-Baker writing to Cecil in late April contended that Drummond's share in the whole affair had been 'quite lamentable'. According to Noel-Baker, Drummond was almost as Japanese as the Japanese and had consistently pressured the Chinese to give in. He had ceased speaking in a hostile manner about the Japanese and had in all things made himself the spokesman and the agent of the policy that Simon pursued. Drummond did not go so far as to advocate a Manchurian state, he noted, but even his closest friends were most worried about him. His behaviour was explained on the grounds that because of financial reasons he had to have Simon appoint him to an embassy position the following year— Drummond had announced his resignation as Secretary-General in January. This kind of talk distressed Noel-Baker who was sure that a way out of the present situation would be for the League to give Drummond a large bonus similar to that awarded Hankey after the war, and beg Drummond not to re-enter the British diplomatic service but to keep himself ready for future League work. Noel-Baker thought this procedure had every

[1] *PRFRUS, 1932*, iv. 7–8.
[2] *DBFP, 1919–1939*, 2, x. 336.

advantage and was right in theory. It was fantastic that Drummond who had served fifty-odd nations should attach himself to the work of one British Embassy.[1]

If Drummond was aware of these criticisms his continual surveillance of the Manchurian situation gave him little time to show it. By early June he pointed out that under Article 15 which the Chinese had invoked the provisions of Article 12 applied to the Assembly's proceedings. Accordingly, the Assembly's report had to be made by 19 August, that is to say, six months from the day the Council deferred the matter to the Assembly. Since this was unlikely to happen and the six months provided for in Article 12 was insufficient owing to the unusual difficulties in the present case, Drummond thought that an attempt ought to be made to obtain a prolongation from both sides of the six months' period. He believed an added three months would be sufficient but thought it might be very difficult for the Japanese to accept such a prolongation. To accept it would be an admission by Tokyo that Article 15 applied to Manchuria, a point which up to the present she had always denied. Drummond thought that the League was bound to submit Japan's objections to the World Court, which would undoubtedly decide that the objections were invalid, and perhaps faced with this alternative the Japanese would automatically agree to the extension.[2] A week later he broached the problem to the Japanese representative, Harukazu Nagaoka, who wished to avoid any specific reference to Article 15 and any Assembly meeting. Drummond thought that perhaps this might be arranged by having Hymans, the Assembly's President, declare that since China and Japan agreed to this arrangement he assumed that no member of the Assembly had any objection, in which case he understood that the prolongation was acceptable to everyone.[3] He then continued his endeavours with Wei-ching Yen, the Chinese representative who had already spoken to Hymans. In view of Yen's desire for a more elastic prolongation

[1] Noel-Baker to Cecil, 30 Apr. 1932, Add. MS. 51107, Robert Cecil Papers, BL.

[2] *DBFP, 1919–1939*, 2, x. 492–3.

[3] E[ric] D[rummond], Record of Interview, 13 June 1932, FO/371/16172. See also, *DBFP, 1919–1939*, 2, x. 493 fn.

Drummond communicated the idea to the Japanese through Sugimura.[1]

The Chinese were alarmed at the necessity of such a step and feared a possible diplomatic recognition by Japan of Manchukuo and the latter's assumption of the excise customs. Drummond realized the seriousness of such steps and assured Yen that he had taken action privately to do everything possible to prevent the diplomatic recognition of Manchukuo's Government. Naturally he could not say whether the steps he had taken would be effective.

Even if these events occurred, Drummond maintained that the prolongation of the six months' period was necessary. The Assembly could not consider the question until the Lytton Commission's report had been received. Yen agreed, but hoped that the prolongation would be short as possible since any delay increased Japan's opportunities for consolidating her Manchurian position, although he anticipated no additional difficulties.[2]

In point of fact the Lytton Commission was apprehensive over press reports that a strong movement was afoot in certain Japanese circles to recognize immediately Manchukuo's Government. Japan's diplomatic recognition of Manchukuo, the commission observed, would greatly reduce prospects for an early and friendly settlement of the Manchurian question and would be difficult to reconcile with Tokyo's December promise to avoid further aggravation of the Manchurian situation.[3]

As it developed the Lytton Commission's fears about Japan's diplomatic recognition of Manchukuo were premature. At about this same time there was conveyed to Drummond a copy of a letter from Lord Lytton to his sister describing and commenting on the Far Eastern situation. In Lytton's opinion Japan would militarily resist any League interference in the Manchurian question. On the other hand, he felt that Japan had 'bitten off more than she can chew and if left alone circumstances will be too strong for her'. Tokyo would be faced by a Chinese boycott,

---

[1] Drummond to Hymans, 16 June 1932 and Eric Drummond, Record of Interview, 16 June 1932, FO/371/16172. See also, *DBFP, 1919–1939*, 2, x. 493 fn.

[2] *DBFP, 1919–1939*, 2, x. 510–11.

[3] Drummond to Cadogan, 15 June 1932, FO/371/16172; *PRFRUS, 1932*, iv. 79.

a hostile population in Manchuria, and a potential guerrilla campaign, all of which would be a terrible drain on Japan's resources and strain her already overstrained economy. With the Japanese disgraced and humiliated but not challenged, and with nothing to show for their violence, he optimistically believed that Japan's liberal opinion would again assert itself and the military party criticized for the mess they had landed the country into.[1] Personally Drummond shared these views. His difficulty was to prevent the extremists in Geneva from 'recriminations or threats' which would only stiffen the Japanese and unite them more. He admitted that he was slightly nervous of the next scheduled meeting of the Committee of Nineteen because the Chinese had requested that action be taken by the committee to stop Japan from recognizing Manchukuo's Government. He thought this Chinese move 'stupid' and sincerely hoped that the committee would not consider it necessary to comply with China's suggestion.[2] Drummond therefore demurred when it was proposed by some of the smaller powers that Hymans insert a warning in his Assembly declaration on prolonging the time limit for the Lytton Commission; a warning that Japan's recognition of the Manchukuo Government would be considered by the League's members as contrary to the understanding not to aggravate further the Manchurian situation until the Lytton Report was received.

Drummond considered that any such warning 'would be dangerous and resented' as an interference with Japan's foreign policy and perhaps propel Tokyo to more important action than it was contemplating. His advice was followed for when the declaration was presented to the Assembly it contained no such warning to Japan.[3] This action as well as some of Drummond's other moves during this period were a recognition that without great power support, including that of the United States, the League was powerless to do anything in the Far East. Under these conditions Fabian tactics would be more in line with the power realities and who knew what future developments might be? A changing alignment might bring the League the great

[1] *DBFP, 1919–1939*, 2, x. 531–5.
[2] Drummond (Geneva) to Ronald, 23 June 1932, John Simon Papers, FO/800/287.
[3] *PRFRUS, 1932*, iv. 122–3, 127.

power support it now lacked making it possible for Geneva to assume a more active role in the Far East *vis-à-vis* Japan. Of course such a stance was not to some people's liking and this undoubtedly explains Drummond's mid-April lament about the 'difficulties that were being created by League enthusiasts, "our unwise friends"'.[1] It was a difficult stance to assume and maintain and could only have contributed to the anti-Drummond attitude reflected in Noel-Baker's comments to Cecil. When in late July the question of amending the Covenant was raised Drummond understandably appeared to agree with those who thought that the League's task was to see that the organization's member states carried out 'their existing obligations'.[2]

Drummond did not again tackle the Manchurian question until late October. By that point the Lytton Commission's report had been signed and distributed by the Secretariat. The report itself was thorough and attempted to satisfy all the disputing parties. Though the report could be read as a severe condemnation of Japan, it conveyed as a whole the impression that as difficult as it might be for Japan to defend the methods she had employed in Manchuria to remedy grievances that she had against China, there was much to be said for the Japanese case if one examined the report carefully.[3]

Drummond proposed that the Assembly adopt the Lytton Report as its own, declaring against any diplomatic recognition of Manchukuo's Government and recommending that the Chinese and Japanese should negotiate on the lines indicated in the report. By doing this the Assembly would have terminated its duties under Article 15. In addition, the Assembly might send copies of the report and its decision thereon to the signatories of the Nine Power Treaty and the Kellogg–Briand Pact in order that these powers, should they desire to do so, might pursue the matter further on their own. Such a procedure, he maintained, was in accordance with the Covenant, and the League for its part would be released from a very troublesome problem. Drummond warned, however, that this procedure could be strongly criticized

[1] Thorne, p. 299.

[2] Riddell (Geneva) to Skelton, 29 July 1932, File 65, Box 265393, Department of External Affairs, PACRMB.

[3] League of Nations, *Appeal by the Chinese Government. Report of the Commission of Enquiry* (Geneva, 1932).

on the grounds that the League had failed to produce a settlement and that it had transferred its task to other parties. Unhappily, he felt that such a 'criticism would not be unjustified' and would go far in weakening the League's position generally.

He asked if it was not likely that each month that passed by would make Japan's position in Manchuria more difficult and would it not increasingly feel the financial drain of her Manchurian adventure?—Lytton's comments to his sister. Morever, could the League really attempt to discover a final solution without American and Russian assistance? As the Lytton Report pointed out, Soviet Russia had large financial and other interests in Manchuria. Of course, it was not possible simply to invite these two states to come to the Assembly or Council because any such move would be strongly and probably effectively resisted by Japan. Drummond's alternate proposal, therefore, was that the Assembly adopt the Lytton Report through chapter eight, that is to say everthing in the report except the proposals for a settlement, as well as the declaration on non-recognition of Manchukuo's Government. Regarding chapters nine and ten, the Assembly would invite those powers especially interested in the Far East, namely, the states adhering to the Nine Power Treaty plus Soviet Russia. They would transmit the results of their examination to the Assembly so it could formulate its final conclusions taking account of all viewpoints. Drummond thought that such a procedure was legally possible as part of the Assembly's report under Article 15.

There were clear advantages, he argued, in adopting such an arrangement. It would bring the Americans and the Russians into the open, forcing both of them to assume their responsibilities. It would also gain time, and lastly, leave the League with the final word. Another special Assembly session in the summer of 1933 might prove necessary, but this difficulty could easily be overcome. This proposal, Drummond observed, would probably be criticized on the grounds that the League had shown weakness by delaying a final judgement and that in the interim Japan would strengthen her Manchurian position. All this aside, he personally believed for reasons that he had given that this was the best procedure. He was sure that considerable opposition would be generated by people like the Spanish representative, Salvador de Madariaga, in favour of a more violent approach.

Suggestions that Tokyo be pressured by a withdrawal of
ambassadors and perhaps by its expulsion from the League
appeared to Drummond 'the negation of wisdom in present
circumstances'.

Though the Foreign Office's reaction was mixed, it essentially
followed Drummond's second proposal. The final decision of
Vansittart, the Permanent Under-Secretary, was to recommend
to Simon that Council discussions be avoided and the Lytton
Report be passed on to the Assembly; at the latter body or at the
Committee of Nineteen to propose acceptance of the report's first
eight chapters avoiding any pronouncements on the last two
chapters; to propose that the last two chapters of recommendations be referred to a commission or conference consisting of
adherents of the Nine Power Treaty plus Soviet Russia, inviting
them to submit their observations or proposals on these chapters
to the Assembly. 'Even if the Soviet Govt were to be troublesome',
Vansittart minuted, 'that should not deter us'.

But Drummond was also concerned about China's future and
during this period he strongly supported a proposal by Frank
Walters, the chief of the Secretary-General's Section, that a
genuine effort be made by League members to establish a strong
central government in China commencing with large scale
financial assistance to the present national government. Drummond's only hesitation was that it would be very difficult to
associate Soviet Russia with any reconstruction work undertaken
by the League and other powers in China. Walters's proposal,
however, did not get off the ground once the combined forces of
the Foreign Office and the Quai d'Orsay made their objections
known.

As to the Nine Power Treaty, if it prove necessary, Drummond
observed, it might be possible while maintaining the procedure
he had spelled out to ascertain separately the advice of Soviet
Russia and the powers adhering to the Nine Power Treaty. The
former might formally be asked for her views on the last two
chapters of the Lytton Report. Likewise the adherents of the
Nine Power Treaty might be asked to come together to advise on
these chapters, and from them might emerge a plan to strengthen
China's central government, especially because if such a step was
adopted it would require the United States' closest co-operation.[1]

[1] *DBFP, 1919–1939,* 2, xi. 18–21, 39–40 and fnn., 49.

Keeping in mind Drummond's notion that the League was essentially a reconstituted but improved concert of powers, his desire to use the Nine Power Treaty is understandable. He held that the 1922 treaty 'had much to recommend it as an instrument governing such a consideration' since the treaty had of course been especially framed for conditions which were peculiar to the Far East. Drummond felt that the adherents of the Nine Power Treaty were, because of their world status and Far Eastern interests, better suited to handle the question than League bodies, including the Committee of Nineteen. This committee was composed of many states, he maintained, whose knowledge of the Far East was on the whole limited, who had no Pacific interests, and whose approach to the problem 'was inclined to be based more on theoretical than on practical considerations'. He noted that to change the present manner in which the question was being handled would probably involve a great deal of delay in the final consideration of the Manchurian affair. At the same time he was not completely sure but that any such delay would be advantageous. He envisaged the financial drain that Manchuria would be for Japan and thought that in time this would modify Japan's aggressive policy. He pictured the Japanese army's difficulties in Manchuria and the consequent loss of enthusiasm that this would produce in Tokyo's military circles. Simultaneously Drummond dismissed the frequently heard argument that any delay would give Japan added opportunity to consolidate her Manchurian position with the observation that Japan had already consolidated herself as far as it was possible to do in Manchuria and that in view of what Tokyo had done he saw no particular disadvantage to any further delay.

As so often in the past Drummond wanted to know Washington's opinion. He also wanted to know, he asked Gilbert, if it agreed with him that further delay in reaching a settlement of the question was not disadvantageous. Drummond really did not see how the Nine Power Treaty could be implemented in this question without a delay of some months. At the same time he did not want the question transferred completely from the League to the 1922 treaty since it was impossible to arrange anything satisfactory which would not give the impression of leaving the League to one side or present the picture of a failure of League endeavours.

On the question of Japan's separation from the League, Drummond observed that while no one could predict what would happen he felt that Japan's attitude had changed. Though Japan's expulsion was entertained in some League circles it was not being seriously considered. His opinion was that Japan would be careful not to place herself in a position the consequences of which would be her withdrawal from the League.

Gilbert's impression was that Drummond was preoccupied with relieving the League from the embarrassments under which the world organization was suffering. At the same time, this did not necessarily mean that Drummond was 'not entirely sincere in feeling that his suggestions are the best means of bringing the problem to a satisfactory conclusion'.[1]

On the day following this conversation, 1 November, Drummond transmitted to Stimson his scheme on how the Lytton Report should be handled by the League. It essentially followed the ideas he had previously expressed, modified, to include Walters's proposal for strengthening the position of China's national government.[2] He then pointed out to Cadogan that Haas, the Lytton Commission's secretary, shared his 'view as to the inadvisability of forcing the pace, or of confronting Japan at the moment with a definite acceptance or rejection of the [Lytton] Report'.[3]

Any hopes that Drummond harboured following conversations in London with Simon that Washington might support his scheme to have the adherents of the Nine Power Treaty play an active role in settling the Manchurian question were soon dashed by Stimson. He had a number of objections to any such move, the main one being that the Nine Power Treaty did not in fact provide for the calling of a conference; hence the parties to the 1922 treaty were not obliged to accept an invitation if one was tendered; and in any case, if such a conference was called, Japan in all probability would refuse to attend. Simon, too, was unwilling to use the Nine Power Treaty for reasons somewhat similar to Stimson's.[4]

---

[1] *PRFRUS, 1932*, iv. 322–5.
[2] Wilson (Geneva) to the Department of State, No. 31, 1 Nov. 1932, File 500.C112/1041, RG 59, NA.
[3] *DBFP, 1919–1939*, 2, xi. 45–6, 48.
[4] *PRFRUS, 1932*, iv. 342–3, 346; *DBFP, 1919–1939*, 2, xi. 71.

Direct contact between Drummond and the Japanese did not take place until 18 November, three days before the Lytton Report was to be discussed by the Council. When informed by the Japanese that if their country was censured Tokyo would leave the League, Drummond retorted that though it was generally recognized that Japan had acute grievances against China in Manchuria and a strong case for action, Tokyo had put itself in the wrong by acting on its own responsibility without initially bringing its case to the League. If it had done this, Drummond felt sure that a reasonable settlement could have been effected which would have given full satisfaction to Japan's claims. He regretted that the Japanese, unlike the British in 1927 when they sent troops to Shanghai, had not informed the League. He believed that this was the main ground for criticism of Japan by those who supported the League. On the question of Japan's recognition of Manchukuo Drummond thought he could make no comments since it was a matter raised by the Lytton Report, but the Japanese were of course aware of the League's position, as well as that of the United States regarding the recognition of a state which had been established by force—an allusion to the Stimson Doctrine. Furthermore, he warned that small powers were represented on both the Assembly and the Council and were free to say what they wanted, and hoped that Japan was big enough to ignore their comments. If Japan departed from the League it would be regretted by everybody and by no one more than himself. On the other hand, he had to state frankly that the League stood for certain principles which could not be abandoned and it would therefore be better for the League to disappear rather than that it should surrender its fundamental conception. Drummond noted that Japan's action in Manchuria did not appeal to the smaller states who could not help but feel that if Japan's action went uncriticized it would endanger their own position *vis-à-vis* more powerful neighbours. He agreed with the Japanese that final recommendations for settling the question could hardly be attempted until conciliation efforts were exhausted.[1]

The Council decided to transmit the Lytton Report to the Assembly without comment. Between 28 November when this

---

[1] *DBFP, 1919–1939*, 2, xi. 88–91 and fnn.

decision was taken and 6 December when the Assembly convened to discuss the Lytton Report, Drummond continued his efforts to execute the scheme he had devised and to associate the Americans and the Russians in the task of settling the Manchurian question. During the Assembly's debate the cleavage between the small and large states became more pronounced. Led by Czechoslovakia, Norway, Spain, and Sweden, the small states demanded that the League take effective action, while Simon with the other Great Powers and Canada in tow moved cautiously. The end result was that the Assembly on 9 December adopted unanimously and without discussion a Czech–Swiss sponsored resolution which requested that the Committee of Nineteen study the Lytton Report, the Chinese and Japanese observations as well as the suggestions that had been expressed in the Assembly's discussions about the report, and draw up proposals for settling the dispute. The committee was then to submit these proposals to the Assembly as quickly as possible. Japanese objections, however, to American or Russian participation in the deliberations of the Committee of Nineteen prevented the fruition of Drummond's scheme. These Japanese objections were accepted provided Tokyo made concessions during the negotiations in the Committee of Nineteen.[1]

During the succeeding weeks the Committee of Nineteen attempted to settle the dispute, but to no avail. Draft resolutions were drawn up accompanied by an explanatory statement and submitted to both China and Japan. As in other situations of this type Drummond played an extremely active role behind the scenes in the complex formal and informal discussions that ensued. Since the committee's endeavours dovetailed with his own desire that some sort of conciliatory settlement might be devised, he was unsympathetic to the wish of the smaller states led by Beneš and Madariaga to force the issue with Japan at this time. To do so, he felt, would lead to Japan's withdrawal from the League.[2]

---

[1] Walters, p. 493; Willoughby, pp. 438–63; Thorne, p. 334; Stimson, p. 225.
[2] E[ric] D[rummond], Record of Conversation, 20 Dec. 1932, and Drummond (Geneva) to Pratt, 21 Dec. 1932, FO/371/16185; Drummond (Geneva) to Cadogan, 9 Jan. 1933, FO/371/17074; *DBFP, 1919–1939*, 2, xi. 150–1, 152–3, 157, 162–3, 164, 190, 217, 228–9, 231, 235, 242, 250–1, 252, 261, 263, 269–75, 302, 304–5, 313–6, 321; *DDF 1932–1939*, I, ii. 573–4, 592, 605;

Both China and Japan proposed amendments to the committee's draft resolution. No agreement could be reached between the two states. These frustrating negotiations finally floundered when Japan replied in the negative to the Committee of Nineteen's query whether she would accept 'as one of the bases of settlement, the establishment in Manchuria of a large measure of autonomy consistent with the sovereignty and administrative integrity of China'.[1] The Japanese occupation of Shanhaikwan in early January 1933 and their invasion of Jehol province beyond the Great Wall in early February could only have contributed to the Committee of Nineteen's decision to terminate its attempts at conciliation and to draft a report to the Assembly stating the facts of the case and its recommendations for a settlement as provided for under paragraph four of Article 15.

Following Japan's occupation of Shanhaikwan Drummond had only the slightest hope that the committee's conciliation procedures would work. Like Hymans, he was convinced 'that every effort towards conciliation must be made in order to forestall if possible the menace of a real war in the Far East'.[2] By mid-February the initial fighting at Jehol caused him to believe a 'very serious war could not be avoided between China and Japan'.[3] Unfortunately for Drummond, his actions during the course of these negotiations did not go unnoticed and the unusual and unjustified cry was raised by the press that he had both exceeded his competence and shielded the Japanese.[4]

The denouement of the Manchurian question now commenced. On 16 February the Committee of Nineteen circulated the draft report to be made by the Assembly. It incorporated the findings of the Lytton Commission and recommended a settlement under which Manchuria would have a large measure of autonomy under Chinese sovereignty. Furthermore, China and Japan would sign a non-aggression pact and there would be

PRFRUS, 1932, iv. 422–4, 429–30, 434, 444, 447–9, 453–4 and *PRFRUS, 1933*, iii. 92–3, 95–7, 107–9, 117, 119, 144, 146–8, 149–52, 161–4, 174–5, 176, 177–180; Baron Pompeo Aloisi, *Journal (25 Juillet 1932–14 Juin 1936)*, trans. Maurice Vaussard (Paris: Plon, 1957), p. 37.

[1] Walters, p. 494; Willoughby, pp. 464–471.

[2] *PRFRUS, 1933*, iii. 93.

[3] Riddell Diary, 14 Feb. 1933, Walter A. Riddell Papers, YUT.

[4] Reginald Bassett, *Democracy and Foreign Policy* (London: Longmans, Green, 1952), pp. 341–3; Thorne, p. 334 and fn.; *PRFRUS, 1933*, iii. 95–7.

temporary international co-operation to assist China in her internal reconstruction. The rights that Japan enjoyed in Manchuria were to be recognized. Conversely, the State of Manchukuo was not to be recognized. Lastly, as soon as China and Japan accepted the Assembly's recommendations, an Assembly committee would be established to assist both sides in reaching a settlement. Drummond was to notify both the Americans and the Russians of this acceptance and then invite each state to appoint a member to the committee should it so desire.[1] Though the Nine Power Treaty, Drummond correctly pointed out, was not actually mentioned in the committee's report, all adherents to this treaty could nominate delegates to sit on the proposed committee. Since Drummond had continuously and unsuccessfully attempted to weld the adherents of the Nine Power Treaty and the League together to help settle the Manchurian question, it would be safe to say that this particular aspect of the committee's report was due to Drummond's influence.[2]

Any hope that this proposed Assembly committee could be established quickly vanished eight days after the committee's report was circulated. Though the committee's report was accepted by the Assembly with Siam (Thailand) abstaining it was rejected by Japan.[3] Japan's rejection meant that this particular aspect of the Committee of Nineteen's report could not be implemented, but it was considered that the report itself had been unanimously accepted by the Assembly since a negative vote by one of the parties to the dispute under Article 15 could not be counted.

As a substitute the Assembly unanimously agreed, following the withdrawal of the Japanese delegation, to establish an advisory committee to follow the Far Eastern situation and to assist it in performing its duties under paragraph three of Article 3 of the Covenant. The Advisory Committee was to include all the states represented on the Committee of Nineteen plus Canada and The Netherlands, but the United States and Soviet Russia were to be invited to co-operate with the Advisory Committee. The invocation of Article 3 paragraph three which stipulated

[1] Willoughby, pp. 472–97.
[2] *DBFP, 1919–1939*, 2, xi. 339–40; *PRFRUS, 1933*, iii. 179–80, 191–3.
[3] Walters, p. 494.

that the Assembly might deal at its meetings with any matter within the League's sphere or affecting the world's peace was drawn up by Drummond in order to make the committee more attractive to Washington and Moscow by excluding from the committee's functions deliberations arising under Article 16.[1] He was only partially successful. Though Washington with qualifications agreed to co-operate with the Advisory Committee, Moscow politely turned it down.[2] On 27 March almost three weeks after the Russian note had been dispatched Japan announced her decision to withdraw from the League.

In his few remaining months as Secretary-General, Drummond continued to work with the Advisory Committee.[3] On 30 June 1933 he departed as Secretary-General. In early January 1932 he had signified to Simon his desire to resign. Six months before he had privately informed the Council's other permanent members that he would take this step in late 1932.[4] Several weeks after writing to Simon he tendered his resignation to the Council. The resignation was accepted with deep regret on the understanding that it would not take effect before 30 June 1933.[5] In early June several weeks before his departure the Council paid Drummond a public tribute.[6]

Since Drummond was returning to the British diplomatic service he offered for Simon's perusal on 21 June the text of a speech he was going to deliver at the League of Nations Union meeting in London on 6 July.[7] He then submitted an amended version to Vansittart some days later.[8] He was back home once more in the bosom of the Foreign Office on 1 July 1933. It had been a long and tiring fourteen-year trek.

As Drummond wrote to Gilbert Murray: 'I am very glad you are ready to go on for another five years, but honestly glad that

[1] *PRFRUS, 1933*, iii. 208–9, 210, 219–20, 227–8.

[2] Willoughby, pp. 500–4.

[3] *PRFRUS, 1933*, iii. 238–9, 257–8, 311–12, 319, 321, 351–2, 356.

[4] James Barros, *Betrayal from Within: Joseph Avenol, Secretary-General of the League of Nations, 1933–1940* (New Haven: Yale University Press, 1969), p. 1.

[5] Secret Meetings of the Council of the League of Nations, 25 Jan., 28 Jan., and 27 Sept. 1932, Council 1928–32: 14/9887/2385, LNA; League of Nations, *Official Journal*, XIV (1933), pp. 170–1.

[6] League of Nations, *Official Journal*, XIV (1933), p. 849.

[7] Drummond to Simon, 21 June 1933, John Simon Papers, FO/800/288.

[8] Drummond to Vansittart, 24 June 1933, ibid.

I have not got to face such a possibility'.[1] This was penned to Murray during the height of the Manchurian crisis. His dejection was understandable but perhaps it might have been tempered had Drummond mused over Niccolò Machiavelli's comment in *The Prince* that there was 'nothing more difficult to take in hand, more perilous to conduct, or more uncertain in its success, than to take the lead in the introduction of a new order of things'.[2]

[1] Drummond to Murray, 4 Oct. 1932, Gilbert Murray Papers, BLOU.
[2] Niccolò Machiavelli, *The Prince*, trans. W. K. Marriott (New York: Dutton, 1948), p. 43.

VIII

SOME THOUGHTS ON DRUMMOND AND HIS SUCCESSORS

In view of Drummond's actions as Secretary-General the erroneous myth that he eschewed political activities, was merely an administrator, or at the most was only a 'trusted private consultant to Governments',[1] can now be safely put to rest. If anything, Drummond was as much a political animal as his French successor, Joseph Avenol, the saving grace being that Drummond was at least committed to the League and the ideals that it represented, which is more than anyone can really say for Avenol.[2]

To a certain extent the view that the League secretaries-general, and Drummond in particular, were non-political can be traced to the rejection of Lord Robert Cecil's idea of a Chancellor. Though the evidence here is somewhat fragmentary there is good reason to suspect that the whole notion of the Chancellor was really an attempt to deal with President Wilson through the charismatic and pro-British Greek Prime Minister, Eleftherios Venizelos, who appeared to be one of the few men able to control and influence the American chief executive. Once Venizelos had, for internal Greek political reasons, rejected the Chancellorship offer and no one else appeared capable of playing the role envisaged for Venizelos the idea of the Chancellor was dropped.

The thinking has been that when the Chancellorship notion was abandoned, the less political and more administrative role projected for the Secretary-General of the League crystallized. This view was seemingly supported by the lack of any public political initiatives at least by Drummond and on the whole by Avenol. In addition, Drummond's prior experience as a Foreign Office official appeared to lend itself to a non-political role. It

---

[1] Andrew Cordier and Wilder Foote (eds.), *Public Papers of the Secretaries-General of the United Nations. Volume I: Trygve Lie 1946–1953* (New York: Columbia University Press, 1969), p. 2.

[2] James Barros, *Betrayal from Within: Joseph Avenol, Secretary-General of the League of Nations, 1933–1940* (New Haven: Yale University Press, 1969), *passim*.

was thought he was the executor not the originator of policy. To a certain extent this was true, but Drummond like any other bureaucrat had discovered after nineteen years in the Foreign Office the indirect power that a bureaucrat can wield by the influence that he has and the advice he gives to the policy maker. One student of the British Foreign Office during the First World War has observed that the official documents 'show Drummond giving advice to the Foreign Secretary on countless occasions and usually having it accepted. How far Drummond initiated policy and how far he merely advised in the sense of translating what he knew to be in Balfour's mind into a practical suggestion for dealing with a given situation can often not be ascertained, but it is doubtful whether any British Foreign Secretary has ever had a more competent or loyal aide than Eric Drummond'.[1] With a few changes in proper nouns the same statement would equally apply to Drummond's actions as Secretary-General.

Of course, during the war Drummond was merely Balfour's private secretary. In this position as well as in his Foreign Office and other government assignments he was as a civil servant under the constant supervision and direct control of his superiors. Such was not the case in Geneva. Here, as one writer has correctly pointed out, there was not 'a single political head in situ to whom he was responsible'.[2] Since the Council met only periodically and the Assembly once a year in the autumn, except when special sessions were called, Drummond was not under constant control as he had been in London. This type of relative isolation, therefore, both from supervision and control made it possible for him to go beyond the actions that he might have taken had he still been a permanent British civil servant. How much his Foreign Office experience or the new situation in which he found himself guided his actions is difficult to say, but obviously both played a part in affecting his behaviour as Secretary-General.

Naturally under the League Covenant, even in what appeared to be essentially an administrative post, Drummond had far greater chances for political actions and initiatives behind the

[1] V. H. Rothwell, *British War Aims and Peace Diplomacy 1914–1918* (Oxford: Clarendon Press, 1971), p. 14.
[2] Christopher Thorne, *The Limits of Foreign Policy: The West, the League and the Far Eastern Crisis of 1931–1933* (London: Hamish Hamilton, 1972), p. 111.

scenes because under the Covenant he was constitutionally the hub of the organization's administrative wheel. As the director of a large multinational staff administering an organization whose primary task entailed the continual surveillance of world events, Drummond, almost inevitably and regardless of whether he did or did not think his actions appropriate to his position as chief administrator of the League, either willingly or unwillingly took part in secret or public discussions with states either in or out of the League involving the use of the organization's political procedure, its facilities, or its staff.[1] How Drummond reacted to the requests, what attitude he assumed, and what resources of the League or its organs he actually made available, immediately drew him, like it or not, into a political vortex where the choices he made furthered the political drives and desires of one state over another. Though he might perhaps rationalize his actions and moves on constitutional or administrative grounds he was nevertheless involved in what were essentially political acts. The very nature of the office was unavoidably political.

This was perhaps the point that was missed by Hankey when he declined the post. He undoubtedly saw a greater future for himself as Secretary to the British Cabinet, the heart of a world empire. Between something that he had experienced and understood, and the unknown, he had understandably chosen the former. As Secretary to the Cabinet he had already tasted the indirect power that a person holding such a key position amasses—the influence that he wielded, the advice that he gave, the access to the power holders that he had, and the person whom policy-makers often consulted since he was the missing link between the very documents for which he was responsible. Hankey was in a way a personification of the twentieth century's organizational man. He was efficient, unobtrusive, dependable, and lacking in an adventurous spirit, which may partially explain his rejection of the Secretary-Generalship.

Naturally, the advice that Hankey received likewise moved him to reject the Secretary-Generalship, but it probably merely confirmed what he had already decided independently. This advice to Hankey, however, covered in the opening pages of this

---

[1] Barros, *Betrayal from Within*, p. 262.

volume, is interesting for the light it throws on British attitudes and opinions toward the League well before the American Senate rejected the Versailles settlement and, with it, the League Covenant. The serious reservations if not outright hostility toward the projected world organization partially mirrored in this correspondence raise some doubts about the often heard contention that Great Britain would have been willing to play a more active and positive role in the League in conjunction with the United States if Washington had assumed its world responsibilities in 1919. These reservations toward the organization, reflected in the highest British political circles and shared by the permanent officials of the Foreign Office, would make it appear that this often heard contention was conveniently sired only after the American rejection of the Versailles Treaty. Perhaps in actual fact American acceptance of the Covenant would have posed for the British Government difficult policy choices. The unfriendly attitude of Lloyd George as well as Lords Curzon and Esher and, one might also add, those of Sir Austen Chamberlain and Ramsay MacDonald, were fairly typical among British policy-makers on both sides of the aisle, while those of Sir Eyre Crowe, Sir William Tyrrell, and Sir Robert Vansittart, the Permanent Under-Secretaries, as well as those of Philip Kerr and Sir Maurice Hankey, reflected the Foreign Office's negative opinions and the negative opinions of those officials who had access to the policy-makers. Lord Robert Cecil and Lord Milner, as well as Balfour, described by one wit as a philosopher to the politicians and a politician to the philosophers, were atypical, while an idealist like Harold Nicolson or even someone like Sir Alexander Cadogan who was willing to co-operate with the League in so far as it helped implement British foreign policy, was an exception.

In this kind of setting and with the United States and Soviet Russia and for a time Germany outside the League system, Drummond had to tread carefully, and this largely explains his methods of operation in what we have said was unavoidably a political position. The keystone of his operations was the maintenance of good relations with London, for of all League states it was Great Britain, despite the reservations or hostility held toward the League in official circles, which potentially was the organization's greatest bulwark. Fortuitously, it was also the one state that he could influence more than any other and it is this factor which largely explains his unceasing contacts with London's official world, including those individuals who by their positions were capable of influencing either the power holder or British public opinion. Kerr was one such person, and Hankey was another. As we have seen in the Saar question, Drummond went to some lengths to explain to both of them the actions that the League had taken in this question and on the whole he successfully defended the organization against the unfair attacks that had been levelled against it.

Though a *status quo* power like France and interested in preserving the peace treaty settlements of 1919, Great Britain unlike France did not view the organization as an instrumentality whose main purpose was to keep Germany in her place. There was an element of flexibility or liberality in Great Britain's attitude toward the League and Germany. This was in line with her historic role as a mediating power and partially dictated by competing empire interests and the insularity of an island people, as well as by her desire to have a balance of forces in Europe so that France's repression of Germany would not lead to France and her allies acquiring a European hegemony. France with less industrial potential than Germany, with a smaller population, and a declining birth rate, and mindful that she had been invaded twice within half a century from across the Rhine, could ill-afford such a British stance. Furthermore, there was in Great Britain, more so than in other countries, a strong popular support for the League which all London governments had to keep in mind and which at the minimum necessitated that any action touching the organization be rationalized as meshing with its principles and purposes even when this was often not the case.

Thus it would have been the height of folly if Drummond had not maintained and expanded the excellent government contacts he had established in London during his wartime work and especially his obvious contacts with the Foreign Office developed over nineteen years of devoted service. But this relationship, as the Foreign Office realized, was a two-way street and if it was in Drummond's interests and therefore the League's to have this close and confidential relationship it was also in the interests of the Foreign Office. A symbiotic relationship therefore developed. To receive one had to give, which largely explains the willingness to allow Drummond to continue seeing the Foreign Office's confidential papers at the British Consulate in Geneva.

If plentiful and accurate information is the indispensable raw material out of which policy is made, in this arrangement it would be safe to say that Drummond had the better of the bargain. Although Drummond's Geneva office, as Sir Alexander Cadogan had pointed out, was visited by the world's leading personalities and was a kind of clearing house for Europe's political ideas, it could never really compare to the vast amount of information flowing into the Foreign Office from Great Britain's world-wide network of embassies, legations, consulates, high commissions, and so forth. The only time Drummond really appears to have been hard pressed for information was during the Manchurian crisis when he repeatedly attempted to tap into the American intelligence line. This was partially a tactical ploy to have greater American co-operation with the League in the Far Eastern crisis, but it was also a wise move. Whereas the Americans could not compare with the British when it came to European intelligence information they were first rate when it came to Far Eastern intelligence, especially during the Manchurian crisis, as a perusal of the *U.S. Foreign Relations* volumes for the inter-war years clearly shows. This was due to many causes. For one, Washington was trusted more and had, unlike London or Paris, played a more balanced role in the area. In addition, like London, Washington had been willing to train people for work in the Far East as it subsequently trained people for work in Soviet Russia well before it diplomatically recognized Moscow. In retrospect, Drummond's successors, and here one might include Avenol since he was not trusted by the Quai d'Orsay,[1] were not as fortunate in this respect. The United Nations secretaries-general being nationals of middle and small powers have had no comparable intelligence tap because of the limited contacts of the diplomatic services of their own countries, though obviously like Drummond, contacts with the organization's delegations, the trips they take, and feedback from the United Nations Secretariat and its overseas missions does supply valuable information.[2]

[1] Ibid., p. 16.

[2] Doubts have been raised as to whether this is true (Leon Gordenker, *The UN Secretary-General and the Maintenance of Peace* (New York: Columbia

There is, however, an important point that should not be missed. When information was conveyed to Drummond by the Foreign Office or by some other source, Drummond practised the greatest tact and discretion in using it. Tact and discretion are two nouns that epitomize his behaviour. From the evidence available it is clear that what the British or anyone else told him was not passed on to the French and vice versa. The only time he appears to have conveyed information received from one source to another is when he wished to impress upon the other party, the Foreign Office, for example, what someone else was doing in order to invoke parallel action.

In a sense Drummond's relationship with successive British Governments and the Foreign Office was a type of holding operation. It allowed the dust to settle in the American internal political arena. Because politics is capricious it was quite possible that with time American hostility to the League might dissolve or be seriously weakened. If this occurred Washington's co-operation with the League in matters both technical and political and especially the latter might increase immeasurably and lead to America's ultimate acceptance of the organization. This was more likely to happen if the League appeared to be, even without America's membership, a viable and vigorous organization. The greater London's involvement with the League and the more it meshed its own policy with and through the organization, the more secure and stable would the organization appear and the more important would it emerge as an instrument for conflict resolution and technical co-operation in a world community of sovereign states. Confidence in the League would increase and its stature and reputation would grow and the custom and tradition of using it would multiply among member states of the organization. At the minimum, Great Britain's toleration would allow the League to survive.

One can perhaps argue that this was the impractical and visionary approach of a Victorian dreamer who had matured in an era that believed that progress was inevitable—a view dealt a body blow by the First World War. Perhaps so. But the passage

University Press, 1967), pp. 89–134), but Urquhart's massive study of Dag Hammarskjöld appears to support it. Brian Urquhart, *Hammarskjold* (New York: Knopf, 1972), pp. 380–1 and *passim*.

of more than fifty years has produced no better alternative approach. Of course in a way it was a very British approach, impregnated as it was by an evolutionary view of the world arena which smacked so much of the slow political development of Drummond's own country.

Yet looking back, it was not all that visionary. As each year passed Washington's hostility to the League perceptibly diminished. Where initially it would not even acknowledge receipt of League communications, let alone reply, in time it slowly began to partake in the League's technical non-political work. There were even exceptions on involvement in political matters whenever questions arose where American interests were concerned as in Liberia, Latin America, or the Far East, and reached its high point with Gilbert's presence at the Council table during the Manchurian crisis. By the summer of 1932, it was decided by the State Department to communicate in a less informal manner with Drummond as a symbolic recognition of his office and of the League.[1] The process of engaging with the League was excruciatingly slow, but it was increasing at a faster rate than before as Drummond departed from the League and a new and friendly administration under President Roosevelt and Secretary of State Cordell Hull assumed the reins of power in Washington. The catch, of course, was that the important time element, so plentiful in the development of Drummond's own country, was lacking as the anti-*status quo* nations during the inter-war period successfully challenged the established international legal and political order and slowly tipped the balance of power in their favour.

In the process of contact and exchange Drummond's relationships with other powers could not for obvious reasons be on the same intimate plane as those he had with the British Government and the Foreign Office. Absent were the equivalent friendly contacts at the Quai d'Orsay, the Palazzo Chigi, the Wilhelmstrasse, the State Department, or the Gaimusho in Tokyo. Here Drummond had to depend on other more circuitous contacts. And what were these contacts? On an everyday basis Drummond's main political contacts with the League's membership

[1] Jay Pierrepont Moffat, *The Moffat Papers,* ed. Nancy H. Hooker (Cambridge: Harvard University Press, 1956), p. 76.

and especially with the Council's permanent members were, as we have seen, the delegates at Geneva, and the members of the League Secretariat and especially its highest officials. Used irregularly but for important political questions were Drummond's personal visits to the capital cities of almost every European League member and especially his periodic trips to Berlin, London, Paris, and Rome—we exclude his hurried visits during his Latin American tour of 1930–1, and distance and the slow transportation of the day precluded any Asian trips.

Under this arrangement it was understood and mutually convenient to have within the Secretariat an individual who was both acceptable to Drummond and to the individual's own country. This selection process was not based on any competitive examination or the candidate's intrinsic qualifications, and although for Drummond competence was a consideration, for the interested state the individual's political loyalty and reliability were of decisive importance. Drummond was forced to compromise with the exigencies of the real world. It was political expediency and it partially explains why Drummond in private, regardless of what he said in public, never for a moment believed or thought that the multinational staff of an international organization like the League could ever be analogous to the non-political civil service of, let us say, Great Britain. Moreover, Drummond as a realist, reflecting his nineteen years of Foreign Office experience, could not believe that the Weberian bureaucratic model exemplified in British government departments could ever really evolve within an international secretariat. Though the League's membership was on the whole homogeneous, composed as it was mostly of European and Latin American states, the Secretariat did not harbour the characteristics and values generally associated with Weber's bureaucratic model of which the Foreign Office was an excellent example.

Imperfect as this system was, in the hands of well-meaning and reasonable men it could have been, if properly used, an instrument for meshing the actions of the Secretariat with the desires of the League's member states. Initially this was the case. The men chosen for service in the Secretariat were, of course, largely picked on nationality grounds and were acceptable to their governments only after they had been scrutinized for their political loyalty. But they were at least committed to the League in the sense that though devoted to their own countries they knew how to conciliate this devotion with international interests, to paraphrase a French Foreign Minister, Louis Barthou, who inscribed this comment in one of his books to a French member of the Secretariat some days before being assassinated.[1]

By October 1922, however, this was no longer the case. Mussolini had come to power in Italy and the system was to be put under increasing stress, not only from Rome, but with Germany's admission to the League also from Berlin. Fascist Italy and Weimar Germany were fundamentally anti-*status quo* so that appointments to the Secretariat for both of them assumed an importance not only in political terms but also in terms of prestige. This was made clear to Drummond when he spoke to Mussolini for the first time in November 1923. Rome's and subsequently Berlin's desires increased the system's rigidity and introduced criteria of state loyalty and state devotion which, though always there, were no longer allowed to go publicly unrecorded and unrecognized. Drummond was then subjected to a new type of negotiation over Secretariat appointments which was now far more difficult than anything previously experienced. Witness the appointment of Paulucci, which was a veritable take-it-or-leave-it proposition from Mussolini.

In that significant case, Italy, a Great Power and a permanent Council member and on the winning side in 1918, was in a strong position. What could Drummond do to resist Paulucci's and other such Italian appointments? If he resisted, Mussolini would have immediately protested to London. Whitehall would have made representations to Drummond and without London's political support he would have had to surrender to the Duce's demands and nothing would have been achieved. The omnipresent threat of an Italian withdrawal from the League first raised by Rome during the Corfu Incident of 1923[2] might have materialized or, at the minimum, there would have been a lack of Italian co-operation with the League until Drummond was removed as Secretary-General. In addition, London and Paris would have viewed his action as irresponsible, because it had annoyed the Duce with whom they wanted, especially under Sir

[1] Barros, *Betrayal from Within*, p. 179.

[2] James Barros, *The Corfu Incident of 1923: Mussolini and the League of Nations* (Princeton: Princeton University Press, 1965), pp. 106–7, 124, 130.

Austen Chamberlain and Aristide Briand, the smoothest relations. It would also have destroyed the Foreign Office's and the
Quai d'Orsay's confidence and trust in his advice and judgement
and likewise undermined his influence. Drummond was boxed in
and he knew it. The best thing to do was to put on a good face
and accept the inevitable. At least when he dealt with Paulucci
he would know that anything and everything he said would
faithfully be reported to Rome. The question of Fascist Italy was
not one that Drummond could handle on his own. The solution
to the Italian problem on the international plane was not to be
found in Geneva; it was to be found in London and Paris.
Drummond was not so mesmerized either by the powers of his
office or by the total influence that he could wield on the
international scene to believe that his actions could be anything
but marginal in handling the Duce. Without control or access to
real power he was in a weak bargaining position that continually
left him at a disadvantage especially in dealing with an anti-
status quo power.

The situation repeated itself to a certain extent with Germany.
There were, however, important differences. Germany, though
a permanent Council member, had been on the losing side in
1918, and though Germany knew she was a weakened Great
Power she did not have to be constantly assured of her potential
greatness as did Rome by an outpouring of verbosity. But French
suspicions of Germany were strong and unlike the Italian case an
appeal to Paris might have furnished Drummond with political
support against Berlin that he could never have mustered against
Rome. Drummond knew that he was in a stronger position *vis-à-
vis* Germany and his comment to the Germans in 1929 'You are
in the League, but not of the League',[1] clearly shows it. Therefore
his bargaining position on the question of German Secretariat
appointments was stronger than it was against the Italians.
Within reason he could negotiate on a more equal footing with
the people in Berlin over candidates acceptable to both of them.
This is not to say that he drove hard bargains or made impossible
demands. He was caught in a less rigid situation, but he would
have been foolish to ignore the fact that Germany as a Great
Power was entitled to the greatest deference in this matter, that

[1] Ernst von Weizsäcker, *The Memoirs of Ernst von Weizsäcker*, trans. John
Andrews (London: Gollancz, 1951), p. 79.

she was also entitled to Secretariat positions commensurate with her political importance, that her nominations would have to be seriously considered, and that Berlin would have to be closely consulted and its advice and recommendations carefully weighed. He did not handle Germany in the same way he handled Ruritania. Under these conditions it was only natural that Drummond would be very circumspect when dealing with his Italian or German associates.

Correspondingly, leaving aside his contacts with London and the Foreign Office, Drummond was probably closest to his French associates in the Secretariat. In this regard he was blessed in the early days with the presence of Jean Monnet. With Monnet's departure and replacement by Avenol, his main contact with Paris and the Quai d'Orsay was Pierre Comert. Though here and there we have glimpses of these relationships they would probably be sharper if access to official French documentation, now closed, were possible. That such documentation exists is clear. Avenol's *chef de cabinet* sent daily reports to the Quai d'Orsay when Avenol subsequently was Secretary-General, giving an analysis of the latest events at the League.[1] One can safely assume that this also occurred but on a more irregular basis during Avenol's tenure as Deputy Secretary-General, since Drummond dealt largely through Comert rather than through Avenol whom he presciently did not hold in high regard.

Next in importance were probably Drummond's American associates, particularly Arthur Sweetser. Here the relationship was somewhat special. If need be, contacts with Washington could have been effected through the American diplomatic missions in Switzerland. Though Sweetser was also a conduit to Washington, his more important role was to be the contact man in the Secretariat, and especially for Drummond, with the pro-League forces in the United States. During the inter-war years these forces were not unimportant and became increasingly influential as Washington's initially hostile attitude toward the League mellowed. In view of Drummond's belief that Washington would in time accept the League if it became a more viable and vigorous organization, the influence that the pro-League

---

[1] Barros, *Betrayal from Within*, p. 178.

forces could wield and the role that they could play in this process was of the greatest importance.

As for Drummond's Japanese associates, they initially also played a special role. Because their country was removed from Europe's political struggles they could be assigned by Drummond to investigate matters and engage in tasks that if delegated to European members of the Secretariat might have led to resentment and tension. As we have seen, when the Manchurian crisis erupted the Japanese Under Secretary-General quickly assumed his role as a conduit to Tokyo and was often used by Drummond not only to maintain the League's contacts with the Japanese Government, but to feed it various proposals and schemes for resolving the crisis and producing a peaceful settlement acceptable to both China and Japan.

So it went through the ranks of the Secretariat. In a sense, Secretariat positions, and places on temporary or permanent League bodies where Drummond might have some influence on who was selected, were a type of spoils system manipulated both to pay off political obligations as well as to assure the continual loyalty or assistance of a particular power. The procedure could at times reach Hallowe'en-like proportions in which a trick or treat format was used, witness as an example Brazilian desires to know if they returned to the League whether assurances could be given by Drummond that a high Secretariat position would be reserved for one of their nationals. Decisions by Drummond on matters of this nature obviously depended on budgetary factors, but the political consideration would naturally be whether the act of placating the suppliant was equal to or exceeded the political advantage that would accrue to the League. Failure to satisfy the suppliant might lead to difficulties which at the minimum could be a re-enactment of Achilles sulking in his tent.[1]

This problem did not disappear with the outbreak of the Second World War. The establishment of the United Nations in 1945 again saw its reappearance. Indeed, under paragraph three of Article 101 of the United Nations Charter the Secretary-General must pay due regard to recruiting Secretariat personnel

---

[1] For a Rumanian example see Nicolae Titulescu, *Documente Diplomatice*, ed. George Macovescu (Bucureşti: Editura Politică, 1967), pp. 125, 209–10.

on as 'wide a geographical basis as possible'. No similar restriction is to be found in the League Covenant, though in practice this is what Drummond did, so that this problem, as the secondary literature on the United Nations testifies, has been as great and inescapable a political issue for the United Nations secretaries-general as it was for Drummond.

In looking at Drummond one is struck by his concentration, at least up to 1931 when the Manchurian crisis erupts, on European affairs. This is understandable for certainly during the early part of his tenure and up to 1931 affairs in Europe occupied the League's and therefore Drummond's attention. Europe had been the principal battleground of the First World War and the scene of post-war problems. It was also the locus of the power struggle and power arrangements, particularly the shifting quadrilateral relations of Great Britain, France, Germany, and Italy, in which such important outside observers as the United States and Soviet Russia had influential and omnipresent roles to play.

By training, experience, and probably by inclination Drummond was better prepared to play his role in this European setting than, let us say, in a Latin American one. Though one of his first assignments when he entered the Foreign Office, as he later admitted, was to write a report for Lord Salisbury, the Foreign Secretary, on the Tacna–Arica dispute between Chile and Bolivia and Peru, his contacts with Latin America had really always been peripheral. His 'feel' was greater for the European situation than for any other part of the world. This may partially explain his reticence in making any concessions to the Brazilians on high positions in the Secretariat during his discussions with them on their returning to the League. Brazil's pressures he must have considered presumptuous, fit perhaps for a Germany, but not for a power which was not among those of the first rank. It may also explain his willingness to use his office with less restraint when dealing with Latin America despite his concern about the Monroe Doctrine and America's role in the southern hemisphere. The caution that was almost innate in him when dealing with European affairs, especially where the Great Powers were involved, seemed to dissolve when dealing with Latin American disputes, if we are to judge by his actions during the Costa Rican–Panamanian dispute in 1921 and the initial stages of the Chaco dispute in 1928. Though important, Latin

America did not hold exactly the same priority position for Drummond that Europe did. Such an outlook could not be maintained for long by his successors, especially his United Nations counterparts, in an increasingly interdependent world.

If Europe was Drummond's centre of concentration until 1931 then the actions that he took in dealing with this political arena warrant some examination. We have already scrutinized his relationship with successive British Governments and the Foreign Office, as well as his recruitment and use of the Secretariat and the opportunities as well as the difficulties that this posed for him.

Following the First World War Drummond unlike his successors in the United Nations never faced a cold war in a bipolar world where the conflicting strategic and military desires of the two sides were disguised in an ideological garb which with the emergence of an Afro-Asian world sometimes led the constituent organs of the organization to delegate power and authority to the Secretary-General. Drummond was, therefore, forced back on whatever powers or influence he could muster or invoke from the very nature of the Secretary-General's office. In this seemingly limited arsenal Drummond proved to be a master of invention. He was an unending source of ideas, advice, recommendations, proposals, schemes, and formulas, not merely to delegations, but often directly to those governments involved or to those governments not involved but interested in peacefully settling a particular question. Most important, Drummond's initiatives were always behind the scenes, and to remove himself from the limelight, were sometimes transmitted through third parties, especially through members of the Secretariat. The advantage of this non-public approach was that if Drummond's proposal was unacceptable to either of the parties it did not exclude amendments or other proposals. It did not drag Drummond into the public arena and thus it allowed him to continue his endeavours, which public failure or public comments, particularly of the interested parties, might have quickly compromised or undercut. Furthermore, this behind-the-scenes approach shielded Drummond, for being human he was open to making mistakes of omission or commission, which if exposed to public view would have damaged both Drummond's own image and the prestige of his office. The longer that Drummond stayed in office, the more that he was trusted, and the more extensive his experience, the greater weight his initiatives carried because they now had added to them the ingredient of wisdom which is largely a product of experience. Certainly in the middle and last years of his tenure, as in the Manchurian crisis for example, he could undertake initiatives and actions that would not have been tolerated during the earlier years.

One can of course argue, as one recent writer does, that Drummond's whole approach was too timid and 'more positive assertion on his part at crucial moments of the obligations member-states owed the League by their acceptance of the Covenant might occasionally have stiffened a backbone or two'.[1] Perhaps so. The assumption of course is that public political activity is more effective political activity in the sense that it is capable of influencing, affecting, or having an impact on other actors in the world community.[2] This of course assumes that the Secretary-General has a public constituency to which he can appeal. However, Drummond believed he had no such constituency. If he did he would have had to weigh the advantages of a public statement against the disadvantages that might accrue not only in the question at issue but in his long-term relationships with the states involved.

But all that said, what would have been the possibilities, one can ask, of Drummond's convincing someone by public moves when he could not convince him by private advice and conversations? Was not this particularly true when Drummond dealt with permanent members of the Council? Indeed, what real power did he have; power defined here as the ability physically or psychically to control other actors in the world community, beyond the weak reed of world public opinion, the appeal to world morality, the tenets of international law that he might be able to invoke to support his position, or the political support that he might be able to muster from some but not all the states of the organization? The last position was of course a

---

[1] George Scott, *The Rise and Fall of the League of Nations* (New York: Macmillan, 1973), p. 252.

[2] For some of the comments that follow see also, James Barros, 'A More Powerful Secretary-General for the United Nations?', *American Journal of International Law (Proceedings of the American Society of International Law)*, 66, No. 4 (September 1972), pp. 81–4ff.

perilous one if Drummond found himself in a head-on collision with a permanent Council member.

In fact, if experience has taught us anything, it is that the United Nations secretaries-general have very often by their public political initiatives undermined their political usefulness. In the case of the first and second holders of that office they became politically impotent once they had crossed swords with Soviet Russia: Trygve Lie because of his actions and attitude following the North Korean invasion of South Korea and Dag Hammarskjöld because of his initiatives and attitudes during the Congo crisis. It could be contended that this was also the case with U Thant, though the clash was not as blatant as it was for his predecessors and it was Washington, rather than Moscow, that was annoyed, largely because of U Thant's attitude toward the American involvement in Vietnam. One would be hard pressed to show how their public initiatives in any of these questions hastened a peaceful settlement which justified the political and personal sacrifice that they made. Their actions, unlike those of an unobtrusive Drummond, may have been more dramatic, but in the long run and certainly in the short run, they were far less useful and practical. They had by their actions exposed themselves to public view, appeared to show favour, and once drawn in, their credibility and usefulness as an impartial bridge between the contending parties was destroyed.

It can be cogently argued from Drummond's time in office that there is no necessary correlation between public political activities by a Secretary-General and political influence. In fact, the contrary might develop. Is it not also possible that the belief in public political activities might propel the Secretary-General into assuming initiatives or undertaking actions that might heighten rather than lessen the tensions of the world community?

The difficulty in appreciating the *modus operandi* of a Drummond is that it is so undramatic. Tedious yes, self-effacing yes, but dramatic it is not. It is a style that demands immense self-control, discretion, continual imagination, tireless energy, and a grasp of international relations as well as a knowledge of the subject under discussion second to none of the Secretariat's technical experts. It also requires the ability to gain and to hold the confidence of all the other participants. Few are capable of doing this, Drummond was one such person. The problem is that this method does not appeal to many investigators of the Secretary-General's office who are more moved by dramatic public acts. Much of this fascination can be traced to what can be called the 'Hammarskjöld model' syndrome. But the Hammarskjöld model is in fact an exception rather than the norm. Indeed, in Hammarskjöld's Sweden, 'undersecretaries are the highest officials in each department immediately under the minister, and the law itself defines their function as "political"'.[1] Keeping in mind that Hammarskjöld before his appointment as Secretary-General had served as Under-Secretary in the Ministry of Finance and Under-Secretary as well as Secretary-General in the Ministry of Foreign Affairs, is it just possible that his later political activities as United Nations Secretary-General might in part be traced to this peculiar aspect of the Swedish constitutional system and its civil service? Of course, to admit to this might weaken the image that Hammarskjöld quickly developed during his second contract period, when he claimed that he had certain implied powers under the Charter in the same way that the President of the United States has certain implied powers under the American constitution. This view has been accepted and lauded then as now.

Nevertheless an examination and a comparison of Hammarskjöld with others who have held the office would soon make it obvious that Hammarskjöld was in many respects a superior Secretary-General and a very unusual person. That is not to say that he was not without faults or that all his actions are beyond criticism.[2] The personal qualities, however, which made Hammarskjöld a superior Secretary-General are not likely to be found in most people chosen for the office. In fact, a close examination of those who have held the office since 1919 will show that it has been held by good men as well as by knaves and fools. The explanation for this wide variation is quite simple: the selection process is based on political expediency and the momentary consensus that can be achieved among the Great Powers. It is not a competitive civil service examination. The Great Powers were

---

[1] Dankwart A. Rustow, *The Politics of Compromise: A Study of Parties and Cabinet Government in Sweden* (Princeton: Princeton University Press, 1955), p. 176. See also, Neil C. M. Elder, *Government in Sweden* (Oxford: Pergamon Press, 1970), pp. 81–7.

[2] Urquhart, *passim*.

fortunate in the hectic days before the Versailles Treaty was signed that in so unstructured a selection process their choice fell on Drummond, who at the minimum was a far better administrator than most of his successors.[1]

In looking at Drummond's style and actions as Secretary-General as well as those of his successors in a changing world it might be fair to say that what the world needs is not secretaries-general who are publicly active but secretaries-general with discretion who are active behind the scenes and yet maintain the trust and confidence of the vast majority of the organization's membership, especially the permanent members of the Security Council. By doing so they might develop some influence and increase the chances that their admonitions and advice would be listened to and perhaps even followed. This is not likely to occur if they take public stands on important issues which can only aggravate one side or the other and in turn strain or compromise their own relations with the involved states.

Like the Bishop of Rome the Secretary-General has no divisions and like the British Monarch his only really effective power is his ability in private to warn, to advise, and to recommend. These were certainly the qualities which made Sir Eric Drummond so successful in his use of the office. It is interesting to observe that though Drummond had no equivalent in the Covenant to Article 99 of the Charter which allows the Secretary-General to bring to the Security Council's attention any matter which may threaten the maintenance of international peace and security, though in actuality this article has been formally invoked only once, in practice Drummond enjoyed just such a power. Having the confidence of the Council's president, an Article 99 was superfluous, for Drummond could influence the Council's president to have important questions examined by the Council. This is what he was undoubtedly attempting to do during the Costa Rican–Panamanian dispute of 1921. It can be safely said that he achieved it during the Greek–Bulgarian Incident of 1925; and he certainly achieved it in the Chaco in 1928, and perhaps in other situations as well about which the available documentation offers little evidence.

---

[1] Barros, *Betrayal from Within*, *passim*; Shirley Hazzard, *Defeat of an Ideal* (Boston: Little, Brown, 1973), *passim*.

To a certain extent the desire for a Secretary-General who takes public initiatives is an escape from reality. It is an attempt to avoid the harsh fact that it is states that run the international community, especially the more powerful ones, and not the directors of international organizations. A Secretary-General who lacks political support and pits himself against almost any state will inevitably lose the struggle. Unlike his successors Drummond never fell prey to the illusion that public actions on his part could have any lasting impact on an imperfect world inhabited by imperfect men. It is a measure of Drummond's success that when he tendered his resignation as Secretary-General in early 1932, the well-known Swiss journalist, William Martin, wrote that even after thirteen years as Secretary-General Drummond was still very much trusted and respected by the League members.[1] Could any of Drummond's successors make a similar claim?

[1] Pablo de Azcárate (ed.), *William Martin: Un grand journaliste à Genève* (Genève: Dotation Carnegie, 1970), pp. 56–8.

APPENDIX

THE COVENANT OF THE LEAGUE OF NATIONS[1]

With Amendments in Force 1 January 1945

THE HIGH CONTRACTING PARTIES,

In order to promote international co-operation and to achieve international peace and security

by the acceptance of obligations not to resort to war,

by the prescription of open, just and honourable relations between nations,

by the firm establishment of the understandings of international law as the actual rule of conduct among Governments, and

by the maintenance of justice and a scrupulous respect for all treaty obligations in the dealings of organised peoples with one another,

Agree to this Covenant of the League of Nations.

ARTICLE 1. MEMBERSHIP AND WITHDRAWAL

1. The original Members of the League of Nations shall be those of the Signatories which are named in the Annex to this Covenant and also such of those other States named in the Annex as shall accede without reservation to this Covenant. Such accessions shall be effected by a declaration deposited with the Secretariat within two months of the coming into force of the Covenant. Notice thereof shall be sent to all other Members of the League.

2. Any fully self-governing State, Dominion or Colony not named in the Annex may become a Member of the League if its admission is agreed to by two-thirds of the Assembly, provided that it shall give effective guarantees of its sincere intention to observe its international obligations, and shall accept such regulations as may be prescribed by the League in regard to its military, naval and air forces and armaments.

3. Any Member of the League may, after two years' notice of its intention so to do, withdraw from the League, provided that all its international obligations and all its obligations under this Covenant shall have been fulfilled at the time of its withdrawal.

ARTICLE 2. EXECUTIVE ORGANS

The action of the League under this Covenant shall be effected through the instrumentality of an Assembly and of a Council, with a permanent Secretariat.

---

[1] Entered into force on 10 Jan. 1920. Subsequent amendments of the Covenant are indicated by italics and footnotes.

ARTICLE 3. ASSEMBLY

1. The Assembly shall consist of representatives of the Members of the League.

2. The Assembly shall meet at stated intervals and from time to time, as occasion may require, at the Seat of the League or at such other place as may be decided upon.

3. The Assembly may deal at its meetings with any matter within the sphere of action of the League or affecting the peace of the world.

4. At meetings of the Assembly each Member of the League shall have one vote and may have not more than three Representatives.

ARTICLE 4. COUNCIL

1. The Council shall consist of representatives of the Principal Allied and Associated Powers [United States of America, the British Empire, France, Italy and Japan], together with Representatives of four other Members of the League. These four Members of the League shall be selected by the Assembly from time to time in its discretion. Until the appointment of the Representatives of the four Members of the League first selected by the Assembly, Representatives of Belgium, Brazil, Greece and Spain shall be Members of the Council.

2. With the approval of the majority of the Assembly, the Council may name additional Members of the League, whose Representatives shall always be Members of the Council; the Council with like approval may increase the number of Members of the League to be selected by the Assembly for representation on the Council.

2. *bis. The Assembly shall fix by a two-thirds' majority the rules dealing with the election of the non-permanent Members of the Council, and particularly such regulations as relate to their term of office and the conditions of re-eligibility.*[1]

3. The Council shall meet from time to time as occasion may require, and at least once a year, at the Seat of the League, or at such other place as may be decided upon. •

4. The Council may deal at its meetings with any matter within the sphere of action of the League or affecting the peace of the world.

5. Any Member of the League not represented on the Council shall be invited to send a Representative to sit as a member at any meeting of the Council during the consideration of matters specially affecting the interests of that Member of the League.

6. At meetings of the Council, each Member of the League represented on the Council shall have one vote, and may have not more than one Representative.

ARTICLE 5. VOTING AND PROCEDURE

1. Except where otherwise expressly provided in this Covenant or by the terms of the present Treaty, decisions at any meeting of the Assembly or of the

---

[1] As amended it went into force 29 July 1926.

Council shall require the agreement of all the Members of the League represented at the meeting.

2. All matters of procedure at meetings of the Assembly or of the Council, including the appointment of Committees to investigate particular matters, shall be regulated by the Assembly or by the Council and may be decided by a majority of the Members of the League represented at the meeting.

3. The first meeting of the Assembly and the first meeting of the Council shall be summoned by the President of the United States of America.

ARTICLE 6. SECRETARIAT AND EXPENSES

1. The permanent Secretariat shall be established at the Seat of the League. The Secretariat shall comprise a Secretary-General and such secretaries and staff as may be required.

2. The first Secretary-General shall be the person named in the Annex; thereafter the Secretary-General shall be appointed by the Council with the approval of the majority of the Assembly.

3. The secretaries and the staff of the Secretariat shall be appointed by the Secretary-General with the approval of the Council.

4. The Secretary-General shall act in that capacity at all meetings of the Assembly and of the Council.

5. *The expenses of the League shall be borne by the Members of the League in the proportion decided by the Assembly.*[1]

ARTICLE 7. SEAT, QUALIFICATIONS OF OFFICIALS, IMMUNITIES

1. The Seat of the League is established at Geneva.

2. The Council may at any time decide that the Seat of the League shall be established elsewhere.

3. All positions under or in connection with the League, including the Secretariat, shall be open equally to men and women.

4. Representatives of the Members of the League and officials of the League when engaged on the business of the League shall enjoy diplomatic privileges and immunities.

5. The buildings and other property occupied by the League or its officials or by Representatives attending its meetings shall be inviolable.

ARTICLE 8. REDUCTION OF ARMAMENTS

1. The Members of the League recognize that the maintenance of peace requires the reduction of national armaments to the lowest point consistent with national safety and the enforcement by common action of international obligations.

2. The Council, taking account of the geographical situation and circumstances of each State, shall formulate plans for such reduction for the consideration and action of the several Governments.

[1] As amended it went into force 13 Aug. 1924.

3. Such plans shall be subject to reconsideration and revision at least every 10 years.

4. After these plans shall have been adopted by the several Governments, the limits of armaments therein fixed shall not be exceeded without the concurrence of the Council.

5. The Members of the League agree that the manufacture by private enterprise of munitions and implements of war is open to grave objections. The Council shall advise how the evil effects attendant upon such manufacture can be prevented, due regard being had to the necessities of those Members of the League which are not able to manufacture the munitions and implements of war necessary for their safety.

6. The Members of the League undertake to interchange full and frank information as to the scale of their armaments, their military, naval and air programmes and the condition of such of their industries as are adaptable to warlike purposes.

ARTICLE 9. PERMANENT MILITARY, NAVAL AND AIR COMMISSION

A Permanent Commission shall be constituted to advise the Council on the execution of the provisions of Articles 1 and 8 and on military, naval and air questions generally.

ARTICLE 10. GUARANTEES AGAINST AGGRESSION

The Members of the League undertake to respect and preserve as against external aggression the territorial integrity and existing political independence of all Members of the League. In case of any such aggression or in case of any threat or danger of such aggression the Council shall advise upon the means by which this obligation shall be fulfilled.

ARTICLE 11. ACTION IN CASE OF WAR OR THREAT OF WAR

1. Any war or threat of war, whether immediately affecting any of the Members of the League or not, is hereby declared a matter of concern to the whole League, and the League shall take any action that may be deemed wise and effectual to safeguard the peace of nations. In case any such emergency should arise the Secretary-General shall on the request of any Member of the League forthwith summon a meeting of the Council.

2. It is also declared to be the friendly right of each Member of the League to bring to the attention of the Assembly or of the Council any circumstance whatever affecting international relations which threatens to disturb international peace or the good understanding between nations upon which peace depends.

ARTICLE 12. DISPUTES TO BE SUBMITTED FOR SETTLEMENT

1. The Members of the League agree that, if there should arise between them any dispute likely to lead to a rupture, they will submit the matter either to arbitration *or judicial settlement* or to inquiry by the Council, and they agree in no case to resort to war until three months after the award by the arbitrators *or the judicial decision*, or the report by the Council.

2. In any case under this Article the award of the arbitrators *or the judicial decision* shall be made within a reasonable time, and the report of the Council shall be made within six months after the submission of the dispute.[1]

ARTICLE 13. ARBITRATION OR JUDICIAL SETTLEMENT

1. The Members of the League agree that, whenever any dispute shall arise between them which they recognize to be suitable for submission to arbitration *or judicial settlement*, and which cannot be satisfactorily settled by diplomacy, they will submit the whole subject-matter to arbitration *or judicial settlement*.

2. Disputes as to the interpretation of a treaty, as to any question of international law, as to the existence of any fact which, if established, would constitute a breach of any international obligation, or as to the extent and nature of the reparation to be made for any such breach, are declared to be among those which are generally suitable for submission to arbitration *or judicial settlement*.

3. *For the consideration of any such dispute, the court to which the case is referred shall be the Permanent Court of International Justice, established in accordance with Article 14, or any tribunal agreed on by the parties to the dispute or stipulated in any convention existing between them.*[2]

4. The Members of the League agree that they will carry out in full good faith any award *or decision* that may be rendered, and that they will not resort to war against a Member of the League which complies therewith. In the event of any failure to carry out such an award *or decision*, the Council shall propose what steps should be taken to give effect thereto.

ARTICLE 14. PERMANENT COURT OF INTERNATIONAL JUSTICE

The Council shall formulate and submit to the Members of the League for adoption plans for the establishment of a Permanent Court of International Justice. The Court shall be competent to hear and determine any dispute of an international character which the parties thereto submit to it. The Court may also give an advisory opinion upon any dispute or question referred to it by the Council or by the Assembly.

[1] As amended it went into force 26 Sept. 1924.
[2] As amended it went into force 26 Sept. 1924.

ARTICLE 15. DISPUTES NOT SUBMITTED TO ARBITRATION OR JUDICIAL SETTLEMENT

1. If there should arise between Members of the League any dispute likely to lead to a rupture, which is not submitted to arbitration *or judicial settlement* in accordance with Article 13, the Members of the League agree that they will submit the matter to the Council. Any party to the dispute may effect such submission by giving notice of the existence of the dispute to the Secretary-General, who will make all necessary arrangements for a full investigation and consideration thereof.[1]

2. For this purpose the parties to the dispute will communicate to the Secretary-General, as promptly as possible, statements of their case with all the relevant facts and papers, and the Council may forthwith direct the publication thereof.

3. The Council shall endeavour to effect a settlement of the dispute, and, if such efforts are successful, a statement shall be made public giving such facts and explanations regarding the dispute and the terms of settlement thereof as the Council may deem appropriate.

4. If the dispute is not thus settled, the Council either unanimously or by a majority vote shall make and publish a report containing a statement of the facts of the dispute and the recommendations which are deemed just and proper in regard thereto.

5. Any member of the League represented on the Council may make public a statement of the facts of the dispute and of its conclusions regarding the same.

6. If a report by the Council is unanimously agreed to by the Members thereof other than the Representatives of one or more of the parties to the dispute, the Members of the League agree that they will not go to war with any party to the dispute which complies with the recommendations of the report.

7. If the Council fails to reach a report which is unanimously agreed to by the members thereof, other than the Representatives of one or more of the parties to the dispute, the Members of the League reserve to themselves the right to take such action as they shall consider necessary for the maintenance of right and justice.

8. If the dispute between the parties is claimed by one of them, and is found by the Council, to arise out of a matter which by international law is solely within the domestic jurisdiction of that party, the Council shall so report, and shall make no recommendation as to its settlement.

9. The Council may in any case under this Article refer the dispute to the Assembly. The dispute shall be so referred at the request of either party to the dispute, provided that such request be made within 14 days after the submission of the dispute to the Council.

10. In any case referred to the Assembly, all the provisions of this Article and of Article 12 relating to the action and powers of the Council shall apply to the action and powers of the Assembly, provided that a report made by the Assembly, if concurred in by the Representatives of those Members of the League represented on the Council and of a majority of the other Members of the League, exclusive in each case of the Representatives of the parties to the

[1] As amended it went into force 26 Sept. 1924.

dispute, shall have the same force as a report by the Council concurred in by all the members thereof other than the Representatives of one or more of the parties to the dispute.

ARTICLE 16. SANCTIONS OF PACIFIC SETTLEMENT

1. Should any Member of the League resort to war in disregard of its covenants under Articles 12, 13, or 15, it shall *ipso facto* be deemed to have committed an act of war against all other Members of the League, which hereby undertake immediately to subject it to the severance of all trade or financial relations, the prohibition of all intercourse between their nationals and the nationals of the covenant-breaking State, and the prevention of all financial, commercial or personal intercourse between the nationals of the covenant-breaking State and the nationals of any other State, whether a Member of the League or not.

2. It shall be the duty of the Council in such case to recommend to the several Governments concerned what effective military, naval or air force the Members of the League shall severally contribute to the armed forces to be used to protect the covenants of the League.

3. The Members of the League agree, further, that they will mutually support one another in the financial and economic measures which are taken under this Article, in order to minimize the loss and inconvenience resulting from the above measures, and that they will mutually support one another in resisting any special measures aimed at one of their number by the covenant-breaking State, and that they will take the necessary steps to afford passage through their territory to the forces of any of the Members of the League which are co-operating to protect the covenants of the League.

4. Any Member of the League which has violated any covenant of the League may be declared to be no longer a Member of the League by a vote of the Council concurred in by the Representatives of all the other Members of the League represented thereon.

ARTICLE 17. DISPUTES INVOLVING NON-MEMBERS

1. In the event of a dispute between a Member of the League and a State which is not a Member of the League, or between States not Members of the League, the State or States not Members of the League shall be invited to accept the obligations of membership in the League for the purposes of such dispute, upon such conditions as the Council may deem just. If such invitation is accepted, the provisions of Articles 12 to 16, inclusive, shall be applied with such modifications as may be deemed necessary by the Council.

2. Upon such invitation being given, the Council shall immediately institute an inquiry into the circumstances of the dispute and recommend such action as may seem best and most effectual in the circumstances.

3. If a State so invited shall refuse to accept the obligations of membership in the League for the purposes of such dispute, and shall resort to war against a Member of the League, the provisions of Article 16 shall be applicable as against the State taking such action.

4. If both parties to the dispute when so invited refuse to accept the obligations of Membership in the League for the purposes of such dispute, the Council may take such measures and make such recommendations as will prevent hostilities and will result in the settlement of the dispute.

ARTICLE 18. REGISTRATION AND PUBLICATION OF TREATIES

Every treaty or international engagement entered into hereafter by any Member of the League shall be forthwith registered with the Secretariat and shall as soon as possible be published by it. No such treaty or international engagement shall be binding until so registered.

ARTICLE 19. REVIEW OF TREATIES

The Assembly may from time to time advise the reconsideration by Members of the League of treaties which have become inapplicable, and the consideration of international conditions whose continuance might endanger the peace of the world.

ARTICLE 20. ABROGATION OF INCONSISTENT OBLIGATIONS

1. The Members of the League severally agree that this Covenant is accepted as abrogating all obligations or understandings *inter se* which are inconsistent with the terms thereof, and solemnly undertake that they will not hereafter enter into any engagements inconsistent with the terms thereof.

2. In case any Member of the League shall, before becoming a Member of the League, have undertaken any obligations inconsistent with the terms of this Covenant, it shall be the duty of such Member to take immediate steps to procure its release from such obligations.

ARTICLE 21. ENGAGEMENTS THAT REMAIN VALID

Nothing in this Covenant shall be deemed to affect the validity of international engagements, such as treaties of arbitration or regional understandings like the Monroe doctrine, for securing the maintenance of peace.

ARTICLE 22. MANDATORY SYSTEM

1. To those colonies and territories which as a consequence of the late war have ceased to be under the sovereignty of the States which formerly governed them and which are inhabited by peoples not yet able to stand by themselves under the strenuous conditions of the modern world, there should be applied the principle that the well-being and development of such peoples form a sacred trust of civilization and that securities for the performance of this trust should be embodied in this Covenant.

2. The best method of giving practical effect to this principle is that the tutelage of such peoples should be entrusted to advanced nations who by reason of their resources, their experience or their geographical position can best undertake this responsibility, and who are willing to accept it, and that this tutelage should be exercised by them as Mandatories on behalf of the League.

3. The character of the mandate must differ according to the stage of the development of the people, the geographical situation of the territory, its economic conditions and other similar circumstances.

4. Certain communities formerly belonging to the Turkish Empire have reached a stage of development where their existence as independent nations can be provisionally recognised subject to the rendering of administrative advice and assistance by a Mandatory until such time as they are able to stand alone. The wishes of these communities must be a principal consideration in the selection of the Mandatory.

5. Other peoples, especially those of Central Africa, are at such a stage that the Mandatory must be responsible for the administration of the territory under conditions which will guarantee freedom of conscience and religion, subject only to the maintenance of public order and morals, the prohibition of abuses such as the slave trade, the arms traffic and the liquor traffic, and the prevention of the establishment of fortifications or military and naval bases and of military training of the natives for other than police purposes and the defence of territory, and will also secure equal opportunities for the trade and commerce of other Members of the League.

6. There are territories, such as Southwest Africa and certain of the South Pacific islands, which, owing to the sparseness of their population, or their small size, or their remoteness from the centres of civilization, or their geographical contiguity to the territory of the Mandatory, and other circumstances, can be best administered under the laws of the Mandatory as integral portions of its territory, subject to the safeguards above mentioned in the interests of the indigenous population.

7. In every case of mandate, the Mandatory shall render to the Council an annual report in reference to the territory committed to its charge.

8. The degree of authority, control or administration to be exercised by the Mandatory shall, if not previously agreed upon by the Members of the League, be explicitly defined in each case by the Council.

9. A permanent Commission shall be constituted to receive and examine the annual reports of the Mandatories and to advise the Council on all matters relating to the observance of the mandates.

ARTICLE 23. SOCIAL AND OTHER ACTIVITIES

Subject to and in accordance with the provisions of international conventions existing or hereafter to be agreed upon, the Members of the League:

(a) will endeavour to secure and maintain fair and humane conditions of labour for men, women and children, both in their own countries and in all countries to which their commercial and industrial relations extend, and for that purpose will establish and maintain the necessary international organisations;

(*b*) undertake to secure just treatment of the native inhabitants of territories under their control;

(*c*) will intrust the League with the general supervision over the execution of agreements with regard to traffic in women and children, and the traffic in opium and other dangerous drugs;

(*d*) will entrust the League with the general supervision of the trade in arms and ammunition with the countries in which the control of this traffic is necessary in the common interest;

(*e*) will make provision to secure and maintain freedom of communications and of transit and equitable treatment for the commerce of all Members of the League. In this connection, the special necessities of the regions devastated during the war of 1914–1918 shall be borne in mind;

(*f*) will endeavour to take steps in matters of international concern for the prevention and control of disease.

ARTICLE 24. INTERNATIONAL BUREAUS

1. There shall be placed under the direction of the League all international bureaus already established by general treaties if the parties to such treaties consent. All such international bureaus and all commissions for the regulation of matters of international interest hereafter constituted shall be placed under the direction of the League.

2. In all matters of international interest which are regulated by general conventions but which are not placed under the control of international bureaus or commissions, the Secretariat of the League shall, subject to the consent of the Council and if desired by the parties, collect and distribute all relevant information and shall render any other assistance which may be necessary or desirable.

3. The Council may include as part of the expenses of the Secretariat the expenses of any bureau or commission which is placed under the direction of the League.

ARTICLE 25. PROMOTION OF RED CROSS AND HEALTH

The Members of the League agree to encourage and promote the establishment and co-operation of duly authorised voluntary national Red Cross organisations having as purposes the improvement of health, the prevention of disease and the mitigation of suffering throughout the world.

ARTICLE 26. AMENDMENTS

1. Amendments to this Covenant will take effect when ratified by the Members of the League whose Representatives compose the Council and by a majority of the Members of the League whose Representatives compose the Assembly.

2. No such amendment shall bind any Member of the League which signifies its dissent therefrom, but in that case it shall cease to be a Member of the League.

BIBLIOGRAPHICAL NOTE

The materials that made this study possible were largely archival in nature. Most of them were examined at the Public Record Office in London, the League of Nations Archives in Geneva, the National Archives of the United States in Washington, D.C., and the Public Archives of Canada in Ottawa.

Wherever possible private papers were also consulted to supplement and elucidate the official record. These papers were largely deposited in university libraries and other public depositories, though some of them were also in private hands.*

Next in importance were the officially published documentary collections of a number of states as well as the published records of the League of Nations. To round out the study, memoirs, biographies, secondary sources, newspapers, and so forth, were also used. Since most of this published material is clearly cited either in the footnotes or in the table of abbreviations found at the beginning of this volume and can be easily consulted it was thought unnecessary to list them in any bibliography. In addition, in examining a footnote, the table of abbreviations easily tells the reader what archival or published source is being cited and if an archival source, whose papers they are and where these papers are to be found.

* Among those I would like to thank are the Beaverbrook Library and the other educational and institutional libraries and archival depositories cited in the Table of Abbreviations. The necessary permission to quote or examine certain materials was kindly given by Lords Balfour, Esher, Hankey, Lothian, Perth, and Scarsdale, as well as by Anthony J. Tennant and Lieutenant Colonel G. I. Malcolm of Poltalloch, while permission to quote from the papers of Lord Robert Cecil was kindly given by Professor Ann Lambton and Francis Noel-Baker.

INDEX